Advance Pr[...]
Oil, Power and Empire

This remarkable account of the trajectory of US and UK policy towards Iraq—from its founding as a British colony after World War I to the immediate present—is brilliantly illuminating, in an almost literal sense. It's as if the author had suddenly turned on the lights in the dark cellar of American foreign policy in the Middle East. Highly readable, studded with cogent, often startling quotations, the story is at the same time soberly told, factual, and horrifying: but above all, enlightening. I can't recommend it too highly, for the many struggling to fathom how America came to the present calamitous role of occupying Iraq against local resistance.

—Daniel Ellsberg, author of
Secrets: A Memoir of Vietnam and the Pentagon Papers

The most thorough and reliable critique of U.S. policy toward Iraq available. Eminently reasonable and coherently argued. Those who have been subjected to the heavy bombardment of U.S. propaganda should read this book—now.

—As'ad AbuKhalil, author of
Bin Laden, Islam, and America's New "War on Terrorism"

Larry Everest's book is a detailed, carefully documented and searing account of the sordid history of American and British involvement in Iraq. It is essential reading for anyone who wishes to understand the background to the latest war and the present occupation.

—Anatol Lieven, senior associate
at the Carnegie Endowment for International Peace

Oil, Power and Empire provides an invaluable analysis of Washington's 60-year drive to secure control over Persian Gulf oil and the underlying factors behind the Bush Administration's decision to invade and occupy Iraq. Goes deep below official rhetoric and media blather to reveal the predatory nature of American policy in the Gulf.

—Michael Klare, author of *Resource Wars: The New Landscape of Global Conflict*

Everest has done an excellent job of putting a lot of pieces together into a readable and informative narrative; an ideal way to fill in all those gaps in your knowledge about a subject obviously of vital importance today.

—William Blum, author of *Rogue State: A Guide to the World's Only Superpower* and *Killing Hope: U.S. Military and CIA Interventions Since World War II*

Excellent...Carefully researched and very well documented. I hope and expect it will be widely adopted as a required text.

—Dwight Simpson, Professor of International Relations, San Francisco State University

What makes Everest's contribution unique is the depth of his research and his seamless integration of disparate sources, from the personal to the documentary. What he has accomplished is all too rare and frankly not less than amazing.

—Thomas J. Nagy, Associate Professor of Expert Systems, George Washington University

OIL, POWER AND EMPIRE

IRAQ AND THE U.S. GLOBAL AGENDA

Larry Everest

Common Courage Press   Monroe, Maine

Cover work by Matt Wuerker and Erica Bjerning
Maps courtesy of *Revolutionary Worker*

Library of Congress Cataloging-in-Publication Data is available
from the publisher on request.

ISBN 1-56751-246-1 paper
ISBN 1-56751-247-x cloth

Common Courage Press
Box 702
Monroe, ME 04951

(207) 525-0900; fax: (207) 525-3068
orders-info@commoncouragepress.com

See our website for e-versions of this book.
www.commoncouragepress.com

Second Printing

Printed in Canada

Contents

Acknowledgments iv

Chapter One 1
    "Go Massive. Sweep It All Up."

Chapter Two 35
    Iraqis—Not Present at the Creation

Chapter Three 55
    Saddam Hussein's American Train

Chapter Four 86
    Arming Iraq:
    Double-Dealing Death in the Gulf

Chapter Five 118
    "We Have to Have A War"

Chapter Six 166
    Germ Warfare:
    America's Weapon of Mass Destruction

Chapter Seven 186
    The Great WMD Flim Flam

Chapter Eight 205
    A Growing Clamor For Regime Change

Chapter Nine 218
    Operation Iraqi Colonization

Chapter Ten 248
    Oil, Power & Empire

Chapter Eleven 277
    The Bitter Fruits of Unjust War

Appendix: Dissecting U.S. Pretexts for War 301

Iraq Chronology 330

Notes 342

Index 377

About the Author 392

Acknowledgments

All intellectual efforts are ultimately much more collective than individual, and this book is no exception. I have benefitted enormously from discussions with and criticism and advice from many colleagues, friends, activists, and scholars. Of course, all omissions or errors of fact or interpretation are my own.

Suggestions by Prof. Dwight Simpson, Daniel Ellsberg, William Blum, Prof. Thomas Nagy, Prof. Elaine Hagopian, Prof. Roger Dittman, Brian Drolet, and Brian Shott have all helped improve this book.

Leonard Innes' research and manuscript assistance has been invaluable. Raymond Lotta's work on global capitalism and his comments on early drafts have helped shape and deepen the analysis presented here.

A particular debt is owed to Bob Avakian. Not long after the events of 9/11, he offered a prescient analysis of the Bush "war on terror" and the broader factors underlying it which greatly influenced my understanding of the seriousness of U.S. plans for war on Iraq, the larger strategic canvas, and the urgency of the moment.

A special thanks to my publisher Greg Bates for his enthusiasm, support and many suggestions.

Finally, the struggles of the peoples of Iraq and the Middle East against foreign domination and for self-determination and liberation have given impetus and inspiration to my work over the years.

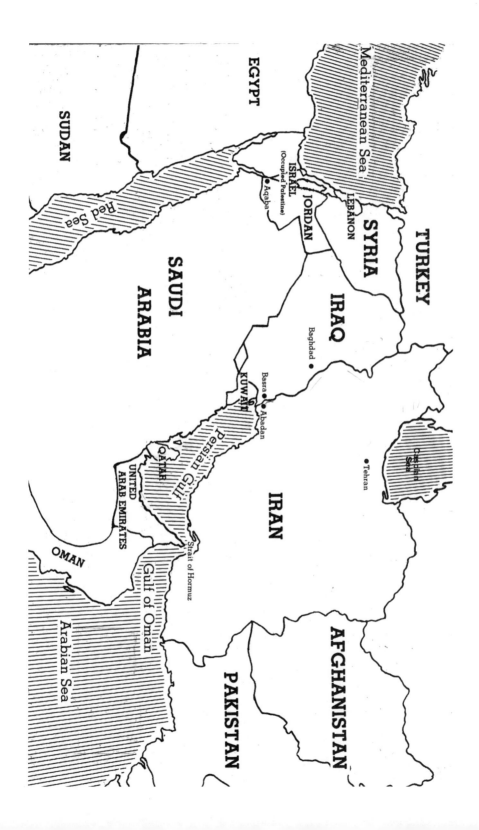

CHAPTER ONE

"GO MASSIVE.
SWEEP IT ALL UP."

[T]he process of transformation, even if it brings revolutionary change, is likely to be a long one, absent some catastrophic and catalyzing event—like a new Pearl Harbor.
    —"Rebuilding America's Defenses, Strategy, Forces and
Resources For a New Century," Project for a New American
Century, September 2000[1]

The Pearl Harbor of the 21st century took place today.
    —Diary entry of President George W. Bush,
September 11, 2001[2]

The 2003 Iraq war was not waged to eliminate "terrorism," destroy weapons of mass destruction, or liberate the Iraqi people. Instead, it was an unjust war of aggression, conquest and greater empire.

Labeled "Operation Iraqi Freedom" by the United States government, this war instead represented phase two, after the Afghanistan war of October 2001, in a sweeping, multi-dimensional campaign, waged under the rubric of a "war on terror," aimed at redrawing the world's geopolitical map in order to extend, strengthen and solidify U.S. imperial dominance.

Iraq is a prize and stepping stone in this audacious grand strategy. Invading and occupying this ancient land are intended to give further momentum to Washington's unbounded war, tighten America's grip on the oil-rich Persian Gulf, turn Iraq into a beachhead for controlling and reshaping the entire arc from North Africa to Central Asia, and strengthen the U.S. hand against rivals—current and future.

The full dimensions and implications of the 2003 war and the global agenda driving it have largely been hidden from the public, but they are both far-reaching and ominous:

- Conquering and occupying Iraq marks an historic escalation of direct American presence in the Middle East, and top Bush officials envision a generation-long campaign to radically restructure the entire region—a more aggressive and intrusive mission that could spark years of opposition and upheaval;
- The U.S. government has many groups, states, and regions in its sights, and radical changes are underway in Pentagon structures and strategies to enable U.S. forces to wage wars more quickly, more frequently, and in more theaters around the world; dramatic shifts are also taking place in U.S. nuclear posture that make nuclear combat more, not less, likely;
- Decades of international law and treaty are being revised wholesale; and
- Plans are afoot to further accelerate capitalist globalization—by force if need be—further widening the chasm between rich and poor, and entailing new, more direct forms of control over Third World countries. Iraq is a proving ground for these designs.

This vision of ongoing war for greater empire has been articulated at the highest levels. Shortly after Sept. 11, 2001, President Bush described the new war as "a lengthy campaign unlike any other we have ever seen."[3] James Woolsey, a former CIA director and one of this agenda's prime supporters, calls it the "fourth world war."[4] It is indeed a kind of world war, different in many respects than World Wars I and II and the Cold War, but a kind of world war nonetheless, fought to shape the destiny of countries, regions, and the entire international order for decades to come.

This book will explore the roots of the Iraq war of 2003 in nearly 100 years of foreign intervention to control the Persian Gulf and its vast oil wealth, and how the difficulties the U.S. encountered in this quest have drawn it into a deepening spiral of military intervention and war. It will dissect the contradictory relationship between Washington and Saddam Hussein's Ba'ath government, including U.S. complicity in many of the regime's crimes, and why it oscillated between collaboration and conflict. It will dissect the

Bush administration's kaleidoscope of fragmented, ever-shifting, and often transparently false renderings of Iraqi intentions and capabilities, and of the history of U.S.-Iraqi relations. And it will examine the interconnection between this history and the new U.S. global agenda, and its long-term implications for Iraq, the Middle East and the world.

Why was Iraq such a key link in this imperial design? Chapter 1 begins with the decision to wage war on Iraq, then analyzes the new global strategy that inspired it in order to answer that question.

A Response to Sept. 11?

The United States government has deliberately obscured the roots of the 2003 Iraq war by presenting it largely as a response to a single event—the attacks of Sept. 11, 2001. As President George W. Bush put it in his May 1, 2003 victory speech aboard the aircraft carrier *USS Abraham Lincoln*: "The battle of Iraq is one victory in a war on terror that began on September the 11th, 2001 and still goes on."[5]

In reality, "War is never an isolated act," as the 19th century German military theorist Karl von Clausewitz wrote, but "a mere continuation of policy by other means."[6] In this case, the invasion of Iraq and the global strategy that shaped it did not originate on Sept. 11, 2001, but grew out of over six decades of U.S. involvement in the region, the global transformations of the 1990s, and more specifically out of planning that began a decade *before* the attacks that brought down New York's World Trade Center towers and damaged the Pentagon.

Tracing the evolution of the U.S. decision to wage war—both before and after Sept. 11, 2001—exposes official justifications on several levels. First, it demonstrates that the Bush II administration cynically used Sept. 11 as an opportunity to launch a sweeping agenda that had been in the making for years before this horrific day.

Second and relatedly, it shows that the U.S. government's real aims were radically different from its public rationalizations for war.

Finally, it shows that Washington's decision to launch the March 2003 war was made well over a year earlier, long before it attempted to secure United Nations support in the fall of 2002.

Agitating For Regime Change—in the '90s

Establishment agitation for war on Iraq and greater global empire began in the 1990s. The 1991 collapse of the Soviet Union was a geopolitical earthquake that suddenly left America the world's only imperial superpower. Officials in the George H.W. Bush administration began mapping out a "new world order" of unchallengeable U.S. global dominance which the 1991 "Desert Storm" war on Iraq, called by the Pentagon "a defining event in U.S. global leadership," was intended to initiate.[7]

This vision was articulated most directly in the Defense Department's 1992 "Defense Planning Guidance." Written by Paul Wolfowitz, Lewis Libby and Zalmay Khalilzad under the direction of then-Defense Secretary Dick Cheney—all later top officials in the Bush II administration—the document argued that the U.S. should insure "that no rival superpower is allowed to emerge in Western Europe, Asia or the territory of the former Soviet Union" and that the United States remain the world's predominant power for the indefinite future. The Defense Guidance envisioned accomplishing these far-reaching objectives by preemptively attacking rivals or states seeking weapons of mass destruction, strengthening U.S. control of Persian Gulf oil, and refusing to allow international coalitions or law to inhibit U.S. freedom of action.[8]

Yet over the next years it became clear that Desert Storm did not usher in the era of unchallenged U.S. supremacy that Washington hoped for—globally or in the Middle East. For various reasons, which we will explore in subsequent chapters, the 1992 Defense Guidance's vision was not fully implemented during the Bill Clinton years. In Iraq, Saddam Hussein remained in power, by the late 1990s Washington's strategy of strangulation pending regime change was unraveling, and the U.S. was facing the prospect of a serious setback in a region key to its global standing. These developments generated enormous frustration within the Clinton administration and outrage among former Reagan and Bush I officials and other powerful currents within the U.S. corporate-political elite, who believed that Clinton was squandering America's global predominance.

While out of office, the strategists of American predominance continued to elaborate and promote their global agenda—and call for more aggressive action against Iraq. Often working through right-wing think tanks, such as the American Enterprise Institute and the Washington Institute for Near East Policy, or prominent publications like the *Wall Street Journal* and the media monopolist Rupert Murdoch-funded *Weekly Standard,* they churned out a stream of commentaries, strategy papers, articles, and books over the decade. In 1995, for example, Khalilzad wrote *From Containment to Global Leadership,* which amplified the theme of U.S. global hegemony.

In 1996, William Kristol, former Vice President Dan Quayle's chief of staff and then-editor of the *Weekly Standard,* and Robert Kagan, another former Reagan official, published an influential article along the same lines in *Foreign Affairs* titled "Toward a Neo-Reaganite Foreign Policy." That same year, Richard Perle, another former high level Reagan official, along with Douglas Feith and David Wurmser, later officials in the Bush II Pentagon and State Department respectively, produced a strategy paper for Israeli Likud Party leader Benjamin Netanyahu titled "A Clean Break: A New Strategy for Securing the Realm," which called for radically reshaping the Middle East and removing the Hussein regime in Iraq. Wolfowitz, meanwhile, opined in the *Wall Street Journal* that the U.S. needed to go beyond "containing" the Hussein regime, and the 2000 Republican party platform called for "a comprehensive plan for the removal of Saddam Hussein."[9]

As discussed below, many of these officials, pundits and strategists would work with the "Project for a New American Century," organized by Kristol in 1997. Its stated mission was shaping "a new century favorable to American principles and interests." In September 2000, it issued a major study titled "Rebuilding America's Defenses, Strategy, Forces and Resources For a New Century" whose contributors would read like a who's-who of the Bush II administration, including the authors of the 1992 Defense Guidance, Wolfowitz and Libby. "Rebuilding" expanded and updated the Guidance's themes and would become a template for the grand strategy embarked on by the Bush II administration.[10]

These strategists, some of whom are labeled neo-conservatives ("neocons") or neo-Reaganites, do not constitute an isolated fringe group, but represent the currently dominant thinking in the U.S. capitalist political establishment on how to deal with the potential opportunities as well as deep challenges confronting their system at home and abroad.[11]

The "Humble" Empire Searches for an Excuse

George W. Bush's seizure of the U.S. presidency in 2000 brought those clamoring for more aggressive action against Iraq and for greater empire back into power. Bush II had campaigned on the promise of a more modest foreign policy: "If we're an arrogant nation, they'll resent us," he said. "If we're a humble nation but strong, they'll welcome us."[12] It would turn out that "humble" was unrelated to his real intentions.

Bush II packed his administration with the strategists of more assertive and expansive empire. Dick Cheney became Vice President, with Libby his top assistant. Donald Rumsfeld was named Secretary of Defense, and he made Wolfowitz, Feith, and Stephen Cambone his top deputies, and appointed Richard Perle as chairman of the Defense Policy Board, a group of some 30 high-level ex-officials and strategists that advises the Pentagon. Khalilzad was made Special Assistant to the President for Near East, South West Asian, and North African Affairs, and would become U.S. emissary to the Iraqi opposition shortly before the war of 2003. Colin Powell, the Chairman of the Joint Chiefs of Staff under Bush, Sr., became Secretary of State.

As soon as his administration took the reins of power in January 2001, it began looking for ways to strike out more forcefully around the world—including against Iraq. The sequence of events shows that Sept. 11 would become the catalyst and opportunity to realize these strategic objectives, long in the works. More than eight months earlier, half of Bush, Jr.'s first national security meeting was spent on Iraq and the Persian Gulf.[13] Shortly before, the *Wall Street Journal* had called reversing "the slide in the Western position against Iraq" Washington's most urgent foreign policy priority.[14] At the Pentagon, Rumsfeld and Wolfowitz immediately began studying military options for ousting Hussein.[15] Containment, in their view, was no longer an option. First, it was breaking down, and second and more importantly, their broader global agenda demanded regime change and a radical transformation of the Middle East status quo. Former Reagan official and Bush II supporter Kenneth Adelman spoke to the global, tone-setting considerations of U.S. actions against the Hussein government: "Ideally, the first crisis would be something with Iraq. It would be a way to make the point that it's a new world."[16]

The new administration also stepped up efforts to link the Hussein regime to al Qaeda—months before Sept. 11, 2001. U.S. intelligence had been attempting to find such a link since the first World Trade Center bombing in 1993, yet according to both The New York Times and the Wall Street Journal, nothing had turned up.[17] Now, in early 2001, the attempt began afresh. The Wall Street Journal reported: "when the Bush administration took office in 2001, officials at the Pentagon immediately began peppering intelligence agencies with requests for studies on Baghdad's links to terrorism. At a meeting of senior administration officials in April 2001 to discuss al Qaeda, a top Defense Department official asked Mr. Clarke [the National Security Council's counter-terrorism coordinator] about whether Iraq had connections to Mr. bin Laden's group. Mr. Clarke said no, according to two people in the room."[18]

In July 2001, the Wall Street Journal editorialized for "swift and serious measures to remove Saddam Hussein from power"[19] and reported that, "Senior officials have held almost weekly meetings on the issue to discuss whether to push for the [Hussein] government's ouster."[20] In August 2001, the U.S. launched its most savage air attack on Iraq in six months.[21]

The Washington Post reported that the week before Sept. 11, Cheney was "worried about the strength of our whole position in the Middle East—where we stood with the Saudis, the Turks and others in the region."[22]

"The Pearl Harbor of the 21st Century"

Then came Sept. 11, 2001. Some five hours after hijacked jets crashed into the World Trade Center and then the Pentagon, Rumsfeld told an aide to begin drawing up plans for war—on Iraq. That afternoon the CIA concluded that it was "virtually certain" that the bin Laden network was responsible, not Iraq or other states,[23] but Rumsfeld wanted to know if U.S. intelligence was also "good enough hit S.H. [Saddam Hussein] at same time. Not only UBL [OBL—Osama bin Laden]." His admonition: "Go massive. Sweep it all up. Things related and not."[24]

Rumsfeld's orientation would encapsulate the U.S. government's response. Sept. 11 triggered a kind of "big bang" in U.S. global policy. In the hours, days and weeks afterward, the Bush team con-solidated a decade of geopolitical planning and debate into a new grand strategy and launched an unbounded "war on terror" to imple-ment it, a war whose varied objectives rapidly expanded far beyond its designated Sept. 11 origins. And Iraq was a key initial target.

The *Washington Post's* Bob Woodward reports that beginning hours after the Sept. 11 attacks and continuing over the ensuing week, top Bush officials held a series of secret discussions to hammer out their response. Woodward's descriptions and, more importantly, the 2003 war on Iraq that ensued 18 months later, make clear that neither punishing those responsible for Sept. 11 nor preventing future attacks were the Bush team's central and overriding goal.

Instead, Bush and his "war cabinet"—which included Vice President Cheney, Defense Secretary Rumsfeld, National Security Advisor Condoleezza Rice, Secretary of State Colin Powell, CIA Director Tenet, and often Deputy Defense Secretary Paul Wolfowitz—worked to translate the shock and grief of Sept. 11 into a mandate for a broad, ongoing war for greater empire.

On the morning of Sept. 11 Bush had stated simply that the U.S. would "hunt down and punish those responsible for these cow-ardly attacks." By the end of that day, however, the Bush II war cab-inet had decided to seize the moment to strike out against a variety of governments and anti-U.S. political forces and to embark on their larger global agenda.[25]

On the evening of Sept. 11 Bush addressed the country. While drafting the speech, he and Rice decided to include a declaration targeting states, not just those responsible for that day's attacks. She argued, "First words matter more than almost anything else." Bush agreed: "We've got to get it out there now." So that night Bush declared: "We will make no distinction between the terrorists who committed these acts and those who harbor them." The *Washington Post* noted, "The declaration was a huge step for the administra-tion...What he outlined that night from the Oval Office committed the United States to a broad, vigorous and potentially long war against terrorism, rather than a targeted retaliatory strike."[26]

The Bush leadership felt the need to respond to Sept. 11 with a vengeance in order to graphically demonstrate U.S. will and "cred-ibility," because its standing around the world is based largely on its military might and demonstrated willingness to use it. These had been challenged on Sept. 11. There is a strong possibility that the attacks were aimed at America's presence and actions in the Middle East, as Christopher Layne put it in the *Los Angeles Times*: "Al Qaeda's actions were coolly calculated to achieve well-defined geopolitical objectives: the removal of the U.S. military presence from the Persian Gulf (and in particular from Saudi Arabia) and an alteration of the U.S. stance in the Israeli-Palestinian conflict. In other words, Al Qaeda's goal was to undermine U.S. hegemony."[27] As Bush said later, he wanted to show "the world that there had been a fundamental change in U.S. policy."[28]

Responding with overwhelming violence (first on Afghanistan, later on Iraq) was inextricably linked with Washington's broader global agenda, which called for employing American military predominance to forcibly recast global economic, political and military relations. Rice, who would draft the official version of this new grand strategy, later spelled out the Bush regime's view of the post-Sept. 11 mix of necessity and opportunity, which was grounded in a decade of geopolitical strategizing:

> [A]n earthquake of the magnitude of 9/11 can shift the tectonic plates of international politics…. The international system has been in flux since the collapse of Soviet power. Now it is possible—indeed probable—that that transition is coming to an end. If that is right, then…this is a period not just of grave danger, but of enormous opportunity…to create a new balance of power that favored freedom.[29]

Bush and company discussed the need to act quickly "to capitalize on international outrage about the terrorist attack."[30] They realized the attacks gave them a once-in-a-lifetime political opportunity to act forcefully to "shift the tectonic plates" of global power. One top Bush official who wished to remain anonymous told *the New Yorker's* Nicholas Lemann, Sept. 11 was a "transformative moment" not because it "revealed the existence of a threat of which officials had previously been unaware," but because it "drastically reduced the American public's usual resistance to American military involvement overseas, at least for a while… Now that the United States has been attacked, the options are much broader."[31]

On the morning of September 12, Bush again escalated his

rhetoric: the attacks "were more than acts of terror. They were acts of war."[32] On September 20, 2001, in an address before a joint session of Congress, Bush pushed the envelope further still by committing the U.S. to an ongoing "war on terror" against "every terrorist group of global reach," and "any nation that continues to harbor or support terrorism." He then issued an ultimatum to the Taliban government of Afghanistan, where Al Qaeda had a base of operations. The U.S. initiated war on Afghanistan October 7, 2001.[33]

The Worldwide Attack Matrix Reloaded

By this time, Bush had already signed a top-secret "Worldwide Attack Matrix" mandating covert counter-insurgency operations in 80 different countries. The *Washington Post* commented that the plan "would give the CIA the broadest and most lethal authority in its history."[34] Bush didn't define "terrorism" in his address to Congress, and his administration has rarely done so publicly in order to maximize its freedom to apply the term to whomever it sees fit, whether Palestinian fighters, Islamic fundamentalists, radical nationalists, Maoist guerrillas, states standing in the way of U.S. designs, or even Iraqis resisting the invasion and occupation of their own country.

In his address to Congress on September 20, 2001, Bush's only reference to Iraq was a brief mention of the 1991 Gulf War. It has since been revealed that his war cabinet had already been debating whether to immediately attack Iraq for over a week, and Bush had already directed the Pentagon to begin initial war planning.

These discussions began on September 12, 2001, the morning after the attacks. According to the *Washington Post*, they centered on whether to "take advantage of the opportunity offered by the terrorist attacks to go after Hussein immediately."[35] Bush's top advisors reportedly agreed in principle, but there were differences over timing.[36]

On September 17, 2001, after six days of debate, the Bush team decided not to strike Iraq—yet. The enormity of their emerging agenda demanded a step-by-step approach, and according to the *Washington Post*, they felt they would "need successes early in any war to maintain domestic and international support." As Bush told

Woodward, "[I]f we could prove that we could be successful in this theater [Afghanistan], then the rest of the task would be easier. If we tried to do too many things—two things, for example, or three things—militarily, then...the lack of focus would have been a huge risk."[37] That day Bush signed secret orders authorizing war on Afghanistan and instructing the Pentagon to begin planning for battle in Iraq.[38]

Bush also told the *Washington Post* that he wanted to make sure that the U.S. Iraq policy was not shaped by a desire to finish what his father hadn't, or, even more importantly, by the approach taken by his father's administration (explored in chapter 5): "one of the things I wasn't going to allow to happen is, that we weren't going to let their previous experience in this theater dictate a rational course for the new war." Here, we can probably take Bush at his word: in his view he had much bigger fish to fry—a global empire to extend—and doing so meant breaking with significant aspects of the Bush, Sr. strategic vision.[39]

Creating Pretexts at Hawk Central

As these discussions were going on within the administration, advocates of war on Iraq and greater global hegemony, in and out of government, began a concerted campaign–publicly and behind the scenes–to make sure that Iraq was indeed targeted in phase two of the war on terror. This campaign was not predicated on Iraqi involvement in Sept. 11, but on the geopolitics of global dominance.

The Pentagon became "hawk central" and kicked off the drive for war just eight days after the Twin Towers collapsed, with a September 19-20 meeting of the Defense Policy Board. *The New York Times* reported that the Board met behind closed doors "for 19 hours to discuss the ramifications of the attacks of Sept. 11. The members of the group agreed on the need to turn to Iraq as soon as the initial phase of the war against Afghanistan and Mr. bin Laden and his organization is over."[40]

Following the meeting, these war plotters dispatched former CIA chief James Woolsey to London on "a mission," the *New York Times* reported, to gather "evidence" linking Hussein to the

September 11 attacks. Woolsey then began raising various charges against Iraq: that Iraqi agents met with Mohammed Atta, the alleged "ringleader" of the September 11 attacks; that Iraq provided fake passports for all 19 hijackers; that an Al Qaeda member traveled to Baghdad in 1998 to celebrate Saddam Hussein's birthday; that Iraq trained Al Qaeda members; and that Iraq was linked to anthrax mailed to U.S. Senators in October 2001. There was no real proof for any of these charges, as detailed in the appendix here—in fact it later turned out that the most likely source for the anthrax letters was someone associated with the U.S. military.[41] Yet these charges were widely repeated in the mainstream U.S. media nonetheless.[42]

The day the meeting concluded, just nine days after Sept. 11, Defense Policy Board members and other prominent right-wingers, including columnists Kristol and Charles Krauthammer, drafted an open letter to Bush arguing, "Even if evidence does *not* link Iraq directly to the [September 11] attack, any strategy aiming at the eradication of terrorism and its sponsors must include a determined effort to remove Saddam Hussein from power in Iraq. Failure to undertake such an effort will constitute an early and perhaps decisive surrender in the war on international terrorism." (emphasis added)[43]

Deciding on War: By November 2001

The "attack Iraq" drumbeat continued over the next months, and the quick U.S. victory in Afghanistan further emboldened hawks in the Bush administration. One official told the *Wall Street Journal*, "the idea of waging a similar small war in Iraq 'stopped looking unthinkable.'" David Frum, the former White House speech writer who coined the phrase "axis of evil" and authored *The Right Man: The Surprise Presidency of George W. Bush*, described the arrogance surging through the corridors of power: "If a few hundred men and a few dozen planes could overthrow the Taliban, what might ten thousand men and a few hundred planes do in Iraq? Or a hundred thousand men and a thousand planes do to the whole Gulf? It suddenly seemed that American power could do *anything*."[44]

By late October or early November 2001, some seven weeks

after Sept. 11, the Bush war cabinet secretly decided to move against the Hussein regime, according to reports in the *Wall Street Journal, USA Today,* and the *New Republic.* By then, the Taliban had been defeated in Afghanistan and Vice President Cheney, who the *Wall Street Journal* reported had become Bush's "war counselor," had joined Rumsfeld and Wolfowitz in urging war on Iraq.[45]

In December 2001, the *New Republic* noted that after late October 2001 the debate within the Administration was no longer over "whether to extend the war to Iraq—that question has largely been settled."[46] On September 12, 2002, *USA Today* reported,

> President Bush's determination to oust Iraq's Saddam Hussein by military force if necessary was set last fall.... He decided that Saddam must go more than 10 months ago; the debate within the administration since then has been about the means to accomplish that.... The course advocated by Rumsfeld and Cheney became policy, despite concerns by Powell and others... But whatever the response, aides say the president's determination to oust Saddam—the decision he made in the seven weeks following the attacks on Sept. 11—hasn't wavered.[47]

The *Washington Post* and *Time* magazine paint a similar picture, but report that the decision to wage war probably came in the spring of 2002. According to the *Washington Post:* "Then, in April, Bush approached Rice. It was time to figure out 'what we are doing about Iraq,' he told her, setting in motion a series of meetings by the principals and their deputies. 'I made up my mind that Saddam needs to go,' Bush hinted to a British reporter at the time."[48]

It may be impossible at this moment to precisely trace the evolution of the decision to go to war because, as *USA Today* reports, it was very closely held and made "without a formal decision-making meeting or the intelligence assessment that customarily precedes such a momentous decision"—and hence without the paper-trail and possibility of leaks that accompanies the process.[49]

However, given other administration actions, it seems most likely that by late October or early November 2001 the Bush administration had decided to move against Iraq in phase 2 of its "war on terror." Bush's January 2002 State of the Union speech targeted Iraq as part of an "axis of evil," and early in 2002 Bush directed the CIA to: step up its financial, military and organizational support for anti-Hussein forces; increase intelligence gathering in Iraq; and plan for the possible use of the CIA and U.S. Special Forces to track down, capture or kill Saddam Hussein.[50]

The meetings and decisions which reportedly took place in April 2002 may well have decided upon a massive assault, as opposed to other means of removing Hussein, or choosing between specific military options. In either case, the choice for war was made months before the U.S. attempted to legitimize its decision by going to the UN, enacting Resolution 1441, and dispatching weapons inspectors to Iraq.[51]

War First, Evidence Later

> [They] lied comfortably, and whenever cornered there was
> no hesitation in lying, and repeating lies, and not caring about
> [whether] what they repeated was true or false.[52]

Former *Washington Post* executive editor Ben Bradlee's description above of the Nixon White House applies doubly to the Bush II White House, Pentagon, State Department, and CIA. Their campaign for war on Iraq took official lying to new depths of cynicism, brazenness, double-speak, and hypocrisy.

The Bush case against Iraq rested on two lies, repeated early and often: first, that Saddam Hussein was linked to Al Qaeda and the attacks of Sept. 11, and second that his possession of dangerous chemical, biological, and possibly nuclear weapons posed a "grave and growing danger" to the Middle East and to the United States itself. The case was made directly by raising the specter that Iraq "could provide these arms to terrorists, giving them the means to match their hatred...the price of indifference would be catastrophic," as Bush did in his 2002 State of the Union address.[53] It was also made indirectly by mentioning Sept. 11 in one breath and Iraq in the next in textbook bait-and-switch fashion.

In fact, U.S. intelligence agencies were well aware, long before Sept. 11, that it was very unlikely that there was any real connection between Iraq and Al Qaeda. In February 2002, the *New York Times* reported that the CIA has "no evidence that Iraq has engaged in terrorist operations against the United States in nearly a decade, and the agency is also convinced that President Saddam Hussein has not provided chemical or biological weapons to Al Qaeda or related terrorist groups."[54]

A Congressional commission set up in February 2002 to investigate the 9/11 attacks found no Iraqi connection, but did find a Saudi connection. According to commission member and former Senator Max Cleland (D-Ga.), the Bush administration delayed the release of their report until after Iraq was invaded and conquered for fear its findings would undermine the government's rationale for war.[55]

As a result of such deceptions, 69 percent of the U.S. public still believed Saddam Hussein was probably involved in Sept. 11 according to a *Washington Post* poll done in September 2003, two years after the attacks.[56] Two weeks after these poll numbers were released, and some six months after the U.S. invaded Iraq, Bush and Rumsfeld were forced to admit—due to lack of evidence and the steady unraveling of their pretexts for war—that there was no evidence of Iraqi involvement in Sept. 11.[57]

Even before the war, it was clear that U.S. claims concerning Iraq's military strength and its possession of weapons of mass destruction were wildly "sexed up," if not outright fabrications.

In his January 2003 State of the Union speech, Bush warned that Saddam Hussein had or could have "biological weapons materials sufficient to produce over 25,000 liters of anthrax; enough doses to kill several million people...materials sufficient to produce more than 38,000 liters of botulinum toxin; enough to subject millions of people to death by respiratory failure...materials to produce as much as 500 tons of sarin, mustard and VX nerve agent...upwards of 30,000 munitions capable of delivering chemical agents." He claimed that during the 1990s, the Hussein regime had "an advanced nuclear weapons development program," and then uttered what would become 16 infamous words: "The British government has learned that Saddam Hussein recently sought significant quantities of uranium from Africa."[58]

Months before, however, a September 2002 assessment by the Defense Intelligence Agency, the Pentagon's primary intelligence arm, concluded that there was "no definitive, reliable information" that Iraq either possessed or was manufacturing chemical or biological weapons.[59]

In 1998, five years before Bush made his nuclear claims, the International Atomic Energy Agency had certified that Iraq no longer had a nuclear weapons program. A year before Bush's speech, former Ambassador Joseph Wilson traveled to Niger at the behest of the CIA to investigate the claim that Iraq had attempted to buy uranium; he found that it was "highly doubtful that any such transaction had ever taken place," and reported as much to the Bush administration.[60] Meanwhile, the Iraqi government denounced charges that it had or would soon have nuclear weapons as a "huge clamour fabricated by the President of the United States" and "the biggest and most wicked slander against Iraq."[61]

After the 2003 war, a team of 1,400 U.S. and British experts scoured Iraq for banned weapons. After four months of searching, none were found.[62] The failure to find any chemical, biological or nuclear weapons or prohibited missiles made a number of things crystal clear:

- first, that no matter what the U.S. finds or doesn't find in Iraq (and most arms experts now feel the U.S. will never find any WMD because they were destroyed by the Hussein regime in the early 1990s), the U.S. had no valid intelligence showing that Iraq possessed chemical, biological, or nuclear weapons;
- second, that the Bush team knew full well that Iraq was not a grave and growing danger;
- third, most, if not all of the Bush administration's specific charges, detailed in the appendix, were deliberate exaggerations, distortions or outright fabrications; and
- fourth, that the United States government had been lying about Iraq's purported WMDs for over a decade, as examined in chapter 7.

The Pentagon leadership was so determined to wage war on Iraq that in October 2001 it set up a new intelligence/operations arm—the Office of Special Plans—directly under the control of Deputy Defense Secretary Wolfowitz and Undersecretary of Defense for Policy Feith. This Office reportedly played a key role in slanting, spinning and concocting "intelligence" that could be used to justify war, and propagating it to the White House and the media.[63]

During the year before the 2003 war, Vice President Cheney pursued a similar objective by paying a number of visits to the CIA to "investigate" the work of analysts assessing Iraq's weapons and possible ties to Al Qaeda. The analysts later reported feeling pressured to skew their findings to fit the White House agenda on Iraq.[64]

As we'll examine in the course of this book, this is but the latest chapter in Washington's long history of misusing, distorting, and concocting "intelligence" in order to achieve its objectives in the Persian Gulf.

In reality and all along, the administration saw a weakened Iraq—a country of 25 million the size of the State of California which had been battered by 20 plus years of war and 12 years of sanctions—as a target of opportunity, not a growing threat. The *New York Times* reported in September 2002 that the "Bush administration's decision to force a confrontation ...reflects its low regard for Iraq's conventional armed forces... American officials are confident that United States forces would quickly prevail" in war.[65]

Rumsfeld and other Pentagon officials "argued that U.S. military forces would overwhelm Iraq's rusting army," *USA Today* reported. In fact, Iraq's military was held in such low regard that Rumsfeld explored attacking as early as August 2002. "The mission would be relatively easy to execute... Rumsfeld envisioned a surgical strike using relatively few troops, many of them from special operations forces." After much internal debate, military planners decided to deploy a more robust force.[66] The Bush II war cabinet calculated that a quick and overwhelming victory over Iraq would give further momentum and legitimacy to their "war on terror."

Like *Alice in Wonderland's* Queen of Hearts who screamed, "sentence first-verdict afterward...off with her head," Bush first decided to decapitate Iraq, then searched for "evidence" to justify it. His administration may even have been gambling that something would turn up after U.S. forces took Iraq that could then be used to validate the war ex post facto. This was even acknowledged in some mainstream accounts: *USA Today* reported that the administration's internal debate over Iraq "left the impression with some that Bush was searching for a justification after deciding to target Saddam."[67]

Finding The Right Way To Do It

In December 2001, the *New Republic* noted that the Bush II orientation was to attack Iraq as soon as "we find the right way to do it."[68] Over the next 17 months, the administration would try to find the right way to do so—developing a military strategy, mustering troops and equipment, preparing public opinion, and trying, unsuccessfully, to build a coalition for war.

Military planning began in November 2001 and was stepped up in April 2002. By late spring a variety of military options were being thrashed out. In late April 2002, the *New York Times* reported that Pentagon planners envisioned "a major air campaign and ground invasion, with initial estimates contemplating the use of 70,000 to 250,000 troops." The attack was to take place in early 2003 to allow "time to create the right military, economic and diplomatic conditions."[69] In September 2002, two days before Bush presented the U.S. case to the United Nations, the Associated Press reported that the Pentagon had given Bush a "detailed set" of military options for overthrowing the Hussein regime.[70]

The decision to proceed through the UN represented an effort to build political and military support for a war the U.S. had already decided to wage, not an effort to disarm Iraq without war. The *Washington Post* reported that in August 2002, Secretary of State Powell convinced Bush to go through the UN, not to avoid war, but to make it possible. According to the *Post*, Powell warned that without UN cover, "the entire region could be destabilized–friendly regimes in Saudi Arabia, Egypt and Jordan could be put in jeopardy or overthrown. Anger and frustration at America abounded. War could change everything in the Middle East."[71]

The U.S. intended the UN weapons inspections, carried out under Resolution 1441 passed on November 8, 2002, to be a "catch-22" situation from which the Hussein regime could not escape. If banned weapons were discovered, Iraq would be in violation of UN resolutions, thereby justifying war.

If Iraq did not admit to having banned weapons, the U.S. would argue that this too constituted a breach of Resolution 1441, which demanded a full and complete disclosure of all chemical, biological and nuclear weapons, as well as missiles with a range of over 150 kilometers. Since the U.S. supposedly had intelligence showing that Iraq did possess banned weapons, Baghdad would be in violation of Resolution 1441 by not declaring them, thus necessitating war in that case as well.

The *Wall Street Journal*, a vociferous advocate of war, spelled out this logic in an editorial on the eve of Iraq's mandated December 8, 2002 weapons declaration to the UN: "If Iraq asserts this weekend that it has no such weapons, then that will be on its face a material breach of UN Security Council resolutions demanding that he disarm. And a material breach means Iraq must be disarmed by force."[72]

But then, disarmament was never Washington's real goal; regime change was. Defense Policy Board Chair Richard Perle let this cat out of the bag in November 2002 when he told British MPs that even a "clean bill of health" from UN weapons inspectors would not stop the U.S. war machine. Perle was right. After more than 600 inspections, UN inspectors came up empty and the U.S. still went to war.[73]

In April 2003, after UN inspectors were pulled from Iraq, chief inspector Hans Blix told the Spanish daily *El Pais*, "There is evidence that this war was planned well in advance... I now believe that finding weapons of mass destruction has been relegated, I would say, to fourth place, which is why the United States and Britain are now waging war on Iraq."[74]

International law and the United Nations Charter provide for only two legitimate reasons for war—individual or collective self defense in response to an armed attack, or an action authorized by the UN Security Council. The U.S. had neither, making its 2003 war on Iraq an illegal act of unprovoked aggression.

One World, One Empire

Neither mystical links with al Qaeda, invisible weapons of mass destruction, reflexive posturing, electoral politicking, nor diverting attention from corporate scandals and a weak economy explained why the U.S. government was hell-bent on attacking Iraq. But the sweep and enormity of its global agenda did.

"They have ambitions of essentially reshuffling the whole deck, reordering the whole situation—beginning with the strategic areas of Central and South Asia and the Middle East that are more immediately involved now—but, even beyond that, on a world scale," Bob Avakian of the Revolutionary Communist Party USA wrote shortly after Sept. 11. "They've set themselves a very far-reaching agenda with gigantic implications."[75]

This momentous shift in U.S. global strategy was crystalized in a new National Security Strategy (NSS) published on September 20, 2002. This new NSS echoed and codified previous strategy papers, including the 1992 Pentagon Defense Guidance and the Project for a New American Century's 2000 paper, "Rebuilding America's Defenses," discussed above. Then it went further.

Taking off from the hegemonic vision developed by Reagan and Bush I officials during the 1990s, the NSS argued that the 1991 Soviet collapse had left the U.S. the world's only superpower—with "unparalleled military strength and great economic and political influence"—and that U.S. policy should be to "work to translate this moment of influence into decades of peace, prosperity, and liberty."[76]

What does this really mean? The document's mantra is creating "a balance of power that favors freedom." Like terrorism, "freedom" hasn't been defined by the Bush regime, but the substance of the NSS, as well as the voluminous writings of the imperial strategists who have shaped it, make clear that it means the freedom of America's dominant corporate-political elite to impose its values, interests, and economic system on all others. As the NSS baldly put it, "These values of freedom are right and true for every person, in every society."

The new National Security Strategy claims that the U.S. will not seek "unilateral advantage," yet it is a doctrine for just that— militarily, politically and economically. It amounts to an audacious declaration that the U.S. aims to remain the world's sole superpower for decades to come. The practical implementation of this new Bush doctrine will no doubt be shaped by internal debates and external events, including the growing unrest and resistance in now-occupied Iraq. Nonetheless, its implications are clearly enormous.

A core thesis, which has been a central theme in neo-conservative theorizing for over a decade, is preventing the rise of rival powers which could challenge the U.S. regionally or globally. The NSS envisions accomplishing this objective by first maintaining overwhelming military superiority over all other countries and combinations of countries, and second by no longer containing possible opponents, but eliminating them before they can emerge: "Our forces will be strong enough to dissuade potential adversaries from pursuing a military build-up in hopes of surpassing, or equaling, the power of the United States." Defense Secretary Rumsfeld elaborates that the U.S. would deter "potential adversaries not only from using existing weapons but also from building dangerous new ones in the first place," and the U.S. would no longer judge states by their actions or intentions, but by their potential "capabilities."[77]

To achieve this staggering goal, the U.S. power structure envisions staggering methods, including disarming various countries, toppling defiant regimes, occupying strategic regions, and waging counter-insurgency wars against a variety of political forces standing in the way of U.S. control.

Marine General Peter Pace, the Joint Chiefs vice chairman, has stated that "the scope for potential anti-terrorist action included—at a minimum—Iran, Iraq, Yemen, Somalia, Sudan, Lebanon, Syria, Libya, Georgia, Colombia, Malaysia, Indonesia, the Philippines and North Korea."[78] Pace knew of what he spoke: The *New York Times* reported that by January 2003, the Pentagon had drafted a "National Military Strategic Plan for the War on Terrorism" which called for 20 to 30 years of war on a variety of states and anti-U.S. groups.[79]

Rule Out Nothing—Including Nukes

To carry out this global campaign of counter-insurgency and "regime change," as well as ensure that no other world power could stand in its way, the Bush II administration has embarked on an enormous military buildup.

For some, the term empire conjures up images of legions of Roman soldiers fanning out across Europe and the Middle East, and when applied to the United States today, seems overblown. Yet at $355.4 billion a year, America's military spending outstrips the combined spending of all other countries, and U.S. troops are stationed in over 120 of the world's 191 nations. The Romans couldn't even dream of such military power and reach.[80]

Radical changes are occurring in military doctrine, organization, and force structure designed to enable the U.S. to launch a number of wars across the globe, quickly and in succession if necessary. The bruising politics of this transformation, concentrated in the reported tensions between Rumsfeld and some of the uniformed military, were at play in the debates that raged within the administration in 2002 over the size of the force needed to seize Iraq.[81]

Ominous changes are also taking place in U.S. nuclear strategy. The latest U.S. "Nuclear Posture Review," leaked to the *Los Angeles Times* in February 2002, advocates scrapping arms control treaties, developing a new generation of nuclear weapons—including more "usable" tactical warheads—more fully integrating nuclear weapons into U.S. war fighting strategies, and planning for the possible preemptive use of nuclear weapons. For the first time, the U.S. stated it would contemplate nuclear strikes on non-nuclear powers. This latter move effectively undermines the Nuclear Non-Proliferation Treaty. The *Los Angeles Times* reported:

> The Bush administration has directed the military to prepare contingency plans to use nuclear weapons against at least seven countries and to build smaller nuclear weapons for use in certain battlefield situations, according to a classified Pentagon report obtained by the *Los Angeles Times*. The secret report, which was provided to Congress on Jan. 8, says the Pentagon needs to be prepared to use nuclear weapons against China, Russia, Iraq, North Korea, Iran, Libya and Syria. It says the weapons could be used in three types of situations: against targets able to withstand nonnuclear attack; in retaliation for attack with nuclear, biological or chemical weapons; or 'in the event of surprising military developments.'[82]

In September 2002, Bush signed Presidential Directive 17, a secret document which states, "The United States will continue to make clear that it reserves the right to respond with overwhelming force—including potentially nuclear weapons—to the use of [weapons of mass destruction] against the United States, our forces abroad, and friends and allies."[83]

Three months later, in December 2002, a new "National Strategy to Combat Weapons of Mass Destruction" was issued which threatened first strikes, possibly with nuclear weapons, against countries thought to be developing chemical, biological, or nuclear weapons.[84]

Top Bush officials radiate, as it were, a vicious eagerness to use military power, including nuclear weapons. "Rule nothing out," Rumsfeld wrote in the May/June 2002 issue of *Foreign Affairs*. "The enemy must understand that we will use every means at our disposal to defeat them, and that we are prepared to make whatever sacrifices are necessary to achieve victory."[85]

It is not widely known that the Bush administration never took the nuclear option off the table in Iraq. Two months before the war, the *Los Angeles Times* reported that the Pentagon was "quietly preparing for the possible use of nuclear weapons in a war against Iraq...including the possible use of so-called bunker-buster nuclear weapons against deeply buried military targets."[86]

Channeling George Orwell: "Pre-Emptive Self-Defense"

The Bush II NSS also spells out that extending U.S. global dominance means striking down adversaries and recasting global political, military, and economic relations, which in turn necessitates trampling on international law, casting aside global treaties, eviscerating international organizations, and reordering traditional alliances.

One of its chilling new double-speak concepts is "pre-emptive self-defense." Throughout its history, the United States has often invaded or attacked other countries, whether they had attacked America or not. The Bush II NSS takes this tradition a huge step further and explicitly makes this doctrine of preemption—really prevention—the norm of U.S. conduct: "America will act against such emerging threats before they are fully formed... We will not hesitate to act alone, if necessary, to exercise our right of self-defense by acting preemptively." In other words, the U.S. has given itself the "right" to launch attacks on other countries without warning, evidence of threat, provocation or international approval. No moral or legal reasoning is offered to explain why other countries should not be able to apply this same doctrine to the U.S.; it is taken as a given that they simply don't have the military power to do so.

A key precept is the NSS's rejection of the principle that other countries have national sovereignty and the right to determine their affairs within their own borders. It proclaimed, instead, the

Orwellian concept that the U.S. will be "convincing or compelling states to accept their sovereign responsibilities." In other words, the U.S. will decide what other government's "responsibilities" are—with the threat that they will face bombs, perhaps even "regime change" and occupation, if they do not comply. Of course, for the U.S. it is different: national sovereignty is assumed to be absolute—unrestrained by treaty, alliance or law.

Well before Sept. 11, the Bush II administration made clear that the U.S. would no longer be impeded by treaties or past alliances. In its first months, Washington walked away from or downgraded its commitments to the International Criminal Court, the Kyoto agreement on global warming, the anti-ballistic missile treaty, and the biological weapons convention.[87]

It is widely understood that the U.S. government is radically breaking with existing international law and practice. Former National Security Advisor and Secretary of State in the Nixon administration Henry Kissinger is no stranger to U.S. intervention. A former member of Bush II's Defense Policy Board, Kissinger outlined the implications of the new strategic doctrine:

> Regime change as a goal for military intervention challenges the international system established by the 1648 Treaty of Westphalia, which established the principle of nonintervention in the domestic affairs of other states. Also, the notion of justified pre-emption runs counter to modern international law, which sanctions the use of force in self-defense only against actual–not potential–threats.[88]

The Bush government is also revising its relationship with its former allies, NATO, and the UN. From now on, the U.S. "mission determines the coalition," as Rumsfeld has put it. Washington will set the terms and then others can sign up—or not.

Europe's insistence on "multilateralism"—that other global powers play a prominent role in shaping international affairs—is derided as the politics of the weak by influential hawks like Robert Kagan. Writing in the June/July 2002 issue of the right-wing *Policy Review*, Kagan argues that, "Europe is turning away from power" and sees the world "through the eyes of weaker powers," while the U.S. "remains mired in history, exercising power in the anarchic Hobbesian world where international laws and rules are unreliable and where true security and the defense and promotion of a liberal order still depend on the possession and use of military might." He argues that Europe lost its "strategic centrality after the Cold War ended." Quoting one historian to make his own point, Kagan argues that Washington should deny it a voice in global affairs and seek "the retirement of Europe from world politics."[89]

The decision to wage war on Iraq without authorization under the UN or international law embodied this orientation. It was aimed in part at relegating other world powers to an even more subordinate status. The intense debate in the UN Security Council and the opposition of France, Germany, and Russia to the Iraq war had more to do with restraining U.S. global power and preserving international institutions in which they had a voice (along with their influence in the Middle East), than concern for the fate of Iraq and its people.[90]

French President Jacques Chirac warned that war on Iraq was an attempt "to legitimize the unilateral and pre-emptive use of force." Referring to the UN debates, the *Washington Post* reported, "the seven-week battle has masked a larger struggle over the projection and containment of U.S. power."[91]

Globalization at Gunpoint

The new National Security Strategy also advocates greater freedom for U.S. business and accelerated capitalist globalization. It states that the U.S. will "use this moment of opportunity" to extend "free markets, and free trade to every corner of the world" and to promote the "efficient allocation of resources, and regional integration." It calls for the promotion of "pro-growth legal and regulatory policies to encourage business investment, innovation and entrepreneurial activity."[92]

Taken together, and placed in the context of the post-Soviet decade of accelerated globalization and privatization, these prescriptions amounts to a demand that U.S. capital have open access to key global markets and raw materials; that trade, investment, ownership and political barriers standing in the way be broken down; that global trade and economic relations be restructured to reflect and perpetuate U.S. dominance; and that conditions be created for the unchallenged exploitation of hundreds of millions of laboring people worldwide. Combined with the NSS's insistence on U.S. military superiority and its right to use it to enforce "regime change," the document's economic principles can best be understood as capitalist globalization on U.S. terms, carried out at gunpoint. As we will explore in chapter 9, this is precisely the vision the U.S. is now carrying out in occupied Iraq.

In the aftermath of the October 2001 war on Afghanistan, acclaimed Indian writer Arundhati Roy described this intersection of globalization and the U.S. "war on terror":

> In the last ten years of unbridled Corporate Globalization, the world's total income has increased by an average of 2.5 percent a year. And yet the numbers of poor in the world has increased by 100 million. Of the top hundred biggest economies, 51 are corporations, not countries. The top 1 percent of the world has the same combined income as the bottom 57 percent and that disparity is growing. And now, under the spreading canopy of the War Against Terror, this process is being hustled along. The men in suits are in an unseemly hurry. While bombs rain down on us, and cruise missiles skid across the skies, while nuclear weapons are stockpiled to make the world a safer place, contracts are being signed, patents are being registered, oil pipe lines are being laid, natural resources are being plundered, water is being privatized...[93]

There are deep connections between the U.S. government's international and domestic agendas. Following Sept. 11 the Bush administration passed the Patriot Act, created a Department of Homeland Security, and enacted a series of repressive measures designed to give the government broad new powers to suppress domestic opposition. Like the international counterpart that restricts sovereignty and broadens U.S. military might, domestic measures restrict privacy and civil rights, while expanding police powers. Such sweeping measures are the domestic version of the doctrine of preemption; the Bush team understands full well that its plan for an ongoing war to reshape the planet will generate waves of opposition—both within the U.S. and around the world—and it is putting in place machinery to attempt to suppress it.[94]

Returning to the international side of the agenda, the U.S. is striving to leverage an historic window of military (and to a lesser degree economic and political) supremacy into all-around political, economic and military dominance for the long term. Half-way measures, negotiated solutions, and diplomatic settlements are anathema to this vision of radical transformation. Michael Ledeen is a former Reagan administration official who was involved in the Iran-Contra affair and is currently a fellow at the right-wing American Enterprise Institute. He put it succinctly: "This is total war. We are fighting a variety of enemies. There are lots of them out there."[95]

The 2002 National Security Strategy was neither voted on by Congress, approved in an election, negotiated with allies, nor authorized by the United Nations. It wasn't even a topic of debate in the November 2002 elections, as right-wing commentator and war supporter Max Boot noted in the *Washington Post*: "Almost no one is criticizing President Bush's pledge to maintain American military hegemony.... The odd thing is that this dominance has occurred quietly and with little public debate."[96]

Instead, politicians and most of the mainstream media treated the NSS as if it were business as usual, and that the U.S. was a "benign" or "reluctant" imperial power that somehow has the right to determine the fate of humanity. Of course, neither U.S. nor world history have ever provided an example of benign imperialism—and the record of U.S. actions in Iraq is certainly no exception.

On September 12, 2002, President Bush went before the UN to condemn Iraq as one of the "outlaw groups and regimes that accept no law of morality and have no limit to their violent ambitions."[97] Eight days later his government made official its new National Security Strategy, which announced that U.S. actions would no longer be bound by existing law or conventional morality, and that there were no limits to the "violent ambitions" of the U.S. corporate-capitalist ruling class. No other empire in history had ever issued such an arrogant, blatant, and chilling declaration of global hegemony. "Go massive. Sweep it all up," Rumsfeld had urged. "Things related and not."

A Laser Focus on Iraq

The NSS mentioned Iraq only once in passing. Yet for any who wonder why the Bush administration was so focused on regime change in Baghdad, it is essential reading, and explains far more than any Colin Powell presentation, British "White Paper," or UN resolution. After its release, Jay Bookman of the *Atlanta Journal-Constitution* remarked,

> The official story on Iraq has never made sense...
> Something else had to be going on; something was missing... In
> recent days, those missing pieces have finally begun to fall into
> place. As it turns out, this is not really about Iraq. It is not about
> weapons of mass destruction, or terrorism, or Saddam, or U.N.
> resolutions. This war, should it come, is intended to mark the
> official emergence of the United States as a full-fledged global
> empire, seizing sole responsibility and authority as planetary
> policeman. It would be the culmination of a plan 10 years or
> more in the making, carried out by those who believe the
> United States must seize the opportunity for global domination,
> even if it means becoming the 'American imperialists' that our
> enemies always claimed we were.[98]

Why was the Bush II administration focused on Iraq—before Sept. 11 and then like a laser after the attacks? War on Iraq was designed to "mark the official emergence" of a more dominant U.S. imperium and much, much more, as we will explore in depth in chapters 9 and 10. In sum, Iraq represented the confluence of regional and global concerns; it can be thought of as a key piece on the chessboard of empire. Toppling the Hussein regime removed a troublesome piece, captured a central square, opened new lines of maneuver and attack—and announced the U.S. intention to checkmate the world.

Enforcing regime change was viewed as essential to solidifying the U.S. position in the Middle East, and thus a continuation of the politics of the 1991 Persian Gulf War. It was also seen as an essential step in implementing Washington's new grand strategy. The U.S. plans to turn Iraq into a client state and a launching pad for the restructuring of the entire Middle East, which includes moving against states like Syria, Iran, and Lebanon; attempting to forcibly resolve the Palestinian people's struggle on Israeli terms; bolstering unsteady allies in Saudi Arabia, Jordan and Egypt; and generally attempting to quash the anti-U.S. anger throughout the region. It was a war intended to "shock and awe" opponents of U.S. domination in the Middle East—and the world.

Of course, where the U.S. turns after Iraq is still an open question, which will be shaped by the outcome of the Iraq war, world events, and ongoing debate within the political establishment. Yet occupying Iraq potentially gives the U.S. direct control of the world's second largest oil reserves and places its armed forces in the center of the Persian Gulf/Central Asia region, home to some 80 percent of the world's petroleum and natural gas. Control of the global flow of oil and natural gas could give the U.S. enormous leverage over Russia, France, Germany, China, Japan, and others, possibly preventing any from challenging it—regionally or globally.

Prior to the war, Kissinger alluded to some of these multiple objectives:

> The overthrow of the Iraq regime and, at a minimum, the eradication of its weapons of mass destruction, would have potentially beneficent political consequences as well: The so-called Arab street may conclude that the negative consequences of jihad outweigh any potential benefits. It could encourage a new approach in Syria; strengthen moderate forces in Saudi Arabia; increase pressures for a democratic evolution in Iran; demonstrate to the Palestinian Authority that America is serious about overcoming corrupt tyrannies; and bring about a better balance in oil policy within OPEC.[99]

"In one place—in one regime," Bush said of Iraq in September 2002, "we find all these dangers, in their most lethal and aggressive forms."[100] Iraq did represent a convergence, but not of terrorism and weapons of mass destruction. It represented a convergence of imperialist needs and ambitions.

All Roads Lead Through Baghdad

It is for all these intersecting regional and global reasons that war on Iraq was deemed essential to the plan for a "New American Century." Different writers, activists and analysts have put forward varying objectives as the "real" reason for the U.S. war on Iraq, including grabbing Iraq's oil, preventing the Hussein regime from acquiring weapons of mass destruction, stabilizing the dollar, strengthening Israel, or retaliating for Sept. 11.

If understood as threads in the fabric of global empire, all these objectives and more are part of the U.S. agenda, although none by itself accounts for this war. Instead, it is the convergence of such necessities and ambitions of empire—in the Middle East and globally—that explains why, in the months following Sept. 11, the U.S. "war on terror" grew increasingly focused on Iraq and increasingly distant from the attack that damaged the Pentagon and destroyed the World Trade Center towers.

Prior to the war, leading Democrats, such as Senator Tom Daschle and Rep. Nancy Pelosi, argued that attacking Iraq would be a "diversion" from the "war on terror." This argument takes official statements that the real objective of this "war" is protecting Americans and eliminating global "terrorism" at face value. Yet, an analysis of the roots and objectives of the "war on terror" and the overarching strategy that it is part of shows the opposite to be true: targeting Iraq reveals the essence of this war.

The representatives of American power who took office with the ascendancy of George W. Bush felt that the alternative to this audacious grab for dominance was strategic drift, mounting opposition, and the erosion of the U.S. grip on global power, and miss an historic opportunity to extend their reach. Without making an aggressive move against Iraq, their game-plan could unravel. "No course open to the United States is free of risk," Wolfowitz argued. "The question is how to weigh the risks of action against the risks of inaction and to be fully aware of both." So for those running the U.S. ship of state, all roads led through Baghdad.[101]

Imperialism By Any Other Name...

After decades of denial, it is now more frequently acknowledged in mainstream discourse that the United States is indeed an imperialist power: "America's entire war on terror is an exercise in imperialism," wrote Michael Ignatieff in the *New York Times Magazine*. "This may come as a shock to Americans, who don't like to think of their country as an empire. But what else can you call America's legions of soldiers, spooks and Special Forces straddling the globe?"[102]

What is still rarely admitted, however, and which we will detail in subsequent chapters in regard to U.S. actions in Iraq and the Persian Gulf, is that the U.S. has been an imperialist power for over a century and this imperialism flows from the exigencies of global capitalism. In 1948, George Kennan, Director of Policy Planning at the State Department under President Truman, bluntly articulated the vision guiding the powers-that-be:

> We have about 50 percent of the world's wealth, but only 6.3 percent of its population. In this situation, we cannot fail to be the object of envy and resentment. Our real task in the coming period is to devise a pattern of relationships which will permit us to maintain this position of disparity... The day is not far off when we are going to have to deal in straight power concepts.[103]

Forty-nine years after Kennan recognized the need for "straight power concepts," former President Clinton painted a similar picture: "We have four percent of the world's population and we want to keep 22 percent of the world's wealth."[104] Then, as now, a central feature of the global order remains the subordination of the bulk of the world's population, living in the oppressed or Third World countries of Asia, Africa, Latin America and the Middle East, to a handful of advanced capitalist states—including the U.S., the European powers, Japan, and Russia. Those countries have some 15 percent of the world's population, yet consume over 80 percent of the world's output.

Today, the U.S. has $5 trillion invested overseas, does $2 trillion in foreign trade a year, and operates networks of manufacturing, finance and commerce that ring the planet. This global system is driven by the interconnected compulsions of economic competition between rival firms and strategic competition between rival nations, whose state institutions represent their nation's dominant corporate and financial interests. In an era of faster and faster global capitalism, this competition has grown more heated as winners rise and losers fall with increasing rapidity—whether products, technologies, corporations, whole industries, countries, even empires. During the past century alone, the British, French, Ottoman, Austro-Hungarian, and two Russia empires—one czarist, one Soviet—have fallen or collapsed. This phenomenon is very much on the minds of those running the U.S. as they attempt to capitalize on what some strategists have called America's "unipolar moment."

Securing ready access to markets, investment opportunities, and natural resources demands influence, even control, which the U.S. has generally secured, through a combination of economic inducements, political alliances, and most of all, military force. As that tireless and tiresome champion of global capitalism, *New York Times* columnist Thomas Friedman, put it, "The hidden hand of the market will never work without the hidden fist. McDonalds cannot flourish without McDonnell Douglas...and the hidden fist that keeps the world safe for Silicon Valley's technologies to flourish is called the U.S. Army, Air Force, Navy, and Marine Corps."[105] This is why some 500,000 U.S. troops are stationed at 700 military bases in 120 of the UN's 189 member states, and why the U.S. spends over $350 billion a year on its military—far more than any other nation in history.

Oil: Greasing the Wheels of Empire

Global capitalism is fueled and lubricated by oil. Of the world's raw materials, none is more vital to economies and armies, none confers greater profit and strategic power. As we will show, it is the lifeblood of modern empire, a crucial prop of U.S. global power and wealth on many levels. Petroleum is an essential economic input whose price impacts production costs, profits, and competitive advantage. It is an instrument of rivalry: controlling oil means exercising leverage over those who depend on it and over the world economy as a whole. And it is impossible to project military power globally without abundant supplies of oil. This is not simply, or even mainly, a question of the U.S.'s growing dependence on imported oil. Even if everyone rode public transportation and the U.S. didn't import a drop of oil, it would still seek to control the global flow of petroleum, if only to prevent others from doing so.

The heart of the world petroleum industry lies in the Persian Gulf, which contains 65 percent of the world's known oil reserves, 34 percent of the world's natural gas reserves, and now accounts for nearly 30 percent of the world output of each.[106] As the world's thirst for petroleum has grown, so has the Gulf's strategic importance. Since the end of World War II, dominating the Middle East and controlling these vast oil supplies have been crucial to U.S. foreign policy under 11 different presidents. In pursuit of these objectives, the U.S. acted covertly and overtly, employing the carrot of aid and the stick of military assault—installing and overthrowing governments, exerting economic, political and military pressure, waging wars, even threatening the use of nuclear weapons. The pillars of U.S. control have included the Shah's regime in Iran, the state of Israel, and the subservience of repressive Arab rulers.

Yet maintaining control of this volatile region of deep poverty, rapid social change, broad popular resistance, and growing anti-U.S. anger has been fraught with difficulties. During the tumultuous decades following World War II, U.S. dominance was repeatedly challenged and often thwarted by the rise of Arab nationalism, the explosion of Palestinian resistance to Israeli colonialism, the 1979 overthrow of the hated Shah of Iran and the subsequent rise of Islamist movements, and by its competition with other global powers—especially its Cold War rivalry with the nuclear-armed Soviet empire.

Iran and Iraq, now labeled part of an "axis of evil," have posed particular challenges to U.S. control. These two Persian Gulf states have adequate water supplies, enormous oil reserves, and relatively large populations. Both have experienced revolutions that put in power forces who sought to tap into nationalist sentiments in the area and turn their country's assets into greater regional power and influence. This course threatened to impede U.S. hegemony and turned Iraq and Iran into frequent targets of American intrigues and interventions.

President Bush and his cohorts have attempted to obscure this history with their talk of a "war on terror" that pits "good versus evil" and champions of "freedom" against those who "hate our freedoms." The history we will explore in the next 7 chapters makes clear why U.S. officials studiously avoid the actual record of American actions in Iraq and the Middle East—in fact they command us to avoid it as well: "Either you are with us or you are with the terrorists," Bush declares. No wonder. This record reveals a starkly different reality than the government fantasies offered to justify intervention and war. Four broad, interconnected themes emerge:

- For over 60 years, U.S. actions in Iraq and the Persian Gulf have been guided by calculations of global empire, regional domination, and overall control of Persian Gulf oil. As a result, they have never brought liberation, but have instead inflicted enormous suffering and perpetuated oppression. There are deep national, social and class divisions running through the societies of the Middle East, but foreign domination—by the U.S. in particular—remains the main obstacle to a more just social order.

- Second, U.S. actions have brought neither peace nor stability, but spawned a deepening spiral of resistance, instability, intervention and war. There are connections here, and a trajectory to events which we will explore, from the 1953 coup that installed the Shah in Iran to the 1979 revolution that overthrew him, to the subsequent Iran-Iraq war, to the first U.S. Gulf War in 1991, and then the second in 2003. The new U.S. National Security Strategy and its offspring—the "war on terror"—are efforts to forcibly resolve these growing impediments.

- Third, this war represents a further, horrific escalation of that deadly spiral of U.S. intervention and it is only the beginning. Washington has dispatched its military to conquer and occupy a country in the heart of the Arab world, perhaps for years to come, and use it as a springboard for further maneuvers and aggressions in the region.

- Finally, the history of foreign intervention in the Persian Gulf demonstrates that grand ambitions of conquest and control are one thing, but realizing them can be quite another. Oppression breeds resistance, actions provoke reactions, and events often careen beyond the control of their initiators in unexpected ways.

It is to that history that we now turn.

CHAPTER 2

IRAQIS—NOT PRESENT AT THE CREATION

On many levels, the roots of the 2003 Iraq war extend back some 80 years to Great Britain's invasion and conquest of the land of Mesopotamia, its 20-plus year occupation, and its creation of the country of Iraq. In 2003 that history has an eerie resonance: today it is the United States that has invaded, conquered, and occupied Iraq, and is now attempting to recreate it to suit U.S. interests.

Iraq's tumultuous history, its bloody conflicts with the U.S., and the growing difficulties faced by U.S. occupation forces today are very much rooted in the story of Britain's conquest and creation of Iraq, which is this chapter's focus.

Why did the British promise "emancipation" and "independence," yet draw borders that led to decades of conflict between Iraq and its neighbors, and ultimately helped lead to the Persian Gulf Wars of 1991 and 2003? Who are the peoples of this ancient land, and why did the British force them together into one state? How did this necessitate the creation of an oppressive configuration of political power, which later shaped U.S. support for Saddam Hussein and created tensions that now threaten to explode in the face of Iraq's new occupiers?

What role was played in all this by Iraq's bountiful oil resources? How did the decisions made then by foreign governments shape Iraq's history and society for decades afterward, and how are they being played out today?

Finally, and perhaps most importantly, this is also the story of how British domination provoked fierce resistance that ultimately led to the overthrow of the monarchy it had installed. Washington is now discovering that this long history of resistance remains very much alive in the 21st Century.

Our Mesopotamian Roots

Most schoolchildren learn of the "cradle of civilization"—the area in today's Middle East where humanity took some of its first steps toward settled communities, writing, architecture, science, and law—the foundations of modern society. Yet how many connect such seminal achievements with the land that is now Iraq? In most U.S. media coverage, the rich history of the area long called Mesopotamia—the Greek term for "land between the rivers"—has been ignored, trivialized, and largely reduced to the cartoonish demonization of one Iraqi—former President Saddam Hussein. How did the cradle of civilization become known as a threat to all civilization?

The Gulf Wars of 1991 and 2003 both generated widespread opposition, and that opposition might have been even broader had more people realized that the U.S. military would be savaging the land where many of our everyday foods were first grown, where writing, law and accounting were invented, and where the authors of the Old Testament placed the "Garden of Eden."

The U.S. government made clear its disdain for this history after its forces took Baghdad on April 9, 2003. American troops carefully guarded Iraq's Petroleum and Interior Ministries—whose records are key to controlling Iraq's economic and political future. However, the U.S. refused to protect Iraq's National Museum, National Library and Archives, or the Ministry of Religious Endowment, despite prior warnings from archaeologists that Iraq's historical treasures could be looted in the event of war. As a result, during the chaos of the U.S. assault, the National Museum was sacked, and the National Library and Religious Endowment ministry set on fire. Irreplaceable records of Iraqi and Islamic history—documents from Ottoman times and a Koranic library—went up in flames; an estimated 3,000 of the National Museum's 170,000 pieces disappeared, and sites across Iraq, such as Nimrud, once the capital of the Assyrian Empire, have been plundered. Even more catastrophic losses were prevented only because Iraqis had secured many of their country's most precious items over the years before the war.[1]

The area that comprised the Fertile Crescent starts in the Tigris-Euphrates plain of today's Iraq, arcs north and west through Syria and southern Turkey, then west through Turkey, and south and west through Palestine and western Jordan. The region's long, hot summers and mild winters are ideal for plant growth. It includes a range of elevations, from the mountains of today's Kurdish areas to the flat plains of the Tigris and Euphrates. This fostered plant and animal diversity in close proximity, hence evolutionary development. A wide variety of species arose, and it was here that humans first cultivated plants and domesticated animals.

As a sign of just how far back the heritage of civilization reaches, it was in this region, around 11,000 BC, that the first tools were invented for harvesting, husking, and storing grain. It was here too, between 8,500 and 8,000 BC, that plants were first domesticated, including peas, chickpeas, lentils and flax. Cereals now make up more than half the calories we consume, and two of the most important—wheat and barley—were first cultivated in the Fertile Crescent.[2] Between 8,000 and 7,000 BC, humanity's first settled communities were established here. Jared Diamond, author of *Guns, Germs and Steel: The Fates of Human Societies*, writes:

> Fertile Crescent peoples profited from an accident of biogeography: they had the good fortune to occupy the world's largest zone of Mediterranean climate, home to the largest number of wild plant and animal species suitable for domestication. Until 8500 BC, all the world's peoples obtained their food by gathering wild plants and hunting wild animals. Then the ancient Iraqis and other fertile crescent peoples began to develop farming and herding, domesticating wild wheat, barley, peas, sheep, goats, pigs and cows. Even today, these species remain the world's staple crops and livestock. Agriculture fueled a population explosion, and also generated food surpluses that could be used to feed full-time professional specialists, who no longer had to devote time to procuring their own food.

He also notes that, "the English we speak today grew out of the Indo-European languages originally spoken by Middle Eastern peoples.[3]

Over the ensuing centuries, numerous civilizations and empires came and went in what is today Iraq—the Sumerians, Akkadians,

Babylonians, Hittites, Hurrians, Kassites, Elamites, Assyrians, Arabs, Persians, and Ottomans—creating much that modern societies rest on. Around 3,000 BC, the Sumerians, one of the world's first great civilizations, invented the earliest form of writing (cuneiform), as well the plough, bronze and perhaps the wheel. Sumerian folklore was later echoed in the Bible and the tales of ancient Greece.

Between 1792 and 1750 BC, Hammurabi united most of Mesopotamia under Babylonian rule and created the world's first legal code, to "cause justice to prevail in the land, to destroy the wicked and the evil, that the strong may not oppress the weak."[4] Babylon, his capital, was built along the Euphrates River about 70 miles south of today's Baghdad. It became the largest settlement in the world, and probably its most famous city. Babylon's hanging gardens were considered by the Greeks one of the Seven Wonders of the World. The Romans called Babylon "the greatest city the sun ever beheld."[5] It was here that King Nebuchadnezzar ruled from 604-562 BC and built monuments whose names are still familiar today—his ziggurat—known as the Tower of Babel—the Temple of Marduk, the Ishtar Gate. Nebuchadnezzar himself is recalled in today's *Matrix* movies, as the name of Morpheus's ship. And it was here that Alexander the Great died in 322 BC, in the city he wished to make his capital.

Mesopotamia also figures prominently in Islamic history. It was conquered by Muhammad's supporters in 632 AD, the year the Prophet died. His death sparked a struggle for succession to the caliphate and leadership of the faith that was battled out in Iraq. Some 30 years after Muhammad's death, his cousin and son-in-law Ali was assassinated near Najaf. Twenty years later in nearby Karbala, Muhammad's grandson Hussein died in a battle over who would succeed Muhammad. These events marked the beginning of the split between Shi'a and Sunni Muslims which still features prominently in the religion's politics and culture.[6] Shi'as consider Ali the sole legitimate caliph after the prophet Muhammed, and hold Ali's tomb in Najaf, Iraq as the faith's most sacred shrine after Mecca and Medina. Hussein's tomb in Karbala is also revered, and his martyrdom is reenacted each year in the commemoration of Ashura.

For over 500 years, from 748 AD until it was sacked by Mongol invaders in 1258, the Abbasid caliphs led the Islamic world from Baghdad, memoralized in *The Thousand and One Nights*. Most children know of the adventures of one of its heroes—Sinbad, most recently through the animated feature *Sinbad: Legend of the Seven Seas*, released the year of the latest U.S. assault on his homeland.

Promises and Betrayal

The modern history of Iraq began after World War I, which was fought in part to determine which European power would control the Middle East, for its vast oil potential, and for its strategic location at the geographic crossroads between Africa, Asia and Europe.

Much of the region had been part of the Ottoman Empire since the 1600s. From 1638 AD until World War I, what is today Iraq consisted of three Ottoman administrative districts (vilayets): Mosul in the north, Baghdad in the center, and Basra in the south. By the turn of the 20th Century the Ottoman Empire was in decline, and the Middle East had become the scene of growing intrigue and rivalry among the world's colonial powers.

This was the time of the "great game"—the rivalry between Czarist Russia and imperial Britain for supremacy in Central Asia, a competition played out most intensely in Afghanistan and Iran for control of India. Initially, Britain's interest in Mesopotamia was to secure lines of communication and defense for India—the "crown jewel" of its Empire. But soon another prize loomed larger: oil.

Oil had been discovered in southwest Persia, and in 1901 William D'Arcy, an Englishman, purchased a 60 year concession covering 500,000 square miles, over five-sixths of what is today Iran. He established Anglo-Persian Oil Company, which later became Anglo-Iranian Oil Company and finally British Petroleum, to exploit the concession. BP became one of the world's largest oil companies, and it was founded solely on Middle Eastern oil.[7]

Anglo-Persian began producing in 1908, but it was World War I that established oil's centrality to empire in the modern age. At the time, navies were the prime instruments of global reach and power, and oil-fueled ships were faster and ranged further than the older coal-fired models. In 1912, Britain's Secretary of the Navy Winston Churchill converted the British fleet to oil. Two years later, the

British Government purchased a half interest in Anglo-Persian Oil to ensure that its fleet would have adequate supplies. For the first time, defending British oil in the Gulf became a key component of state policy.

Airplanes and tanks made their first combat appearances in World War I, increasing petroleum's strategic value. As Daniel Yergin points out in his comprehensive history of the oil industry, *The Prize*, oil helped decide the war's outcome: Britain had abundant supplies, while Germany ran short. The lesson of oil as a strategic resource was immediately understood: Britain's Lord Curzon declared that the Allies had "floated to victory upon a wave of oil."[8]

During World War I, the British, most famously T. E. "Lawrence of Arabia," promised the Arabs freedom and independence if they fought with the British against the Ottoman Empire, which had allied with Germany. Between 1915 and 1916, Sir Henry McMahon, Britain's High Commissioner in Cairo, wrote to Sherif Hussein of Mecca, the leader of the Arab forces, explicitly promising British support for an independent Arab state over most of what is today Syria, Iraq, Saudi Arabia, Palestine/Israel, Lebanon and Jordan.[9]

During the war, the British made similar promises to the peoples of Mesopotamia. In 1914 British forces landed there as part of the campaign against the Ottoman Empire, and fought for the next four years before capturing the whole country. When the British entered Baghdad in 1917, their commanding officer, Sir Stanley Maude, told the city's residents, "Our armies do not come into your cities and lands as conquerors or enemies, but as liberators... The Arab race may rise once more to greatness!"[10]

The Arabs took the British at their solemn word, while the British considered these communications, which were never formalized in treaties or binding agreements, as empty promises to be discarded when they were no longer useful. As Gilbert Clayton, the head of English intelligence put it, "Luckily we have been very careful indeed to commit ourselves to nothing whatsoever."[11]

Unbeknownst to the peoples of the Middle East, in 1916 Britain, France and Czarist Russia met secretly and carved up the Middle East between them. The general public is rarely privy to the most secret deliberations of state, but in 1917 Lenin's Bolsheviks overthrew Russia's Czar and as an act of internationalism quickly renounced—and published—the Czar's secret treaties. One, which the Bolsheviks found in the Foreign Ministry's archives, was the Sykes-Picot Agreement (after its principal architects, the Englishman Mark Sykes and the Frenchman Francois Georges Picot), hammered out in May 1916.[12]

Sykes-Picot gave Russia Constantinople (now Istanbul) land on either side of the Bosporus Straits and large chunks of the Turkish provinces bordering Russia. Britain got the Ottoman provinces of Basra and Baghdad, and the French took greater Syria (including today's Lebanon) and much of Turkey. Palestine was initially split between Britain and France. Later Britain received a mandate from the League of Nations, which was dominated by World War I's victors—Britain and France—for the area comprising Palestine and Transjordan (now Jordan).

Sykes-Picot was not Britain's only betrayal of its promises to the Arab peoples. In November 1917, a month before the Bolsheviks published Sykes-Picot in *Izvestia*, Lord Balfour declared that Britain would "view with favor the establishment in Palestine of a national home for the Jewish people"—the same land it had promised to Sherif Hussein as part of a future Arab state.[13] The British felt that a Zionist settler-colonial state—similar to those in South Africa and Rhodesia—would help Britain solidify its control of the Middle East by securing Iraq's flank and provide transit routes to the Gulf.

The needs and desires of the peoples of the region were contemptuously dismissed in the interests of empire. Balfour articulated this imperial arrogance best: "The four great powers are committed to Zionism, and Zionism...is rooted in an age-long tradition, in present needs, in future hopes, of far profounder import than the desires and prejudices of the 700,000 Arabs who now inhabit that ancient land."[14]

WMDs Then as Now: Mostly an Invader's Tool

The disclosure of Sykes-Picot triggered outrage and revolt in the Arab world, and Iraq soon became its epicenter. An Arab Independence Party was formed in 1919 and demanded independence for Syria, Palestine, and Iraq, the renunciation of the Sykes-

Picot agreement and the Balfour Declaration, and the withdrawal of Britain and France from the region.

Britain's response was two-fold (foreshadowing the dual-track employed by the U.S. against Iraq 70 years later): it convened the League of Nations to ratify its colonial actions, then sent troops to forcibly put down an uprising in Iraq. A May 1920 League of Nations conference at San Remo condemned the Arab demands and upheld Sykes-Picot and Balfour. This provided Britain and France with "a legalistic cloak of respectability for their de facto partition of the Middle East," as British author Geoff Simons put it in his insightful 1996 history, *Iraq: From Sumer to Saddam*.[15]

A month later, over 100,000 Shi'as, Arab nationalists (many who had been officers in Hussein's Arab army), and tribal leaders rose up against the British forces which had occupied Mesopotamia during World War I. Jihad was proclaimed, imperial posts overrun, lines of transit and communication cut, and British soldiers shot. By August, the rebels proclaimed a provisional government.

The British response was swift and brutal. British forces were reinforced and went on a rampage—destroying, sometimes burning whole villages, and executing suspected rebels on the spot. The Iraqis fought fiercely, so fiercely that British leaders demanded chemical weapons be used—shortly after their horrors had been graphically demonstrated in World War I. T. E. Lawrence, generally portrayed as a friend of the Arabs, offered, "By gas attacks the whole population of offending districts would be wiped out neatly; and as a method of government it would be no more immoral than the present system."[16] Winston Churchill, that icon of the established order, declared, "I do not understand this squeamishness about the use of gas. I am strongly in favour of using poison gas against uncivilized tribes."[17]

The Royal Air Force didn't drop gas bombs on the Iraqis—but only because they hadn't yet perfected the necessary technology. British forces did, however, bombard Shi'a rebels with artillery shells filled with poison gas.[18]

The RAF's conventional air assaults may have been even more indiscriminate and lethal. One British wing commander bragged, "Within forty-five minutes a full-size village can be practically wiped out and a third of its inhabitants killed or injured." Another officer declared, "the attack with bombs and machine guns must be relent-less and unremitting and carried on continuously by day and night, on houses, inhabitants, crops and cattle." The RAF dropped 97 tons of bombs and fired 183,861 rounds against the insurgency, crushing it by March 1921. Between 6,000 and 9,000 Iraqis were killed. Estimates of British losses run from 500 to 2,000.[19]

Installing a King in Baghdad

In 1921, the country of Iraq was created, its first government chosen, and its future determined—not in Baghdad, or anyplace else in Iraq for that matter. These plans were made at a closed-door meeting of British officials and Middle East specialists in the Semiramis Hotel in Cairo, Egypt. Two pro-British Iraqis were pres-ent.[20]

After crushing the uprising in Iraq, then-Colonial Secretary Winston Churchill called some 40 British Middle East experts together in Cairo to plan the administration of their new conquest. At this meeting, which came to be known as the Cairo Conference, Mesopotamia was formally christened "Iraq" (meaning "cliff" in ancient Arabic).[21] The area between Palestine, Syria and Iraq was renamed Transjordan (later Jordan). The Cairo Conference never considered self-determination for the peoples of Mesopotamia. Instead the discussion focused on the best means of ensuring British control. Simons sums up,

> There was a broad consensus...that the Iraqis were not fit to govern themselves; nor, it was assumed, would they be able to do so in the foreseeable future... The broad framework of European colonialism was to be preserved while at the same time both strengthened and rendered more economically man-ageable.[22]

Britain had originally planned to run Iraq as a direct colony as it was then doing with India. But World War I weakened the empire and politically awakened a broad movement for self-rule in the col-onized countries. So it was decided that a somewhat more indirect and cost-effective approach was needed: an Iraqi government, con-trolled by the British. The British decided to crown Sherif Hussein's son Faisal the monarch of Iraq. Faisal had no real roots in the area—

he'd been born 800 miles from Baghdad in what is now Saudi Arabia—and was dependent on British troops to protect his throne.

The British organized a "plebiscite" to provide a patina of legitimacy. However, during the runup to the vote, the Iraqi nationalist Sayyid Talib raised the radical slogan "Iraq for the Iraqis!" and was gaining broad popular support. So the British invited Talib to tea, then arrested and deported him to Ceylon.[23] Faisal won 96 percent of the rigged vote (with Kurdish areas largely boycotting). Faisal was then coronated in ceremonies in Baghdad. There was no Iraqi national anthem, so a British military band struck up "God Save the King."[24]

In 1918, forces led by Faisal's brother Abdullah (the great grandfather of Jordan's current King Abdullah II) entered the area east of the Jordan River, which was then under British mandate. The British decided to support Abdullah as monarch, providing him with money and troops. In return, the British demanded that Abdullah accept Britain's mandate over Transjordan and Palestine, submit to British political officers, agree to British air bases, and promise to suppress anti-French and anti-Zionist struggles. For London, Transjordan was a useful buffer and transit route between Palestine and the Mediterranean on one side, and the oil fields of Iraq on the other, one which enabled transhipment of oil if the Suez Canal was ever closed. Meanwhile, the patriarch Sherif Hussein, along with ibn Saud of what would soon become the Kingdom of Saudi Arabia, were each paid 100,000 pounds a year to go quietly along with Britain's agenda in the region.[25]

The British built up a small, loyal clique of rural landowners and tribal sheikhs (chiefs), as the monarchy's social base by deeding them huge plots of land, previously shared communally by the various tribes. British historians Peter Sluglett and Marion Farouk-Sluglett write that "some of the largest private estates in the Middle East" were "created by the stroke of a pen between 1915 and 1925." In 1920, one British political officer noted condescendingly, "Many of them were small men of no account until we made them powerful and rich." Wealth, privilege and authority were concentrated in this tiny percentage of Iraq's population.[26]

Real power, however, remained firmly in British hands. British political officers held key positions in the Iraqi government, controlled Iraq's foreign relations, and had veto power in military and financial matters. And British-owned firms dominated the main sectors of Iraq's economy.[27]

Most importantly, the British took control of all of Iraq's most valuable resource—oil. It had been known that Iraq possessed vast oil potential since the turn of the century, after a 1901 German exploration team reported that Mesopotamia sat on "a veritable 'lake of petroleum' of almost inexhaustible supply."[28] In 1925, the British forced the new King Faisal to sign a 75-year concession granting the foreign-owned Iraq Petroleum Company (IPC) all rights to Iraq's oil, in return for modest royalties—but no ownership. Iraq's first major oil fields were discovered near Kirkuk in 1927.[29]

Borders of Conflict and War

The artificial borders drawn by the British in the wake of World War I still haunt the region—a source of war and conflict ever since. During the five years after the 1921 Cairo Conference, a series of international conferences, backroom meetings, and armed conflicts took place that led to the formation of the Iraq that we know today. The key decisions—delineating the border between Iraq and Kuwait and the incorporation of the Kurdish population—have had an enormous impact on Iraq's history, its relations with its neighbors, and its dealings with the world's imperial powers.

In 1922, Sir Percy Cox, Britain's High Commissioner for Iraq, met with the future leaders of Iraq, Saudi Arabia, and Kuwait to resolve their border disputes. With the stroke of a pen on his map, Cox finalized their common borders, but certainly didn't end the tensions between them.

Kuwait had originally been settled in the early 1700s by nomadic tribes, led by the al-Sabah clan, who later became its rulers. During the 18th and 19th centuries, Kuwait was an autonomous principality, loosely under Ottoman control until 1899 when the British made it a colonial protectorate. Because the Ottomans had considered Kuwait the southern part of the administrative unit of Basra, many Iraqis felt it should rightly have been incorporated into Iraq.[30] The British ignored these claims.

To make matters worse, Kuwait was given a Gulf coastline line of 310 miles, while Iraq, the much larger state, was given only 36 miles. This made Basra, a city 50 miles up the Shatt al-Arab waterway, Iraq's principal point of entry to the Persian Gulf.[31] The British goal was plain: keep the emerging state of Iraq weak in order to ensure British supremacy. An Iraqi political scientist, cited by the *Washington Post's* Glenn Frankel, came to this conclusion after studying British historical records: "It was British policy to prevent Iraq from becoming a Gulf state because Britain thought Iraq would be a threat to its own domination of the Gulf."[32] This was in keeping with the British strategy of creating a series of small, weak states throughout the Middle East. London's strategy, in short, was that time-tested means of imperial control: divide-and-conquer.

Cox's borders would wreck havoc for decades to come. Iraq's claims on Kuwait and its desire for greater access to the Gulf nearly led to conflicts with Britain and the U.S. in 1958 and 1961. They contributed to tensions between Iran and Iraq during the 1970s and to Iraq's invasion of Iran in 1980. And they were a major reason for Iraq's August 1990 invasion of Kuwait, which triggered the U.S. "Desert Storm" assault five and a half months later.

Incorporating—and Subordinating—the Kurds

In 2003, Saddam Hussein's history of brutality against Iraq's Kurdish population would feature prominently in Washington's indictment of Ba'ath rule and its case for "regime change." What Bush and company hypocritically ignored and what is rarely mentioned in mainstream coverage, however, was Britain's role in deepening Kurdish oppression and the U.S. role in perpetuating it.

The Kurdish people have lived in the rugged mountains and valleys of northeast Iraq, western Iran, eastern Turkey and northeast Syria since the 7th century BC. This contiguous area, often called "Greater Kurdistan," is nearly the size of Iraq. The Kurds are historically a pastoral and nomadic people, raising sheep and goats. Over time many have become peasants, others urban dwellers. Today numbering some 25 to 30 million, Kurds make up the fourth largest ethnic group in the Middle East, behind Arabs, Persians, and Turks. The Kurds converted to Islam in the 7th century AD (around 80 percent are Sunnis, the rest Shi'as), while retaining their national identity. The Kurdish language, a branch of Indo-European family close-ly related to Iran's Farsi and Afghanistan's Dari, is distinct from Arabic and Turkic. Kurdish culture, dress, and history are also dis-tinct.

The Ottomans ruled most of Kurdistan from the 1600s until their empire collapsed following World War I. In 1880, during one Kurdish uprising, Sheikh Ubaidullah wrote the British:

> "The Kurdish nation is a nation apart. Its religion is dif-ferent from that of others, also its laws and customs.... We want to take matters into our own hands. We can no longer put up with the oppression which the governments [of Persia and the Ottoman Empire] impose on us."[33]

Unfortunately, subsequent history, explored here and below, would demonstrate that neither the British nor the American empires, despite their claims to benevolence, would bring justice to the Kurds.

Like the Arabs, the Kurds had been promised independence by the world's major powers following World War I. Point 12 of President Woodrow Wilson's 1918 "Fourteen Points" declared that "the nationalities now under Turkish rule should...be assured...an absolutely unmolested opportunity of autonomous development."[34] The August 1920 Treaty of Sevres formally recognized, for the first time, that the Kurds formed a distinct nationality and forced Turkey to renounce possessions comprised of non-Turkish populations, such as Kurdistan, and stipulated that the Kurds be given "local autono-my."[35]

However, Kurdish aspirations, like those of the Arabs, were betrayed and then suppressed for British imperial interests. The Treaty of Sevres would have effectively dismembered Turkey—par-titioning it between Italy and Greece, with independent states (or autonomous areas) in the Armenian and Kurdish areas.[36] However, the treaty was never ratified and Turkish nationalists, led by Ataturk, rose in revolt and defeated the Greek Army in 1923, mak-ing the Sevres agreement moot.

A new treaty was signed by the allies and the new Turkish gov-ernment at Lausanne, Switzerland on July 23, 1923. It made no mention of Kurdish independence. Instead, it ceded much of Kurdistan to the new Turkish government, which promptly banned all Kurdish schools, organizations, and publications. For decades after, Turkey refused to even acknowledge Kurdish ethnicity— instead calling them "mountain Turks"—and outlawed the Kurdish language. Ataturk's government brutally crushed a 1925 Kurdish revolt against the Lausanne Treaty, and government assaults, mass deportations, and massacres against the Kurds continued during the 1920s and 1930s.[37] Turkey, one of the U.S.'s closest allies in the region, has continued its grim oppression of the Kurds to this day. The *Los Angeles Times* reported that in December 2001, during the buildup to the 2003 war on Iraq, Turkish military police began scouring Kurdish villages and checking birth records for any newborns given traditional Kurdish names, and then forcing their parents to rename and re-register them with Turkish names. The Turkish regime warned that use of traditional Kurdish names would be considered "terrorist propaganda."[38]

Kurds in Iraq also rose for self-rule. In 1919, Sheikh Mahmoud Barzinji declared himself the ruler of an independent Kurdistan and began administering the area around Suleimanieh in north east Iraq. London's main political officer in Baghdad wrote at the time: "the Kurds wish neither to continue under the Turkish government nor to be placed under the control of the Iraqi government." He estimated that 80 percent of the Kurds supported independence.[39] The British quickly removed Barzinji from power.[40] Subsequent revolts were also crushed by British forces in 1922 and by the RAF bombing of Suleimanieh in 1924.

The British were fundamentally no more interested in Kurdish self-determination than the Turks. Rather, they were interested in making sure that the former Ottoman Province of Mosul, an area populated by Kurds and Turkomans, was incorporated into the new state of Iraq, not Turkey. The reason was oil. The British feared that without the oilfields near the cities of Mosul and Kirkuk, the new state of Iraq would not be economically viable.[41]

The British promised the Kurds that the new Iraqi government under their control would recognize "the right of the Kurds who live within the frontiers of Iraq to establish a Government within those frontiers." And in December 1925, the League of Nations decided in favor of the British: the Mosul region was incorporated into the new state of Iraq with the understanding that the British, whose mandate would continue for 25 years, would ensure Kurdish rights. "The desire of the Kurds that the administrators, magistrates and teachers in their country be drawn from their own ranks, and adopt Kurdish as the official language in all their activities," the League declared, "will be taken into account."[42]

This was the first and only time an international body formally promised the Kurds, of any country, a degree of autonomy. Yet such promises proved as empty as the others made by the British and the League to the peoples of the Middle East. Nor has the League's successor, the United Nations, ever taken serious steps to uphold the Kurdish peoples' right to self-determination. Today the Kurdish people remain the largest ethnic group in the world never to have achieved statehood.

Cobbling Together a Country

The new state of Iraq that emerged from these post-war years of foreign rivalry and maneuvering was born with deep internal fault lines, which have frequently been exploited by outside powers in the decades since. Britain had no desire to see a strong state arise in the midst of the world's greatest oil fields. The British had created Iraq by combining three demographically distinct administrative units of the Ottoman Empire: Basra in the Shia south, Baghdad in the Sunni center, and Mosul in the Kurdish north.

The result was a patchwork of polities: the Kurdish areas comprised roughly 17 percent of Iraq's 438,446 square kilometers, and some 20 percent of its population. Sixty percent of Iraqis were Shi'a Arabs living in the south; and some 20 percent were Sunni Arabs living in the center. Turkomans, who mainly live in the north, made up some 2.4 percent of the population, Persians 1.7 percent, and Chaldean Christian and Assyrians another 3.6 percent. In *A History of the Modern Middle East*, author William Cleveland notes that these groups "did not constitute a political community in any sense of the term," yet the formation of Iraq drastically changed their political worlds.[43]

The British held this agglomeration together by relying on the Sunni Arab-based monarchy, backed by British arms, to rule over the Shi'a south and the Kurdish north. This oppressive configuration was supported by London and Washington—most glaringly in the aftermath of the 1991 Gulf War as explored in chapter 5—up until the 2003 overthrow of the Hussein regime. The point of this arrangement was to prevent the emergence of a Kurdish state, which could threaten the stability of Iran to the east and Turkey to the north; and also to prevent the rise of Shi'a power. Prior to 1979, this could have destabilized the Shah's rule in Iran; after his fall it could have increased the regional influence of Iran's Islamic Republic. Today, the U.S. occupation of Iraq has not resolved these deep ethnic and religious tensions; instead, they have the potential to help turn Washington's conquest into a quagmire.

The new state lay at the head of the Persian Gulf, soon to become the heart of the world oil industry, and was bordered by Turkey to the north, Iran to the east, Kuwait and Saudi Arabia to the south, and Jordan and Syria to the west. Three of these states— Turkey, Iran, and Syria, shared overlapping Kurdish populations with Iraq—a demographic that the U.S. has frequently exploited to weaken Iraq.

In 1932, Britain's League of Nations mandate ended and Iraq became formally independent, but London still effectively ruled. Its armed forces remained in Iraq to ensure the continuation of the monarchy, which was widely hated and rightly considered a tool of British interests.

There were repeated uprisings against the British and the King, which British forces violently put down. In July 1931, RAF planes buzzed towns along the Euphrates River to intimidate an Iraqi general strike. That year and the next, the RAF bombed Kurdish rebels in Barzan.[44] British planes were deployed against numerous uprisings, mainly in Kurdish areas, between 1936 and 1941. And during World War II, British troops invaded and occupied Iraq to depose the nationalist and pro-German government of Prime Minister Rashid Ali, who had seized power in 1941 with support from reformist intellectuals and nationalist army officers. During the war, preventing Iraq's oil from falling into German hands became an important military objective.

Beyond Dreams of Avarice

After World War I, the world's major powers not only carved out spheres of influence in the Middle East, they also battled for control of its most prized resource: oil. The decade after 1918 saw the first serious U.S. foray into the region, and Iraq was at the center of the intrigue.

The region's oil had proved to be immensely profitable and strategically vital. In 1918, after oil had proved critical to the outcome of World War I, Britain's foreign secretary Balfour declared, speaking of Mesopotamia's then untapped petroleum, "I do not care under what system we keep the oil. But I am quite clear it is all-important for us that this oil should be available."[45]

In *The Control of Oil*, his 1976 study of the monopolization of the global petroleum industry, John Blair writes that Anglo-Persian Oil Company had been pumping Iranian oil since 1908, and by 1917, one Iranian well was producing "more than the entire prewar production from the whole of Rumanian and Galician oil fields with 10 times the number of wells and invested capital." In 1923 Churchill reported that the British government had earned 25.6 million pounds on an investment of 2 million pounds. They were, John Blair notes, "profits beyond the dreams of avarice."[46]

U.S. firms had not been active in the region, due mainly to their abundant supply of domestic oil, although they had conducted explorations there. This changed after World War I when fears rose of a global oil shortage. The rivalry between Britain, the U.S. and other powers for control of Middle East oil quickly became intense (and is still at work today in Iraq).

In September 1919, for example, Standard Oil of New York geologists were dispatched to explore in Iraq. One wrote his wife, "I am going to the biggest remaining oil possibilities in the world...the pie is so very big." When the British got wind of the expedition, they blocked its work.[47]

Much worse in American eyes was the discovery that the 1920 San Remo conference had not only approved Sykes-Picot, but had also ratified agreements monopolizing Middle East oil for the British. U.S. politicians and businessmen understood that domestic oil supplies wouldn't last forever, and after the war discovered to their great dismay that other powers were in the process of gaining a stranglehold on much of the world's future supply.

When Standard Oil of New Jersey obtained a copy of the secret San Remo oil agreement, the petroleum giant protested vigorously, and a titanic behind-the-scenes struggle between oil monopolies ensued. Britain's Lord Curzon argued the region's oil should belong to Britain because "Britain controlled only 4.5 percent of world oil production and the U.S. controlled 80 percent, and the U.S. excluded non-American interests from areas it controlled." Standard Oil retorted that no matter the extent of U.S. control over current production, the more important fact was that American firms controlled only one-twelfth of the world's oil reserves and therefore deserved more.[48]

A U.S. Senate investigating committee was formed and concluded unsurprisingly that "American interests were indeed being systematically excluded from foreign oil fields."[49] A 1920 bill established a government corporation to develop foreign oil resources, and pressure was brought to bear upon the British to cut the U.S. in on Middle East oil.[50] The U.S. demanded an "Open Door" to Middle East oil, and by 1928 the British were forced to agree, due to America's rising global power and the enormous leverage exerted by U.S. firms: Exxon supplied half of the United Kingdom's oil.[51]

The result was the 1928 "Red Line Agreement"—after a line drawn in red pencil on a map of the region. It divided Middle East oil between American, British, Dutch, and French companies. As their economic futures were being determined, no Iraqis, Iranians, Saudis, or Kuwaitis were present. Such blatant colonialism may seem an outdated relic of the past, but similar discussions are taking place at this writing between the U.S., Russia, and France over how to parcel out oil spoils in post-Saddam Iraq.

In the late 1920s, the Red Line Agreement provided that no single power would develop the region's oil without the participation of the others. For the first time, U.S. firms got a slice of Middle East oil: Exxon and Mobil would share 23.75 percent of the Iraq Petroleum Company (IPC). British Petroleum, Royal Dutch Shell, and the Compagnie Francaise des Petroles (CFP) received equal 23.75 percent shares.[52] The open door demanded by the U.S. was now, as C. S. Gulboukian, an Armenian businessman who owned a five percent share of IPC, put it, "hermetically sealed" to other competitors.[53] The French called the agreement the beginning of "a long-term plan for the world control and distribution of oil in the Near East."[54] John Blair described it as "an outstanding example of a restricted combination for the control of a large portion of the world's supply by a group of companies which together dominate the world market for this commodity."[55]

The IPC and the oil cartel deliberately restricted Iraq's oil production and development for decades in order to prevent an oil glut which could weaken prices and lower their profits. At the time, Iranian oil was more profitable, so Iranian production was favored. This decision, made without Iraq's consent or even knowledge, cost it hundreds of millions of dollars in lost revenues and is one reason Iraq's oil fields remain relatively untapped to this day.

Surveying the record of foreign domination of the region's petroleum wealth, Simons concludes,

> The oil bounty that should rightly have liberated the Arab peoples (and the Persians and others) was destined to lead to their subjugation and humiliation.[56]

A Testing Ground of Empire

Iraq has been a testing ground for the tactics—and crimes—of empire.

The U.S. got its first Middle East oil supplies and profits from Iraq, and the British-U.S.-controlled IPC became a model for oil cartel operations in other Third World countries. As Blair concluded, "The pattern of control through joint ventures [throughout the Middle East] was first established by the formation of the Iraq Petroleum Company."[57]

Iraq was one of the first colonies policed with air power, and the British developed a number of anti-personnel weapons specifically for use in Iraq. Britain's Air Ministry acknowledged:

> Phosphorus bombs, war rockets, metal crowsfeet [to maim livestock] man-killing shrapnel, liquid fire, and delay-action bombs. Many of these weapons were first used in [Iraqi] Kurdistan.[58]

The U.S. continued this bloody tradition in the 1991 Persian

Gulf War—first using certain depleted uranium munitions, "bunker buster" bombs and precision guided missiles—including its Multi-Launch Rocket System (MLRS), Standoff Land-Attack Missile (SLAM), and Army Tactical Missile System (ATACM)—against Iraq and its people.[59]

In 2003, Iraq was used as a test case of the new Bush II doctrine of preventive war and the new Pentagon strategies of blitzkrieg-like warfare. The U.S. again field tested new weapons, sensors, and communications equipment. The deadly array reportedly included new satellite-guided bombs and missiles; the Air Force's newest attack jet—the F-18 Super Hornet; new unmanned spy planes including the Predator, the Global Hawk, and the Shadow; and the latest model of the helicopter-launched Hellfire missile, which reportedly creates a blast wave that kills people, while leaving buildings intact. And not to be forgotten were old standbys like napalm.[60]

This deadly arsenal helped quickly overpower Saddam Hussein's battered and demoralized forces, and put the United States in charge. Yet the occupiers quickly found out what the British discovered decades before: that conquest and occupation does not bring thanks and acquiescence, but generates new waves of Iraqi resistance.

CHAPTER 3

SADDAM HUSSEIN'S AMERICAN TRAIN

In making their case for "Operation Iraqi Freedom," President George W. Bush and his supporters repeatedly invoked Iraqi history—or at least their version of Saddam Hussein's part in that tragic story. Their silence, however, was deafening when it came to another telling side of that history—the record of U.S. intrigue and intervention between 1945 and 1979.

Bush II and company claimed that U.S. actions in Iraq have been guided by "friendship" for the Iraqi people and support for their liberation. Yet if this were truly the case, why did Washington oppose the popular removal of another Iraqi tyrant in 1958 with near nuclear vehemence? Why, in 1967, did the administration of Lyndon Baines Johnson dispatch a former Treasury Secretary to Baghdad to help Saddam's Ba'ath Party grab power? And why, in the 1970s, did President Richard Nixon and his chief collaborator Henry Kissinger cynically double-cross Iraq's Kurds in favor of keeping Hussein and his people in power?

The answers to these questions, explored in this chapter, cast American motives and goals in a very different light, reveal the real reasons for the U.S. hatred of Saddam Hussein (which have very little to do with the cardboard villain of U.S. propaganda), and help explain why the Bush II government was so anxious to remove him from power in 2003.

Middle East Oil: A "Basic Premise" of American Prosperity and Power

The post-World War II history of the U.S. in the Middle East and Iraq begins with three seismic global shifts: first, the ascendance of the United States as the world's dominant imperial power; second, the centrality of petroleum to that global power; and third, the shift of world petroleum production from the continental U.S. to the Persian Gulf.

Before World War I, the United States was the world's leading oil producer, while Third World countries accounted for only 15 percent of world output.[1] On the eve of World War II, the U.S. still produced 61 percent of the world's oil, imported little, and was able to meet its needs, as well as those of its allies, from wells in the continental United States, Mexico and Venezuela.

Yet world demand was growing, while U.S. reserves—petroleum which could be profitably extracted given the technology of the day—were shrinking. During World War II, Washington was taken by the realization, as Daniel Yergin records in *The Prize*, that oil was "the critical strategic commodity for the war and was essential for national power and international predominance."[2]

A 1944 U.S. State Department memo called oil "a stupendous source of strategic power, and one of the greatest material prizes in world history." A year later a State Department official commented, "a review of the diplomatic history of the past 35 years will show that petroleum has historically played a larger part in the external relations of the United States than any other commodity."[3]

Yet Washington was gripped by fear that its petro-supremacy was slipping away. What was the solution? "In all surveys of the situation," State's Economic Advisor Herbert Feis said, "the pencil came to an awed pause at one point and place—the Middle East." A single Saudi well, it would turn out, could produce more oil than half the wells in Texas put together. By 1950, Middle East reserves were equal to the rest of the world's combined, and double U.S. reserves.[4]

Oil's strategic power is multi-dimensional, and understanding this is crucial to understanding six decades of U.S. strategy in the Middle East, including the 2003 war on Iraq.

For one, petroleum's military and economic importance grew enormously following World War I. "Petroleum was central to the course and outcome of World War II in both the Far East and Europe," Yergin writes. Japan and Germany sought to secure sources of petroleum, but "America's predominance in oil proved decisive."

New oil-based industries had arisen and expanded—auto, rubber, petro-chemicals, plastics—and the economies and militaries of the West—the U.S., Europe, and Japan—had become ever more dependent on a growing supply.[5]

Thus, oil's power as a geopolitical weapon also increased exponentially. Carl Solberg, a former editor at *Time* and author in 1976 of *Oil Power—The Rise and Imminent Fall of an American Empire*, calls oil "the link between the Truman Doctrine for the Middle East and the Marshall Plan for Europe." In short, plentiful and inexpensive Middle East oil was essential to the success of America's efforts to revive Europe and prevent it from falling into the Soviet orbit.[6]

Control of oil was also essential in ensuring American leadership of a revived Europe and a rebuilt Japan. "Europe in the next ten years may shift from a coal to an oil economy," Secretary of Defense James Forrestal wrote in 1947, "and therefore whoever sits on the valve of Middle East oil may control the destiny of Europe."[7] MIT Professor Noam Chomsky, the author of numerous works on the U.S. in the Middle East, writes that in 1948, George Kennan, head of the State Department's Policy Planning staff, argued that "U.S. control over Japanese oil imports would help provide 'veto power' over Japan's military and industrial policies."[8]

The U.S. would exert its oil "leverage" over Europe and Japan many times over the ensuing decades, and the 1956 Suez crisis provided a telling example. Two-thirds of Europe's oil passed through the Suez Canal, then controlled by the British. In April 1956, Egyptian President Gamel Nasser seized the canal for Egypt, and Britain, France, and Israel dispatched troops to retake it. No oil flowed through the Canal during the conflict, so Europe turned to Washington for relief. The Eisenhower administration refused. Determined to assert U.S. regional primacy, it instead demanded the withdrawal of European and Israeli forces. Facing crippling oil shortages, Britain and France had no choice but to comply. "Petroleum would provide the way for Washington to punish and pressure its allies in Western Europe," Yergin concluded.[9]

Persian Gulf oil was not only abundant, it was also enormously profitable. During the mid-1950s, it was estimated that Persian Gulf oil cost between 5 and 15 cents a barrel to produce—while selling on the world market for around $2.25 a barrel.[10] Between 1948 and

1960, Western capital earned an estimated $12.8 billion in profits from the production, refining and sale of Middle Eastern oil, while investments in fixed assets during that period amounted to only $1.3 billion.[11] In 1957, half of Gulf Oil's profits came from Kuwait, and in 1960 nearly 28 percent of Exxon's earnings came from Middle East oil (on a much smaller percentage of its total investments). Between 1952 and 1963, the Iraq Petroleum Company's (IPC) profits (which went to Western oil companies) averaged 56.6 percent of net assets per year.[12] One oil financier bragged, "Oil *is* almost like money."[13]

Plentiful and inexpensive Middle East oil helped lower production costs and raise returns for Western capital generally, not just for oil corporations. In his path-breaking analysis of global capitalism, *America in Decline*, Marxist political economist Raymond Lotta argues that such superprofits from oil and other Third World investments "stimulate and activate the entire mass of capital anchored in the imperialist countries." In his memoirs, Henry Kissinger, President Nixon's National Security Advisor and later his Secretary of State in the late 1960s and early 1970s, makes essentially that point: "cheap and plentiful oil" was the "basic premise" on which post-World War II Western capitalism was built.[14]

In sum, military power, political leverage, and economic profit all flowed, and continue to flow, from the control of oil. And oil gushes most copiously and most profitably from wells in the Middle East.

The Indelible Imprint of Three Middle East Challenges

Ensuring control of the Middle East and its oil has been a central pillar of U.S. foreign policy for more than 50 years. In the decades following World War II, the U.S. faced three major, inter-related challenges in realizing this aim: British and French influence; the Soviet Union and its allies in the region; and the struggles of the region's peoples, who sought, by one means or another, to control their own destinies. Iraq would soon become a focal point of these last two challenges to American regional dominance.

During World War II and in the years immediately afterward, the U.S. maneuvered to replace Britain and France, both greatly weakened by the war, as the region's predominant power and principal beneficiary of its oil wealth. This struggle included negotiations, legal actions, political arm-twisting, economic threats and covert coups against pro-British and French regimes.

One front was a complex battle for control of Persian Gulf oil concessions, which had been dominated by the British since early in the 20th century. A 1944 meeting between President Roosevelt and Britain's Ambassador Lord Halifax crystallized both the nakedly imperialist nature of these negotiations and the tectonic shift taking place in global power relations. Roosevelt sketched out a map dividing the region's oil, and according to Yergin, informed Halifax: "Persian oil is yours. We share the oil of Iraq and Kuwait. As for Saudi Arabian oil, it's ours."[15] In 1940, Britain controlled 72 percent of the Middle East's oil reserves, while the U.S. only held 10 percent. By 1967 their positions were reversed: the U.S. controlled nearly 60 percent, while the British share had fallen below 30 percent.[16]

In 1945 President Roosevelt solidified U.S. control of Saudi Arabia by making a deal with King Saud: the U.S. would protect his throne in exchange for exclusive access to the Kingdom's enormous oil wealth. For the next 50 plus years, ensuring the stability of this stifling and oppressive feudal tyranny would be a pillar of U.S. strategy in the Middle East.[17]

The U.S. assumed control of the colonial setup bequeathed by the British and French—maintaining the borders they had drawn across the region, continuing (even while renegotiating) the oil concessions they had imposed, and generally defending the regimes they had installed. However, in order to diminish British and French influence, the CIA also secretly encouraged anti-colonialist struggles in Syria and Egypt, including Gamel Nasser's 1952 coup against Egypt's pro-British King Farouk. It was neither the first nor the last time that Washington would back forces that would later turn against it.

At the same time, the U.S. didn't want things to go too far. So it worked to contain or suppress the nationalist and anti-imperialist fervor sweeping the colonized countries and the popular upheavals that rocked Palestine, Egypt, Iran, Syria, Lebanon, and by 1958, Iraq.

Iran provided the textbook case of the CIA's Middle East operations. There, the U.S. worked to both edge out the British, who had monopolized Iranian oil through the Anglo-Iranian oil company, and to suppress Iranian nationalism.

Britain's enrichment from Iran's vast oil wealth, juxtaposed with the crippling poverty which was the lot of most Iranians, had engendered explosive popular anger and widespread demands for nationalization. Here is one measure of Britain's plunder: in 1949 Anglo-Iranian Oil paid more to the British government in taxes than it paid to the Iranian government in royalties.[18]

After receiving 99.5 percent support in a plebiscite on his government, in 1953 Iran's Prime Minister Mossadegh attempted to nationalize Anglo-Iranian. In response, the CIA organized a coup overthrowing his government and restoring the Shah Mohammad Reza Pahlevi to the throne. The Shah would rule Iran for the next 25 years as an absolute monarch, imprisoning, torturing, and murdering many of his opponents, while loyally working for U.S. interests in the region.[19]

Following the 1953 coup, a new petroleum agreement voided Roosevelt's 1944 promise to Halifax and gave five American companies 40 percent of Iran's oil, reduced British Petroleum's (formerly Anglo-Iranian) share to 40 percent, and gave French and Dutch companies the remaining 20 percent.[20]

The U.S. also fought to suppress pro-Soviet political forces and to prevent the Soviet Union from gaining influence in the region. The first post-war confrontation between the U.S. and the Soviets took place over the Middle East in 1946, when President Truman threatened to drop a "super-bomb" if Soviet forces were not withdrawn from northern Iran. Though the threat may seem overblown today, Truman made it a year after he had dropped not one, but two atomic bombs on Japan.

A year later he articulated the "Truman Doctrine," which promised to oppose "international communism" wherever it challenged U.S. interests. In 1955, the "Baghdad Pact" created a military alliance of states on the Soviet Union's southern border, including Iran, Iraq, Turkey, and Pakistan, anchored by Britain and the U.S.[21] In the event the Persian Gulf's oil installations fell into Soviet hands, the U.S. even secretly planned to cap or destroy them.[22]

The creation of Israel, which was based on the violent dispossession of the Palestinian people, served all three U.S. aims: suppressing Soviet influence, curbing Arab nationalism, and reducing British and French power.

Israel's 1948 victory over armies from Egypt, Jordan, Syria, and Iraq led to the expulsion of 800,000 Palestinians—two-thirds of the entire population—from their historic homeland and the subsequent razing of most of their homes and villages. U.S. imperial strategists saw opportunity in this ethnic cleansing. Palestine had been ruled under a British mandate since World War I, and Israel's creation undercut remaining British influence in the region. One of President Truman's aides also argued that Israel "could become a strategic asset—a kind of stationary aircraft carrier to protect American interests in the Mediterranean and the Middle East."[23]

Over time, Israel became a key U.S. gendarme against the peoples of the region, as well a military outpost against the Soviet Union. Between 1949 and 1997, the U.S. provided Israel over $84 billion in economic and military aid, far more than to any other country in the world.[24] Although the United States demanded that Israel stay out of its wars on Iraq in 1991 and 2003, Israel's services over the years have included not only assaulting the Palestinian people and attacking neighboring Arab states, but also arming and training the brutal Guatemalan military during the 1980s after Congress had made it illegal for the U.S. to do so directly, aiding the South African apartheid regime, and facilitating Washington's secret dealings with Iran's Islamic Republic during the Iran-Iraq war.

Iraq on the Eve of Revolution

By the mid-1950s Iraq had suffered under the British installed monarchy for 40 some years, and the country was seething. Wealth and power were concentrated in the hands of a tiny land-owning elite linked with the monarchy, while the vast majority of Iraqis toiled in desperate rural poverty as tenant farmers or landless peasants. Iraq's vast oil wealth remained in foreign hands, its potential untapped for those who should rightfully have benefited from it. The country was poor and undeveloped. Opposition to this oppressive status quo was met with violent state repression.

In 1952, 55 percent of all privately held land belonged to one percent of all landowners, just 2,480 families. In one province in central Iraq, two families—one a relative of the monarch—owned over 500,000 acres each. Eighty percent of Iraq's population lived in the countryside, where the conditions were abysmal.[25] The landed class bled the peasantry and kept Iraqi agriculture in a state of stagnation, if not ruin. So many Iraqi peasants tried to flee this wretched existence that the monarchy passed a law forbidding them from leaving the land if they owed any debt. This effectively made most rural-to-urban migration illegal.

Iraq's rural population still found ways to escape, but when they reached the cities their poverty didn't end. Most could only find jobs as manual laborers. Over 10 percent of greater Baghdad's population—some 92,000 people at the time—lived in shacks made from palm branches. Over 80 percent of Iraqis were illiterate; there was but one doctor for every 6,000 people. Meanwhile, urban wealth was concentrated in the hands of a small class of landowners, merchants and government officials, some of them newly rich from oil money. At the time, according to the British historians Peter Sluglett and Marion Farouk-Sluglett, 17 Baghdad families owned wealth equal to "55-65% of all private corporate commercial and industrial capital."[26]

The Iraqi people felt this pervasive poverty was all the more intolerable and unnecessary because their country was sitting on the world's second largest pool of oil. This potential was being denied them because control of Iraq's output, pricing, revenues, and development remained in the hands of the British-U.S. owned Iraq Petroleum Company—which was looking after its own global interests, not Iraq's. Under a 50-50 split, Iraq received some $200 million a year in oil income, then half the government's annual revenues.[27] But the U.S.-dominated oil cartel refused to boost Iraq's production and revenues. They found Saudi and Iranian production more profitable, so they kept Iraq's oil output "down" in order to maintain higher global prices and higher profit margins.[28]

Over the years, the IPC had discovered wells capable of producing 50,000 barrels of oil a day, but capped them without informing Iraq's government. The U.S. State Department admitted that IPC had not exploited Iraq's oil "solely according to the requirements of Iraq and the intention of the concession, but in accordance with the overall interests of the participating companies."[29] Iraq was deprived of hundreds of millions of dollars in oil income annually as a result. This bitter history is worth remembering with the U.S. now in control of Iraq's vast oil fields.

The Iraqi people repeatedly fought for self-determination against the British and U.S.-backed monarchy, which violently suppressed their struggles. In July 1946, IPC workers in Kirkuk struck, demanding a union. The strike ended after one of their meetings was attacked by police and 10 workers were killed. In 1948, when the monarchy accepted the so-called Portsmouth Agreement ratifying the ongoing presence of British troops in Iraq, tens of thousands took to the streets in what came to be known as "al-wathbga"—the leap. This upsurge reflected the rising nationalist, anti-imperialist, and revolutionary sentiments of Iraq's growing urban working and middle classes. A huge anti-government demonstration on January 27, 1948 turned into a fierce street battle in Baghdad, with demonstrators fighting police with stones, barricades and burning cars. Between 300 and 400 people were killed that day alone by the regime's police and military.[30]

In November and December 1952, massive demonstrations against Britain and the monarchy again rocked Baghdad and spread to other cities. The movement, called "al-Intifada" or the uprising, was again viciously repressed, with scores of demonstrators gunned down.[31]

Liberating the Beloved Homeland from Imperialism's Corrupt Crew

In the mid-1950s, nationalist fervor was sweeping through the Middle East. In April 1956, Egyptian President Gamel Nasser seized the Suez Canal, then controlled by Britain and France. British, French, and Israelis troops were dispatched to regain the canal, but when the U.S. refused to back their action—because it had not been initiated under U.S. leadership—the intervention collapsed. Meanwhile, a nationalist-leaning government had come to power in Syria and in 1958 Syria and Egypt merged into the "United Arab Republic" (which dissolved in 1961). And in 1957 and 1958, there were mass uprising against Lebanon's pro-U.S. government.

Millions of Iraqis were emboldened by the changes sweeping

the region and Nasser's calls for Arabs to rise up.[32] By 1958, they had had enough of the pro-Western monarchy. On July 14, General Abdul Karim Qasim and the secret "Free Officers" group within the Iraqi military seized power and declared a republic. A military-based Revolutionary Council, made up of nationalist and pan-Arabist officers, took charge. The King and the Crown Prince were shot dead in their palace. Qasim declared that the army had liberated "the beloved homeland from the corrupt crew that imperialism installed."[33] Crowds poured into the streets, and the new regime initially received broad popular support. The monarchy and its rubber-stamp parliament were abolished, and the top levels of the government and military were purged.

Over the next 5 years the new government took steps to loosen foreign capital's stranglehold on Iraq, break the grip of the old feudal ruling elite, and promote state-sponsored industrial and military development. Iraq withdrew from the Baghdad pact and the British Sterling areas, demanded the removal of British forces, established relations with the Soviet Union and Mao tse-Tung's People's Republic of China, and pursued a neutralist foreign policy. The Qasim government enacted land reform, greatly reducing the power of the old landed elite. Rents and food prices were reduced, and new housing programs were enacted. The new Republic recognized trade unions and peasant organizations, lifted the ban on Iraq's pro-Soviet Communist Party (one of the largest in the Middle East), and amnestied Iraq's political prisoners.[34]

Qasim also opened negotiations with the foreign-owned Iraq Petroleum Company for increased royalties, part ownership, and the return of undeveloped areas in the IPC concession.[35] In 1960, frustrated by the cartel's refusal to budge, Iraq invited Saudi Arabia, Iran, Kuwait, Venezuela and other oil-producing nations to meet in Baghdad. This meeting led to the formation of the Organization of Petroleum Exporting Countries (OPEC). In 1961, Iraq withdrew the IPC's concession rights in areas where it was not producing, renewed Iraq's claims to Kuwait, and blocked Kuwait's entry into the UN and Arab League.[36] The new government also planned to create a new, Iraqi-controlled, national oil company (which was accomplished in 1964, after Qasim's downfall).[37]

U.S. Threatens Iraq's Revolution

How did the United States government respond to the fall of a hated monarch, this dramatic manifestation of the sentiments of the vast majority of Iraqis, and these steps toward greater Iraqi self-seter-mination? With joy that the Iraqi people has taken steps to "liberate" themselves? With satisfaction that a bit of democracy had reared its head in the region? With delight that a hated despot was no more? Hardly. The U.S. reacted to these events with military deployments—which included nuclear weapons—threats of war, and a covert campaign to undermine the new republic.

Iraq's monarchy had been one of the U.S.'s closest regional allies. The *New York Times* called it an "irreplaceable source of oil," the "keystone of the Baghdad Pact," and "the last bastion of Western influence" in the Middle East.[38] The three most powerful Arab states—Egypt, Syria and Iraq—were now led by nationalist forces who had taken measures against Western interests and opened relations with the Soviet Union. The U.S. position in the region suddenly seemd quite vulnerable.

The U.S. responded with military force and covert operations. The year before, in March 1957, Congress approved the new "Eisenhower Doctrine" designating "the independence and integrity of the nations of the Middle East" a vital interest that the U.S. would use force to defend.[39]

The U.S. invoked this doctrine in deploying the Sixth Fleet and a battalion of Marines to Lebanon in response to anti-government rioting in April 1957. Later that year, when a pro-Egyptian faction of the army came to power in Syria, the U.S. again deployed the Sixth Fleet to the Eastern Mediterranean, rushed arms to Jordan, Lebanon, Iraq, Turkey, and Saudi Arabia, and encouraged Turkey to mass 50,000 troops on Syria's northern border.[40] In *Killing Hope*, his blistering accounting of U.S. global intervention spanning six decades, author William Blum writes that U.S. covert operations against Egypt and Syria were also stepped up:

> Between July 1957 and October 1958, the Egyptian and Syrian governments and media announced the uncovering of what appear to be at least eight separate conspiracies to overthrow one or the other government, to assassinate Nasser, and/or prevent the expected merger of the two countries.[41]

Then, when the Iraqi monarchy was overthrown, Washington threatened war against the new republic. U.S. forces—including the Strategic Air Command—were put on worldwide alert. Shortly before Iraq's revolution, 70 naval vessels, hundreds of aircraft and 14,000 Marines had been dispatched to Lebanon. They arrived in mid-July in position to intervene in Iraq.[42]

In his study of the U.S. reaction to Iraq's revolution, Micah Sifry, formerly Middle East editor at *The Nation*, notes that these forces reportedly included an "atomic unit" with artillery capable of firing nuclear shells. Eisenhower had in fact issued a secret directive to the Joint Chiefs of Staff ordering them to prepare to use nuclear weapons to prevent an Iraqi takeover of Kuwait's oil fields.[43] Two days later, British troops entered Jordan.

The *New York Herald Tribune* reported that the U.S. was giving "strong consideration" to "military intervention to undo the coup in Iraq." Eisenhower stated that the U.S. was ready to employ "*whatever* means might become necessary to prevent any unfriendly forces from moving into Kuwait," a country whose oil and investments were essential to British financial stability. A secret cable from British Foreign Secretary Selwyn Lloyd to his home office in London stated, "at all costs these oilfields [in Kuwait, Bahrain and Qatar] must be kept in western hands."[44]

So a secret plan for a joint U.S.-Turkish invasion of Iraq was drafted shortly after the 1958 coup. General Nathan Twining, the Chairman of the Joint Chiefs of Staff, raised the possibility of an "area-wide counteroffensive." U.S. forces would be deployed to Lebanon, British troops would go into Iraq and Kuwait, the Israelis to the West Bank, and Turkish forces into Syria.[45]

In response to U.S. threats and deployments, the Soviet Union began large-scale maneuvers on its borders with Turkey and Iran. Sifry concluded, "Until the makeup and intentions of the new Republic of Iraq became clear, 'general war' was a real possibility."[46] In April 1959, CIA Director Allen Dulles told Congress that the situation in Iraq was "the most dangerous in the world today."[47]

The U.S. didn't end up directly attacking Iraq for a number of reasons, and U.S. troops were withdrawn from Lebanon by October 1958. Roger Morris, a National Security Council staff member under Presidents Johnson and Nixon, writes that the U.S. tolerated Qasim "as a counter to Washington's Arab nemesis of the era, Gamal Abdel Nasser of Egypt."[48] The Soviet presence near Iraq as well as declarations by the new United Arab Republic that it would fight on Iraq's side against any foreign intervention, also raised the specter that a U.S. assault could have triggered wider fighting in the region.[49]

Finally, Iraq's new republic did not immediately move against Western oil interests—in Iraq or Kuwait. On July 18, 1958, four days after the revolution, the *New York Times* reported that "intervention will not be extended to Iraq as long as the revolutionary government in Iraq respects Western oil interests." Sifry writes that "later that day Baghdad Radio announced Iraq's intentions to 'respect its obligations.'"[50]

The CIA Forms a "Health Alterations Committee"

Over the next several years, however, Qasim's government took a number of steps, mentioned above, to assert Iraq's independence, and by 1961, the U.S. had decided to counter-attack. Morris writes:

> [T]he Kassem [Qasim] regime had grown more assertive. Seeking new arms rivaling Israel's arsenal, threatening Western oil interests, resuming his country's old quarrel with Kuwait, talking openly of challenging the dominance of America in the Middle East—all steps Saddam Hussein was to repeat in some form—Kassem was regarded by Washington as a dangerous leader who must be removed.[51]

So the U.S. began a covert campaign to destabilize and overthrow Qasim—a campaign which ultimately brought the Ba'ath Party and ultimately Saddam Hussein to power.

Qasim's government was an unstable mixture of military officers from different political tendencies—some leaning toward Nasser's Arab nationalism, others toward the right-wing Ba'ath Party. Washington worked behind the scenes to exploit these contradictions.

With State Department backing, the Iraq Petroleum Company slowed down production in an effort to bankrupt the new regime. The State Department tried to prevent Iraq from turning to non-IPC oil companies for help; U.S. officials warned oil companies outside the Seven Sisters cartel—the so-called independents—to "stay out of Iraq."

Later, during a 1964 State Department meeting on Iraq, Averell Harriman, Governor of New York from 1955-1959 and a pillar of the establishment, argued against tolerating the nationalization of Iraq's oil: "We could not wish governments, such as Iraq, to get the impression that American oil companies can be pushed around."[52]

The U.S. also sought to weaken Qasim by encouraging a Kurdish insurgency. The Kurds had initially welcomed the 1958 revolution, but it soon became clear that Qasim and the military would not grant their demands for autonomy and a share of the country's oil wealth. By 1960, the U.S. and the Shah of Iran were arming the Kurds and supporting their revolt.[53] According to Morris, the CIA plotted against Qasim and tried—unsuccessfully—to assassinate him:

> In Cairo, Damascus, Tehran and Baghdad, American agents marshaled opponents of the Iraqi regime. Washington set up a base of operations in Kuwait, intercepting Iraqi communications and radioing orders to rebels.... The CIA.'s 'Health Alteration Committee,' as it was tactfully called, sent Kassem a monogrammed, poisoned handkerchief, though the potentially lethal gift either failed to work or never reached its victim.[54]

Hussein's "American Train"

The CIA also focused on cultivating contacts within Iraq's Ba'ath Party.

The Ba'ath Party had been founded in Damascus, Syria in 1944 by Michel Aflaq, and organized its first Iraqi branch in 1949. Its ideology was pan-Arabism, a variant of secular Arab nationalism which held that all Arabs constituted one nation. In social terms, it represented the interests and outlook of newly emerging bourgeois forces based in Iraq's military and state sectors. Iraq's Ba'ath Party put forward vague promises of socialism and sharing the wealth under the slogan "unity, freedom, socialism." It was also virulently anti-communist and upheld private property and inherited wealth as "natural rights." The Ba'ath pursued a state-sponsored, oil-funded form of capitalist industrial development and continued the nationalization program begun under Qasim. By the mid-1960s all of Iraq's banks, insurance companies and large industrial firms, including its oil industry, were state-run.[55]

The overthrow of the monarchy, Qasim's reforms, and the loosening of restrictions on left-wing organizations led to the political awakening and activation of millions of Iraqis. The Iraqi Communist Party (ICP) soon emerged as the "best-organised party in the country." Qasim found the ICP a useful ally, but never fully legalized it or included it in his government.[56]

Yet the Ba'ath, like the U.S., feared that Qasim was taking things too far and that the left, especially the ICP, was becoming too strong. Ba'ath Party founder Aflaq had warned, "Communist Parties will be banned and suppressed with the utmost severity in any country where the Ba'ath Party comes to power," and the Ba'ath soon began denouncing Qasim as a "tool of the communists."[57] The Ba'ath and other right-wing elements also worried that Qasim's claims against Kuwait were alienating other Arab regimes, and they feared pushing too hard against Western interests or moving too quickly toward the Soviet Union.

One avid participant in this anti-Qasim conspiring was hardcore Ba'ath party cadre Saddam Hussein. He had been born in 1937 to a family of landless peasants living near Tikrit, a town on the Tigris River northwest of Baghdad, and raised by an uncle who had once been imprisoned for participating in Ali Rashid's 1941 uprising against the British.[58] Hussein joined the Ba'ath Party during the political upsurge leading to the 1958 revolution. In 1959, he took part in a Ba'ath attempt to assassinate Qasim, fleeing to Cairo when it failed. There, he apparently initiated contact with U.S. officials.[59] Morris corroborates these reports of Hussein's ties with the CIA:

> According to the former Ba'athist leader Hani Fkaiki, among party members colluding with the C.I.A. in 1962 and 1963 was Saddam Hussein, then a 25-year-old who had fled to Cairo after taking part in a failed assassination of Kassem in 1958.... I often heard C.I.A. officers, including Archibald Roosevelt, grandson of Theodore Roosevelt and a ranking C.I.A. official for the Near East and Africa at the time, speak openly about their close relations with the Iraqi Ba'athists.[60]

The CIA's efforts proved successful. On February 8, 1963, a combination of Ba'athists, Nasserists, and right-wing nationalists staged another military coup, seized power, and summarily executed Qasim. According to Palestinian journalist and Saddam Hussein biographer Saïd Aburish, Qasim "refused to arm the tens of thousands of Communists, peasants and workers who had trekked to his headquarters to offer to defend him...."[61]

Some 40 years later, the U.S. would denounce Ba'ath Party tyranny and call for regime change. In February 1963, however, the U.S. directly assisted in the establishment of that tyranny by providing the Ba'ath Party with lists of suspected communists, left-leaning intellectuals, progressives, and radical nationalists. On the night of the coup, with the CIA-provided lists in hand, the new Ba'ath regime unleashed a reign of terror.

U. Zaher, a researcher in Iraq's contemporary political history, writes that on the night of February 8, Radio Baghdad broadcast "Order Number 13" stating that "communist agents" and "supporters of God's enemy 'Abd al-Karim Qasim" were disobeying orders and disturbing the peace. "We hereby confer authority on the commanders of military units, Police and National Guards to annihilate anyone who disturbs the peace." Following the broadcast:

> Armed with the names and whereabouts of individual communists, the national guards carried out summary executions. Communists held in detention...were dragged out of prison and shot without a hearing. Iraqi Communist Party sources put at 5,000 the number of their members and supporters killed during the first three days of the coup while resisting the Ba'ath take-over or the house-to-house witch-hunt. Other sources claimed that by the end of the rule of the Ba'th, its terror campaign had claimed the lives of an estimated 3,000 to 5,000 Communists.[62]

The Slugletts paint a similarly gruesome picture:

> Rank and file [ICP] members and sympathisers were rounded up in their homes, or shot in the streets in the first few days if they went out to join the crowds in brave but futile attempts to 'defend the revolution'....many members of the Central Committee were arrested and subsequently murdered. It is impossible to establish exactly how many people were killed, but many thousands were arrested, and sports grounds were turned into makeshift prisons to hold the flood of detainees. People were killed in the streets, tortured to death in prison, or executed after mock 'trials.' Many of those who escaped with

their lives were condemned to long periods in prison under atrocious conditions. The killings, arrests, and torture continued throughout the Ba'athists' period in power, and their direct responsibility for these crimes is not in doubt. As almost every family in Baghdad was affected—and both men and women were equally maltreated—the Ba'athists' activities aroused a degree of intense loathing for them that has persisted to this day among many Iraqis of that generation.[63]

Aburish cites estimates of the number executed ranging from 700 to 35,000, adding "Those killed included people who represented the backbone of Iraqi society—lawyers, doctors, academics and students—as well as workers, women and children."[64]

The United States government has never acknowledged its culpability in this slaughter—and the Bush II administration never included it in its indictment of the Hussein regime—but the evidence of direct American involvement is abundant. King Hussain of Jordan told Egyptian journalist Muhammad Haikal that "an American espionage service" had been in communication with the Iraqi Ba'ath and, according to Zaher, "conveyed to the latter, on a secret broadcasting service, the names and addresses of the Iraqi Communists."[65]

The Slugletts describe a "closely coordinated campaign" of Ba'ath Party repression:

> it is certain that some of the Ba'ath leaders were in touch with American intelligence networks...and it is also undeniable that a variety of different groups in Iraq and elsewhere in the Middle East had a strong vested interest in breaking what was probably the strongest and most popular Communist Party in the region.[66]

France's *L'Express* stated outright that, "The Iraqi coup was inspired by the CIA." London's *Guardian* reported some years later that newly declassified British cabinet papers "disclose that the coup had been backed by the British and the CIA." Aburish calls the U.S.-Ba'ath conspiracy against the Qasim government "one of the most elaborate CIA operations in the history of the Middle East."[67]

If there were any doubts concerning U.S. complicity, Washington dispelled them by quickly demonstrating its approval of the 1963 coup and subsequent massacre. The day of the coup, one NSC official wrote President Kennedy that it was "Almost certainly a gain for our side," and Washington offered diplomatic recognition to the coup plotters within hours of Qasim's execution.[68] The State Department applauded the new regime's promises to honor Iraq's agreements with the IPC and its decision to recognize Kuwait's independence and drop Iraqi objections to Kuwait's membership in the UN and the Arab League. Apparently, part of the price for this newfound harmony was an $85 million loan from Kuwait, probably with encouragement from the U.S. and Britain.[69]

Two years earlier, in 1961, the U.S. had encouraged the Kurds to rebel against Qasim. Now, in April 1963, just months after the Ba'ath massacre, the U.S. turned against the Kurds and flew arms from Iran and Turkey to northern Iraq to help the new Ba'ath regime put them down. American and British companies were also pleased: "Soon, Western corporations like Mobil, Bechtel and British Petroleum were doing business with Baghdad," Morris reports.[70]

One Ba'ath Party cadre later admitted, "we came to power on an American train."[71]

The Brutal Ascent of Saddam Hussein

The new regime, made up of different factions from within Iraq's military, proved as unstable as Qasim's and series of coups followed over the next several years. Nine months after overthrowing Qasim, another coup, led by Abdul Salam Arif and his allies in the military, ousted the Ba'ath forces. Arif's brother Abdul Rahman (who had taken over in 1966 after Abdul Salam's death in a helicopter crash), in turn, was overthrown in another military coup in July 1968, again by a combination of Ba'ath and nationalist forces.

Saddam Hussein was again closely involved in the intrigue. He had returned to Iraq shortly after the February 1963 coup and reportedly took part in some of the anti-leftist massacres. He was again arrested in 1964 in the wake of a November 1963 coup that forced the Ba'ath Party from power. After escaping from prison in 1966, Hussein was appointed Deputy Secretary General of the Ba'ath by its leader, General Ahmad Hasan al-Bakr, a relative who was also from Tikrit. There are reports that at the time Hussein wrote the U.S. Consulate in Basra urging help for Ba'ath efforts to overthrow the regime.[72]

The U.S. was open to such entreaties and was particularly concerned about General Arif's invitation to French and Russians concerns to help develop Iraq's oil industry.[73] So Washington continued to conspire to put the Ba'ath Party more firmly in control and in 1967 dispatched former Treasury Secretary Robert Anderson to Baghdad to supervise the operation.

On July 30, 1968, the Ba'ath faction, led by acting President al-Bakr, ousted the non-Ba'ath elements from the government. Iraq's chief of military intelligence later wrote, "for the 1968 coup you must look to Washington."[74]

The Ba'ath Party soon consolidated power and has ruled Iraq ever since. It purged the military and civil service, and placed party loyalists in all key government positions. The Slugletts write that a new constitution made the Ba'ath Revolutionary Command Council (RCC) the "supreme legislative and executive authority," giving it in effect, "an absolute monopoly of all judicial, legislative and executive authority."[75]

By then Saddam Hussein was a Vice Chairman of the RCC and head of the Party's internal security apparatus—the dreaded Mukhabarat or National Security Bureau and the Ba'ath regime forcibly suppressed its opponents and extended its reach into all corners of society, taking control of labor unions, student federations, women's groups, and most especially the military. Historian William Cleveland writes, "From the very outset, the regime was ruthless in its treatment of those whose loyalties were suspect. Hundreds were sentenced to lengthy prison terms, and others were hanged in public executions...."[76]

Hussein's control of the Mukhabarat enabled him to gain more and more power. By the early 1970s, he was the most powerful figure in Iraqi politics. Hussein forced al-Bakr to resign in 1979, became Iraq's President, and then promptly purged RCC and Ba'ath ranks.[77]

Like the monarchy before it, Ba'ath rule was based in Iraq's Sunni Arab center, which made up about 20 percent of the population, while Iraq's Shi'a and Kurdish populations were essentially excluded from power. These were the first years that the U.S. allied with Saddam's Ba'ath Party against the people of Iraq, but they would not be the last.

From Collaboration to Conflict

The U.S. preferred Ba'ath rule to the prospect of millions of politically energized Iraqis, of various political persuasions, taking Iraq in a more democratic, anti-imperialist, or revolutionary direction. Yet tensions would soon grow between Washington and Baghdad. Iraq came to embody some of the important challenges to U.S. hegemony that emerged in the Middle East during the late 1960s and early 1970s: the spread of Arab nationalism, expanding Soviet influence, and the nationalization of the region's petroleum industry.

Ba'athist Iraq was becoming a problem, and the U.S. would spend the next 30 plus years trying to subordinate it—sometimes with the carrot of aid and weapons, more often with the stick of force.

The Ba'ath took power a year after Israel's lightning victory over Egypt and Syria in the June 1967 "Six-Day War." Israel's U.S.-backed victory and seizure of the West Bank, Gaza and East Jerusalem—the remaining 23 percent of historic Palestine—along with Egypt's Sinai Peninsula and Syria's Golan Heights triggered a wave of anti-U.S. and anti-Israeli anger across Iraq and the Middle East, impacting Arab governments and creating opening for further Soviet inroads. As Kissinger put it:

> Arab radicalism grew exponentially in the wake of the 1967 war... The Soviet Union implanted itself more firmly in the region by sending massive military supplies to Egypt, Iraq, and Syria; the Arab front-line states, having cut their ties to the U.S. in 1967, became dependent on Soviet support, diplomatic as well as material.[78]

Iraq, having broken diplomatic relations with the U.S. in 1967, became a leader of the "rejectionist front" of Arab states that refused to recognize or negotiate with Israel, and Iraq would over the years provide some aid to the Palestinian struggle. However, its anti-Zionist and anti-imperialist rhetoric far outstripped its actual support of the Palestinians, and masked a more contradictory relationship with foreign powers in general, and with the U.S. in particular.

The Ba'ath-ruled Republic of Iraq sought to build its military and economic strength and to assert the interests of the Arab regimes in the struggle with Israel. These positions frequently put

Iraq into conflict with the U.S. regional agenda. Yet Ba'athist Iraq also remained dependent on foreign capital and technology and open to having relations with the world's major powers, although that often took the form of trying to play them off against each other to achieve Baghdad's objectives. Hussein's Ba'ath Party, in short, represented the interests and outlook of a comprador, or dependent, bourgeoisie with its own necessities and goals.

Two major developments in 1972 exemplified this agenda and impacted US-Iraqi relations throughout the 1970s. The first was the signing of a 15-year friendship treaty between Iraq and the Soviet Union. The second was the nationalization of Iraq's oil industry.

The Soviet Union under Khrushchev and then Brezhnev sought to expand its imperial reach into the Middle East.[79] Although unable to frontally challenge America's regional predominance, and seeking to avoid a direct military confrontation, Moscow instead worked to increase its influence by offering political, military, and economic support to local regimes, as well as anti-U.S. resistance movements. For three decades this superpower rivalry shaped U.S. strategy in the Middle East, and it became so intense during the 1970s and 1980s that Washington warned the Soviets that it would use nuclear weapons during at least two Middle East crises—the 1973 Arab-Israeli war and in 1980 during the tense aftermath of the Iranian revolution (explored in chapter 4).

In Iraq, the Soviets agreed to provide extensive military, technical, and economic assistance, and by the mid-1970s, Moscow supplied 95 percent of Iraq's arms and many of its modern weapons.[80] In return, the Soviets gained access to Iraqi oil, political leverage in Baghdad, and permission to use Iraqi ports. Iraq became one of the Soviet Union's most important Middle East allies and its prime entry point to the Persian Gulf.[81]

Iraq's 1972 nationalization of the foreign-owned Iraq Petroleum Company was another point of tension with the U.S. In the early 1970s, the "Seven Sisters" oil cartel—Royal-Dutch Shell, British Petroleum, and the U.S. multinationals Exxon, Mobil, Texaco, Standard Oil of California, and Gulf Oil—controlled two-thirds of world oil reserves and production and still produced 91 percent of the crude pumped in the Middle East.[82] These oil transnationals paid royalties on their oil income to the host governments, but still owned all the production facilities and refineries, and made all the key decisions concerning oil prices, production, marketing, and development.

By the mid-1970s, however, most Middle East crude was owned by national petroleum companies which formally determined price and output levels and received income directly from crude sales. Libya's 1969 revolution, followed by Iraq's 1972 nationalization were key moments in this shift. Blair described its significance: "Thus forty-five years after it had brought in its first well in Iraq, the Iraq Petroleum Co. lost its rights in a land that was not only the original sources of Mideast oil but remains a repository of 'fantastic' reserves."[83]

Nationalization and the growing weight of Middle East oil in the world market were key factors in OPEC's decision to sharply raise crude prices, which skyrocketed from $1.26 a barrel in 1970, to $9.40 per barrel in 1974, to $24 in 1979.[84] Iraq's oil output was also boosted dramatically thanks in part to Soviet (and some European) technical aid. By 1979, Iraq's oil production—which had long been held down by the IPC—had grown to 3.48 million barrels a day, second only to Saudi Arabia's. This combination of soaring prices and rising output meant that between 1968 and 1980, Iraq's oil revenues rose from $476 million to $26 billion a year.[85]

This by no means turned Iraq into an industrial power or gave it economic clout that in any way approached that of the world's industrialized powers. Iraq, like other Middle East oil producers, still relied on oil revenues for the bulk of its foreign exchange earnings— 90 percent in Iraq's case—and budget revenues. Its petroleum and industrial sectors remained heavily dependent on foreign capital, technology, markets, and expertise. And its technical-industrial base lagged far behind those in the major capitalist countries.

The surge in oil income did, however, give Iraq's industrial, social, and military development a major shot in the arm. Other big oil producers, notably Saudi Arabia and Kuwait, "recycled" much of their new oil income, or "petro-dollars," back to the West via loans and investments. This was encouraged, if not demanded, by Washington because the U.S. bill for imported oil had shot up from $2.8 billion in 1970, to $24.3 billion in 1974 and by 1979 it was 20 times more than it had been a decade earlier. This cash outflow weakened the dollar and worsened the U.S. balance of payment deficit (i.e., more money was flowing out of the U.S. in the form of payments for imports and for capital investment abroad, etc., than was flowing in from export sales, foreign investment in the U.S., and income from overseas investments). So petro-dollar recycling became quite important for maintaining America's global monetary preeminence and stabilizing world financial markets.[86]

Iraq, on the other hand, mainly invested in its own development—and loudly urged other Arab countries to do the same. It expanded a host of economic projects and sought a wide variety of joint ventures with foreign firms, from both the Soviet bloc and the West. In addition to its dealings with the Soviet Union, Iraq engaged in manufacturing projects with French, German, and Japanese concerns. The French were also heavily involved in Iraq's military sector. At one point Iraq even enlisted the U.S. engineering giant Brown & Root to build offshore oil terminals.[87]

"What we want is the best technology and the fastest possible fulfillment of orders and contracts," Iraq's Minister of Planning declared in 1975. There was even talk that Iraq could become one of the world's minor industrial powers by the turn of the century. The Hussein regime was also able to expand many social welfare programs in an attempt to dampen popular discontent, although its extensive repressive apparatus remained the foundation of its power.[88] And oil wealth allowed Iraq to boost its military spending—and thus its capacity to exert influence in the region.

This tension between Iraq's overall integration into the imperialist-dominated global economy and its own national agenda helps account for its shifting relations with the world's major powers—allies at some points, enemies at others.

Nixon and Kissinger Target Iraq

The challenges of Arab nationalism, growing Soviet influence, and the oil price explosion took place when the U.S. was embroiled in Vietnam and in no position to mount a major counter-offensive in the Middle East. Kissinger felt that defeating the 1973-74 Arab embargo and rolling back oil prices hikes would have entailed domestic gasoline rationing and supplying Europe with petroleum, and didn't think the U.S. was capable of such discipline and sacrifice "in a country racked by Vietnam."[89]

Forceful action was also hindered by conflicting agendas and strategies of the U.S. and its European allies in the Middle East—divisions which remain to this day. In addition, the U.S. realized some advantages from the rise in oil prices. According to Kissinger, one internal U.S. government study found that "the rise in the price of energy would affect primarily Europe and Japan and probably improve America's competitive position." Answering charges that the U.S. secretly supported the oil price hikes to either weaken Europe and Japan or bolster Saudi Arabia and Iran, Kissinger claimed, "The United States never saw the price rises as anything but a disaster, and no one welcomed them as a means to finance Iranian military purchase or for any other purpose."[90]

Kissinger may not have felt military action was possible, but he apparently considered it. Robert Dreyfuss writes in the March 2003 issue of *Mother Jones* that in a 1975 *Business Week* interview Kissinger "delivered a thinly veiled threat to the Saudis, musing about bringing oil prices down through 'massive political warfare against countries like Saudi Arabia and Iran to make them risk their political stability and maybe their security if they did not cooperate.'" Dreyfuss also reports that *Harper's* ran an article the same year titled "Seizing Arab Oil," which argued that the U.S. could solve its economic problems by taking over Middle East oil fields—an argument that experienced a post-September 11, 2001 revival on the Washington think-tank circuit. The article, it turned out, had been inspired by a background briefing by Kissinger.[91]

The U.S. may have been constrained, but it was neither helpless nor inactive. On the Mediterranean side of the region, it increasingly relied on Israel. Its June 1967 and October 1973 wars were intended to bludgeon the surrounding Arab countries—in particular Egypt and Syria—and to demonstrate as Kissinger put it, "the limits of Soviet influence."[92] They were also aimed at the Palestinian liberation struggle, then the region's most revolutionary and broadly influential movement, as were its invasions of Lebanon in 1976 and 1982, during which over 20,000 Lebanese and Palestinians were killed.

In the Persian Gulf, U.S. difficulties were compounded by

Britain's announcement in 1968 that it could no longer be responsible for protecting Western interests there and that it would withdraw its forces by 1971. Iraq was becoming a particular concern. Kissinger and the Shah of Iran worried that the Ba'ath regime, newly strengthened by rising oil revenues and Soviet arms:

> would be used as a battering ram against all moderate prowestern regimes in the area. Though not strictly speaking a Soviet satellite, once fully armed with Soviet weapons Iraq would serve Soviet purposes by intimidating pro-western governments, such as Saudi Arabia; simultaneously, it would exert pressure on Jordan and even Syria, which, while leaning to the radical side was far from being a Soviet client. The Soviet Union would try to squeeze Iran between Afghanistan and its Iraqi client... We must try to prevent the fertile crescent—Iraq, Syria, and Jordan—from being ruled from Baghdad.[93]

Yet U.S. options for dealing with Iraq were limited:

> To keep Iraq from achieving hegemony in the Persian Gulf, we had either to build up American power or to strengthen local forces... Creating a credible military capability for the defense of the Persian Gulf by America alone is a task of enormous, perhaps insuperable, practical and logistical difficulty in the best of circumstances.[94]

In 1972, the U.S. chose "local forces"—Iran and Saudi Arabia—as its "Twin Pillars" in the Persian Gulf. These client regimes were the region's two largest oil producers, would soon become flush with billions in additional oil income thanks to soaring crude prices. Between 1970 and 1978, the Shah bought some $20 billion worth of U.S. arms (amounting to one-quarter of total U.S. arms sales at the time). "Our choice in 1972," Kissinger argued, "was to help Iran arm itself or to permit a perilous vacuum."[95] The U.S. and Saudi Arabia also began constructing an extensive network of military bases and supply depots, built to U.S. specifications. These facilities became crucial to the projection of American military power in the Persian Gulf over the next decades—especially during the 1991 and 2003 wars on Iraq.[96]

Playing the Kurdish "Card" (Again!)

To hear the Bush II administration tell it, Iraq's Kurds could have no better allies than their self-proclaimed friends in Washington. Bush and company repeatedly denounced the Hussein regime's "persecution of its civilian population, including Shi'a, Sunnis, Kurds, Turkomans and others," as Bush put it before the United Nations in September 2002, and argued that war, conquest, and regime change were needed to assure Kurdish freedoms.[97]

The proponents of the 2003 war never saw fit, of course, to mention the actual, sordid record of Washington's manipulation and betrayal of the Kurds during the 1970s, which we delve into below. That history not only makes U.S. promises ring hollow and hypocritical, but casts Washington's true intentions toward the Kurds in a starkly different light.

In 1972, Nixon, Kissinger and Iran's Shah also came up with a cynical plan to deal with its concerns in the Persian Gulf: encouraging an insurgency by Iraq's Kurds in order to weaken Baghdad. In May, Nixon and Kissinger visited Moscow and promised that the U.S. would join the Soviets to "promote conditions in which all countries will live in peace and security and will not be subject to outside interference." Seymour Hersh, a long-time investigative journalist for the *New York Times* and later the *New Yorker*, writes in his biography of Kissinger that, "The next day, Nixon and Kissinger flew to Tehran and made a secret commitment to the Shah to clandestinely supply arms to the Kurdish rebel faction inside Soviet-supported Iraq...."[98] The goal, Kissinger later explained, was for the Shah to "keep Iraq occupied by supporting the Kurdish rebellion within Iraq, and maintain a large army near the frontier."[99]

Since Iraq's creation by the British, its Kurdish population has suffered systematic discrimination and oppression. Much of Iraq's oil flows from fields around Kirkuk in Iraqi Kurdistan. Yet Iraqi Kurds saw few benefits from Iraq's petroleum wealth and had no voice in its oil policy. Kurdistan remained undeveloped, with fewer industries, roads, schools, and hospitals than the rest of Iraq. Kurds were discriminated against in government employment and had little control over even their local affairs.

Following the Ba'ath takeover in 1968, the new regime promised Kurds that their lot would improve. Iraq's new 1970 constitution recognized "the national rights of the Kurdish People and the legitimate rights of all minorities within the unity of Iraq." A 1974

"Law for Autonomy in the Area of Kurdistan" promised that Kurdish would be an official language, used in Kurdish schools.[100] These actions marked Iraq's broadest official recognition of Kurdish identity and rights. (In contrast, neighboring Iran and Turkey, then staunch U.S. allies, have never even formally recognized the Kurds as a distinct nationality, let alone promised them national rights.)

However, during negotiations in 1971 between the Ba'ath regime and Kurdish representatives, it became clear that the key issues of Kurdish control of local security forces, receiving a fair portion of Iraq's oil income, and sharing national power were not on the table. The Ba'ath also began encouraging Iraqi Arabs to move to Kurdistan and attempted to assassinate Kurdish leader Mustafa Barzani.[101] Barzani, who had been in contact with the U.S. and the Shah (and perhaps Israel) since the early 1960s, turned to them once again for help against Baghdad. Barzani even promised the *Washington Post* that if the U.S. backed the Kurdish struggle, "we are ready to do what goes with American policy in this area if America will protect us from the wolves. If support were strong enough, we could control the Kirkuk field and give it to an American company to operate."[102]

The Kissinger-Shah plan went into effect in 1972. Iran and the U.S. encouraged the Kurds to rise against Baghdad and provided them millions of dollars in weapons, logistical support, and funds. Over the next 3 years, $16 million in CIA money was given to Iraq's Kurds, and Iran provided the Kurds with some 90 percent of their weapons, including advanced artillery.[103]

The U.S. goal, however, was neither victory nor self-determination for Iraqi Kurds. The CIA feared such a strategy "would have the effect of prolonging the insurgency, thereby encouraging separatist aspirations and possibly providing to the Soviet Union an opportunity to create difficulties" for U.S. allies Turkey and Iran.[104] A Congressional investigation of CIA activities, headed by New York Congressman Otis Pike, concluded that "none of the nations who were aiding [the Kurds] seriously desired that they realize their objective of an autonomous state."[105] Rather, the U.S. and the Shah sought to weaken Iraq and deplete its energies. According to CIA memos and cables, they viewed the Kurds as "a card to play" against Iraq, and "a uniquely useful tool for weakening [Iraq's] potential for international adventurism."

To this end, Iran instituted "draconian controls" on its military assistance and never gave the Kurds more than three days worth of ammunition in order to deny them the freedom of action needed for victory.[106] At one point in 1973, Kissinger personally intervened to halt a planned Kurdish offensive for fear it would succeed and complicate U.S. machinations in the wake of the October Arab-Israeli War.[107] The Pike investigation concluded:

> The president, Dr. Kissinger, and the Shah hoped that our clients would not prevail. They preferred instead that the insurgents simply continue a level of hostilities sufficient to sap the resources of our ally's [Iran's] neighbouring country. The policy was not imparted to our clients, who were encouraged to continue fighting.[108]

"Ours Was a Cynical Enterprise"

By 1975, the Kurdish insurgency posed the gravest threat the Ba'ath Regime had yet faced. Some 45,000 Kurdish guerrillas, aided by two Iranian divisions, had pinned down 80 percent of Iraq's 100,000 troops, severely straining Iraq's economy and military.[109] Kissinger and the Shah wanted neither all-out war, nor the collapse of the Iraqi regime. Rather, they sought to force Iraq to curb its anti-Israeli Arab nationalism and to pry it from its Soviet patrons, demonstrating to others in the region that being a Soviet client didn't pay. The Shah also wanted to prove that Iran was the Gulf's strongest power and a reliable regional gendarme for the U.S., as well as to renegotiate the Sa'dabad Pact of 1937, which had given control of the entire Shatt al Arab waterway between the two countries to Iraq.[110]

The Shah planned to abandon the Kurds "the minute he came to an agreement with his enemy over border disputes," one CIA memo noted. Eight hours after Iraq did agree to U.S.-Iranian terms, which were formalized in the Algiers Agreement of March 1975, the Shah and the U.S. cut off aid—including food—and closed Iran's border, cutting off Kurdish lines of retreat.[111]

The Kurds had no idea that they were about to be abandoned. But Iraq knew, and the next day it launched an all-out, "search-and-destroy" attack. The Kurds, who had been led to believe that the U.S. was acting as a "guarantor" against betrayal by the Shah, were taken by complete surprise. Deprived of Iranian support, Kurdish forces were quickly decimated and between 150,000 and 300,000 Kurds were forced to flee into Iran.[112]

The U.S. coldly betrayed its erstwhile Kurdish "allies," but even then, as the Pike Commission sardonically noted, "The cynicism of the U.S. and its ally had not yet completely run its course." Barzani had written to Kissinger, pleading desperately for help. Kissinger didn't bother replying.

Washington then "refused to extend humanitarian assistance to the thousands of refugees created by the abrupt termination of military aid," the Pike Commission reported. One CIA cable acknowledged, "[O]ur ally [Iran] was later to forcibly return over 40,000 of the refugees and the United States government refused to admit even one refugee into the United States by way of political asylum even though they qualified for such admittance."[113]

The U.S.-Iranian covert campaign further poisoned relations between Baghdad and Iraq's Kurds. The Pike Commission concluded that if the U.S. and the Shah hadn't encouraged the insurgency, the Kurds "may have reached an accommodation with the central government, thus gaining at least a measure of autonomy while avoiding further bloodshed. Instead, our clients [the Kurds] fought on, sustaining thousands of casualties and 200,000 refugees."[114]

Baghdad also retaliated with a massive pacification campaign: some 250,000 Kurds were forcibly relocated to central and southern Iraq, while many Arab Iraqis were forced to move to into traditionally Kurdish areas.[115]

In what became an infamous remark, Kissinger dismissed the Pike Commission's concerns: "Covert action," he said, "should not be confused with missionary work." Nonetheless, the Commission concluded, "Even in this context of covert operations, ours was a cynical enterprise."[116] It is important to note here that as these events were taking place (beginning in September 1973), Kissinger's top aide was General Brent Scowcroft, who would later become National Security Advisor under Bush, Sr. and an architect of the 1991 Persian Gulf war on Iraq. It is also important to note that if the U.S. government had had its way, the Pike Commission's damning

exposures would have never seen the light of day. First, the House of
Representatives voted not to release the document. The, when CBS
correspondent Daniel Schorr obtained a leaked copy and gave it to
the *Village Voice*, he was promptly fired by CBS and threatened with
contempt of Congress for refusing to reveal his sources. A new
Director of Central Intelligence had just been appointed when this
attempted cover-up took place. His name was George H.W. Bush.[117]

As we'll explore in the next chapter, the United States govern-
ment again resorted to a cynical "no win" strategy during the Iran-
Iraq war of the 1980s with even more horrific consequences for
Iranians, Iraqis and Kurds.

OPEC's "Pivotal" Price Hike

The economic shocks from petroleum's steep price climb rever-
berated well into the 1980s, and still color U.S. strategy in the
Middle East. Kissinger even called OPEC's December 1973 decision
raising the price of crude from $5.12 to $11.65 a barrel, "one of the
pivotal events in the history of this century:"

> The statistics were staggering enough. Within forty-eight
> hours the oil bill for the United States, Canada, Western
> Europe, and Japan had increased by $40 billion a year; it was a
> colossal blow to their balance of payments, economic growth,
> employment, price stability, and social cohesion...all the coun-
> tries involved, even the producers themselves, faced seismic
> changes in their domestic structures.[118]

These price hikes, he adds, "altered irrevocably the world as it
had grown up in the postwar period. The seemingly inexorable rise
in prosperity was abruptly reversed."[119]

Western capitalism found ways to cope with these rising oil
prices, and giant global oil monopolies continued to dominate world
production, marketing, and supply. By 1990, inflation adjusted crude
prices had returned to pre-1972 levels. Yet the price shock of the
1970s, as well as the 1973-74 embargo, highlighted the western
industrialized countries' dependence on cheap Middle East crude,
and the devastating impact that severing that economic lifeline
could have. Today, some 30 years later, establishment think-tanks
warn that another severe energy crunch is on the horizon, and avert-

ing such a crisis and strengthening U.S. control of global energy sources was a major objective in the 2003 Iraq War and the Bush Doctrine that inspired it, as we examine in chapter 10.

Over the 1970s, rising crude prices, frustrations with nationalistic regimes such as Iraq and Syria, sharpening rivalry with the Soviet Union, and the constraints that forced the U.S. to work through local proxies contributed to a growing sense among America's rulers that they needed to deal more forcefully with these challenges to their power. Former Reagan National Security Council staffer Howard Teicher, in a study of U.S. Middle East policy written with his wife, states that America's inability to block OPEC price increases "helped convince Middle East leaders and others that the United States would not act forcefully to defend important interests."[120]

This concern over the erosion of U.S. power took on even greater urgency in the wake of three dramatic regional shocks that took place in 1979. The U.S. would then spend the 1980s and 1990s forging the strategic doctrine and building the military presence and capability to deal with them, laying the groundwork for two wars on Iraq in the process.

CHAPTER 4

ARMING IRAQ

DOUBLE-DEALING DEATH
IN THE GULF

The 1980s were a goldmine for U.S. propagandists and spin-meisters during the months of buildup for the 2003 war. Saddam Hussein was condemned for invading Iran, for accumulating weapons of mass destruction, and for using them against Iranian troops and Iraqi Kurds, "leaving the bodies of mothers huddled over their dead children," as George W. Bush put it in his 2002 State of the Union message.[1]

The only fly in the ointment was that these crimes took place when Hussein's government was closer to Washington than ever before—or since—and the U.S. directly facilitated every one of them, as detailed in this chapter.

The story of the 1980s, however, is much more than a chronicle of U.S. hypocrisy. It is also the story of how Washington fueled the Iran-Iraq War and helped turn it into one of the longest and bloodiest conventional wars of the 20th century. It's the story of secret dealings between Ronald Reagan's supporters and the Khomeini regime which helped Reagan get elected president, and of the mind-boggling and Machiavellian twists and turns of U.S. policy—first supporting Iraq, then Iran, and then back to Iraq again. It is the story of how Washington—including Donald Rumsfeld, the man later put in charge of destroying Saddam's regime for the Bush II administration—helped Iraq obtain and use the very weapons of mass destruction that provided the alleged *casus belli* for war in 2003.

The record of the 1980s offers a unique window into the real concerns of the world's largest empire, concerns that are quite different than the second Bush administration's moralistic condemnations of Iraqi behavior. And it also illustrates the potential for U.S.

imperial interventions to backfire. This decade marked the beginnning of a cycle of greater and more direct American military intervention in the Persian Gulf. And finally, it is the story of how Washington's actions over the decade helped set the stage for another devastating Persian Gulf War—Operation "Desert Storm" of 1991.

1979: Seismic Jolts to Empire

The 1980s were a decade of extreme tension across the Persian Gulf/Southwest Asian region, marked by revolutionary upheaval in Iran, the bloody Iran-Iraq war, and intense superpower competition. U.S.-Soviet rivalry reached its most intense peak during this decade, thanks in no small measure to events in this region. World war loomed as a real danger, and there may not have been any other place where a direct U.S.-Soviet conflict was more likely to begin. Iraq was at the vortex of these tumultuous events.

The decade was ushered in by three seismic jolts to U.S. power which occurred in rapid succession in 1979: the February revolution that toppled the pro-U.S. Shah of Iran; the November seizure of the American Embassy in Tehran; and the Soviet invasion of neighboring Afghanistan in December.

In December 1977, President Jimmy Carter called the Shah's Iran an "island of stability" in a sea of turmoil. A year later more than 10 million people—a third of Iran's entire population—took to the streets demanding an end to his U.S.-backed tyranny. In January 1979, the hated Shah was forced to flee, and February's revolution put Ayatollah Khomeini and the Shi'a clerics in power. Nine months later, on November 4, 1979, Islamic students seized the U.S. embassy in Tehran with Khomeini's blessing, took its personnel hostage, and demanded the exiled Shah be returned to face trial. A month later, on Christmas Eve, Soviet troops rolled into neighboring Afghanistan.

All three events were, in large measure, reactions to 25-plus years of U.S. interventions in the region. Nowhere was the U.S. more deeply involved in imposing and maintaining a dictatorial regime than in Iran, and nowhere was it more hated. The Shah's subservience to U.S. interests, his reliance on repression and torture

by the despised secret police, SAVAK, and his squandering of billions on Western arms while millions of Iranians remained impoverished all helped fuel the 1979 revolution. Anti-U.S. anger that
accumulated over decades, fears of an attempted repeat of the CIA's
1953 coup, and Khomeini's efforts to consolidate clerical power all
contributed to the embassy seizure.

I traveled to Iran in the spring of 1980 and interviewed a leader
of the students holding the expansive walled compound in the middle of downtown Tehran that was once the U.S. embassy. This former University of California Berkeley student told me, "We felt that
in order [for Washington] to bring the Shah back to Iran [where he
could be reinstated as ruler], the U.S. imperialists needed international acceptance of him. Bringing him to the U.S. was the way to
do that."[2] These students argued that seizing the embassy and its
personnel would call attention to Iran's grievances and prevent the
former Shah from being returned to power.

The Soviet invasion, in turn, was motivated by a combination
of Moscow's own imperial ambitions and its concern over stepped-
up U.S. covert operations in Afghanistan and possible military
action in Iran. In his book *Iran Under the Ayatollahs*, author Dilip
Hiro argues that Moscow feared that following the embassy seizure,
Washington was preparing a military assault on Iran, which in turn
would "have encouraged President Hafizollah Amin of Afghanistan
to loosen his ties with Moscow. Forestalling such a move was one of
the main considerations which led Soviet officials to order their
troops into Afghanistan."[3]

All three events were severe blows to U.S. regional power. The
Shah's fall collapsed the more important of its "twin pillars" in the
Persian Gulf and unmoored one of the region's most strategically
important countries from American control—something
Washington is still trying to deal with. Zbigniew Brzezinski,
President Carter's National Security Adviser, also sensed "growing
vulnerability" in its Saudi pillar after anti-government Islamists
seized Mecca's Grand Mosque and held it for 10 days in November
1979, only weeks after the seizure of the U.S. embassy in Tehran.[4]
Making matters worse, Iran's new Islamic Republic began agitating
against the pro-U.S. oil sheikdoms in the Gulf.

The U.S. power structure viewed the seizure and holding of the

Tehran embassy and 52 of its personnel for 444 days as a global humiliation. The media labeled it "America held hostage," and establishment commentators complained that the U.S. had been turned into a "pitiful giant," incapable of imposing its will even on a Third World country. The hostage drama ended Jimmy Carter's presidential career, raised questions among allies and rivals about American strength, and helped propel a U.S. counter-attack under President Ronald Reagan during the 1980s.

The Soviet invasion came in the wake of stepped up "competition for influence with the United States throughout the Middle East, Indian Ocean, Horn of Africa, Arabian Peninsula and Southwest Asia regions," as the former Reagan NSC staffer Howard Teicher and his wife put it in their book on U.S. policy in the Gulf.[5] Taking over Afghanistan rescued a pro-Soviet government in Kabul, gave Moscow control of a key buffer state between Iran and Pakistan, and put its forces closer to the Persian Gulf. For the U.S., the fertile crescent had become, as Brzezinski labeled it, an "arc of crisis" stretching from Afghanistan through Iran to Saudi Arabia— a label that is once again being applied to this region in the wake of the U.S. wars on Afghanistan and Iraq.

The Empire Strikes Back

Intervention in the Iran-Iraq War was one facet of a multi-dimensioned and aggressive U.S. response to the shocking turn of events in 1979. Washington's overarching goals were protecting the Gulf's pro-U.S. oil sheikdoms while preventing the Soviet Union from turning regional turmoil into geopolitical gain.

In July 1979, some five months before the Soviet invasion, the U.S. had initiated a covert campaign to destabilize Afghanistan's pro-Soviet government by arming and funding the Islamist opposition. The goal, according to Brzezinski, was "to induce a Soviet military intervention." When the Soviets did intervene in December, Brzezinski wrote Carter: "We now have the opportunity of giving to the USSR its Vietnam War."[6]

Over the next decade, the U.S. government funneled more than $3 billion in arms and aid to the Islamic Mujahideen, helping create a global network of Islamist fighters, some of whom would form the core of Osama bin Laden's al Qaeda. When the Soviets finally pulled out of Afghanistan in 1989, more than a million Afghans (along with 15,000 Soviet soldiers) had been killed and one-third of the population driven into refugee camps.

The U.S. also began a regional military buildup that has continued ever since. In 1980 a "Rapid Deployment Joint Task Force" was organized and assigned 100,000 troops ready for deployment to the Gulf. The U.S. gained access to facilities in Bahrain, Oman, Saudi Arabia, and the Indian Ocean island of Diego Garcia. Military equipment and supplies were pre-positioned and bases built that could be quickly utilized by U.S. forces. The Navy's presence was augmented, and according to the Teichers, the U.S. began a "discreet strategic dialogue" with Israel to "enhance the ability of the U.S. to project power into southwest Asia."[7] These supplies, bases and alliances would all come into play during U.S. wars on Iraq in 1991 and 2003.

These steps were components of a more assertive U.S. global posture, begun under President Carter, but ultimately personified by Ronald Reagan—whose administration was staffed by many who became prominent "Iraq hawks" in the Bush, Jr. administration. Its focus was a belligerent "full court press" against Soviet power and interests, backed by the massive Reagan military buildup. "For the first time," Brzezinski later wrote, "the United States deliberately sought for itself the capability to manage a protracted nuclear conflict."[8]

In his January 23, 1980 State of the Union address, President Carter underscored the Persian Gulf's centrality to U.S. global power, and Washington's willingness to wage war to maintain its regional dominance: "Any attempt by any outside force to gain control of the Persian Gulf region will be regarded as an assault on the vital interests of the United States and such an assault will be repelled by any means necessary, including military force." In 1981, Reagan added his own corollary stating that the U.S. would intervene militarily to ensure pro-U.S. rule in Saudi Arabia. (The Teichers argue that this "Carter Doctrine" and the subsequent Reagan Corollary laid "the policy groundwork" for the 1991 Persian Gulf War.)[9]

Brzezinski called U.S. actions in 1979-80 and the enunciation of the Carter Doctrine a "strategic revolution in America's global position." Controlling the Gulf was now as important to the empire as its alliances with Europe and Japan. During the internal government debates leading up to Carter's declaration, Brzezinski argued that "losing" the Persian Gulf would lead to the loss of Europe as well. The Gulf's importance to U.S. global power has, if anything, grown in the years since.[10]

"Headlong into World War III"

After Iran's revolution and then the embassy take-over, Brzezinski felt that pressure on Tehran should be stepped up. Gary Sick, who was Carter's chief National Security Council aide on Iran at the time, wrote that Brzezinski argued "Iran should be punished from all sides," and "made public statements to the effect that he would not mind an Iraqi move against Iran."[11] The U.S. cast about for ways to strike at the Islamic Republic, force it to release the embassy personnel, and stop its destabilizing agitation in the region.

During the hostage crisis, the U.S. considered various military actions, including imposing a naval blockade or launching air strikes against Iran's main oil facilities at Kharg Island.[12] The atmosphere was thick with threats and plots, including conspiracies to restore the monarchy involving the CIA and a variety of generals, officials and hangers-on from Pahlevi days.

On April 24, 1980, the U.S. mounted a covert operation to extract the captured embassy personnel by helicopter, but the mission was aborted shortly after it began when three of the eight helicopters were knocked out of action by a dust storm and mechanical problems. President Carter called it "a strange series of mishaps—almost completely unpredictable."[13]

The U.S. did not mount a major military campaign against Iran for several reasons. First, it did not have the extensive military infrastructure and presence in the region that it does today. Second, Washington's strategy was to punish Iran, but not to overthrow the Khomeini regime because in important ways it didn't threaten U.S. interests: the new Islamic Republic had brutally clamped down on Iranian leftists, maintained its distance from the Soviet Union, and kept Iranian oil flowing West. Many U.S. strategists felt that

Washington would eventually be able to rebuild ties with Tehran. Avoiding an all-out clash with the Islamic regime in Iran took on added importance following the Soviet invasion of Afghanistan, when Brzezinski argued that a key U.S. strategic task was to "forge an anti-Soviet Islamic coalition."[14]

The U.S. also feared that any major military move against Iran could be, as Brzezinski put it, "strategically damaging" by creating "additional opportunities to the Soviets in their drive toward the Persian Gulf and the Indian Ocean."[15]

Looming over all these considerations was the fear that an American invasion of Iran might provoke a U.S.-Soviet military confrontation that could slide into nuclear combat. This was no idle concern. During the tumultuous years of the Iranian revolution and its immediate aftermath, the U.S. and the Soviets engaged in a series of high-stakes warnings and threats, backed by military maneuvers and nuclear alerts, as each tried to block the other from gaining ground in Iran.

When the Iranian revolution was gaining momentum in November 1978, Soviet Premier Brezhnev warned the U.S. that "any interference, especially military, in the affairs of Iran, a state which directly borders the Soviet Union, would be regarded as affecting its own security," thereby raising the specter that the Soviets could invoke the 1921 treaty giving them the right to move troops into Iran in the event of foreign armed intervention. The U.S. replied that it would not interfere, weakening the Shah's regime and bolstering its opponents.[16]

The enunciation of the Carter Doctrine and the U.S. military buildup prior to its April raid raised Soviet fears of a U.S. invasion of Iran. Moscow responded by moving half its 100,000 troops in Afghanistan to the Iranian border. The Soviet response to the failed April raid underscored just how tense relations between the two superpowers had become in the region: the Soviet news agency Tass called it "a reckless gamble which might have started a war." U.S. actions, Tass declared, are "balancing on the brink of madness, and there is no need to say what a serious danger is posed to peace."[17]

Soviet fears of U.S. military action against Iran were apparently sparked again on August 16, 1980 when columnist Jack Anderson published an article reporting that, "A startling, top-secret plan to invade Iran with powerful military forces has been prepared for President Carter. The ostensible purpose is to rescue the hostages, but the operation also would exact military retribution." Anderson reported that the assault, tentatively scheduled for October, called for seizing and holding Kharg Island, through which 90 percent of Iran's oil flowed, and possibly other oil fields in southern Iran. Anderson called it a "desperate political gamble.... There already have been ominous rumblings out of the Kremlin, warning of retaliation if Iran should be attacked. A Soviet-U.S. clash over Iran, of course, could become the opening skirmish of World War III."[18]

The Carter administration claimed it had no such plans,[19] but the Soviets seem to have responded to Anderson's exposé by placing their forces near Iran in a higher state of readiness, perhaps as a warning. In late August, Brzezinski writes that Washington detected Soviet forces deployed "in a mode suited for intervention in Iran" and decided to warn the Soviets that any move into Iran "would lead to a direct military confrontation" and to "develop military options both for the defense of Iran itself and for retaliatory military responses elsewhere, in the event of a Soviet move." Those options included the use of tactical nuclear weapons.[20]

The atmosphere was so fraught with tension that when the Carter team was debating whether to move AWACS planes to Saudi Arabia following the September 1980 outbreak of the Iran-Iraq war (thus directly inserting advanced U.S. weapons in the region), Brzezinski writes that then-Secretary of State Muskie "exploded and said that we are plunging headlong into World War III."[21]

During the 1980s, the U.S. considered Iran one of the most likely places for a direct conflict with the Soviets to occur. In 1983 the Pentagon organized five light divisions designed for quick deployment to confront Soviet forces in Iran and developed plans for using nuclear weapons to block a Soviet invasion. "In short," Hiro concludes, "when it came to keeping the Soviets out of Iran the Reagan administration [like the Carter administration before it] was prepared to go to the furthest limit, including nuclear warfare."[22]

Exploiting Iran-Iraq Tensions—Once Again

The tense U.S.-Soviet face-offs of 1978-80 led the Carter

administration to drop plans for further military attacks on Iran, fearing they could create chaos and present the Soviets with the need and opportunity to step in.[23]

These constraints on U.S. power created enormous frustration in the U.S. ruling class. A decade later, with the Soviet Union spiraling into crisis and eventual collapse, the U.S. no longer faced such impediments and, as a consequence, unleashed its Desert Storm slaughter on Iraq. But in 1979-80, the U.S. was not in a position to launch a massive and direct military assault on Iran. So it turned to less direct means: exploiting regional tensions as it had during the 1970s with Iraq's Kurds. Only this time it would be using Iraq against Iran.

Iraq had its own issues with Iran and the new Islamic Republic. The Hussein regime had long wanted to abrogate the humiliating 1975 Algiers Agreement, which had been forced on it by the CIA-Shah backed Kurdish insurgency, and regain full control of the Shatt al-Arab waterway.[24]

Tensions between Baghdad and Tehran grew worse after Iran's Shi'a clerics came to power. Ayatollah Khomeini, who had been expelled from a 13-year exile in Najaf, Iraq in 1978, began denouncing the "infidel Ba'ath Party" and calling for its overthrow—a call which Baghdad feared might resonate with Iraqi Shi'as.

The Ba'ath seizure of power in 1968 had exacerbated longstanding tensions between Iraq's ruling Sunni minority and its Shi'a majority. Iraq's Shi'a are a diverse population, but religious leaders remain influential. These clerics and their supporters were never comfortable with the Ba'ath Party's secularism, its alliance with the Soviet Union, or its effort to tightly control all Iraqi institutions, including religious organizations. In addition, Islamic revivalist current had grown in Iraq during the 1970s.[25]

These undercurrents were manifested in open protests in 1974 and 1977 when 30,000 Shi'as demonstrated against the regime during a traditional religious procession. They were met with harsh repression. In 1980, following the attempted assassination of Deputy Prime Minister Tariq Aziz by the underground Islamic Call (al-Da'wa) organization, the regime executed the prominent Shi'a cleric Mohammed Baqir al-Sadr along with his sister (their family remains prominent in Shi'a politics today) and then expelled an estimated 40,000 Shi'as to Iran.[26]

Baghdad calculated that war might put a halt to the Islamic Republic's destabilizing agitation, and perhaps even topple Tehran's diplomatically isolated regime before it could fully consolidate power. If Iraq had succeeded in capturing Iran's southwest Khuzestan province, the heart of its oil industry, Iraqi oil production capacity could be boosted from 4 to 11 million barrels a day. This would put Baghdad in control of about 20 percent of world production and greatly increase its global and regional leverage—while gravely weakening Iran's. Iraq would also control deep water ports and off-shore oil terminals which it had been long denied by the legacy of its British-drawn borders, reducing its dependence on oil pipelines running through other, sometimes hostile, neighbors.[27]

Saddam: the New "Principal Pillar of Stability"

Shahram Chubin, the co-author with Charles Tripp of *Iran and Iraq at War*, described Iraq's motives in attacking Iran as a mixture of "fear, opportunism and overconfidence...a compound of a preventive war, ambition and punishment for a regional rival."[28] Iraq's decision to invade Iran was also made with an eye toward building stronger relations with the U.S. Baghdad understood that America was the dominant power in the Gulf and sought to advance its ambitions in that context—as well as with explicit support from Washington. Iraq, in short, did not act as an "unpredictable rogue," as the Bush II administration would claim in 2002-2003.

Iraq's desire for closer relations with the U.S., which Iraqi officials articulated in meetings with U.S. representatives, flowed from a number of developments. By the late 1970s, Baghdad had grown unhappy with its relationship to Moscow, in part because the West offered much more of the capital and advanced technology Iraq needed for its industrialization programs. The 1978 pro-Soviet coup in Afghanistan also alarmed the Hussein regime, which then cracked down on Iraq's pro-Soviet Communist Party to make sure the Soviets couldn't make a similar move in Iraq.[29] Defeating Iran could have turned Iraq into the West's favored protector in the Gulf states against the new threat of anti-U.S. Islamic revivalism ema-nating from Tehran, and open up new opportunities for Western aid and investment.

U.S. officials were well aware of this potential. In 1979, Brzezinski began arguing that the U.S. should reconsider its "nonre-lationship" with Iraq. He felt it might be possible to use Iraq to weaken the Islamic Republic and force it to release the U.S. hostages.[30] With the right mix of incentives, he argued, Iraq could also be extracted from the Soviet orbit. "Iraq was poised," he felt, "to succeed Iran as the principal pillar of stability in the Persian Gulf."[31] (Moscow understood what Washington was trying to accomplish and opposed Iraq's invasion of Iran.)

On April 14, 1980, five months before Iraq's invasion, Brzezinski publicly signaled a new U.S. willingness to work with Iraq: "We see no fundamental incompatibility of interests between the United States and Iraq...we do not feel that American-Iraqi rela-tions need to be frozen in antagonisms." In June, Iranian students revealed a secret memo found in the embassy from Brzezinski to then-Secretary of State Cyrus Vance recommending the "destabi-lization" of Iran's Islamic Republic via its neighbors.[32]

In the next weeks and months, there were numerous indica-tions that the U.S. encouraged Iraq to attack Iran, although much is still shrouded in secrecy. Abol Hassan Bani-Sadr, then President of the Islamic Republic, writes that his government received an intel-ligence report describing secret talks that had taken place in Paris during the summer of 1980 between U.S. and Israeli military experts, Iranian exiles, and Iraqis to prepare an attack. Bani-Sadr also states that Brzezinski met with Saddam Hussein in Jordan two months before the Iraqi assault to assure him that the U.S. "would not oppose the separation of Khuzestan from Iran."[33]

Kenneth R. Timmermann, author of *The Death Lobby: How the West Armed Iraq*, supports the essentials of Bani-Sadr's account, writ-ing that Brzezinski met with Hussein in July 1980 in Amman, Jordan to discuss joint efforts to oppose "Iran's reckless policy." Saddam Hussein biographer Said Aburish agrees that the Amman meeting did take place, but says that according to a member of King Hussein's cabinet, Hussein met with three CIA agents, not Brzezinski.[34]

The U.S. go-ahead may also have come through its close allies Saudi Arabia and Kuwait. Investigative journalist Robert Parry reported that in a secret 1981 memo summing up a trip to the

Middle East, then-Secretary of State Al Haig noted, "It was also interesting to confirm that President Carter gave the Iraqis a green light to launch the war against Iran through [then Prince, later King] Fahd."[35]

Saddam Hussein traveled to Saudi Arabia on August 5, 1980 and reportedly secured Saudi and Kuwaiti backing for an attack. Both Gulf states had been shaken by the Iranian revolution, the seizure of the Grand Mosque in Mecca, and Khomeini's condemnation of their monarchies.[36] Iran had become a menace to both.

Hussein and the Saudis may also have shared intelligence estimates of Iran's military capabilities. The U.S. had passed such intelligence to Jordan and Saudi Arabia in the months leading up to Iraq's invasion with the expectation, according to the Teichers, that they "would reach Baghdad." These assessments painted the picture of an Iranian military in disarray and vulnerable because shipments of spare parts for its American-made weapons had been frozen by the U.S. and much of the Shah's officer corps had been purged. The Iraqis were led to believe that Iran could quickly be defeated.[37]

Finally, would Iraq have undertaken such a major action in a region considered "vital" to U.S. strategic interests without feeling it either had a "green light," or that Washington would go along? Possibly. The confusion surrounding its later moves into Kuwait certainly suggest that Hussein could act against Washington's wishes, or at the very least that the two parties could miscommunicate, an issue that will be discussed later. But in this instance, the U.S. did give Hussein either an explicit or, at the very least, an implicit go-ahead, as Sick has revealed. He denies that Washington directly encouraged Iraq's attack, but instead let "Saddam assume there was a U.S. green light because there was no explicit red light."[38]

On September 22, 1980 Iraq invaded Iran. One of the longest conventional war of the 20th century had begun—the product of Iraqi fears and ambitions, coupled with American regional intrigues.[39]

Reagan's "October Surprise"

The U.S. attitude toward Iraq's 1980 invasion was markedly different from its response to Iraq's 1990 invasion of Kuwait. In 1980, there were no U.S. cries of outrage, no imposition of punitive sanctions, and certainly no massive deployment to defend Iran's Islamic Republic. The U.S., in short, found Iraq's aggression useful.

However, the war was marked by many unexpected twists and turns—beginning in its first weeks. Contrary to U.S. intelligence estimates, Iranian forces did not collapse, and Iraq's assault quickly bogged down outside the main cities in southwest Iran. Instead of destabilizing the new regime, Iraq's invasion ended up helping it consolidate power as Iranians rallied to the defense of their country. Later exposures of the CIA's practice of providing both Iran and Iraq with doctored intelligence, discussed below, also raise the possibility that the U.S. lured Iraq into the war by deliberately underestimating Iranian capabilities.[40]

The Carter administration made clear that it was not after a decisive Iraqi victory. Instead, it initially saw Iraq's invasion as a way to pressure Iran to release the U.S. hostages prior to the November 1980 U.S. presidential election. So, in the first of many double-crosses, after initially encouraging an Iraqi invasion, Carter and other officials began signaling Iran that the U.S. was prepared to help its war effort if it would release the embassy personnel.

On September 28, 1980, the UN called for a cease-fire and mediation of the conflict. The U.S. stated it was against "any dismemberment of Iran," and on October 18, Carter said that Iraq had gone beyond its initial goal and that the U.S. wanted "any invading forces withdrawn." Ten days later, Carter stated that if the Americans were released, the U.S. would airlift $300-$500 million worth of arms to Iran which had already been ordered and paid for by the former Shah.[41]

Nothing, however, came of this proposal because of behind-the-scenes wheeling and dealing—not in Baghdad or Tehran, but in Washington—what former Carter official Sick called "nothing less than a political coup." In his book, October Surprise—America's Hostages in Iran and the Election of Ronald Reagan, Sick details the actions of "an organized cabal among individuals inside and outside the elected government of the United States to concoct an alternative and private foreign policy with Israel and Iran without the knowledge or approval of the Carter administration." Their goal: to ensure Ronald Reagan's victory in the 1980 presidential election over incumbent Jimmy Carter.

During the summer of 1980, candidate Reagan's campaign feared that Carter was about to pull off an "October surprise" release of the hostages, which might well guarantee his reelection. So Reagan's top advisors made a secret agreement with the Islamic Republic: if Iran continued to hold the hostages through November's election and Reagan won, he would lift the economic sanctions imposed by Carter and allow Israel to ship arms to Iran. Reagan did win, and on January 21, 1981, the day he was inaugurated, Iran sent the U.S. embassy personnel home.[42]

This secret deal may have helped sabotage an early-negotiated end to the war, with devastating consequence for hundreds of thousands of Iraqis and Iranians. Saddam Hussein had quickly grasped that the war was not going as planned, so when the UN called for a cease-fire, he offered to end the war if Iran accepted Iraqi control of the Shatt al Arab and agreed not to interfere in Iraqi affairs. Although Iran initially refused to stop the war so long as Iraqi troops were on its soil (and also because the Khomeini government had its own motives for continuing the conflict), a diplomatic solution still may have been possible if the U.S. had been onboard.

However, since Tehran was still holding the U.S. hostages and Carter's efforts to win their release had secretly been undercut, the U.S. neither had an incentive to pressure Iraq to withdraw, nor the leverage to demand that Iran come to terms. So, thanks in part to political jockeying by Democrats and Republicans, as well as other machinations explored below, the war dragged on for eight years.

In the end, neither Iran nor Iraq would win a clear victory, but the suffering was enormous on both sides. Conservative estimates place the death toll at 367,000—262,000 Iranians and 105,000 Iraqis. An estimated 700,000 were injured or wounded on both sides, bringing the total casualty figure to over one million.[43]

The Stockholm International Peace Institute estimates that Iran spent between $74 and $91 billion on the war, including $11.3 billion on weapons imports. Iraq, meanwhile, spent $94 to $112 billion.[44] Others put the direct and indirect cost of the war for both countries at $1.19 trillion—$627 billion for Iran and $561 billion for Iraq.[45] Is it any wonder that in 2003—following two more devastating wars on Iraqi soil—the U.S. would find a country in ruins?

Arming Iraq

Most would assume that the U.S. government had a moral responsibility to help stop the bloodshed it had encouraged and fueled. But moral responsibility wasn't what counted. Washington may have initially envisioned a relatively short war, but once the election and hostage dramas were over, it did little to halt the killing. As one State Department official put it later, "We don't give a damn as long as the Iran-Iraq carnage does not affect our allies or alter the balance of power."[46]

For two years, the war was a stalemate fought on Iranian territory. But in 1982, the momentum shifted and did threaten to affect U.S. allies and alter the regional balance. Iran had taken the war into Iraq and threatened Basra, Iraq's second largest city—aided by hundreds of millions of dollars in arms that were secretly shipped from Israel as part of the Reagan hostage deal.[47]

The fall of Basra could have destabilized nearby Kuwait and Saudi Arabia, upset the regional balance of power, and undermined U.S. "credibility" in the region. The *New York Times* reported, "Iran's rout of Iraqi forces threatened the stability of Persian Gulf states and was creating a situation potentially more dangerous to Western interests than the unresolved Arab-Israeli conflict."[48]

Teicher later stated in a legal affadavit that the U.S. feared that Iraq "teetered on the brink of losing its war with Iran," so in June 1982 President Reagan "decided that the United States...would do whatever was necessary and legal to prevent Iraq from losing the war with Iran," and signed a secret National Security Decision Directive 114 to that effect.[49] After the Directive was signed, "the United States actively supported the Iraqi war effort by supplying the Iraqis with billions of dollars of credits," Teicher stated, and "by providing U.S. military intelligence and advice to the Iraqis, and by closely monitoring third country arms sales to Iraq to make sure that Iraq had the military weaponry required."[50]

In 1982, Iraq was removed from the State Department's list of alleged sponsors of "terrorism," where it had been placed in 1979 for supporting some Palestinian resistance groups. This made Iraq eligible for U.S. government-backed credits and so-called dual-use technology, which could be used for either civilian or military purposes.[51] In short, Iraq had been removed from the U.S. "terrorism" list so it could be better supplied with weapons of terror! And so the flow of weapons to Baghdad—both conventional and unconventional—began in earnest.

Over the next eight years, the U.S. gave Iraq some $5 billion in economic aid and encouraged its allies to provide billions of dollars worth of arms. The British sold Iraq tanks, missile parts, and artillery; the French provided howitzers, Exocet missiles, and Mirage jet fighters; and the West Germans supplied technology used in Iraqi plants that reportedly produced nerve and mustard gas.[52]

(Soviet conventional arms also flowed into Iraq, despite an initial cutoff. Since the early 1970s, the Soviets had been Iraq's main arms supplier, accounting for roughly 90 percent of its major weapons imports during the 1970s. After the outbreak of the Iran-Iraq war, the Hussein regime turned increasingly to Western firms for advanced and unconventional weapons. However, between 1981 and 1985, 55 percent of Iraqi imports of major conventional arms still came from the Soviet Union.)[53]

Much of this hardware was paid for by Saudi Arabia and Kuwait, which loaned Baghdad between $50 and $60 billion during the war, and also transferred millions of dollars in U.S. military hardware to Iraq.[54]

Meanwhile, in 1983 the U.S. launched "Operation Staunch" to stem the flow of arms to Iran. The next year, it added the Islamic Republic to the ever-malleable State Department list of "terrorist" states. A U.S. official explained, "We do not want to see the government in Baghdad destabilized. We want to see a stable and internally secure Iraq. We see it as the first line of defense against Iranian expansionism."[55]

Supplying Anthrax & Calibrating Chemical Attacks

The full extent of American military involvement in the Iran-Iraq slaughter is still emerging, but it is clear that the U.S. and its European allies were directly complicit in many of Iraq's worst wartime atrocities, including its use of chemical weapons.

CIA Director William Casey was "adamant," according to Teicher, that Baghdad receive one of the most savage weapons of war-anti-personnel cluster bombs. Casey considered them a "perfect 'force multiplier' that would allow the Iraqis to defend against the 'human waves' of Iranian attackers." Accordingly, "the CIA authorized, approved and assisted Cardoen [a Chilean weapons company] in the manufacture and sale of cluster bombs and other munitions to Iraq."[56]

U.S. firms also directly supplied Iraq with biological weapons. Author William Blum writes that according to a May 25, 1994 Senate Banking Committee report, "From 1985, if not earlier, through 1989, a veritable witch's brew of biological materials were exported to Iraq by private American suppliers pursuant to application and licensing by the U.S. Department of Commerce."

According to Blum, the Senate report detailed 70 shipments from the U.S. to Iraq over three years, including anthrax, botulism, and *E. coli* bacillus. Although there is no evidence that Iraq ever used these agents, the report concluded that, "It was later learned that these microorganisms exported by the United States were identical to those the United Nations inspectors found and recovered from the Iraqi biological warfare program."[57]

The U.S. and its allies also helped provide Iraq with chemical weapons. Iraq's December 2002 arms declaration to the United Nations stated that since 1983 it had imported 17,602 tons of chemicals which could be used in making chemical weapons (mainly from Singapore, the Netherlands, Egypt, India, and Germany); 340 pieces of equipment used to make chemical weapons (primarily from Germany, France, and Austria); and 200,000 artillery shells for delivering deadly chemicals (mainly from Italy and Spain).[58]

Between 1985 and 1990, U.S. corporations—with government approval—supplied Iraq with precursor chemicals for weapons, including for nerve gas. They also supplied $782 million in dual-use technology and equipment, including helicopters used in chemical attacks, computers which could be used in ballistic missile and nuclear weapon development, machine tools, graphics terminals, and lasers for designing and building ballistic missiles.[59]

A 2002 investigation by the *Washington Post* concluded, "The administrations of Ronald Reagan and George H. W. Bush authorized the sale to Iraq of numerous items that had both military and civilian applications, including poisonous chemicals and deadly biological viruses, such as anthrax and bubonic plague."[60]

Nathaniel Hurd, a Cambridge University researcher, writes in his compilation of U.S. dealings with Iraq during the 1980s, "One study lists 207 firms from 21 countries that contributed to Iraq's non-conventional weapons programs during and after the Iran-Iraq war." Included were 86 West German, 18 British, 17 Austrian, 16 French, 12 Italian, 11 Swiss, and 18 American companies.[61] It seemed none of these firms wanted to be left out when it came to profiting from the bloodletting in the Gulf.

The U.S. not only supplied Iraq with a variety of weapons, it also helped it maximize their deadly impact on the battlefield. According an August 2002 story in The *New York Times*, over 60 U.S. Defense Intelligence Agency [DIA] officers "were secretly providing detailed information on Iranian deployments, tactical planning for battles, plans for airstrikes and bomb-damage assessments for Iraq."[62]

Accounts of Iraqi chemical attacks began surfacing in 1982, and one 1983 State Department report cited Iraq's "almost daily use of CW [chemical weapons]." In 1984, the Reagan administration publicly condemned the use of chemical weapons in the war.[63]

Yet, despite such occasional public pronouncements, U.S. military assistance to Iraq kept increasing—including assistance Iraq used in waging chemical warfare. According to the August 2002 *New York Times* story, "critical battle planning assistance" provided by U.S. intelligence officers, continued even after it was clear that Iraq "had integrated chemical weapons throughout their arsenal and were adding them to strike plans that American advisers either prepared or suggested."[64]

The *Washington Post* reported that Iraq used U.S. intelligence to "calibrate attacks with mustard gas on Iranian ground troops." Iranian estimates of the dead and wounded from these gas attacks range between 50,000 and 100,000, including many civilians.[65]

The U.S. understood and supported Iraq's reliance on imported high-tech weapons, including chemical arms, because Iraq's population was only a third the size of Iran's, and Baghdad was in no position to match Tehran casualty for casualty so it had to rely on its technological advantages.

Iraq used some 100,000 chemical shells and bombs during the

war, mainly mustard and nerve gas.[66] One DIA officer interviewed for the August 2002 *New York Times* story, said that the Pentagon "wasn't so horrified by Iraq's use of gas. It was just another way of killing people—whether with a bullet or phosgene, it didn't make any difference." Col. Walter P. Lang, then a senior defense intelligence officer, said, "The use of gas on the battlefield by the Iraqis was not a matter of deep strategic concern." The *New York Times* continued, "What Mr. Reagan's aides were concerned about, he said, was that Iran not break through to the Fao Peninsula and spread the Islamic revolution to Kuwait and Saudi Arabia." And for that goal, Iraq's chemical attacks served a vital purpose.[67]

Between 1984 and 1988, the UN Security Council passed six resolutions on the Iran-Iraq war, followed by another four in the nearly two years leading up to Iraq's invasion of Kuwait. Some of the resolutions expressed "dismay" at the use of chemical weapons, others "deplored" their use, and some didn't mention the subject at all. None of them explicitly condemned Iraq or called for punitive sanctions, inspections, or disarmament. And none mentioned the major powers—including most of the permanent members of the UN Security Council—that facilitated and supported Iraq's chemical warfare.[68]

Mr. Rumsfeld Goes to Baghdad

The U.S. program of arming Iraq was facilitated by one who would become a leading proponent of war on Iraq in 2003: Donald Rumsfeld. In 2002, Rumsfeld called Saddam Hussein one of "the world's most dangerous dictators." But in December 1983 and again in March 1984, Rumsfeld, who had been Secretary of Defense under President Ford, traveled to Baghdad as President Reagan's special Middle East envoy to assure Hussein of U.S. support and its readiness to restore diplomatic relations, which Iraq had broken after the 1967 Arab-Israeli war.

Bush, Jr. claimed that Saddam Hussein "holds an unrelenting hostility toward the United States."[69] Other commentators argue that Hussein envisioned himself as a modern day Saladin, who "vows to 'liberate' Jerusalem, vanquish the United States, and rule over a united Arab world."[70] Certainly Hussein has his dreams and regional ambitions, but in the main he attempted to pursue them in league with foreign powers, not in opposition to them. During their meetings with Rumsfeld, the Iraqi leadership expressed their desire for better relations with the U.S.—not animosity.

Teicher traveled to Baghdad with Rumsfeld, and he and his wife write that during the visit Deputy Prime Minister Tariq Aziz made clear that "Baghdad required a stable, long-term relationship with the United States in order to promote economic development and rebuild after the end of the war." Teicher also reports that Saddam Hussein was "visibly pleased" at receiving a letter from Reagan, and told Rumsfeld he hoped that "bilateral relations would continue to improve and move toward full restoration on the basis of mutual respect and dignity."[71] Rumsfeld later told the *New York Times* that Hussein "made it clear that Iraq was not interested in making mischief in the world."[72]

Iraq retained its own objectives, as well as continued ties to the Soviet Union. However, during the 1980s it shifted its stance on a number of regional issues in order to strengthen its links with the West. Baghdad sought better relations with the pro-U.S. states in the Gulf and resumed relations with Egypt-after having initially condemned the 1978 Camp David agreement between Egypt and Israel.[73] Iraq also indicated a willingness to modify its refusal to recognize Israel. In August 1982, Hussein told U.S. Congressman Steven Solarz that "a secure state is necessary for both Israel and the Palestinians."[74]

According to the *Washington Post*, months before Rumsfeld's meetings in Baghdad, the U.S. government was well aware of Iraqi chemical attacks against Iranian troops. In a September 2002 interview on CNN, Rumsfeld claimed that he had "cautioned" Hussein against using chemical weapons. In fact, State Department notes show that Rumsfeld said nothing to Hussein about chemical weapons and only mentioned them in passing to Tariq Aziz.[75] There is little doubt that Hussein and Aziz understood this as U.S. approval for their continued use.[76]

Rumsfeld's visits led to renewed U.S.-Iraq diplomatic relations in November 1984, which opened the door to increased U.S. aid. Between 1985 and 1990, Iraq received some $4 billion in U.S. government-guaranteed agricultural credits. These credits freed up Iraqi resources for its war effort and were sometimes secretly used to purchase weapons.[77]

In September 2002, Senator Robert Byrd asked Rumsfeld whether the U.S. had helped Iraq "acquire the building blocks of biological weapons during the Iran-Iraq war?" "Certainly not to my knowledge," Rumsfeld replied with a lie: "I have no knowledge of it whatsoever, and I doubt it." As for his trips to Baghdad, Rumsfeld claimed he was only acting as a "private citizen," interested in combating terrorism in Lebanon.[78]

During the post-Sept. 11 run up to war on Iraq, Rumsfeld's meetings in Baghdad and what they revealed about the U.S. role in arming Iraq with "weapons of mass destruction" received only passing coverage in the U.S. media and were never examined by Congress.

Tilts and Counter-Tilts

During Rumsfeld's Baghdad meetings, Aziz was especially happy that President Reagan affirmed "U.S. opposition to the continuation of the Iran-Iraq War." Aziz specifically asked Rumsfeld if Washington would work to end the war sooner rather than later. Rumsfeld replied that the U.S. "would work harder to stop the flow of arms to Iran."[79] A year later, the U.S. did just the opposite. It began secretly shipping arms to Iran. And rather than end the war, these secret arms shipments, like previous U.S. actions, helped prolong it. Iraq may have aspired to a partnership with the U.S. to police the Gulf, but it ended up getting double-crossed.

In the mid-1980s, the U.S. still did not want either Iran or Iraq to score a decisive victory in the war. Yet it also had new concerns: the possibility of a Soviet-Iranian rapprochement after Ayatollah Khomeini's death (which would come in 1989).

In May 1985, Graham Fuller, the CIA's National Intelligence Officer for Near East and South Asia (with assistance from Teicher), prepared a special intelligence estimate that argued for a shift in U.S. policy toward Iran: "The U.S. faces a grim situation in developing a new policy toward Iran," Fuller wrote. "The Khomeini regime is faltering and may be moving toward a moment of truth; we will soon see a struggle for succession. The U.S. has almost no cards to play; the USSR has many." Fuller warned that whichever super-power first gained the trust of Iran's leadership was "in a strong position to work towards the exclusion of the other" and argued it was time to make some bold moves to regain the initiative:

> It is imperative, however, that we perhaps think in terms of a bolder—and perhaps riskier policy which will at least ensure greater U.S. voice in the unfolding situation. Right now—unless we are very lucky indeed—we stand to gain nothing, and lose more, in the outcome of developments in Iran, which are all outside our control.[80]

In a conclusion that laid bare the cold imperial calculus guiding U.S. actions, Fuller wrote: "Our tilt to Iraq was timely when Iraq was against the ropes and the Islamic revolution was on a roll. The time may now have to come to tilt back."[81]

A sharp debate ensued within the Reagan administration over Fuller's memo, and how to maintain U.S. dominance and prevent Soviet advances in the complex and rapidly changing waters of the Persian Gulf. Some argued in favor of strengthening ties with Iraq, which they believed could "replace Iran as America's pillar in the Gulf."[82] The Soviet Union was then trying to bolster its long-time ally, and the pro-Iraq faction in Washington argued for expanding ties with Baghdad to "counter Soviet influence."[83]

Others favored tilting toward Iran. It was the larger strategic prize in the region: four times the size of Iraq, with 1,000 miles of Persian Gulf coastline, and standing between the Soviet Union and the oil fields of the Middle East. Further, Iraq was not to be trusted—in all likelihood, the Hussein regime was playing the U.S. and Soviets off against each other to gain Western assistance, survive the war, and advance its own regional agenda.[84]

Regardless of the intensity of the debate, the consensus undergirding it was more noteworthy. The key issue was how to maintain U.S. dominance in the region, not concern over the carnage of war, attacks on human rights, or spreading democracy—the principles Democratic and Republican administrations both routinely claim as their central motivations.

By 1985, the Iran faction gained the upper hand. A June 1985 draft National Security Directive spelled out the U.S. rulers' worst fears: "Soviet success in taking advantage of the emerging power struggle to insinuate itself in Iran would change the strategic balance in the area."[85]

The White House and the CIA then came up with a nefarious and soon infamous plan to implement this shift: supplying Iran with arms and military intelligence in return for the release of U.S. hostages held in Lebanon. Washington felt this arms-for-hostages gambit might lead to a geopolitical coup in Tehran. Reagan's Deputy National Security Adviser at the time, Adm. John Poindexter, spelled out the administration's strategic thinking to one CIA official: "We have an opportunity here that we should not miss...if it doesn't work, all we've lost is a little intelligence and 1,000 TOW missiles. And if it does work, then maybe we change a lot of things in the Mideast."[86]

Beginning in the fall of 1985, the U.S. began secretly shipping TOW anti-tank missiles, Hawk missile parts, and Hawk radars to Iran, first via Israel, and beginning in early 1986 directly to Tehran. One CIA official feared the arms shipments would give Iran "a definite offensive edge" and "could have cataclysmic results."[87] In February 1986, Iran scored a major military victory by capturing the Fao Peninsula in southern Iraq.

When the U.S. arms-for-influence plot was exposed in November 1986, Iraqi officials were shocked that their would-be patron was secretly supplying their enemies, and blamed their February 1986 defeat at Fao, according to the New York Times, on "misleading intelligence reports provided by the United States."

First Deputy Prime Minister Taha Yassin Ramadan told the New York Times, "A few months before the Iranian offensive we detected movements of Iranian troops, but the U.S. kept on telling us that the Iranian attack was not aimed against Fao." According to the New York Times, Baghdad concluded that "American arms sales to Iran and the provision of false intelligence information to Iraq were part of a deliberate policy to prolong the war and increase United States influence in the region." Ramadan said that the Iraqis were outraged by "the lack of morals on the part of the U.S," and called the Reagan administration's duplicity "a treachery and conspiracy that started from the very day" after Iraq and the U.S. restored diplomatic relations.[88]

It turned out that manipulating intelligence was standard U.S.

operating procedure during the Iran-Iraq War. The *New York Times* reported, "American intelligence agencies provided Iran and Iraq with deliberately distorted or inaccurate intelligence data in recent years to further the Reagan Administration's goals in the region." One method was altering satellite photos to make them "misleading or incomplete"—including by cropping images "to leave out important details."[89] In a memo to Poindexter, Oliver North called it "a mix of factual and bogus information."[90]

U.S. double-dealing reached mind-numbing proportions. In August 1986, while U.S. arms shipments to Iran were in full swing, the U.S. also set up a direct top-secret intelligence link to give Baghdad near real-time battlefield intelligence, and Casey met with senior Iraqis to urge increased attacks against Iranian economic targets. In 1986, according to Teicher, "President Reagan sent a secret message to Saddam Hussein telling him that Iraq should step up its air war and bombing of Iran."[91]

Then, two months later, in October 1986, Reagan National Security Council staffer Oliver North told Iranian officials that Reagan's position was that "Saddam Hussein is a [expletive]," that the U.S. sought peace in a way that made "very evident to everybody that the guy who is causing the problem is Saddam Hussein," and that Washington knew "that Saddam Hussein must go." North even offered a plan for toppling Hussein.[92]

In reality, the U.S. was lying to both sides and had no intention of allowing either to win. As one *New York Times* headline put it in 1987, the U.S. goal was "Keeping Either Side from Winning the Persian Gulf War."[93] Victory could embolden the winner, destabilize the loser, upset the regional balance of power, and possibly create opportunities for Soviet intrigue. At the same time, the U.S. was also trying to strengthen its leverage in both Baghdad and Tehran.

The *New York Times* reported that the Reagan leadership hoped such covert double-dealing and intelligence manipulation "could bring about major geopolitical changes, such as an opening to Iran." At one point, for instance, the U.S. supplied Iran with intelligence which was "'doctored' to exaggerate the size of Soviet troop concentrations on the Iran border."[94]

So cooking and fabricating "intelligence" did not begin with the 2003 Iraq war; rather, it has become a well-honed weapon in the

American arsenal of empire, which would also be deployed during the 1991 Persian Gulf War, examined in the next chapter.

The more devastating the war, the more both sides might be forced to turn to the U.S. for help. For instance, Reagan's August 1986 message encouraging stepped-up Iraqi attacks may have been designed to prevent an Iranian victory; it may have been primarily intended to pressure Iran to come to terms with the U.S.; or it may have been an attempt to do both.[95]

These U.S. maneuvers contributed mightily to the war's murderous toll. "Doling out tactical data to both sides put the agency in the position of engineering a stalemate," the *Washington Post's* Bob Woodward writes in *Veil*, his study of CIA covert operations in the 1980s. "This was no mere abstraction. The war was a bloody one... almost a million had been killed, wounded or captured on both sides. This was not a game in an operations center. It was slaughter."[96]

One *New York Times* editorial succinctly summed up the U.S. establishment's overarching—and cold-blooded—approach in the Gulf:

> In Henry Kissinger's apt phrase, the ultimate American interest in the war between Iran and Iraq is that both should lose. The underlying hope is that mutual exhaustion might rid the Middle East of the aggressive regimes of both Ayatollah Khomeini and Saddam Hussein, yet leave their nations intact to avoid a superpower rush into any vacuum.[97]

Tilting Back to Baghdad

The U.S. tilts during the Iran-Iraq War may have been deadly and duplicitous, but they did not put Washington in firm control of developments in the Gulf. The Soviet presence forced the U.S. to work through Iran and Iraq, which each had its own agenda. U.S. actions often had unintended consequences, and events sometimes careened in unexpected directions. During the 1980s, the U.S. veered from one crisis to another, shifting tactics to keep up with the changing tides of war and politics in the region.

On November 3, 1986, the Lebanese magazine *Al-Shiraa* exposed the Reagan arms-for-hostages deal with Iran. Its revelation doomed the U.S. gambit in Iran, sparked a furor in the region, trig-gered serious infighting over strategy within the U.S. power struc-ture and helped turn the "Iran-Contra" affair, which included using the proceeds from weapons sales to Iran to illegally fund the count-er-revolutionary Contras of Nicaragua, into a major scandal.

The collapse of the Iran initiative, the need to reassure stunned Gulf allies that the U.S. was indeed committed to their stability, and growing fears of an Iraqi defeat, forced the U.S. to tilt decisively back to Iraq. Other major players also felt it was time to end the war. France and the Soviet Union poured arms into Iraq, and in 1987 American forces directly intervened on Iraq's side by deploying 42 combat ships to the Gulf. This was ostensibly to protect Kuwaiti tankers, which had been re-registered as American ships, from Iranian attacks. The primary goal, however, was to pressure Iran to end the war. The Navy began engaging Iranian naval vessels and attacking Iranian facilities. And the U.S. again stepped up efforts to block arms shipments to Iran.

In early 1988, Iraq retook the Fao Peninsula with American intelligence and planning help. Then, on July 2, the U.S. adminis-tered the coup de grace. The warship *Vincennes* shot down an unarmed Iranian passenger jet—killing all 290 onboard. The U.S. claimed it was an accident, but the Iranian leadership apparently interpreted it as a signal to halt the war or face further American attacks.[98] On July 18, just 16 days later, Iran accepted a UN cease-fire resolution. The cease-fire formally went into effect on August 20, 1988, a month short of eight years after the war had begun.

Gas Massacres in Kurdistan

In 2003, the heinous gassing of Iraq's Kurds during the Iran-Iraq War ranked high on the Bush, Jr. administration's list of charges against the Hussein regime. Yet when these attacks were actually taking place, the U.S. government was not only supporting the Hussein regime, it was directly complicit in the gas massacres them-selves.

During the war, Iraq's Kurds took advantage of Baghdad's focus on Iran to take control of Kurdish areas near the Iranian and Turkish borders. When Iranian forces moved into sections of Iraqi Kurdistan, as they sometimes did, they were often aided by Kurdish forces. By 1986, Baghdad held only the cities in Kurdistan, while Kurdish peshmergas controlled the surrounding countryside. In the midst of war, with the regime under great stress, the Kurdish insurgency forced Iraq to divert troops from the Iranian front and again posed a serious challenge to Baghdad. It responded viciously.

In 1983, Hussein put his cousin Ali Hasan al-Majid in charge of reasserting Ba'ath control, and he earned the sobriquet "Chemical Ali" for his murderous efforts. One of his first actions was rounding up some 8,000 males from the clan of Kurdish Democratic Party (KDP) leader Masoud Barzani. They were never seen again.[99] Kurds claim that the Hussein regime first used chemical weapons against them a year later. Chemical attacks further escalated in the spring of 1987.

Beginning in February 1988, as the war was winding down and momentum had shifted back to Iraq, the Hussein regime unleashed its "Al-anfal" (spoils of war) campaign—a seven-month rampage of murder, destruction, and scorched-earth vengeance against Iraq's Kurds. Chemical attacks were stepped up, fields were destroyed, villages bulldozed, and survivors forcibly transferred to government resettlement camps outside of Kurdistan.

Charles Tripp, author of A History of Iraq, writes that by the time the campaign ended in August 1988, the Kurdish resistance had been crushed and "roughly 80 percent of all the villages had been destroyed, much of the agricultural land was declared 'prohibited territory' and possibly 60,000 people had lost their lives."[100]

An estimated 3,800 Kurdish villages—the foundation of Kurdish life-were affected. In the 12 months from March 1987 until March 1988, Kurds were subjected to chemical attacks on 211 separate days.[101] When I traveled around Suleiymeniah in Iraqi Kurdistan in the summer of 1991, I saw piles of stone rubble where Kurdish villages had once stood—grim testimony to the ferocity of the regime's campaign.

The most notorious Iraqi attack took place on March 16, 1988 in the Kurdish town of Halabja. Iranian troops and Kurdish fighters had taken control of Halabja, some 15 miles from the border with Iran, and Iraq mounted a chemical weapons counter-attack to retake it. Some 5,000 Kurds were massacred in a few hours by a lethal combination that may have included mustard gas, cyanide, and the first recorded military use of nerve gas. People reportedly died where they had been standing, and bodies littered the streets.[102]

Independent journalist and *Democracy Now* contributor Jeremy Scahill reports that in 1991 U.S. intelligence sources told the *Los Angeles Times* that they believed U.S.-built helicopters had been used to drop chemical bombs.[103]

Washington's Silence and Complicity

In September 2003, Secretary of State Colin Powell made a much-publicized trip to Halabja to visit the mass graves of those killed in the Hussein regime's gassing; he even lit candles in memory of the victims. Given Washington's complicity in creating those mass graves—and Powell's own as a Defense Department official in the Carter, Reagan and Bush I administrations—his posturing in Iraqi Kurdistan was yet another display of the shameless hypocrisy of those running the U.S. empire.[104]

Throughout the 1980s, the U.S. supported attacks on Kurds throughout Greater Kurdistan, and steadfastly opposed recognizing their basic rights, let alone self-determination. This was done in service of overall U.S. objectives: preserving the "territorial integrity" and ruling governments of Iraq, Iran and Turkey and thus a regional balance of power that maintained U.S. dominance.

Iran's Kurdish population rose up with millions of other Iranians to overthrow the hated Shah in 1979, but when they demanded their national rights, the U.S. government publicly supported the Khomeini regime's efforts to crush them. This was brought home to me during trips to Iranian Kurdistan in 1979 and 1980, when, traveling with Iranian *peshmergas*, we were forced to drive with lights out in the dead of night to evade U.S. fighter jets, sold to the Shah and then utilized by the Khomeini regime, which streaked overhead strafing Kurdish positions along our route.

The picture was similar in Turkey. Its Kurdish population rose against the dictatorial Turkish regime in 1984, and the U.S. supported Ankara's brutal suppression campaign with increased U.S. aid, which included supplying 80 percent of Turkey's heavy weapons.[105]

Former U.S. Marine and UN weapons inspector Scott Ritter

says that the U.S. assisted the Hussein regime in its chemical attacks on the Kurds: "Wafiq Samarai the former head of the Iraqi intelligence service responsible for Iran—I have met with him many times—and he has said that U.S. advisers were sitting there as Iraq planned the inclusion of chemical weapons in the *Anfal* offensive [of 1987-88]."[106]

Throughout the Iran-Iraq War, the U.S. maintained a "no-contacts" policy and refused to even meet with Iraqi Kurdish representatives. Washington's approach was spelled out in the recently declassified, National Security Directive 26 (NSD-26), signed by President George H. W. Bush in October 1989:

> We should oppose Iraqi military activities against the civilian population and the destruction of hundreds of villages in Kurdistan. But bearing in mind the historical context, in no way should we associate ourselves with the 60-year-old Kurdish rebellion in Iraq or oppose Iraq's legitimate attempts to suppress it. [107]

NSD-26 stated that Iraqi use of chemical or biological weapons or development of nuclear arms, would "lead to economic and political sanctions," but these provisions were not enforced because they conflicted with overall U.S. strategy.[108] For instance, after the gassing at Halabja, Secretary of State Schultz condemned the attack as "abhorrent and unjustifiable," and the Senate passed the "Prevention of Genocide Act of 1988," which would have imposed economic sanctions on Iraq (reflecting concerns of some strategists that the Hussein regime might not be a reliable client). The Reagan and Bush administrations, however, were still committed to turning Iraq into a strategic ally and blocked any action against Baghdad. U.S. officials argued that sanctions were "premature" because Washington needed "solid, businesslike relations" with Iraq. As one government memo stated, "there should be no radical policy change now regarding Iraq."[109] No sanctions were imposed and the "Genocide Act" died in Congress.

Instead, U.S. aid and trade increased. Guaranteed U.S. agricultural exports to Iraq peaked in 1988 at $1.1 billion. By early 1990, Iraq had become America's third leading Middle East trade partner, after Saudi Arabia and Israel, purchasing $433.6 million worth of U.S. goods. The U.S., meanwhile, was importing 500,000 barrels of Iraqi oil a day by 1988.[110]

Covering Up the Carnage

Washington's machinations in the Iran-Iraq war never became the public scandal that the Iran-Contra affair did, and consequently the record of U.S. responsibility for the war's enormous carnage has never been fully aired. Several Congressional investigations revealed details of the Reagan administration's support for Iraq, and in 1987 the report on Iran-Contra concluded, "The Administration...pledged that the United States would not arm either side, but would maintain a policy of strict neutrality, and would urge U.S. allies and friends to do the same. The Iran initiative broke both of these pledges and violated both of these policies."[111]

A few high government officials were indicted for their roles in the Iran-Contra affair; none were ever indicted for helping to fuel an eight-year slaughter in the Persian Gulf.

(In 1990, Deputy National Security Adviser Poindexter was convicted in federal court of conspiracy, obstruction of justice, and destruction of evidence for his role in the Iran-Contra affair. These convictions were later overturned and Poindexter received a complete pardon from President Bush, Sr. In 2002, Poindexter's government career was revived by Bush, Jr., who appointed him the head of the "Office of Total Information Awareness," later renamed the "Office of Terrorist Information Awareness," created under the Homeland Security Act of November 2002. Poindexter was forced to resign in August 2003 after it was revealed that the Defense Advanced Research Projects Agency (DARPA), which he headed, had created "FutureMAP"—Futures Markets Applied to Prediction—an online market for speculating on future international events, including assassinations, terror attacks, and coups.

Another Iran-Contra figure reemerged, even more briefly, on Bush II's watch. In August 2003, it was revealed that Pentagon officials had secretly met with Manucher Ghorbanifar, the Iranian arms merchant who had helped arrange the covert Iran-Contra arms devices, reportedly to discuss strategy toward Iran.[112])

There was a brief flap in Washington after Iraq invaded Kuwait in August 1990. The issue then was not the catastrophic suffering inflicted on the peoples of Iran and Iraq and the U.S. share of responsibility for it, but whether the Reagan and Bush I administrations had helped arm Iraq, thus complicating U.S. planning for the coming "Desert Storm" assault.

The Bush, Sr. administration was mandated to investigate the charges, but its November 1990 report concluded that Europe was to blame and that U.S. "suppliers did not contribute directly to Iraq's conventional or nonconventional weapons capability." Texas Congressman Henry Gonzales, the only official to seriously investigate the U.S. role in supplying Iraq, called the Bush report "patently false... U.S. firms, at the urging of the Administration, played a considerable role in arming Iraq."[113]

Government attempts to coverup Western complicity in arming Iraq in the 1980s continue to this day. Iraq's December 2002 report to the UN detailing its weapons programs included a list of some 150 foreign firms that had supplied it with technology, equipment, and materials for making missiles and chemical, biological, and nuclear weapons. U.S. officials excised this information from the report—removing 8,000 of the declaration's 11,800 pages-before it was made public or even passed to most members of the UN Security Council. The UN also refused to make this information public.[114]

Andreas Zumach of the Berlin daily *Die Tageszeitung* did obtain an unexpurgated copy of Iraq's declaration. It listed 24 of America's most prominent corporations (as well as 80 German firms), which helped build Iraq's "weapons of mass destruction" programs. The list reads like a who's who of American business: Honeywell, Spektra Physics, UNISYS, Sperry Corp., Tektronix, Rockwell, Hewlett Packard, Dupont, Eastman Kodak, International Computer Systems, Bechtel, and EZ Logic Data Systems, Inc. *Die Tageszeitung* also reported that the U.S. Departments of Energy, Defense, Commerce, and Agriculture had also helped arm Iraq, and that Iraqi nuclear scientists had received assistance from U.S. nuclear weapons laboratories Lawrence Livermore, Los Alamos and Sandia.[115]

"A Great Moral Cause..."

In the summer of 2002, Bush II's National Security Advisor Condoleezza Rice argued that there "is a very powerful moral case for regime change" in Iraq. Bush repeated the morality theme in his September 2002 address to the UN: "Liberty for the Iraqi people is a great moral cause and a great strategic goal."[116]

One only need examine the history of deceit, manipulation and complicity in mass slaughter that comprises the record of U.S. actions during the Iran-Iraq war to get an inkling of the kind of "morality" that has guided Bush, Rice and the rest of the U.S. establishment for decades in the Persian Gulf.

CHAPTER 5

"WE HAVE TO HAVE A WAR"

T he tortured twists and turns of U.S. policy during the Iran-Iraq War were Machiavellian to be sure, but they also reflected the profound difficulties the American empire confronted in controlling a volatile region half way around the globe. For all Washington's machinations, it still didn't have a firm grip on either Iran, Iraq, or the Persian Gulf region.

This was brought home in dramatic fashion in the early morning hours of August 2, 1990, when six elite Iraqi Republican Guard divisions crossed into Kuwait heading south. Four hours and 75 miles later they entered the capital of Kuwait City, and by morning had effectively taken over the whole country. Overnight, Baghdad was transformed from a sometime U.S. ally into its main enemy in the region. Iraq's lightning invasion led to the first Persian Gulf War—Operation Desert Storm of 1991—and began a confrontation with the U.S. that led to the war of 2003 and continues, albeit in a different form, as of this writing in September 2003.

Critically, what role did U.S. actions in the Iran-Iraq War play in setting the stage for the invasion of Kuwait? Did the U.S. give Saddam Hussein the green light to invade Kuwait? How did the Bush I administration's secret war aims extend far beyond its public pronouncements and explain what came after: why the U.S. sabotaged numerous peace proposals; why they dictated a military strategy which led to literally hundreds of thousands of Iraqi deaths during the war and in the years after; and why Coalition forces did not march on Baghdad, but instead allowed Hussein to remain in power?

Equally important to explore are the striking similarities as well as profound differences between the Persian Gulf wars of 1991 and 2003: the 1991 Gulf War represented a radical escalation of U.S.

intervention in the region and an attempt to usher in a "new world order" of unfettered U.S. dominance. Yet, as we'll examine, U.S. ambitions were frustrated and this paved the way for an even more aggressive and far-reaching grand strategy under Bush II, and another, different kind of war in 2003.

From Gulf War to Gulf War

> When planned and deliberate policy forces the price of oil down without good commercial reasons, then that means another war against Iraq. Because military war kills people by bleeding them, and economic war kills their humanity by depriving them of their chance to have a good standard of living...We know that the United States has nuclear weapons. But we are determined either to live as proud men, or we all die.
> —Saddam Hussein, July 25, 1990, meeting with U.S. Ambassador April Glaspie

> Iraqi armed forces, without provocation or warning, invaded a peaceful Kuwait....There is no justification whatsoever for this outrageous and brutal act of aggression.
> —George H.W. Bush, August 8, 1990

> Twelve years ago, Iraq invaded Kuwait without provocation.
> —George W. Bush, September 12, 2002[1]

Iraq's brutal seizure of Kuwait may have been a surprise, but it was no bolt from the blue, coming without provocation or warning.

In large part, it grew out of the destruction and tensions spawned by the eight-year Iran-Iraq War.

When that earlier war with Iran began, Iraq had $36 billion in reserves, making it one of the world's richest Third World countries. By the war's end, it was $80 to $90 billion in debt.[2] The regime had been forced to abandon development and social projects, and inflation was running at 100 percent.[3] The war caused enormous suffering in Iraq, and anti-Ba'ath slogans reportedly appeared on Baghdad walls for the first time since 1969. In a country where verbally abusing the President is punishable by death, this dissent was no small matter.[4]

Iraq's economic problems had mushroomed during the war, but

so had its military. Its armed forces had expanded from 190,000 to 1 million men; it had imported at least $42 billion—perhaps as much as $102 billion—in weapons; and, thanks in part to aid from the U.S. and its allies, Iraq had built an arms industry capable of turning out everything from light arms to Scud missiles and chemical weapons.[5]

The 1980-88 war raised Iraq's regional profile as never before. Afterward, the Hussein regime expected to play a more prominent role in the Gulf, perhaps as the favored U.S. "policeman," and to strengthen its leadership in the Arab world. Baghdad felt its Gulf neighbors were in its debt. After all, it had just fought a bloody war to defend them from Iran's Islamic Republic.

Instead, Iraq found its interests under attack. Saudi Arabia and Kuwait refused to forgive its billions in debt. Iraq also charged that Kuwait had been slant drilling into the Iraqi portion of the Rumaila oil field and had extracted some $2.4 billion in crude.[6] Adding insult to injury, the United Arab Emirates (UAE) and Kuwait were exceeding their OPEC oil production quota by 30 and 40 percent respectively, driving crude prices down from OPEC's 1989 target of $18 to $12 a barrel, and costing Iraq some $14 billion in lost revenues when it could least afford it. Saddam Hussein called it "another war against Iraq." [7]

Tensions had existed between Iraq and Kuwait since their creation in the aftermath of World War I. The British-drawn borders had given Kuwait, a country smaller than the state of Vermont, an extensive coastline and ready access to the Gulf, while greatly limiting Iraq's. Iraqi indignation was further aroused by the feeling, among many Iraqis, that Kuwait should rightly be part of their country, as it had been the southern-most section of the vilayet, or province, of Basra during Ottoman rule.

The Ba'ath Party renounced Iraqi claims to Kuwait when it first came to power in 1963, but never formally delineated their common border. In 1973, when the British withdrew from the Gulf, Iraq briefly deployed troops to Warbah and Bubiyan Islands, located at the head of the Gulf between the two countries, and demanded that it be able to lease the islands and have deep-water access to the Gulf. Kuwait, with support from Britain and the U.S., refused, but offered Iraq a substantial "loan," and Iraq then withdrew its forces.[8]

Following the Iran-Iraq War, Iraq's need for Gulf access was especially acute. Basra, its main gateway to the Gulf, had been heavily damaged during the war, leaving it dependent on oil pipelines running through U.S. clients Saudi Arabia and Turkey, which could be shut down at any time.[9] (Indeed, one of the U.S.'s first actions following Iraq's August 1990 invasion was to successfully demand that these pipelines be closed, crippling Iraq's economy.)

Given the Kuwaiti royal family's utter dependence on foreign protectors, Iraq feared that its belligerent demands for repayment of its $12-14 billion war loan and to finalize its border with Iraq represented a U.S.-backed effort to humiliate and weaken Iraq. Baghdad may have had good reason to be suspicious; during their negotiations, the Kuwaitis warned Iraq that it had "very powerful friends."[10]

(Iraq later claimed to have discovered an internal Kuwaiti government memo that detailed agreements it made with CIA Director William Webster in November 1989. "We agreed with the American side that it was important to take advantage of the deteriorating economic situation in Iraq," the memo read, "to put pressure on that country's government to delineate our common border." The CIA claimed it was a forgery.[11])

International developments also worried Baghdad. Hussein warned that the crisis in the Soviet Union had created a dangerous situation for the Arab world: "It is now clear that the U.S. can exert influence over the Soviets and make them abandon any position contrary to the U.S.," he told the *Wall Street Journal* in June 1990. "So, America thinks it can cast things anyway it wants in the region and in alliance with Israel can suppress any voice in support of Arab rights."[12]

Iraq was particularly concerned that Israel would seize on Moscow's weakness to forcibly crush or expel the Palestinians, or to attack Iraq—perhaps as it had in 1981 when it bombed the Osiraq nuclear reactor near Baghdad. The first Palestinian Intifada had begun in December 1987 and was being met with harsh Israeli repression and the continued expansion of Jewish settlements in the West Bank and Gaza. Israel's new right-wing Likud government talked of needing a "bigger Israel" to accommodate Jewish immigration from Russia, which was surging under Gorbachev's "Glasnost," and it proclaimed "The eternal right of the Jewish people to Eretz

Yisrael [which includes the West Bank] is not subject to question."[13] In April 1990, Hussein threatened to turn half of Israel into an "inferno" if Iraq was attacked.

The *Wall Street Journal* summed up:

> Both King Hussein [of Jordan] and President Hussein believe the Palestinian uprising in Israel and the wave of Soviet Jews emigrating to the country have convinced Israel's government that it must find a pretext to push Palestinians out of the West Bank and into neighboring Jordan. Some of King Hussein's ministers anxiously describe scenarios that could lead to war, including an Israeli attack on either Jordan or Libya followed by an Iraqi military response... Both Arab leaders see Iraq as the best deterrent and the only real defense should Israel attack. And both leaders insist the U.S., and to a lesser extent Great Britain, are conducting a campaign to smear Iraq and thus create international support for an Israeli attack.[14]

Meanwhile, as UN weapons inspectors discovered after the 1991 Gulf War, Iraq secretly stepped up its efforts to develop a nuclear bomb, and was trying to build a "supergun" that could hit Israel with chemical or biological shells. Hussein told the *Wall Street Journal* that he was willing to recognize Israel, but also warned that unless the U.S. curbed Tel Aviv's "aggressive policies," another Middle East war was inevitable.[15]

Strains in U.S.-Iraqi relations added to this tense and uncertain atmosphere. The Iran-Iraq war ended with a defacto alliance between Washington and Baghdad, but the U.S. considered it an alliance of convenience and never fully trusted the Ba'ath regime, much less envisioned it becoming a regional power that could hinder U.S. dominance.

After the Iran-Iraq War, U.S. intelligence concluded that Iraq sought to "dominate" the Persian Gulf, but probably wouldn't attempt new military actions due to the ongoing strains from its war with Iran.[16] In October 1989, President Bush, Sr. signed National Security Directive 26 which concluded that "Normal relations between the United States and Iraq would serve our longer-term interests and promote stability in both the Gulf and the Middle East," and directed government agencies to "propose economic and political incentives for Iraq to moderate its behavior and to increase our influence with Iraq."[17]

For its part, the Hussein regime also gave the U.S. a one-dollar-per-barrel discount on oil, verbally supported an Arab-Israeli peace process it had condemned in years past, stopped supplying arms to Lebanon, and promised to strengthen human rights protections in Iraq.[18]

Yet the U.S. remained wary, and there were divisions within the government over Iraq's reliability. Bush officials pressured Iraq to more fully cooperate with Washington's regional agenda, criticized Iraq's threats against Israel, and raised concerns about its reported pursuit of nuclear arms. Hussein wrote Bush assuring him that Iraq was not about to wage war and offering to destroy his nonconventional weapons if Israel would do the same. Neither the U.S. nor Israel bothered to respond to this offer, a fact rarely mentioned in discussions of Iraq's pursuit of "weapons of mass destruction."[19] In May 1990, the Department of Agriculture announced it would delay Iraq's request for an additional $500 million in agricultural credits. And in July the Pentagon stopped selling Iraq parts that could be used for missiles.

Another "Green Light" for Saddam

By July 1990, tensions between Iraq and Kuwait were rising after several failed negotiations, and Iraqi troops were mobilizing near Kuwait's border. Yet before he took action, Saddam Hussein consulted with the U.S., as he had a decade earlier before moving against Iran. On July 25, he summoned U.S. Ambassador April Glaspie for their soon infamous meeting during which he spelled out his complaints against his neighbor to the south and threatened to take action.

There has been controversy ever since over whether Glaspie gave Hussein a "green light" to invade Kuwait. U.S. officials deny any such responsibility. Former Secretary of State James Baker claims it's "ludicrous" to charge that "somehow the United States was responsible for or contributed to Saddam Hussein's invasion of Kuwait."[20] In their book, A World Transformed, published seven years after the Gulf War, President George H. W. Bush and his National Security Advisor Brent Scowcroft argued that, "It is a total misreading of this conversation to conclude that we were giving

Saddam a green light to seize his neighbor." They charge instead that "Saddam had made an abrupt change in his policy to the United States."[21]

The public is rarely privy to discussions between governments, yet in this instance Iraq released the transcript of the Hussein-Glaspie meeting in September 1990 to show that it had gotten a U.S. go-ahead for its invasion. At the time, U.S. officials denounced it as misleading and incomplete. When Glaspie later testified before the Senate Foreign Relations Committee in March 1991, she claimed that she had firmly warned Hussein not to take action against Kuwait and that the Iraqi transcript "was largely fabricated." Yet, the veracity of the Iraqi account was soon confirmed, in part by Glaspie's own cables back to the U.S.[22]

This transcript shows that Hussein was neither making an "abrupt" change in his relations with the U.S., nor acting as an "unpredictable rogue." Rather, it shows the head of a small state trying to defend its regional interests, while trying to maintain a relationship with the world's dominant superpower. And the transcript makes clear that the U.S. did indeed give Iraq a green light for some sort of military action against Kuwait.

Hussein began by telling Glaspie of Iraq's desire for better relations with the U.S. and reminded her of Iraq's value: "You know you are not the ones who protected your friends during the war with Iran." He assured her that he understood that the U.S. needed "an easy flow of oil," and offered that he was the first Arab leader to support lower oil prices.[23]

Yet Hussein was also concerned that the U.S. might abandon Iraq as it had during the Iran-Contra affair of the mid-1980s: "We accepted the apology, via his envoy, of the American President regarding Irangate, and we wiped the slate clean," Hussein stated, but "new events remind us that old mistakes were not just a matter of coincidence." He worried that "repeated American statements last year made it apparent that America did not regard us as friends." The Iraqi leader complained about U.S. media coverage of his regime, think tank studies of "Who will succeed Saddam Hussein," and American support for Israel against the Arab states: "When will humanity find its real chance to seek a just American solution that would balance the human rights of two hundred million human beings with the rights of three million Jews?"

The focus of Hussein's complaints centered on Kuwait and the UAE and their "deliberate policy" to force "the price of oil down without good commercial reasons." Iraq, he complained, came out of the Iran-Iraq War "burdened with a $40 billion debt, excluding the aid given by Arab states." Yet while Iraq was "busy at war, the state of Kuwait began to expand at the expense of our territory." This, he concluded, "means another war against Iraq." Iraq, Hussein declared, "cannot understand the attempt [by the U.S.] to encourage some parties to harm Iraq's interests." He then bluntly warned that if the UAE and Kuwait "try to weaken Iraq," then "Iraq has the right to defend itself."

Hussein told Glaspie that Iraq was even prepared for war with America: "We know that the United States has nuclear weapons. But we are determined either to live as proud men, or we all die." While Hussein also offered some pro forma reassurances that the solution to these conflicts "must be found within an Arab framework and through direct bilateral relations," it would be hard to imagine a clearer signal that major military action was in the offing.

The first thing Glaspie said to Hussein's warnings of war was that she understood and agreed: "I clearly understand your message. We studied history at school. They taught us to say freedom or death." In other words, fighting for one's interests is legitimate.

She then reassured him concerning U.S. intentions toward Iraq: "I have a direct instruction from the President to seek better relations with Iraq," and she apologized for U.S. media coverage critical of the Iraqi regime. Glaspie concluded, "We have no opinion on the Arab-Arab conflicts, like your border disagreement with Kuwait... We hope you can solve the problem using any suitable methods," then mentioned reports of discussions with other Arab leaders. Glaspie's defenders argue that in raising "suitable methods," she was warning Hussein against war. Yet in the context of their entire discussion, she neither made this clear, nor emphasized it. Instead, she flashed a U.S. green light—not only by promising to stay out of Iraq's border dispute with Kuwait, but by assuring Hussein of overall U.S. support.

Glaspie was not free-lancing, but expressing U.S. policy, which was mainly shaped by NSD-26. After Glaspie's meeting, Bush sent

Hussein a secret, conciliatory message stating, "We believe that differences are best resolved by peaceful means and not by threats involving military force or conflict," and reiterating, "My Administration continues to desire better relations with Iraq."[24] And on July 31, 1990 Assistant Secretary of State for Near Eastern and South Asian Affairs John Kelly told Congress, "We have no defense treaty relationship with any Gulf country. That is clear... We have not historically taken a position on border disputes."[25]

Glaspie later told the *New York Times*, "Obviously I didn't think and nobody else did, that the Iraqis were going to take all of Kuwait."[26] Glaspie may have been telling the truth in this instance. On July 28, 1990, the CIA reportedly informed Bush that an invasion of Kuwait was imminent, but that Iraq would probably only take the disputed Rumaila oil field and Warbah and Buybian islands.[27]

There were other, more belligerent, signals coming from the U.S. as well: on July 19, then-Defense Secretary Dick Cheney stated that the U.S. was committed to defending Kuwait if attacked, and on July 31, the U.S. stated it was committed to "supporting the individual and collective self-defense of our friends in the Gulf." These statements show that the U.S. was well aware that Iraqi military action could be in the offing, and were probably efforts to dissuade Iraq, or warn it against going too far. These somewhat mixed U.S. signals could also have represented confusion or conflicting views within the government, or both. Woodward writes that in the late 1980s, "U.S. policy toward Iraq was muddled." Yet overall, the U.S. had signaled its willingness to tolerate limited Iraqi military action.[28]

A subsequent report by the right-wing Washington Institute for Near East Policy concluded, "It is unlikely that Saddam Hussein would have invaded Kuwait had he not calculated both that the regional balance of power stood in his favor and that local and outside powers would not act vigorously."[29]

Some have argued that the U.S. deliberately lured Hussein into Kuwait in order to then crush Iraq. In his book *The Fire this Time: U.S. War Crimes in the Gulf*, former Attorney General Ramsey Clark wrote, "The U.S. government used the Kuwait royal family to provoke an Iraqi invasion that would justify a massive assault on Iraq to establish U.S. dominion in the Gulf." Sami Yousif, an Iraqi critic of the Hussein regime, wrote, "My contention is that the U.S. administration encouraged Saddam's new criminal adventure because it suited U.S. interests to do so. Simultaneously, the administration was backing and encouraging Kuwait to resist Iraqi demands. Saddam was the perfect bogeyman."[30]

There were certainly forces in the U.S. ruling class who wanted to undercut Iraq in the region (and Hussein complained bitterly to Glaspie about "certain parties" in the U.S. with "links with the intelligence community and with the State Department" who were campaigning against Iraq).[31] Given U.S. double-dealing during the 1980s, such cynical manipulation is not out of the question. However, the unfolding of events is better explained as a U.S. effort to limit Iraq's ability to make trouble in the region following the Iran-Iraq war, even as it sought some form of relationship with Baghdad.

So, overall the evidence—including NSD-26, the Glaspie meeting and follow-up cables, and the Bush administration's shock at the invasion (explored below) points more to miscalculations by both the U.S. and the Iraqis in a situation where their interests clashed and when major geopolitical changes were taking place in the world.

Global Shifts, Strategic Miscalculations

Iraq's invasion meant that, at least momentarily, its debts to Kuwait were canceled, its border issues were solved, it had deep-water access to the Persian Gulf, and it now controlled some 20 percent of world oil reserves.

In a speech on August 10, Hussein justified the invasion as a blow against the legacy of British colonialism:

> The foreigner entered their lands, and Western colonialism divided and established weak states ruled by families that offered him services that facilitated his mission.... The colonialists, to insure their petroleum interests...set up those disfigured petroleum states. Through this, they kept the wealth away from the masses of this nation.[32]

Seizing Kuwait was also a way for Hussein to redefine Iraq's relationship with the U.S. on more favorable terms. Four days after his invasion, Hussein told Joseph Wilson, the deputy chief of mission at the U.S. embassy in Baghdad (who in 2002 was sent to Niger by the Bush II administration to investigate claims that Iraq had purchased uranium there, and subsequently exposed these charges as unfounded), that "in exchange for keeping Kuwait, he would give the U.S. oil at a good price and would not invade Saudi Arabia." Hussein also argued that it wasn't in U.S. interests to wage war—the region would be destabilized and Washington should negotiate instead: "You are a superpower and I know you can hurt us," Hussein reportedly told Wilson, "but you will lose the whole area. You will never bring us to our knees. You can destroy some of our economic and industrial base but the greater damage you cause, the greater the burden to you. In such a situation, we will not remain idle in the region."[33]

There is also speculation that Hussein was prepared to withdraw in return for a strip of northeast Kuwait and control of Bubiyan and Warbah Islands. The *Washington Post* noted, "By seizing the entire country, Saddam thought he would have Kuwait under his thumb and force its rulers to agree to cede the northern area."[34]

In sum, Hussein may have felt that he had been backed into a corner and had little choice but to invade Kuwait, the easiest target in his vicinity and one that could potentially help resolve Iraq's economic crisis and increase its strength in the region.

Yet the Iraqi leadership also miscalculated and greatly overplayed its hand. Hussein had come to power in an era when it was possible to play one superpower off against the other to a certain degree. But the Soviet Union's crisis and impending collapse had radically altered that calculus. Hussein did understand that the ground he stood on was shifting, but may not have grasped the full extent of the Soviet Union's weakness and retreat from its global rivalry with the U.S.—which included Moscow's backing for U.S.-sponsored UN resolutions and cutting off arms shipments to Iraq.

Hussein apparently didn't believe the U.S. had the will to fight a major war in the Gulf: "Yours is a society which cannot accept 10,000 dead in one battle," he told Glaspie. Ambassador Wilson writes that when he met the Iraqi leader, "He mocked American will and courage, telling me that my country would run rather than face the prospect of spilling the blood of our soldiers in the Arabian Desert."[35]

This assessment gravely underestimated the U.S. rulers' determination to break out of their "Vietnam syndrome" (or difficulty mustering domestic political support for foreign military interventions in the wake of their defeat in Vietnam), deploy their military more forcefully in the post-Cold War world, and risk upheaval in the Middle East. Nor, apparently, did Hussein understand the extent to which new high-tech weapons would allow the U.S. to massively attack Iraq, while limiting its own casualties.

Saddam was a Third World ruler trying to defend his interests and muscle his way to greater regional status. However, he was attempting to do so at a time when past constraints on American military power no longer existed; when the U.S. no longer had to balance Iran and Iraq off against each other, but could intervene more directly; and when Washington wasn't going to tolerate his effrontery, but was determined instead to turn it into a lesson for others around the world.

Talking Diplomacy, Preparing for War

The Bush I administration was apparently stunned by the boldness of Iraq's attack, and took several days to grasp both the enormity of the stakes involved, and the new possibilities opened by the Soviet eclipse. President Bush's initial public response to the invasion was muted, and the first meeting of the National Security Council afterward was fairly low-key: "Hey, too bad about Kuwait, but it's just a gas station," one participant reportedly said, "and who cares whether the sign says Sinclair or Exxon?"[36]

Scowcroft, who had been Henry Kissinger's top National Security Council deputy in the early 1970s, later described the tenor of this first NSC meeting:

> I was frankly appalled at the undertone of the discussion, which suggested resignation to the invasion and even adaptation to a fait accompli. There was a huge gap between those who saw what was happening as the major crisis of our time and those who treated it as the crisis du jour. The remarks tended to skip over the enormous stake the United States had in the situation, or the ramifications of the aggression on the emerging post-Cold War world.[37]

The next morning, after consulting with Bush, Scowcroft apparently set his colleagues straight. From the early days of the crisis, there were two tracks to U.S. policy: the public theater of diplomacy and secret preparations for war. Within a week of Iraq's invasion, the U.S. had frozen Iraqi and Kuwait assets in the U.S., sponsored UN resolutions condemning Iraq's action and imposing sanctions, and begun beefing up its forces in the Gulf. It demanded an "immediate, unconditional and complete withdrawal of all Iraqi forces from Kuwait," but claimed that U.S. forces were being dispatched to Saudi Arabia solely for defensive purposes. "America does not seek conflict. Nor do we seek to chart the destiny of other nations," Bush stated on August 8, 1990. He also claimed the U.S. would not "initiate hostilities." He told reporters that American troops were not there to force Iraq from Kuwait—UN sanctions would do that job.[38]

In reality, the Bush team had already set a course for war, not merely to expel Iraq from Kuwait but to crush it as a regional power and forcefully assert U.S. global power in the post-Soviet world. Labeled the "Gang of Eight," this leading core included Bush Sr., Scowcroft, Cheney, Powell, Vice President Dan Quayle, Secretary of State James Baker, Scowcroft's deputy Bob Gates, and White House Chief of Staff John Sununu.[39] According to Woodward, on August 3, the day after Iraq's invasion, Bush ordered the CIA to draft plans for overthrowing the Hussein regime through an "all-fronts effort to strangle the Iraqi economy, support anti-Saddam resistance groups inside or outside Iraq, and [to] look for alternative leaders in the military or anywhere in Iraqi society."[40]

Three days later, on August 6, Bush met with NATO leaders to begin planning a massive troop deployment—labeled "Operation Desert Shield," which reached 100,000 by September 6 and 230,000 by November. Air Force Chief of Staff General Michael Dugan let slip the administration's real intentions in mid-September when he revealed that he was preparing a massive bombing campaign against Iraqi cities which would target the country's leadership and civilian infrastructure. Defense Secretary Cheney promptly fired Dugan for his momentary lapse of truth-telling.[41]

Gulf Oil and "Vital Interests"

The U.S. said it was sending troops to the Gulf to protect Saudi

Arabia from an Iraqi attack, even though Bush and company understood that Hussein's immediate objectives were limited to Kuwait.
In one internal discussion, General Norman Schwarzkopf, the commander of the U.S. Central Command, which was charged with
prosecuting the Gulf War, noted Baghdad's goals: adjusting Iraq's
border with Kuwait, debt forgiveness, payment of $4 billion and
control of Kuwait's Warbah and Bubiyan Islands. In his book *The
Commanders*, Bob Woodward writes that Chairman of the Joint
Chiefs of Staff Colin Powell argued that Hussein thought he might
be able to take Kuwait, but that he "would know that Saudi Arabia
was another matter entirely.... Attacking Saudi Arabia would be
overreaching; it would be a direct assault on the oil-dependent
west." In fact, Hussein had made that very point during his August
6 meeting in Baghdad with U.S. charge d'affairs Wilson.[42]

The Bush team may not have been concerned about an Iraqi
attack on Saudi Arabia, but they were concerned that if Iraq were
allowed to take Kuwait, or even withdraw with its military intact, it
could then exert greater influence over Saudi Arabia and the small
Gulf emirates, eroding U.S. hegemony, and bolstering its own
regional stregnth.

The Gulf states, Saudi Arabia in particular, are crucial to U.S.
petro-dominance and global power. Bush's National Security
Directives 45 of August 20, 1990 and 54 of January 15, 1991, which
spell out U.S. interests in the Gulf, both begin with oil. NSD 54
authorized U.S. forces to commence military action against Iraq,
which they did the next day:

> Access to Persian Gulf oil and the security of key friendly
> states in the area are vital to U.S. national security...the United
> States remains committed to defending its vital interests in the
> region, if necessary through the use of military force, against any
> power with interests inimical to our own. Iraq, by virtue of its
> unprovoked invasion of Kuwait on August 2, 1990, and its sub-
> sequent brutal occupation, is clearly a power with interests
> inimical to our own.[43]

Saudi Arabia sits on some 260 billion barrels of oil—a *fourth* of
world reserves. It pumps around eight million barrels of crude a day,
more than any other country. And it is located in the heart of the
region's oil fields, and astride petroleum transit routes through the
Persian Gulf.

Saudi oil production capacity is so vast that the Royal Kingdom can quickly increase or decrease daily production by as much as two to three million barrels. The Energy Information Administration calls this spare capacity, which amounts to 70 to 90 percent (depending on global production levels) of global spare capacity, even "more significant" than Saudi reserves because it allows this U.S. client to quickly ramp up oil production to head off shortages or price explosions which could disrupt the global economy.[44] Former CIA analyst and Clinton National Security Council official Kenneth Pollack succinctly sums up just how economically crucial Saudi production and spare capacity are:

> [T]he sudden loss of the Saudi oil network would paralyze the global economy, probably causing a global downturn at least as devastating as the Great Depression of the 1930s, if not worse. So the fact that the United States does not import most of its oil from the Persian Gulf is irrelevant: if Saudi oil production were to vanish, the price of oil in general would shoot through the ceiling, destroying the American economy along with everybody else's.[45]

Saudi spare capacity also effectively gives Washington enormous leverage in world energy markets and against rivals who depend on oil revenues or imported petroleum. In the mid-1980s, this spare capacity was used to savage effect against the Soviet Union: the Saudis launched a price war to prevent competitors from cutting into the Saudi's market share and drove oil prices down by more than half to under $10 a barrel. Writing in *Foreign Affairs*, energy industry analysts/investors Edward L. Morse and James Richard note, "The aforementioned Saudi-engineered price collapse of 1985-86 led to the implosion of the Soviet oil industry—which, in turn, hastened the Soviet Union's demise."

Morse and Richard conclude: "Saudi spare capacity is the *energy equivalent of nuclear weapons*... It is also the centerpiece of the U.S.-Saudi relationship. The United States relies on that capacity as the cornerstone of its oil policy." (emphasis added)[46]

The U.S. reaps other benefits from its dominant position in Saudi Arabia as well. Professor Michael Klare, author of *Resource Wars—The New Landscape of Global Conflict*, writes, "The United States has enjoyed preferred access to Saudi petroleum reserves, obtaining about one-sixth of its crude-oil imports from the kingdom. ARAM-

CO [Arabian American Oil Company] and its U.S. partners have reaped immense profits from their operations in Saudi Arabia and from the distribution of Saudi oil worldwide. Saudi Arabia also buys about $6-10 billion worth of goods per year from U.S. companies."[47]

The Gulf states also play a critical role in the world capitalist financial system. The Saudis have invested between $700 billion and $1 trillion abroad, mainly in the West, and Kuwait and the UAE have done likewise to the tune of $200 to $300 billion. This recycling of oil revenues, or "petrodollars," helps keep the dollar stable and helps enable the U.S. to run huge trade deficits. Iraq's invasion and its calls to invest petrodollars in Arab countries—rather than the west—imperiled these arrangements.[48]

As one CIA assessment in the fall of 1990 put it, Iraq's invasion "posed a threat to the current world order and that the long-run impact on the world economy could be devastating."

Saddam was striving to strengthen Iraqi—and Arab—power by taking control of 20 percent of world oil reserves and possibly having political and military influence over another 20 percent in Saudi Arabia—even without threatening to invade the Royal Kingdom—shifting the region's political-military balance and countering Israel. Cheney felt that the "marriage of Iraq's military of 1 million men with 20 percent of the world's oil presented a significant threat."[49]

Iraq had committed the cardinal sin of overstepping its bounds, asserting its own interests in the region, and demonstrating just how fragile and artificial the U.S. client states in the Gulf really are. So merely forcing it out of Kuwait wasn't enough; the U.S. wanted to destroy its future economic and military capabilities as well, goals which continued to drive U.S. Iraq policy during the 1990s. Scowcroft acknowledged that the Bush team's objectives went well beyond expelling Iraq from Kuwait:

> The over-all strategic political objectives were set out in the UN resolutions: principally, to eject Iraq from Kuwait and restore the Kuwaiti government. But beyond this there were strategic military objectives for the coalition forces, and our own war aims—what outcome the United States wanted to see...foremost among these was to reduce the Iraqi military as much as possible, starting with an air campaign...destroying as much of the Iraqi military machine as possible would have other benefits as well. One was to reduce the threat Saddam posed to

his neighbors. The trick here was to damage his offensive capability without weakening Iraq to the point that a vacuum was
created and destroying the balance between Iraq and Iran, further destabilizing the region for years.[50]

New World Order—Take One

Global considerations also loomed large in U.S. Gulf strategy.
The Berlin Wall had fallen the year before, and when Iraq invaded
Kuwait the Soviet Union was mired in a deepening crisis and was
retreating from its global rivalry with the U.S. This signaled a major
historical juncture and an enormous shift in the global balance of
power in favor of U.S. imperialism, and it had profound implications
for Washington's strategy in the Middle East.

Bush, Scowcroft, and other top government officials understood that this was a momentous time, and they shaped the U.S.
response to Iraq's invasion in light of these larger global events.
Scowcroft wrote that they "were both struck with the thought that
we were perhaps at a watershed of history. The Soviet Union was
standing alongside us, not only in the United Nations, but also in
condemning and taking action against Iraqi aggression. That cooperation represented fundamental change."[51]

On one hand, they were concerned that the Soviet collapse
could trigger "violent centrifugal tendencies," like Iraq's invasion,
since smaller states were no longer "worried about the involvement
of the superpowers," as Deputy Secretary of State Lawrence
Eagleburger put it in one NSC meeting.[52]

On the other, they were well aware the U.S. had been handed
a rare opportunity to extend its imperial reach and control: Bush and
Scowcroft acknowledge: "In the first days of the crisis we had started self-consciously to view our actions as setting a precedent for the
approaching post-Cold War world."[53]

The precedent they wanted to set was that "the United States
henceforth would be obligated to lead the world community to an
unprecedented degree."[54] In plain language this meant that crushing
Iraq would serve as notice that the U.S. had overcome its "Vietnam
syndrome," was no longer seriously impeded by the Soviet Union,
and would now forcefully assert its global designs.[55]

The 1991 Gulf War was shaped by the rapid weakening of the Soviet empire, and the war in turn demonstrated to the world just how weak the Soviet Union had become. This in turn helped speed its collapse, which came in August 1991, just six months after the war's end.

On September 11, 1990, a month and a week after Iraq's invasion, Bush proclaimed the beginning of a "new world order." This new order really meant preserving much of the existing—and old—world order with the U.S. more firmly on top. While arrogant and sweeping, this declaration was conceived before the contours of the post-Soviet world had taken shape and a new U.S. grand strategy had emerged, so it was not nearly as ambitious and comprehensive as the Bush, Jr. National Security Strategy of 2002.

Going the Last Mile for War

Washington's objectives demanded war, not peace. The last thing Bush wanted was for Iraq to negotiate its way out of Kuwait with its military in one piece, its political weight increased, and its weak neighbors intimidated. War would also send a much clearer message of U.S. power and will than simply pressuring Iraq into withdrawing. By September 1990, probably even earlier, the U.S. leadership had decided to attack.

Waging full-scale war in the Persian Gulf posed new military and political challenges. The U.S. had never deployed such massive forces to the region, and it needed time to make the necessary basing and logistical arrangements with regional allies, and to build its military presence around Iraq.

The U.S. also had to fend off efforts to resolve the crisis short of war, yet appear willing to go "the extra mile to achieve a peaceful solution," as President Bush said. Scowcroft put it this way: "The question of how we would initiate the use of force, should it come to that, remained. How could we act without it appearing as aggression on the part of the [U.S.-led] coalition?"[56]

The U.S. dealt with these obstacles by sabotaging peace efforts, demonizing the Hussein regime, and carrying out its war preparations under cover of UN resolutions. Some—although not all—of the pages from this playbook were pulled out again during the runup to the 2003 Iraq war and carried out by some of the same 1991 players.

Between Iraq's invasion on August 2, 1990 and the end of the Gulf War in late February 1991, the U.S. rejected at least 11 peace proposals from a variety of countries, including Iraq, the Soviet Union, Jordan, Libya, France, Morocco, and Iran.[57]

The day after its invasion, Iraq offered to withdraw if it wasn't condemned or attacked, and announced that Saddam Hussein would meet with King Hussein of Jordan, President Mubarak of Egypt, and King Fahd of Saudi Arabia in Jeddah on August 5 to resolve the crisis. The U.S. immediately, and forcefully, blocked the meeting and warned its Arab clients not to deal with Hussein.

Two days later Bush dispatched Cheney to Saudi Arabia to tell the Royal family they were in imminent danger and to strong-arm them into accepting the stationing of tens of thousands of American troops. The satellite intelligence Cheney presented to show that an Iraqi attack was imminent was apparently doctored—a tactic the U.S. had perfected during the Iran-Iraq war. Two Soviet satellite photos obtained by the *St. Petersburg Times* (FL) showed no evidence of any Iraqi buildup along the Saudi border.[58]

In his recent survey of American actions in the Middle East, *Tinderbox—U.S. Middle East Policy and the Roots of Terrorism*, University of San Francisco Professor Stephen Zunes notes that, "Arab leaders were apparently very close to convincing Iraq to withdraw... According to then-Crown Prince Hassan of Jordan, the America-Saudi decision to implement what became known as 'Operation Desert Shield' scuttled a tentative agreement he had made with Saddam Hussein to withdraw from Kuwait." Under this agreement, Iraq reportedly would have annexed a small piece of Kuwait and then withdrawn.[59]

On August 12 and August 23, Iraq again offered to negotiate. It would withdraw from Kuwait and release the foreigners it was then holding, if UN sanctions were lifted and Iraq was given control of the Rumailah oil field and unimpeded access to the Persian Gulf. The U.S. summarily rejected both offers as "non-starters."

A number of peace proposals linked Iraq's withdrawal with negotiations over Israel's withdrawal from the West Bank and Gaza and called for the banning of all weapons of mass destruction in the region, including Israel's 200-plus nuclear warheads. The U.S.

rejected any such linkage. It would, as Scowcroft put it, change the U.S. "path" and possibly give Hussein a "political victory." The point for the U.S., after all, was dominance, not "even-handedness."

The U.S. government provided a textbook demonstration of its war/peace two-step in late October 1990. On October 30, the Bush leadership secretly mapped out a timetable for launching a war in mid-January, starting with massive air strikes, followed by a ground war in February. Nine days later Bush announced the dispatch of another 200,000 U.S. troops to join the 230,000 already in the Gulf. He claimed it was merely to give the U.S. an "offensive military option," while insisting "I would love to see a peaceful resolution."[60]

On January 9, 1991, at a meeting in Geneva, Switzerland, Secretary of State Baker presented Iraqi Foreign Minister Tariq Aziz with a U.S. ultimatum that Iraqi forces withdraw unconditionally from Kuwait. On hearing the news that Aziz had refused Washington's demands and a diplomatic resolution to the crisis had been averted, Woodward writes that "Bush was jubilant because it was the best news possible, although he would have to conceal it publicly."[61]

Three days later, on January 12, 1991, with prospects for a negotiated settlement fading, Congress voted to give Bush the authority to use force against Iraq (53-47 in the Senate and 250-183 in the House).

Iraq never simply withdrew from Kuwait. Even as the U.S. military buildup proceeded, the Iraqi leadership apparently never fully understood the scope and determination of U.S. war plans, and overestimated the effectiveness of French, German, and Russian opposition—in part because Baghdad did not grasp how profoundly the international balance of power had changed due to the Soviet crisis. So until the war was well underway, Baghdad felt it could emerge with something to show for its invasion, and continued to insist on a negotiated settlement.

Former UN weapons inspector Scott Ritter writes that as late as January 1991, the Iraqis still believed the U.S. would only launch limited air strikes against a few targets. Military analyst Michael Vickers told the *San Francisco Chronicle* that Hussein may have doubted the U.S. would attack, despite its threats: "He thought all along that the international anti-war movement and French and

German opposition would forestall a war."[62]

Iraq also made Bush's job of appearing the peacemaker easier in a number of ways. On August 8 it annexed Kuwait, the first annexation of a sovereign state since World War II. It initially held thousands of U.S., British, and other foreigners as human shields against a U.S. attack, until it realized the tactic was backfiring politically and began releasing them in late August.

The U.S. bombing campaign began on January 16, 1991. That night, Bush told the nation that war had been forced on the U.S. after "months of constant and virtually endless diplomatic activity" had been "totally rebuffed" by Iraq. The U.S.-led coalition, he said, had "exhausted all reasonable efforts to reach a peaceful resolution," but "Saddam Hussein met every overture of peace with open contempt."

"While the world prayed for peace," Bush declared, "Saddam prepared for war." Bush used variations on the word "peace" 11 times in his speech as bombs rained down on Baghdad and other Iraqi cities.

Jobs, Hitler & Kuwaiti Babies

During the run-up to war, Scowcroft and Bush agonized over their difficulties in rallying the population behind their imperial agenda. Later Scowcroft described how they deliberately "added" various reasons in hopes of convincing the public to back the war:

> The core of our argument rested on long-held security and economic interests: preserving the balance of power in the Gulf, opposing unprovoked international aggression, and ensuring that no hostile regional power could hold hostage much of the world's oil supply. President Bush...added the Hitler, holocaust, and morality arguments, and Baker expanded the grounds to include American jobs.[63]

Comparing Hussein to Hitler was a deliberate absurdity on a number of levels. It vastly exaggerated Iraq's military strength and equated a small Third World country with an advanced industrial power like Nazi Germany. The notion that Iraq had ambitions of conquering Europe or becoming a global power was ludicrous on the face of it and ignored Iraq's specific grievances in the region, against

Kuwait in particular.

After supporting the Hussein regime throughout the 1980s, America's rulers acted as if they had suddenly become alarmed at its record of brutality. And when the regime's real crimes weren't dramatic enough, others were invented. In October 1990, a 15-year-old woman identified only as Nayirah, supposedly to protect her from reprisals, told a congressional committee that Iraqi soldiers in Kuwait "took the babies out of the incubators, took the incubators and left the babies to die on the cold floor!" These charges sparked a furor of official and media outrage. It was later discovered that Nayirah was actually the daughter of Kuwait's ambassador to the U.S., and that her incubator story was a fabrication concocted by the public relations firm of Hill & Knowlton, which was paid for its creative services by Kuwait's government. But the damage had already been done; the "story" had become a staple of administration statements and mainstream media coverage.[64]

This hoax became so deeply "embedded" in mainstream coverage that it was even repeated a decade later during the runup to the 2003 war on Iraq. HBO's made-for-TV movie on CNN's coverage of the 1991 Gulf War—"Live From Baghdad"—aired in December 2002. It referred to the incubator story, but didn't mention that it had been exposed as a fabrication, leaving viewers to conclude that it actually may have taken place.[65]

The vilification of Saddam Hussein also served another purpose: to keep the focus on Iraq and away from the imperial agenda being pursued by the U.S. and the nature of the Kuwaiti regime it was defending. After all, for the U.S. "liberating" Kuwait meant restoring a despotic and decadent monarch ruling a country where a mere 3.5 percent of the population—literate male citizens over the age of 21—were allowed to vote, where nearly two-thirds of the prewar population of 1.9 million were noncitizens who performed 80 percent of the labor, and where women were relegated to inferior, second class status.[66]

Seeking a UN "Cloak of Acceptability"

The Bush administration viewed the UN Security Council as its primary vehicle for building a coalition against Iraq and for giving Desert Storm a veil of legitimacy. As Scowcroft put it, "Building an international response led us immediately to the United Nations, which could provide a cloak of acceptability to our efforts and mobilize world opinion behind the principles we wished to project."[67]

The Security Council passed 12 resolutions on Iraq's invasion, including on August 2, 1990 Resolution 660 demanding that Iraq "immediately and unconditionally" withdraw from Kuwait; on August 6, 1990 Resolution 661 which imposed a stringent embargo and economic sanctions; and on November 29, 1990 Resolution 678 approving the use of "all necessary means" to force Iraq from Kuwait.[68]

The U.S. claimed that these Security Council resolutions represented the will of the world's people, but the Security Council was, and remains, dominated by its five permanent members—the U.S., Britain, France, the Soviet Union (now Russia), and China. Except for China, all are imperialist countries in their own right, and the U.S. was dominant among them. The Bush administration secured support from these permanent members, as well as other imperialist powers like Germany and Japan, based in part on their shared interest in suppressing an upstart Third World country and maintaining Western control of Persian Gulf oil.

These allies were also strong-armed with what *The Godfather's* Michael Corleone might have called an "offer they couldn't refuse": be part of the war coalition or have no voice in post-war decisions in the Gulf. Kissinger put the matter accurately:

> Not waiting for an international consensus, the U.S. had unilaterally dispatched a large expeditionary force. Other nations could gain influence over America's actions only by joining what was in effect an American enterprise.[69]

Regional clients like Saudi Arabia, Kuwait, and Turkey came on board because their very existence depended on U.S. muscle and support. The U.S. received pledges for $50 billion to cover its war costs, including $16.8 billion from Saudi Arabia, $16 billion from Kuwait, $10.7 billion from Japan, and $6.6 billion from Germany.[70]

International sanctions imposed by the United Nations were particularly useful in giving U.S. allies "security cover," as Bush put it. "They will give some spine to Saudi Arabia and others to take difficult actions," he said, such as shutting down Iraqi oil pipelines running through their countries, agreeing to the massive deployment of U.S. forces on their soil, or allowing attacks on Iraq to be launched from their territories. All these actions were highly unpopular in the region and would have been very difficult without the political cover the UN provided.[71]

Where shared interests weren't enough, the U.S. hammered together its coalition with bribes, like forgiving billions of Egypt's foreign debts; by threatening to cut aid to those who didn't go along, like Jordan; and by cutting off aid to those who refused. Minutes after Yemen voted against Resolution 678 authorizing "all necessary means" to implement UN resolutions regarding Iraq's invasion, Washington's UN Ambassador angrily warned its delegate, "that will be the most expensive vote you would ever cast." The next day the U.S. abruptly suspended its $70 million aid package to this impoverished country.[72]

When all was said and done, the U.S. assembled a coalition of 28 countries from six continents, as Bush bragged, that participated in one way or another in the war on Iraq. Yet countries like France, Germany and the Soviet Union, while part of the Coalition, also had long-standing ties to the Ba'ath regime, extensive economic interests in Iraq, and their own interests in the region that were not identical to those of the U.S. They agreed on the need to punish Iraq and drive it from Kuwait, but not to permanently cripple it or overthrow Hussein. These tensions within the Coalition would come into play over UN sanctions after the war, and even more sharply in the runup to a second war on Iraq in 2003.

The U.S., however, was not about to be encumbered by the desires of its coalition partners, the fine points of international law, or even the text of the UN resolutions it pushed through. When any of these stood in the way of U.S. objectives, Washington simply ignored them.

In August 1990, the International Red Cross denounced the imposition of sanctions under UN Resolution 661 as a flagrant violation of the UN Charter because the sanctions blocked food and medicine for Iraqi civilians. Sanctions were imposed anyway. Resolution 661 didn't give the U.S. authorization to enforce sanctions by military means, and the Security Council refused to grant such authority. So the U.S. simply went ahead unilaterally.

Resolution 660 called for Iraq and Kuwait to "begin immediately intensive negotiations for the resolution of their differences," and stated that the Security Council "supports all efforts in this regard, and especially those of the League of Arab States." Subsequent resolutions carried similar language calling for a negotiated end to the crisis without war. The U.S. torpedoed all such efforts. No UN resolution authorized the U.S. to destroy Iraq's military and civilian infrastructure, yet the U.S. did so anyway.

Resolution 678 stated that the Security Council would "remain seized of the matter"—in other words in control of what would happen next. Yet, the U.S. went ahead and attacked Iraq without further UN authorization.

The UN provided a "cloak of political cover," Scowcroft later wrote. Scowcroft also acknowledged that the U.S. was not bound by the UN: "Never did we think that without its blessings we could not or would not intervene."[73] Neither Scowcroft nor other U.S. officials spoke so frankly while their war preparations were unfolding.

Vietnam Nightmares and Nuclear Threats

U.S. objectives necessitated a military strategy that Greenpeace would later call "the most efficient killing campaign ever executed by any military force." This strategy made the Gulf War one of the most one-sided slaughters in history and insured that tens of thousands of civilians would be killed—many during the war and far more afterward.[74]

The Bush leadership was acutely concerned about restoring the confidence of the U.S. armed forces and rebuilding public support for military action abroad. This dictated a strategy of overwhelming force, minimal U.S. casualties, and quick victory. Woodward reports that Colin Powell argued for maximizing U.S. forces and options, not halfway measures: "If the U.S. military did not succeed in a pretty clear-cut way, it could be devastating," Powell warned. "A spectacular victory was required."[75]

"[T]his will not be another Vietnam," Bush declared when the war began, "Our troops...will not be asked to fight with one hand tied behind their back. I'm hopeful that this fighting will not go on for long and that casualties will be held to an absolute minimum."

Schwarzkopf agreed: the goal was to "achieve the absolute minimum number of casualties on our side."[76] Neither remarked on the other side of the coin: this strategy meant maximizing the destruction of Iraq's military capabilities and inflicting enormous casualties.

The U.S. was so determined to prevail that it was prepared to use nuclear weapons. According to military researcher William Arkin, the U.S. had more than 100 nuclear bombs at air bases in Turkey and nearly 500 naval nuclear weapons aboard the armada deployed in the Gulf. During the buildup to war, Defense Secretary Cheney instructed Powell to draw up plans for their possible use,[77] and on August 14, told troops leaving for combat that the U.S. had a "wide range of military capabilities" and would "respond with overwhelming force" should Saddam "be foolish enough to use chemical weapons on United States forces."[78]

On January 9, 1990, a week before the war started, Secretary of State Baker warned Iraq's Foreign Minister Tariq Aziz that the U.S. would use nuclear weapons if Iraq employed chemical or biological weapons—a warning that may have deterred the Iraqis from doing so.[79]

Iraq attempted some deterrence of its own. On August 6, 1990, Hussein warned the U.S. charge d'affaires that Iraq "reserved the right to use every weapon in its arsenal if invaded, just as it had against Iran and later the Kurds," a threat the Iraqi leadership reportedly felt helped deter a U.S. march on Baghdad.[80]

In August 1990, Hussein also began a crash program to build at least one nuclear warhead to be targeted on Israel if his rule was threatened, and, according to Pollack, during the war Iraq's military readied biological and chemical weapons in case Baghdad came under ground attack. Hussein later reportedly said it had been a mistake to invade Kuwait before Iraq had nuclear weapons. The Iraqis reportedly hoped to produce a bomb by April 1991, but lacked the necessary nuclear fuel and components.[81]

Apocalypse Now—and Later

The war began on January 16, 1991 with an unprecedented bombing assault code-named "Instant Thunder." Forty-six percent of the U.S. Air Force's combat planes were deployed, and for the next 43 days and nights, U.S. and British bombs and missiles pummeled Iraq from above. Coalition planes flew 109,876 combat sorties, dropping some 250,000 weapons—6,000 a day. The 88,500 tons of bombs were the explosive equivalent of six Hiroshimas. Afterward, Greenpeace stated, "the Gulf War was unprecedented in the amount of destruction inflicted on a nation with conventional weapons in so short a period of time."[82]

Bush claimed this air war was aimed at "Saddam's vast military arsenal," and its goal was driving Iraq from Kuwait and protecting Coalition forces.[83] America's fight, he insisted, was with Iraq's government, not its citizens. "We have no argument with the people of Iraq," he stated the night the bombs began falling, "Indeed, for the innocents caught in this conflict, I pray for their safety."[84]

The U.S.-led Coalition did target Iraq's leadership; command, control and communication; air defense; airfields; nuclear, biological and chemical weapons; Scud missiles; conventional military production and storage facilities; naval ports; and Republican Guard forces. But they also targeted Iraq's economic and social infrastructure—the foundations of its civilian life.

Iraq was a predominantly urban society with fairly well developed electrical, transportation, water, and medical systems that covered most of the country. These networks, however, relied heavily on Western equipment and technology. The U.S. systematically destroyed or crippled much of this infrastructure—including Iraq's electrical grid, power system, bridges, and telecommunications network.

Veteran French Middle East journalist and diplomat Eric Rouleau called the bombing the "latest descent into hell" for Iraqis, and detailed the losses, which the Arab Monetary Fund estimated at $190 billion:

> Electric power stations (92% of installed capacity destroyed), refineries (80 percent of production capacity), petrochemical complexes, telecommunications centers (including 135 telephone networks), bridges (more than 100), roads, highways, railroads, hundreds of locomotives and boxcars full of goods, radio and television broadcasting stations, cement plants, and factories producing aluminum, textiles, electric cables, and medical supplies...[85]

The assault on Iraq's electrical system proved to be enormously deadly for the Iraqi people. Coalition bombs and missiles destroyed 11 of Iraq's 20 power generating stations and damaged another six. By the war's end, Iraq's electrical generation had been slashed by 96 percent and reduced to 1920 levels.[86]

This electrical system powered Iraq's water, sewage and medical system, so without electricity, water could not be pumped, sewage could not be treated, and hospitals could not function. This destruction was compounded by U.S. attacks on plants making water purification chemicals such as chlorine. During the war, a World Health Organization investigation reported that "the whole of the Iraqi drinking water system is in or near collapse." Shortly after the war, a study team from Harvard University reported, "with the destruction of the country's electrical power plants in the Gulf War, Iraq's water purification and distribution system came to a virtual standstill." Iraqi deaths, particularly among the young and the elderly, from the devastating combination of contaminated water and crippled medial care began soaring.[87]

I visited Iraq in June 1991, three months after the war's end. Talking to Iraqi authorities and various international relief officials, I learned that if the Allies had simply wanted to cripple Iraq's war effort, they could have easily bombed the electrical transmission lines leading from power generating stations. This would have cut electricity during the war, but allowed Iraq to restore power afterward.

Instead, the allies bombed the main generation and control facilities of many power plants—with an estimated five-year repair time. During the war, some of these targets were acknowledged, but as the *Washington Post* put it, "the purposes and consequences of their destruction were not divulged."[88] Instead, this strategy of massive destruction was justified by government officials as a way to shorten the fighting and "save American lives."

Later, Air Force strategists admitted that this was part of a deliberate strategy to give the U.S. post-war "leverage" over Iraq by destroying "valuable facilities that Baghdad could not repair without foreign assistance."[89]

Col. John A. Warden II, Deputy Director of Strategy, Doctrine and Plans for the Air Force, told the *Washington Post*, "Saddam Hussein cannot restore his own electricity. He needs help. If there are political objectives that the UN coalition has, it can say, 'Saddam, when you agree to do these things, we will allow people to come in and fix your electricity.' It gives us long term leverage." Another Air Force planner went further: "We're not going to tolerate Saddam Hussein or his regime. Fix that, and we'll fix your electricity."[90]

The *Washington Post* noted, "The worst civilian suffering, senior officers say, has resulted not from bombs that went astray but from precision-guided weapons that hit exactly where they were aimed—at electrical plants, oil refineries and transportation networks."[91]

This directly contravened Article 54 of the Geneva Convention which prohibits attacks on essential civilian facilities including "drinking water supplies and irrigation works." Thus, the U.S. bombing campaign constituted a war crime that would contribute to the deaths of hundreds of thousands of Iraqis in the decade after the war, as detailed in the next chapter.

Hiding the War's Horrors

The extent of the death and destruction being visited on Iraq and its people was carefully hidden from the American people by the tightest wartime control of media coverage in U.S. history up to that point. The Bush administration fought to control the news flow through high level briefings run by Powell and Cheney, by restricting press access to the battlefield, and by feeding the media so-called "gun camera" footage (from cameras mounted on planes or held by military cameramen), which had been carefully selected by U.S. generals to present an image of a clean, surgical war.[92]

U.S. officials refused to show or even discuss Iraqi casualties—the press was certainly never given footage of B-52s carpet bombing Iraqi troops. And the U.S. mainstream media mostly acted as cheerleaders for the war, repeating official disinformation as if it were hard fact, dutifully broadcasting hours of Pentagon-selected footage of smart bombs unerringly striking their nonhuman targets, and refusing to show footage of Iraqi deaths even when it was readily available in the Arab media. It also refused to interview grieving Iraqi victims. CNN's decision to keep reporter Peter Arnett in Baghdad and show some footage of civilian casualties was condemned by much of the U.S. establishment as bordering on treason.

These briefings and the media coverage of the war were carefully crafted to avoid one dreaded aspect of the Vietnam syndrome: identification with the victims of U.S.-sponsored wars and popular revulsion at the horror and bloodshed that they entail. The U.S. government's solution to this "Vietnam syndrome," however, was not to stop slaughtering people; it was to stop showing it on TV.

Dumb Bombs and Civilian Death

The picture of the air war presented to the public was captured in one post-war Pentagon report:

> Careful targeting and expert use of technological superiority—including precision guided munitions—throughout the strategic air campaign minimized collateral damage and casualties to the civilian population.[93]

This picture was false and distorted in several different ways. First, U.S. "smart" weapons turned out to be much dumber than advertised. While the war raged, the Pentagon claimed a 98 percent success rate for its cruise missiles. In fact, at least 10 percent missed their targets, perhaps double that number.[94]

It also turned out that only six to eight percent of the munitions used were "smart," or guided, weapons. The rest were gravity bombs, usually dropped from 15,000 to 35,000 feet, and 70 percent went astray.[95]

During my trip to Iraq shortly after the war, I saw bombed-out water systems, power plants, hospitals, bridges, homes, roads, factories, and schools. Workers living on a small side street in downtown Baghdad showed me where a bomb or missile had hit their neighborhood—totally destroying a half dozen apartment buildings, collapsing their own roof, and damaging a nearby church.

In Basra, I saw residential areas dotted with bomb craters, food storage facilities that had been destroyed, and a Pepsi warehouse which had been reduced to a bombed-out shell. Iraqis said that 14 were killed, 46 wounded, and 128 homes damaged or destroyed on the day of the Pepsi attack. The director of Basra's Teaching Hospital showed me wards in his facility that had been extensively damaged in another U.S. attack.

Overall, a third of all U.S. air attacks were directed at Iraq's densely populated cities, and the UN reported that at least 9,000 homes were destroyed and that 72,000 Iraqis had been left homeless.[96]

My grimmest experience was a visit to a quiet upper middle class neighborhood in Baghdad. With its wide streets and comfortable two story homes, it was hard to imagine that anything untoward had ever happened there. But on the night of February 13, 1991, it did. Two U.S. cruise missiles scored direct hits on the Amiriya air raid shelter and incinerated some 408 civilians inside.[97]

The shelter's massive, two-story exterior, decorated with triangular patterns of brown, beige and tan, looked fine from the outside, save for a few spots blackened with soot. But on the roof there was a single hole, some six feet across, blasted through four or five feet of concrete and steel. It looked into a dark cavern. A strange odor hung faintly in the air, and I began to visualize how in a single moment, a place of safety was turned into an inferno for hundreds of men, women and children—an inferno with heavy steel doors, thick concrete walls, and no way out. The U.S. still insists the Amiriya shelter was a military command and control center and a "legitimate" military target. I saw no evidence whatsoever to support that claim, and none has been produced by Washington.

Terrorizing Iraqi Children

Iraqis described nights of terror under the U.S. bombardment—being trapped underground, never knowing when the bombs or missiles would come, where they would strike, or who would fall victim.

In many ways children were most affected. Iraqi doctors said the bombing had caused a wide range of psychological traumas, from increased bed wetting to severe phobias. In one Baghdad hospital I saw a 10-year-old boy from Kurdistan who had stopped eating and talking when his neighborhood was attacked. "He looked like a ghost when he first came to the hospital," one doctor said. He was being kept alive by intravenous fluids but still wouldn't speak.

Dr. Ameed Hamid, the Director of Iraq's Red Crescent Society (the Islamic equivalent of the Red Cross), told me what happened to his family:

> I have a son 5 years old. During the air raid he was shak-
> ing, shivering, saying 'Bush is coming, Bush is coming.' After
> the cease-fire American airplanes were flying over Baghdad,
> crossing the sound barrier, making this explosive sound, fright-
> ening the children and writing with blue smoke, 'USA.' What
> was the purpose except frightening Iraqi children?

There was a method to this madness. Air Force Lt. General
Charles A. Horner, who had overall command of the air campaign,
called such psychological terror a "side benefit" of the air assault.[98]

Refusing to Take "Yes" for an Answer

"Instant Thunder" had roused waves of protest around the
world and frantic efforts in January and February 1991 to negotiate
a cease-fire in the Gulf War. The U.S. rejected them all in order to
finish the job of decimating Iraq's armed forces with a ground
assault. "We have to have a war," Bush told his top advisers.
Woodward writes, "Scowcroft was aware that this understanding
could never be stated publicly or be permitted to leak out."[99] Only
years later did Scowcroft acknowledge their determination to wage
a ground war whether or not Iraq withdrew from Kuwait:

> Cheney and I also believed that a ground campaign would
> be necessary no matter what air power accomplished, because it
> was essential that we destroy Iraq's offensive capability. This was
> also a major objective, *although it had not been feasible to list it
> openly as such while a peaceful solution to the crisis was possible.*
> (emphasis added)[100]

U.S. air strikes had degraded Iraq's military by an estimated 40
percent, but this was not enough for the Bush leadership. Their
biggest worry was that Hussein would withdraw Iraqi forces from
Kuwait "before we had managed to grind down his armor and heavy
equipment," as Bush put it. Scowcroft agreed: even if Iraq agreed to
U.S. demands, "it would be a disaster to take 'yes' for an answer..."
Bush told Powell he preferred a ground war to Iraqi compliance with
U.S. demands because if Iraqi forces "crack under force, it is better
than withdrawal."[101]

Bush was determined to end the war "definitively" no matter

what other Coalition members wanted. "Our credibility is at stake," he wrote. "We don't want to have another draw, another Vietnam, a sloppy ending."[102] But a "sloppy" ending would be what the U.S. got.

Bush and Scowcroft write that the Soviets were "furious" because the bombing campaign had exceeded the scope of the UN resolutions by hitting not only Iraq's military, but its cities as well.[103] Although the Soviet Union had for now retreated from the struggle for global supremacy and was supporting the Gulf War coalition, its objectives were not identical to Washington's, and it remained a formidable presence in the region. Moscow had long-standing ties with Iraq, did not want to see the Hussein regime destroyed, and sought to impose some restraints on the U.S. in the region.

On January 30, 1991, Secretary of State Baker and Soviet Foreign Minister Bessmertnykh issued a joint statement calling for a cease-fire provided Iraq agreed to leave Kuwait. It also stated that solving the Israeli-Palestinian conflict should be a priority after the resolution of the Gulf crisis. Bush and Scowcroft hadn't approved this initiative, and Scowcroft recounts watching Bush when they heard about it: "the anger—as sharp as I'd ever seen in him—started to rise." A ground war apparently didn't infuriate Bush; but the prospect of peace did. The administration 'brushed off' the declaration and proceeded with the war.[104]

On February 15, the Iraqi leadership indicated that it was willing to accept Resolution 660 and withdraw from Kuwait. On hearing the news than the war could be halted, Bush recalled, "Instead of feeling exhilarated, my heart sank.... We've got some unfinished business.... I don't see how it will work with Saddam in power, and I am very, very wary."[105] Bush dismissed Iraq's offer as a "cruel hoax."[106]

On February 18, the Soviets, who Scowcroft noted "were searching, with increasing desperation, for some way to head off a ground war," informed the Bush administration that Iraq was prepared to withdraw without any conditions except that their forces not be attacked. But Bush and Scowcroft felt that "If Saddam withdrew with most of his armed forces intact, we hadn't really won." So the U.S. quickly announced four new criteria—"no cease-fire until the withdrawal was complete, no more launching of Scuds, no use of chemical weapons, and an immediate swap of POWs." Scowcroft later acknowledged that these new criteria were "beyond the UN resolutions with which the Iraqis would have to comply to show their good faith."[107]

On February 21, the Soviets announced that Iraq had agreed to pull out of Kuwait within 21 days in return for a one-day cease-fire and the lifting of sanctions. There was no linkage to Palestinian issues. Colin Powell described the quandary faced by the U.S. leadership: "The President's problem was how to say no to Gorbachev without appearing to throw away a chance for peace." Powell proposed giving Iraq a deadline they couldn't possibly meet. "If, as I suspect, they don't move," Powell said, "then the flogging begins."[108]

On February 22, the U.S. rejected Iraq's offer, and issued its new ultimatum: Iraq would have until noon the next day to start withdrawing—while the air war continued. Early the next morning Gorbachev told Bush that "Saddam has caved" to U.S. demands for an unconditional withdrawal and asked for time to work out the details. Bush dismissed the effort: "It was too late for that."[109]

Slaughter and Censorship

The next day, February 24, at 4:00 a.m. local time, the U.S. launched its ground war from Saudi Arabia. "The liberation of Kuwait has now entered its final phase," Bush declared. Over the next three days, Marine and Army units attacked with infantry and armor along several fronts, retaking Kuwait and moving some 100 miles into southern Iraq to engage and cut-off retreating Iraqi forces.[110]

New peace proposals continued to be floated after the ground war started. On February 25, Iraq announced it was pulling out of Kuwait, repeated its acceptance of resolution 660, and requested—through the Soviets—a UN sponsored cease-fire. Bush rejected the joint Soviet-Iraqi plea the next morning. For the U.S., any cease-fire before Iraq's military had been annihilated was a deal-breaker, even as it continued to insist that it was Hussein who hadn't met one condition or another.[111]

The war's single worst atrocity occurred on February 26—the day Iraq said it would accept any terms the U.S. dictated.[112] Iraqi forces were retreating north from Kuwait City to Basra in a long con-voy of tanks, personnel carriers, trucks, buses, and cars. General Powell declared, "we shall cut them off and then kill them." U.S. planes attacked both ends of the convoy, blocking off any escape, and for the next 48 hours the strip of roadway became a free-fire zone for Coalition aircraft and ground forces.

Bush declared a cease-fire at midnight on February 27, 100 hours after the ground war had begun. By that time, thousands had been slaughtered and the six-lane "highway of death" was littered with burnt-out vehicles and charred bodies. Many were non-com-batants from a variety of countries, just trying to escape. One U.S. soldier said it was like "a medieval hell."[113]

Greenpeace estimated that between 25,000 and 50,000 Iraqi soldiers were killed during the ground war—mostly during the retreat from Kuwait—half of Iraq's total military casualties. Hiro puts Iraqi casualties during the retreat between 25,000 and 30,000. The London Observer labeled the slaughter "one of the most terrible harassments of a retreating army from the air in the history of war-fare."[114]

This slaughter of retreating Iraq forces constituted a violation of the Fourth Geneva Convention of 1949's prohibition on attacks on soldiers who have withdrawn from combat, as well the 1907 Hague Convention, which declared it illegal to give "no quarter" to withdrawing forces. According to the Washington Post, many Iraqi troops had fled their positions 36 hours before the U.S. assault, yet were hunted down mercilessly anyway. In short, the "highway of death" massacre constituted another U.S. war crime.[115]

This massacre and other ground war atrocities were largely hid-den from the public by the government's wartime control of the media and by the press blackout instituted by Defense Secretary Cheney at the start of the ground war. Reporters in the official press pool were banned from the front, and their dispatches were vetted by the military. Newsday reporter Patrick Sloyan found that "More than 70 reporters were arrested, detained, threatened at gunpoint and literally chased from the front lines when they attempted to defy Pentagon rules."[116]

As a result, all the press accounts of the highway of death came from reporters working outside the Pentagon pool. "More than 150 reporters who participated in the Pentagon pool system failed to produce a single eyewitness account of the clash between 300,000 allied troops and an estimated 300,000 Iraqi troops," Sloyan writes. "There was not one photograph, not a strip of film by pool members of a dead body—American or Iraqi."

For Cheney, it was "the best-covered war ever. The American people saw up close with their own eyes through the magic of television what the U.S. military was capable of doing." Yet several months after the war, 17 major news organizations issued a report concluding that the Pentagon restrictions constituted "real censorship." The report, whose signers included ABC, CBS, and NBC News, CNN, the New York Times, the Associated Press, the Washington Post, the Los Angeles Times, the Wall Street Journal, and USA Today, argued that "By controlling what journalists saw and when they saw it, the military exercised great power to shape and manage the news."[117]

Burying the Living and Dead

In the months and years following the war's end, other U.S. massacres have come to light. In June 1991, Dr. Salem Mohammed al Saedi, the regional health director in the southern Iraqi city of Amarah, told me that soldiers had been killed 100 miles north of the highway of death. "They [the U.S.] bombed the soldiers when they were retreating, and that was a tragedy I saw in front of my own eyes," Dr. Saedi said. "We're 186 kilometers from Basra and it's 40 kilometers from Basra to Sufwan [Iraq's border with Kuwait], and they attacked soldiers who were retreating on foot." He and his colleagues counted 504 casualties in the 13 hours leading up to the cease-fire at just one small clinic outside Amarah. I saw the grim evidence while traveling north of Basra: burnt-out wrecks of every type of vehicle imaginable—from tanks to school buses—strewn along the roadsides.

On February 25, 1991 the Pentagon prevented UPI reporter Leon Daniel and other journalists from witnessing a 1st Infantry Division (Mechanized) assault on some 8,000 Iraqi soldiers at the tip of the Neutral Zone between Saudi Arabia and Iraq. Daniel became suspicious after reporters were allowed to visit the battle scene the next afternoon: there were no bodies, no blood, and no evidence of fighting, only some 2,000 Iraqi soldiers who had surrendered.

Daniel later learned that, "Thousands of Iraqi soldiers, some of them alive and firing their weapons from World War I-style trenches, were buried by plows mounted on Abrams battle tanks. The Abrams flanked the trench lines so that tons of sand from the plows funneled into the trenches. Just behind the tanks, actually straddling the trench line, came Bradleys pumping 7.62mm machine gun bullets into the Iraqi troops." Army Col. Anthony Moreno, the commander of the lead brigade in the assault, later told him, "What you saw was a bunch of buried trenches with people's arms and land [sic] things sticking out of them. For all I know, we could have killed thousands." The army attempted to cover up the slaughter by leveling the ground with earthmovers. Moreno estimated that 70 miles of trenches and bunkers were filled in.[118]

In 2000, Seymour Hersh reported in the *New Yorker* that US forces under General Barry McCaffrey (later President Clinton's "drug czar") killed hundreds of retreating Iraqi forces, including by firing into a crowd of 350 disarmed Iraqi prisoners, in two separate attacks—several days *after* the cease-fire.[119]

The U.S. military quickly exonerated McCaffrey, who told CNN shortly afterward that he thought that 400 Iraqis had been killed. The *New York Times* reported that "Some Army officers complained after the war that General McCaffrey had used the episode as an excuse to pummel the Iraqis" and that "discomfort over the attack also ran deep within General McCaffrey's own 24th Infantry Division." McCaffrey called Hersh's charges "both unfair and untrue."[120]

Not Counting the Dead

Neither Baghdad nor Washington, each for their own reasons, had an interest in detailing how many Iraqis died during the war, and so the war's precise toll remains unknown. During the Vietnam War, the Pentagon's daily "body counts," often intended to show that the U.S. was supposedly winning, ended up bringing home that war's horror and fueling opposition. So in the Gulf War, the Pentagon refused to provide estimates of either Iraqi civilian or battlefield casualties. "I'm never going to get into the body count business," Schwarzkopf said at one briefing.[121]

Afterward, the U.S. would only say that its forces buried 577 Iraqis on the battlefield, while providing no estimates of Iraqi civilian deaths. In June 1991, after a Freedom of Information Act request, the Defense Department acknowledged an estimate of 100,000 Iraqi soldiers killed and 300,000 wounded. The Pentagon never provided an accounting of Iraqi civilian casualties.[122]

An in-depth study by a team of Greenpeace researchers concluded that between 100,000 and 120,000 Iraqi soldiers were killed during the war. This was more in 43 days, according to Greenpeace, than died during the eight years of the Iran-Iraq War, and three times the daily Vietnamese casualty rate during the Vietnam War. The organization estimated that between 5,000 and 15,000 Iraqi civilians were also killed, mainly during Coalition air attacks, as well as 2,000 to 5,000 Kuwaitis as a result of Iraq's invasion and the U.S. counter-attack.[123]

In 1991, Census Bureau demographer Beth Osborne Daponte estimated that 158,000 Iraqis were killed in the war and its immediate aftermath. Her findings were summarized in the *Philadelphia Inquirer*:

> 86,194 men, 39,612 women, and 32,195 children died in one year as a direct and indirect result of the U.S.-led attack and the ensuing Shiite and Kurdish rebellions. About a quarter, 40,000, were Iraqi soldiers killed in combat. The rest were civilians, including 13,000 who got caught in the crossfire. About 70,000 civilians died after the war due mainly to the destruction of water and power plants.

According to the *Philadelphia Inquirer*, after Daponte's estimate was leaked to the press, she was reprimanded by the Census Bureau, and then "saw her report rewritten and her career sidetracked."[124]

Meanwhile, the U.S. lost 79 killed, 212 wounded, and 45 missing in action.

Toxic Clouds & Depleted Uranium

Death, illness and suffering resulting from the war continued right up until the war of 2003, when it became impossible to assess the ongoing damage from the first Persian Gulf War. Coalition forces flew 518 sorties and dropped 1,200 tons of explosives on 28 Iraqi oil refineries, and also attacked chemical weapons depots.[125] Iraqi forces, meanwhile, are accused of torching some 700 of Kuwait's 1,000 oil wells during their retreat. These actions resulted in massive oil spills and environmental destruction concentrated in southern Iraq, affecting perhaps 800 miles of Persian Gulf coastline. They also released a toxic stew of chemical agents, pesticides, acid rain, soot, and smoke from burning oil wells into the atmosphere.[126]

There is some dispute about who set Kuwait's oil wells on fire. On February 23, 1991, Iraq denied responsibility for setting them afire and called for a UN investigation; none was undertaken. Some 12 years later, on February 19, 2003, the American Gulf War Veterans Association issued a press release stating that some U.S. vets had come forward to claim that U.S. forces, not the Iraqis, had set at least some of these fires in order to discredit the Hussein regime.[127]

Shortly after the 1991 war, Michael Renner of Worldwatch Institute wrote, "Satellite pictures showed that by mid-March, clouds of toxic smoke were stretching from Romania and Bulgaria to Afghanistan and Pakistan." The Arms Control Research Center (ARC) states, "Black snow fell in the Himalayas that year, 2,000 kilometers from Kuwait, and smaller quantities of smaller soot particles traveled longer distances." In May 1991 *Scientific American* reported that at the start of the war, the U.S. government issued a memo instructing all Department of Energy facilities and contractors to "immediately discontinue any further discussion of war-related research and issues with the media until further notice," and authorized them to say only:

> Most independent studies and experts suggest that the catastrophic predictions in some recent news reports are exaggerated. We are currently reviewing the matter, but these predictions remains speculative and do not warrant any further comment at this time.[128]

To these horrors was added another: the U.S. use of depleted uranium shells. Depleted uranium—or DU—shells are 1.7 times denser than lead and when fired at high velocity can quickly penetrate and destroy armored combat vehicles such as tanks. During the Gulf War, U.S. forces fired 1 million DU rounds, destroying approximately 4,000 Iraqi armored vehicles. Overall, some 320 tons of such DU shells were fired by U.S. forces, generating tens of thousands of pounds of dust and debris that are both radioactive and toxic. (It takes 4.5 billion years for DU to lose half of its radioactivity.)[129]

Upon impact roughly 70 percent of their uranium catches fire and oxidizes—forming clouds of black uranium oxide particles of varying sizes. James C. Warf, Professor Emeritus of Chemistry at the University of Southern California and an expert on nuclear issues, writes, "It is the smallest, those about one micrometer in size, which are the most dangerous. They tend to lodge in the lungs and become embedded. The slow and constant exposure of the lung tissues to the alpha particles [a form of radiation] forms pockets of tissue prone to become cancerous."[130]

The Pentagon claims that DU is harmless, but a 1991 study by Britain's Atomic Energy Authority estimated that 500,000 "potential deaths from cancer" could eventually result from 40 tons of DU weapons—one-eighth the amount actually fired in the Gulf War. The report was suppressed by the British government until 1998. By then, Iraqi doctors were reporting a surge in cancer deaths and birth defects. In January 2003, Iraqi doctors told Robert Collier of the *San Francisco Chronicle* that the cancer rate among children had increased five-fold throughout Iraq since 1990 (and 38 percent for all Iraqis), while congenital birth defects and leukemia rates had tripled. In December 2002, Scott Peterson of the *Christian Science Monitor* reported that one Basra gynecologist told him that birth defects were six times more frequent than before the 1991 Gulf War.[131]

In 1996, the UN Subcommission on the Promotion and Protection of Human Rights classified depleted uranium as a "weapon of mass destruction."[132] Doug Rokke, who was responsible for the U.S. military's DU cleanup and decontamination operations in Kuwait, says, "What happened in the Gulf was a form of nuclear warfare."[133]

Exposure to the toxic atmospheric stew and to depleted uranium may also have caused—or helped cause—"Gulf War Syndrome," which afflicts between 175,000 and 210,000 of the 700,000 U.S. soldiers who served in the Gulf War and has recently been linked to Lou Gehrig's disease (ALS or amyotropic lateral sclerosis).[134]

Symptoms include chronic fatigue, aching joints, diarrhea, migraines, dizziness, memory loss, and problems with balance and muscle control. Chalmers Johnson, the author of *Blowback: The Costs and Consequences of American Empire*, writes in May 2003:

> [A]s of May 2002 the Veterans Administration (VA) reported that an additional 8,306 soldiers had died and 159,705 were injured or became ill as a result of service-connected 'exposures' suffered during the war. Even more alarmingly, the VA revealed that 206,861 veterans, almost a third of Gen. Schwarzkopf's entire army, had filed claims for medical care, compensation, and pension benefits based on injuries and illnesses caused by combat in 1991. After reviewing the cases, the agency has classified 168,011 applicants as 'disabled veterans.' In light of these deaths and disabilities, the casualty rate for the first Gulf War is actually a staggering 29.3 percent.[135]

During the war, Coalition forces placed over 117,000 land mines and dropped 60,000 to 80,000 cluster bombs, which scattered 12-16 million anti-personnel "bomblets." Even those the U.S. claimed to be rescuing became their victims: unexploded munitions killed 1,700 *Kuwaitis* and injured another 2,300 in the decade after the war. In Iraq, half of its agricultural land reportedly became unusable because of unexploded munitions from first the Iran-Iraq warand then the 1991 Gulf war.[136]

Retired Admiral Eugene Carroll of the Center for Defense Information argues that antipersonnel land mines and weapons of mass destruction are "equally indiscriminate and dangerous." Carroll, writing in February 2003 noted, "Antipersonnel land mines emplaced by the U.S. during the Gulf War in 1991, as well as those from the Iran-Iraq war, now continue to kill or maim up to 30 Iraqis each month."[137]

Betraying the Iraqi Uprising

Iraq accepted U.S. terms for a cease-fire on March 3, 1991, officially ending the war (although no formal peace treaty was signed). Iraqi forces had been decimated and driven from Kuwait, and Iraq's economic and social infrastructure had been devastated. The Hussein regime remained, but its grip on power was severely shaken by uprisings in the Shi'a and Kurdish areas that erupted—with U.S.

encouragement—on March 2.

Bush I's actions during these anti-Hussein uprisings represented yet another cynical U.S. manipulation of the Iraqi people, which (along with his refusal to march on Baghdad) has been hotly debated by government officials and establishment strategists ever since. The U.S. government's strategic vision at that time also stands in sharp contrast to the war for regime change waged by Bush II in 2003. The reasons for Bush, Sr.'s choice illustrate both the unjust character of the 1991 U.S. war and how U.S. strategy has evolved in the years since.

On February 15, 1991, in the midst of the war, President Bush called upon the Iraqi people to rise up: "And there's another way for the bloodshed to stop," he said, "and that is for the Iraqi military and the Iraqi people to take matters into their own hands and force Saddam Hussein, the dictator, to step aside..."[138]

Afterward, Scowcroft and other administration officials argued that Bush's remark was simply "impulsive ad lib," which neither constituted encouragement for an Iraqi uprising nor had a significant impact. Even Bush himself claimed there was "never a promise to aid an uprising."[139]

In reality, encouraging an anti-Hussein uprising was one component of U.S. war planning, and, as the *Wall Street Journal* reported, Bush's call for an uprising was "one of many such statements."[140] NSD-54 spelled out that one U.S. war objective was to "weaken Iraqi popular support for the current government."[141] According to military planners interviewed by the *Washington Post*, the U.S. bombing campaign was designed in part to "incite Iraqi citizens to rise against the Iraqi leader," and Bush and Scowcroft acknowledge that the U.S. also tried to assassinate Hussein during the war.[142]

As U.S. and British bombs pounded Iraq from above, the "Voice of America" broadcast calls for Iraqis to rise against Hussein from below. The CIA, working through Saudi intelligence, also set up a clandestine "Voice of Free Iraq" on Saudi soil which began transmitting on January 1, 1991. In mid-January, American planes began dropping the first of some 21 million propaganda leaflets. One pictured a dove and read: "Saddam is the cause of the war and its sorrows. He must be stopped. Join with your brothers and demonstrate rejection of Saddam's brutal policies. There will be no peace with

Saddam." With Radio Baghdad knocked out by the Coalition air assault, these U.S. stations had little competition inside Iraq.[143]

Saif Ataya, a Shi'ite resister, later talked to the *San Francisco Chronicle* about his experience: "Ataya recalls waking up one day in early March 1991 and finding the streets of his town littered with white flyers dropped by the Americans. 'Rise up, oh brothers," the flyers read in Arabic. 'This is your time. The American armed forces will help you. We need your help to change for democracy and freedom.'"[144]

Many Iraqis took these declarations of U.S. support for an uprising at face value, and one came quickly after the fighting stopped. On March 2, with Coalition forces still in Kuwait and Iraq, retreating Iraqi soldiers rebelled. They were quickly joined by civilians and before long a largely spontaneous revolt had erupted across southern Iraq. By mid-March the insurgents had taken control of most of southern Iraq, including Basra, Karbala, and Najaf. The uprising in the south was quickly followed by a Kurdish revolt in the north, and within weeks the Kurds were in control of the major cities and towns in the northern Kurdish areas.

To the insurgents surprise, however, the U.S. refused to provide them with captured Iraqi weapons or support their actions. Instead, General Schwarzkopf gave the Iraqi military permission to fly helicopters, as long as they didn't approach U.S. forces.[145] The regime had managed to preserve its most elite Republic Guard units, and with helicopter support they were able to mount a brutal counterattack beginning in the south on March 9. Several months later, when I traveled through Najaf and Karbala, burnt out buildings pockmarked with bullet holes testified to widespread and ferocious fighting.

On March 27, with the fighting still raging in Kurdistan, the White House claimed the U.S. "had made no promises to the Shi'as or Kurds" and declared that it had no intention of placing U.S. forces in the midst of a civil war. By April 6 the rebellions in the Shi'a south and the Kurdish north had been crushed. Estimates of the death toll range from 20,000 to 100,000.[146]

Two to three million Kurds and Shi'ites fled their homes to escape Baghdad's counter-attacks, fearing the regime might again use chemical weapons, including hundreds of thousands of Kurds who ended up trapped in make-shift camps in frigid winter conditions in the mountains near Turkey and Iran. Between 15,000 and 30,000 Kurds and others died in refugee camps or during their escape—mainly the very old and the very young. Over 800,000 people left Iraq entirely within three days. Jeff Chenoweth of the Catholic Legal Immigrant Network told the *San Francisco Chronicle*, "It was at the time the largest, swiftest mass exodus recorded in history."[147]

The Kurdish winter, however, was not as cold as the strategic calculations guiding Bush, Scowcroft and company, who allowed Baghdad to suppress these revolts. For all their demonization of the Hussein regime, they actually wanted to preserve it as a bulwark of the regional status quo. They feared that the regime's overthrow by a mass uprising from below could strengthen Kurdish forces in the north and the Shi'a opposition in the south, perhaps even lead to the fragmentation of Iraq. Either outcome could fuel the Kurdish struggle in NATO ally Turkey, or strengthen Iranian influence in the south and the Gulf—undermining U.S. regional dominance. "Neither the United States nor the countries of the region wished to see the breakup of the Iraqi state," Scowcroft explained. "We were concerned about the long-term balance of power at the head of the Gulf. Breaking up the Iraqi state would pose its own destabilizing problems."[148]

The U.S. government didn't have a problem with the Hussein regime's repression in Iraq. Washington's problem with Hussein's regime came when it sought to exert influence beyond Iraq's borders. The Bush administration wanted to be rid of Saddam Hussein because he embodied those regional ambitions and because he had defied the U.S. before the world—but they did not want to be rid of his Ba'ath regime. In February 1991, Richard Haass, director for Middle East Affairs on the Bush I National Security Council (and a top State Department official under Bush II), said bluntly: "Our policy is to get rid of Saddam, not his regime."[149] And if Hussein was to go, the U.S. wanted the job done by the Iraqi military—not the Iraqi people. "It is true that we hoped Saddam would be toppled," Scowcroft said, "But we never thought that could be done by anyone outside the military and never tried to incite the general population."[150]

A December 1991 assessment by the *Wall Street Journal* concluded:

> Washington also was caught off guard by the revolt.
> Alarmed by the rebels' Islamic fervor, and fearful that aiding
> them would force the U.S. to occupy Iraq, the administration
> balked just as the Baghdad regime appeared to teeter. 'The Iraqi
> people alone have the responsibility and the right to choose
> their own government—without outside interference,' declared
> a Voice of America editorial on March 7, when the Shiites con-
> trolled almost all of southern Iraq.

According to officials interviewed by the paper, that message of
no outside interference "flashed a green light to Baghdad" to suppress the revolt.[151]

One defense analyst later interviewed by the *San Francisco
Chronicle* on condition of anonymity painted a similar picture: the
CIA argued that the Hussein regime was near collapse and "all we
have to have is an uprising and then one of the generals will shoot
Saddam." When this didn't happen, the U.S. reversed course and
allowed Hussein to crush the rebellion.[152] So once again, U.S. imperialism came to Saddam Hussein's aid, and once again helped dig the
mass graves it would shed crocodile tears over a decade later.

The Bush administration didn't think Hussein could survive in
power for more than a few months following his Gulf War defeat,
and they had major concerns about the ramifications of invading
and occupying Iraq. Bush felt the Gulf Coalition would shatter if it
were stretched so far beyond its original mission. And for all their
talk about overcoming the Vietnam syndrome, the Bush team still
feared getting bogged down in a protracted ground war and occupation of Iraq, with the potential for heavy U.S. casualties. As noted
earlier, the U.S. was also concerned that Iraq might employ chemical and biological weapons against an invading army.[153] This could
not only have led to significant losses, but could also have—especially given Baker's threat of a nuclear response—triggered an
unpredictable and perhaps devastating spiral of escalation.

"Had we gone the invasion route, the United States could conceivably still be an occupying power in a bitterly hostile land,"
Scowcroft later wrote. "It would have been a dramatically different—and perhaps barren—outcome."[154] In 2003, with its occupation
troops suffering daily attacks, the U.S. may be starting to experience
that "dramatically different outcome" that Scowcroft warned of.

Preserving an Unjust Status Quo

Bush promised that America's 1991 Gulf War would usher in a "new world order" in which "the nations of the world, East and West, North and South, can prosper and live in harmony."[155] In reality, Desert Storm was a war by the imperialist "north" against an upstart regime of the Third World "south" designed to tighten the U.S. hold on the Middle East and preserve an oppressive regional order.

In Kuwait, the Sabah family was restored to the throne, and it unleashed a campaign of terror and reprisals against Palestinians living there, (thanks in part to the PLO's support for the Hussein regime), that included imprisonment, torture, and murder. Of the 400,000 Palestinians living in Kuwait prior to the war, 350,000 were forced to flee by the war and subsequent Kuwaiti repression.

There were other huge displacements across the region, impacting hundreds of thousands of impoverished laborers and their often-extended families. Some 300,000 Egyptian workers were expelled from Iraq after Egypt joined the U.S. war coalition. Under U.S. pressure, Saudi Arabia expelled 800,000 Yemeni workers when their country refused to support the war.[156]

In Saudi Arabia, the corrupt House of Saudi was kept in place, and the Kingdom's continued subordination to the U.S. ensured. Thus, one of the world's most oppressive social orders had been preserved—a social order in which Saudi women must be veiled at all times in public, cannot drive, travel alone, check into hotels, or mix with men in any public or work setting; a society where banks, schools and hospitals are all segregated by sex, and where women doctors, teachers, or bank tellers can only tend to other women.[157]

James Schlesinger, formerly head of the departments of Defense and Energy, as well as the CIA, and currently a member of the Defense Policy Board, was forthright about the U.S. establishment's agenda there: "Do we seriously want to change the institutions of Saudi Arabia? The brief answer is no; over the years we have sought to preserve these institutions, sometimes in preference to more democratic forces coursing throughout the region."[158]

Following the Gulf War, the U.S. continued to support Turkey and its scorched-earth counter-insurgency campaign against its Kurdish population. Turkey's Kurds lived under military rule from

1987 until late November 2002. During that time, the Turkish military destroyed more than 2,300 Kurdish villages and forced more than 2 million Kurds to flee or be relocated. Some 30,000 people, overwhelmingly Kurds, were killed in those 15 years of emergency rule.[159]

The U.S. victory strengthened Israel's hand in the region by striking down a major Arab state. As a result, in October 1991 in Madrid, Spain, direct peace talks were begun for the first time between Israel and the Arab countries bordering it. These negotiations led to the Oslo Agreements of 1994, which were advertised as a first step toward ending the Israeli-Palestinian struggle and creating a Palestinian state. Instead, Israel used the agreements, which led to the ending of the first Palestinian *Intifada*, to accelerate its efforts to settle and incorporate wide swaths of the West Bank and Gaza. Rashid Khalidi, professor of Middle East history at the University of Chicago, calls Oslo an effort to "protect the expansion of settlements and the continuation of occupation."[160]

In May 1991, the U.S. and its allies created a "safe haven" zone in Iraqi Kurdistan after images of thousands of Kurds driven into freezing, snowy mountains sparked a worldwide outcry. Here, as at other junctures when the U.S. government claimed the moral high ground, its actions were instead guided by strategic imperial interests. In this case, Washington's goal was not a liberated Iraqi Kurdistan, but protecting Turkey from a flood of Kurdish refugees. The Bush administration supported Turkey's decision to close its borders immediately after the Gulf War as well as its refusal to grant Iraqi Kurds asylum, decisions which prevented tens of thousands from escaping the wrath of the Iraqi military.

Turkey didn't even offer refugee status to the 350,000 Iraqi Kurds who did manage to cross the border, but instead forced many of them into squalid internment camps surrounded by barbed wire and armed guards.[161] There, Kurdish children were denied an education and their parents were denied employment. "Denial of asylum is a human rights violation," states Bill Frelick, an analyst with the U.S. Committee for Refugees. "The U.S. supported Turkey's violation of the Kurds' right to asylum."[162]

Most importantly, the end of the Gulf War didn't bring a halt to U.S. assaults on Iraq. Rather, it opened a new 12-year chapter of economic strangulation and military attacks whose main victims were the Iraqi people.

Escalating Intervention, Fraying Control

The U.S. won a decisive military victory in 1991, and in the wake of the Soviet collapse it reigned as the planet's dominant imperial power. In *World Transformed*, Scowcroft wrote:

> The final collapse of Soviet power and the dissolution of its empire brought to a close the greatest transformation of the international system since World War I and concluded nearly eight decades of upheaval and conflict. The world we had encountered in January 1989 had been defined by superpower rivalry. The Cold War struggle had shaped our assumptions about international and domestic politics, our institutions and processes, our armed forces and military strategy. In a blink of an eye, these were gone. We were suddenly in a unique position, without experience, without precedent, and standing alone at the height of power.[163]

The Pentagon bragged that Desert Storm was "a defining event in U.S. global leadership." Scowcroft saw it as "the bridge between the Cold War and the post-Cold War eras." Bush said the Vietnam syndrome "had been put to rest and American credibility restored."[164]

Yet for all its brutality and swagger, a firm grip on Iraq and the Persian Gulf eluded the U.S. in the decade after the war. Like the Iran-Iraq war before it, the Gulf War did not bring peace, justice or stability—quite the opposite. It spawned enormous suffering, weakened the very regimes the U.S. fought to protect, triggered new rounds of U.S. intervention, and paved the way for yet another Gulf war 12 years later.

CHAPTER 6

GERM WARFARE

AMERICA'S WEAPON OF MASS DESTRUCTION

> Let me also make clear that the United States has no quarrel with the Iraqi people.
> —George H.W. Bush, September 11, 1990

> Since the war Iraqi children have been exposed to biological warfare, massive biological warfare. When you destroy the infrastructure of a country, sewage with all its germs will flow into the streets; you stop pure water from reaching the children; you give them malnutrition; you prevent medicines from reaching the country. So it's an excellent environment for death and disease.
> —Dr. Ameed Hamid, Director of Iraq's Red Crescent Society, June 1991

After 13 years of hearing U.S. officials and the media routinely and repeatedly demonize Saddam Hussein, most Americans would be shocked to learn that, in reality, their own government was responsible for more Iraqi deaths than all Hussein's atrocities combined. And they would be equally shocked to learn that Washington had been systematically lying about the nature, terms, and purpose of the United Nations sanctions that have been responsible for the staggering suffering inflicted on the Iraqi people.

Washington's line has been that it would have gladly lifted sanctions if only Hussein had complied with UN demands. Iraq instead "answered a decade of U.N. demands with a decade of defiance," according to George W. Bush.

This official storyline stands reality on its head. For all practical purposes, the U.S. never stopped waging war against Iraq even after the 1991 Gulf War formally ended. UN resolutions became weapons in this ongoing conflict, even as they were being violated more frequently by Washington than by the Hussein regime. In fact, Baghdad complied with UN demands more than it defied them, including on arms inspections and disarmament, as detailed in chapter 7. This compliance is the simple reason why no weapons of mass destruction have yet been found in Iraq and most likely will never be found. Most, if not all, were destroyed early in the 1990s—a fact the Bush II administration knew perfectly well.

Dissecting 13 years of lies and excavating the truth about sanctions not only illuminates U.S. objectives in Iraq and the actual nature of the conflict between Baghdad and Washington, a conflict that culminated in the war of 2003, but also helps explain why the U.S. found Iraq in such ruin after its invasion, as well as the deep roots of Iraqi resistance to occupation. These years, in short, constitute one of the most shameful chapters in the history of U.S. intervention in the Middle East.

War By Other Means

Iraq agreed to a cease-fire with the US-led coalition on March 3, 1991 and formally accepted the terms for ending the Gulf War—UN Resolution 687—on April 6, 1991. America had won the war, and Iraq was severely weakened, yet Saddam Hussein had managed to survive. Washington's imperial strategists felt his survival was a long-term threat to U.S. control of the Gulf, and a blot on its "new world order." The day the Gulf War ended, Bush, Sr. wrote in his diary, "It hasn't been a clean end—there is no battleship Missouri surrender. That is what's missing to make this akin to WWII, to separate Kuwait from Korea and Vietnam... Saddam. He's got to go..."[1]

So the aims of the 1991 Persian Gulf War—crippling Iraq as a regional power, eliminating Saddam Hussein, shoring up U.S. regional control, and demonstrating U.S. military might—continued in the post-war years under Bush I and Clinton via sanctions, arms inspections, and military attacks.

Washington called its new Persian Gulf strategy "dual containment," and it was was built on what Scowcroft and others understood during the 1991 Gulf War: the absence of the Soviet Union changed what was possible. Rather than having to balance Iran and Iraq against each other as it had in decades past, the Soviet collapse meant that the U.S. could more directly intervene to weaken and control both. "The elimination of the Soviet Empire also eliminated a major strategic consideration from our calculus in the Gulf," explained Clinton National Security Council official Martin Indyk in 1993. "We no longer have to worry that our actions would generate Soviet actions in support of our adversaries in the region." The Iran-Iraq and Gulf wars had also created a "regional balance of power...at a much lower level of [Iranian and Iraqi] military capability," he argued, making it "easier to balance the power of both of them."[2]

As detailed in this chapter and the next, the UN resolutions that dictated the terms of the post-war "peace," the U.S. interpretation and implementation of those resolutions, and U.S. actions outside the UN framework were all shaped by and served this "dual containment" strategy.

These UN resolutions left vague exactly what constituted Iraqi compliance, and to ensure that they remained in force, the U.S. continually moved the "goalposts" for what constituted that compliance. If Iraq met some UN demands, others were added. When Security Council resolutions stood in the way of U.S. aims, they were reinterpreted, selectively enforced, or simply ignored. No matter what Iraq did, so long as Hussein remained in power, the U.S. kept the heat on—despite the fact that no UN resolution authorized regime change in Baghdad.

The goalposts were first shifted after the 1991 war. When it began, George Bush, Sr. promised that when Baghdad complied with UN resolutions, it would be able to rejoin "the family of nations." The UN resolutions Bush, Sr. referred to concerned Iraq's withdrawal from Kuwait. Yet following the war and Iraq's withdrawal, UN Resolution 687 imposed new conditions: Iraq was to be stripped of its nuclear, chemical and biological weapons and ballistic missiles with a range of more than 150 kilometers.[3] No prior UN resolutions mentioned Iraq's "weapons of mass destruction" (and Iraq had not used any during the war; the Scuds it fired at Israel and Saudi Arabia were armed with conventional warheads).

Resolution 687 affirmed "the sovereignty, territorial integrity and political independence of Kuwait and Iraq," but this was ignored in Iraq's case. Over the decade, the U.S. used punitive economic sanctions, a stringent disarmament program, and frequent military attacks to keep Iraq under a perpetual state of siege. It was prevented from rebuilding its economy or military, controlling its territory and airspace, or determining its economic and political destiny.

Iraq had little choice other than accept Resolution 687, but bridled under its punitive terms. The Hussein regime initially defied UN disarmament demands by attempting to hide and protect some advanced weapons and its military-scientific infrastructure, but soon mainly caved in. For five years, it wouldn't agree to an oil-for-food program that gave control of its economic lifeline—oil sales—to the U.S.-dominated UN. Over time, Iraq was forced to agree to and mainly go along with various UN stipulations, yet compliance brought it no relief.

Resolution 687 stated that upon "completion" of its disarmament obligations, sanctions "shall have no further force or effect." This did not happen. The U.S. repeatedly made clear that there would be no end to the crippling embargo as long as Hussein ruled. Shortly after the war, President Bush, Sr. declared, "My view is we don't want to lift these sanctions as long as Saddam Hussein is in power."[4] The Clinton administration continued this policy in violation of the terms of Resolution 687.

The U.S. also acted outside the UN framework. No UN resolution authorized the U.S. to overthrow the Hussein regime, but nonetheless, in 1991, the White House issued a "finding" ordering the CIA to begin covert operations "to create the conditions for the removal of Saddam Hussein from power." The next year the CIA organized and funded the Iraqi National Congress as a "democratic" alternative to the Hussein regime. (This is the same Iraqi National Congress, or INC, that has proffered much "false intelligence" on the Hussein regime's weapons capabilities and that the Pentagon is now trying to install as a dominant voice in Iraq's post-Saddam government.) These efforts were continued during the Clinton years and led to several unsuccessful coup attempts. Sanctions were also intended to weaken and undermine the Hussein regime, in hopes that life would become so unbearable that Iraqis (preferable elite military units) would overthrow the regime.[5]

In April 1991, the U.S. and Britain prohibited Iraq from flying aircraft in the northern part of the country (north of the 36th parallel), and in August 1992 created a similar "no fly" zone in southern Iraq (south of the 32nd parallel). The U.S. has claimed that its unilateral imposition of these no-fly zones was authorized under Security Council Resolution 688, passed in April 1991, which demands that Iraq end its repression of "all Iraqi citizens." In fact, the resolution authorizes no specific action against Iraq; nor did it make any such demands on the U.S.'s repressive and tyrannical allies in the region.

Over the decade, the U.S. maintained a large military presence around Iraq averaging over 20,000 troops, 200 planes, and 150 tanks, and frequently attacked it. Between 1991 and 2001, U.S. and British planes flew over 280,000 sorties against Iraq, routinely bombing military and civilian targets, killing hundreds of civilians.[6]

In sum, the clash between the U.S. and Iraq during the 1990s was not a clash between a rogue state and the "just demands of the international community." It was a confrontation between a global imperialist power seeking total control of the Persian Gulf, and a Third World Iraqi regime retreating, maneuvering, and resisting in order to preserve itself and some shred of Iraqi sovereignty.

"A Legitimized Act of Mass Slaughter"

During the 1990s, the UN embargo proved to be Washington's most deadly weapon against the Iraqi people. U.S. officials propagated three main myths about sanctions. First, their purpose was simply to compel Iraq to abide by UN resolutions and disarm. Second, they are aimed at Iraq's rulers, not its people. Third, they were continued because Iraq did not comply with UN resolutions. None were true.

The UN Security Council first imposed economic sanctions on Iraq on August 6, 1990, four days after its invasion of Kuwait. Resolution 661 embargoed all financial transactions and trade with Iraq, as well as "commercial, industrial or public utility undertaking" in Iraq.

Because Iraq's economy depended so heavily on foreign trade, investment and technology, the UN embargo had an immediate and crippling impact. Before the war, selling oil on the world market had accounted for 90 percent of Iraq's foreign exchange income. These oil revenues funded Iraq's industrial development and its military strength; supported extensive electrical, transportation, water, sewage, and medical systems; and fed its largely urban population. Iraq spent between $3 and $4 billion a year to import nearly three-quarters of its foods and medicines, and at the time was the region's largest market for U.S. food exports. During the 1980s, according to *Middle East Report,* Iraq had the "highest rate of food availability per capita in the region."[7]

All this was brought to a screeching halt by sanctions. Coalition bombs then amplified sanctions' devastating impact by savaging Iraq's bridges, roads, power systems, electrical grid, and industrial infrastructure. Sanctions in turn blocked their repair. Iraq was formally allowed to import food and other humanitarian goods. Yet this meant little. Iraq couldn't obtain loans or credit, and it didn't have the cash to buy them because oil sales were embargoed until 1996.

A horrifying spiral of disease and death quickly resulted. In March 1991, UN Under Secretary General Martti Ahtisaari reported:

> The recent conflict has wrought near-apocalyptic results upon the economic infrastructure of what had been, until January 1991, a rather highly urbanized and mechanized society. Now, most means of modern life support have been destroyed or rendered tenuous. Iraq has, for some time to come, been relegated to a pre-industrial age, but with all the disabilities of post-industrial dependency on an intensive use of energy and technology.[8]

The UN Security Council responded to Ahtisaari's report by continuing the most comprehensive economic sanctions in recent history. Originally enacted to force Iraq from Kuwait, they were then continued under Resolution 687, enacted in April 1991, to advance U.S. post-war aims.

One *New York Times* editorial, written in the summer of 1991 following numerous reports of the enormous suffering being inflicting on ordinary Iraqis, captured the U.S. political elite's ruthless consensus on Iraq: "To accept human suffering as a diplomatic lever is tormenting—but preferable to leaving the Persian Gulf allies with no credible way to compel Iraqi compliance but resuming military attacks...this is the wrong time to relax the embargo."[9]

Sanctions gave the U.S.-dominated UN control of virtually all of Iraq's imports and exports. Over the next decade, Washington would use them to prevent Iraq from rebuilding its civilian, industrial, and military infrastructures so it could not reemerge as a regional power. The embargo was also intended to make life so miserable that Iraq's elite would be prompted to remove Hussein from power. Robert Gates, Bush, Sr.'s Deputy National Security Advisor, said as much in 1991: "Iraqis will be made to pay the price while Saddam Hussein is in power. Any easing of sanctions will be considered only when there is a new government."[10] This orientation bluntly underscored that Washington would fight to maintain sanctions whether Baghdad fulfilled its UN obligations or not.

This post-war U.S. agenda has meant devastation and death for Iraq's people, especially the young, the sick, and the elderly. This enormous human catastrophe has been documented by an ever-growing literature from the UN, non-governmental organizations (NGOs), academics, medical professionals, religious organizations, and many eyewitnesses. After an extensive analysis, Fairfield University Professor Joy Gordon concluded that U.S. policymakers had turned UN sanctions into "a legitimized act of mass slaughter."[11]

Biological Warfare—American Style

The destruction of Iraq's water system may be the single most criminal act committed by the U.S. in Iraq. The evidence is overwhelming that culpability for this crime lies squarely at Washington's feet, not at Saddam Hussein's.

Before the 1991 Gulf War, 96 percent of Iraqis had access to abundant supplies of safe drinking water, thanks to a national network of electrically powered pumping stations and treatment plants.[12] Three years later less than half had such access.

The U.S. had bombed Iraq's electrical grid, power stations, and dams—and Iraq's water and sewage systems nearly ground to a halt. Shortly after the war, a UN team reported, "In Baghdad untreated sewage has now to be dumped directly into the river—which is the source of the water supply...and all drinking-water plants there and throughout the rest of the country are using river water with high sewage contamination..." Sanctions were then used to prevent their repair.[13]

During my trip in the summer of 1991, I saw people in Kurdistan and in southern Iraq collecting water from polluted rivers. Sewage plants had either been destroyed, or lacked the spare parts or power to function. Urban families showed me how they had to scrounge for water. In one Basra neighborhood everyone collected water from one tap, located at the lowest point in the area. In a middle class neighborhood in Baghdad, people collected water a bit at a time in pots and pans. In the hospitals I visited, children were dying from the diseases of contaminated water: cholera, typhoid, and diarrhea. Doctors told me that diarrhea alone was four times as prevalent as it had been the year before.

At the Children's Welfare Hospital in Baghdad, I met Satenya Naser, as she was trying to comfort her emaciated, one-and-a-half-year-old son Hamid, who cried at the slightest touch. She'd only been able to feed Hamid rice water since January. "Milk isn't available," she explained, "but even if it is available it is too expensive for me." After four months of diarrhea, Hamid was down to 15 pounds—he'd lost half his body weight and, it seemed, looked half his age. His blotchy skin and distended belly were characteristic of kwashiorkor—severe protein deficiency. Hamid was so weak he couldn't even lift his bony arm.

For several weeks, I wandered through hospitals in Baghdad, Basra, and Amarah shooting video footage and talking to people. In ward after hospital ward I saw hopelessly frail children slowly wasting away, dying the agonizing deaths induced by not enough food, clean water, or medicine, their mothers sitting helplessly beside them, their doctors denied the means to treat them.

I was on a shoestring budget, without government minders, but with lots of help from Iraqis I met along the way. Evidence of the lethal impact of war and sanctions wasn't hard to find, but I never ran across anyone from the mainstream U.S. media even trying to report this atrocity. This willed-ignorance would not change significantly over the next 12 years. The post-war U.S. war on Iraq has been under-reported, misreported, and hidden from most Americans. Even in the fall of 2002, when the press descended on Baghdad after UN weapons inspectors returned, few bothered to visit hospitals or cover the deadly impact UN sanctions have had on the Iraqi people.

Horrifically, the situation did not change significantly over the next 12 years. Gordon writes, "By 1996 all sewage plants had broken down," and "UNICEF reported that up to 40 percent of the purified water run through pipes is contaminated or lost through leakage."[14]

In April 2002, A.C. Maturin, reporting for Quakers in Aotearoa/New Zealand, found that electrical power is still intermittent, causing leaks in water mains and preventing waste treatment facilities from running continuously, and was told by UNICEF that the water in the southern city of Basra is sometimes 40 percent sewage.[15]

Iraqis pointed out to me that destroying a country's water system is a form of germ warfare and a violation of the Geneva Convention's prohibitions against attacks on civilian populations. What's most chilling is that the U.S. government planners did so deliberately, knowing the likely consequences.

Many years after the war, Associate Professor Thomas Nagy of George Washington University discovered a number of declassified or partially declassified Pentagon studies concerning Iraq's water system. (One, from January 22, 1991 was labeled "Iraq Water Treatment Vulnerabilities.") These documents revealed that U.S. military and intelligence agencies carefully studied Iraq's water system, assessed its potential weaknesses, predicted the catastrophic health impacts of disrupting it, and studied the means to prevent its reconstruction. The U.S. then went ahead and bombed Iraq's electrical system, virtually shutting down its water and sewage treatment systems, while maintaining the sanctions that prevented its rehabilitation. The documents further show that government analysts tracked the resulting spread of disease. According to Nagy, they even set forth "a timetable for the destruction of Iraq's water supplies." Nagy concluded that the U.S. "*intentionally* used sanctions against Iraq to degrade the country's water supply after the Gulf War." (emphasis added)[16]

Washington's intentions with regard to Iraq's water supply are not in doubt. One Pentagon planner bluntly spelled out U.S. strategy shortly after the 1991 Gulf War: "People say, 'You didn't recognize that it was going to have an effect on water or sewage.' Well, what were we trying to do with sanctions—help out the Iraqi people? No. What we were doing with the attacks on infrastructure was to accelerate the effect of the sanctions." Defense Secretary Cheney said every target the U.S. attacked was "perfectly legitimate," and added, "If I had to do it over again, I would do exactly the same thing."[17]

Clinton and Bush administration officials have argued that sanctions permitted humanitarian goods. However, behind this facade of benevolence, the U.S. continued to pursue its "water denial" strategy in the years following Desert Storm, and ignored one report after another detailing its catastrophic impact, especially on children. Gordon reports that since August 1991, the U.S. "has blocked most purchases of materials necessary for Iraq to generate electricity," without which no modern water system can function. Iraq was allowed to buy a sewage-treatment plant, but not the generator needed to run it, even though it was dumping 300,000 tons of raw sewage into its waterways every day. The U.S. also prevented Iraq from importing water pipes, the earth-moving equipment needed to install them, and chemicals for water treatment.[18]

Given all this, it is hardly surprising that in August 2003 U.S. occupation authorities would estimate that restoring Iraq's electrical grid and meeting current demand would cost $2 billion, and rebuilding Iraq's water system and delivering clean water to the whole country would take another $16 billion.[19] Yet Washington's responsibility for the devastation and suffering that U.S. and British forces found when they took control of Iraq in 2003 is rarely—if ever—mentioned in the mainstream press, which is only too happy to repeat Bush II and company's charges that it's all Saddam's fault.

Twisting the Knife of Dependence

War and sanctions have wreaked havoc with Iraq's import-dependent economy. Relief officials told me in 1991 that 70 to 80 percent of the industrial workforce was unemployed. Eight years later, little had changed. UNICEF reported in 1999 that, "Economic development has come to a virtual halt and the physical and human capital stock of the country have witnessed serious deterioration." Meat and grain production had fallen. Much of Iraq's oil industry was either destroyed or in disrepair. Unemployment stood at 50 percent, and annual per capita income had fallen from $3,500 in 1989 to less than $500, making oil-rich Iraq one of the world's poorest countries.[20]

Before the 1991 Gulf War, Iraq was one of the region's most literate societies, with an extensive educational system. That too was devastated by the war and sanctions. Iraqi teachers, once well-paid professionals, were earning on average $3 a month in 1999, and their schools were falling apart. Classrooms were overcrowded, most lacked rudimentary heating and cooling, and one principal estimated that seven or eight students fainted every day from hunger. As a result, by the time of the 2003 war, 65 percent of Iraq's secondary-school students had dropped out and nearly half of all Iraqi girls over 15 had no schooling at all.[21]

In January 2001, the *San Francisco Chronicle* reported that the "income of shoeshine boys and cigarette salesmen routinely exceeds that of doctors and teachers. The Iraqi middle class has virtually disappeared."[22]

Economic collapse has had a particularly harsh impact on Iraqi women, who once enjoyed greater legal and social equality than women in any other Arab country. Middle class jobs previously open to women disappeared, along with various state programs to support them, such as childcare. Many Iraqi men can no longer support a family, so are not marrying.

Hunger in the Fertile Crescent

Iraq is not without arable land. Driving south from Baghdad one travels through rich, flat plains of green and yellow, watered by the Tigris and Euphrates rivers. Forests of date palms line the Shaat al-Arab further south in Basra. In Iraqi Kurdestan to the north and east, the flat plains of central Iraq give way to rolling, fertile hills and then mountains. There is ample rainfall, and much of Iraq's grains are now grown here.

The stage was set for disaster during the 1980s, when U.S. agricultural aid and imports—by the end of the decade, the U.S. was selling 20 percent of its rice crop to Iraq—encouraged the Iraqi government to move from collective to private farming, and shift agricultural production from staples to more profitable crops for export. This, coupled with continued migration off the land and into the cities, gravely weakened Iraqi agriculture and made the country more dependent on imported food—and thus much more vulnerable to the UN embargo.[23]

War and its aftermath then devastated Iraqi agriculture. In 1991 I visited the village of Al Quds—Jerusalem—outside of Amarah in southeastern Iraq. There, as in other villages, crops had been ruined by the lack of water, electricity, fertilizer and pesticides, reducing their harvest to a third of the previous year's. The village water pump had been idle for months while the electricity was out and then broke down. Thanks to sanctions, replacement parts were unavailable. At the time, the UN estimated that half of Iraq's farm equipment was idle because they lacked spare parts. A few months later, the Harvard Study Team reported that the 1990-91 harvest was 80 percent smaller than 1989's.[24]

Reports from the late 1990s paint a similar picture. "Major constraints on agricultural production include the lack of functioning agricultural machinery, particularly of essential replacement and spare parts," writes Dr. Peter L. Pellett, a professor in the Department of Nutrition at the University of Massachusetts at Amherst who served on three UN Food and Agriculture Organization missions to Iraq, "as well as high-quality seeds, fertilizers, pesticides, and herbicides, all of which have resulted in declines in output." Other observers reported that Iraq's veterinary diagnostic and control infrastructure had collapsed, and disease had devastated much livestock.[25]

Economic collapse and shortages caused food prices to skyrocket. When I met Satenya, she lived with her husband and nine children in a two-room house on the outskirts of Baghdad. Her husband, an unskilled laborer, was making 120 dinars a month. A tin of powdered milk cost 35 dinars—over $100 at the official exchange rate. "How can I buy milk for my children?" she asked me.

The devastating impact of contaminated water, economic collapse, and food shortages was starkest in Iraq's hospitals. I saw hundreds of sick and malnourished children who were trapped in a vicious cycle: food shortages made them susceptible to disease, while diarrhea from contaminated water made it impossible to absorb the food they did consume.

Dr. Ayman al Beiruti, a pediatrician at Saddam General Hospital in Amarah, explained: "An undernourished baby is an immune compromised baby. That's why typhoid fever hits babies hard, as well as intestinal bleeding, convulsions and gastro-intestinal disease. The situation in the pediatric age group is horrible, especially if I remind you that we have no drugs to treat them." Dr. Beiruti told me that before the 1991 war he had only seen cases of malnutrition in textbooks.

After the war, Iraq's government began rationing food. This prevented mass famine, but not malnutrition. In 1999, UNICEF found that 23 percent of all Iraqi infants were born underweight and that among children under five years of age, one in four—over one million children—suffered from chronic malnutrition.[26]

In 2000, the head of the UN "oil-for-food" program told the *New York Times*, "People have become so poor in some cases that they can't even afford to eat the food that they are given free, because for many of them the food ration represents the major part of their income." In other words, many were forced to sell rationed food to pay for other necessities.[27]

Blaming the Victims

The enormous toll of UN sanctions has received scant attention in the mainstream media, but has generated torrents of protest and outrage around the world. U.S. officials have reacted to this growing outcry, not by altering their policies or objectives in Iraq, nor by taking responsibility for the suffering their actions have caused, but by trying to shift the blame onto Saddam Hussein, claiming that he misused resources destined for Iraq's civilian population. This was no more truthful than their now-discredited "weapons of mass destruction" charges against the former Ba'ath government.

Washington claims that the UN's oil-for-food program, which Iraq accepted in 1996, allows it to sell enough oil to meet Iraq's humanitarian needs. Any shortfall is Hussein's fault. "He has more money today than he did before the embargo," former President Clinton argued in 2000, "and if they're hungry or they are not getting medicine, it is his own fault."[28] President Bush made similar charges at the UN in September 2002: "Saddam Hussein has subverted this program, working around the sanctions to buy missile technology and military materials. He blames the suffering of Iraq's people on the United Nations, even as he uses his oil wealth to build lavish palaces for himself, and arms his country. By refusing to comply with his own agreements, he bears full guilt for the hunger and misery of innocent Iraqi citizens."[29]

These arguments are disingenuous, distorted and untrue. In March 2000, the UN finally lifted restrictions on the amount of oil Iraq could sell. However, since Iraq's oil industry remained in a state of disrepair, it could not significantly raise oil production. Before the 1991 war, Iraq could produce 3.8 million barrels of crude a day (mbd), but production capacity fell significantly afterward. Even as late as 2003, production capacity was still at only 2.8 mbd according to a former Iraqi Oil Minister. Daily production completely collapsed after the 1991 war, and only modestly recovered once the oil-for-food program was established in 1996. Production in late 2002/early 2003 was only about 1.7 mbd, and peaked at around 2.1 mbd under the oil-for-food program.[30]

This was no accident. The U.S. has consistently blocked imports and opposed foreign investments that could repair Iraq's petroleum sector. In April 1999, Peter Burleigh, Deputy U.S. Ambassador to the UN, rejected a proposal to allow direct foreign investment in Iraq's oil sector, designed to enable Iraq to bring its oil revenues closer to the allowed ceiling of $5.26 billion every 180 days, even though Iraq had not come close to approaching the ceiling since it was established in 1998.[31]

Hans von Sponeck, who was the UN's Humanitarian Coordinator supervising Iraq's oil-for-food program from October 1998 until March 2000, called raising Iraq's oil ceiling a "political ploy." "They are not allowing the rehabilitation of the Iraqi oil industry," he told me, "and therefore Iraq cannot extract the oil as it wishes."[32]

Adding insult to injury, Iraq only received a fraction of its oil revenues. Under the UN program, 30 percent of Iraqi oil sales went to war reparations; five to ten percent to UN operations in Iraq, and 13 percent for humanitarian supplies for Iraq's 3 million Kurds (giving them, on a per capita basis, 50 percent more aid than other Iraqis). That left barely half for Iraq's humanitarian and rebuilding needs.[33]

Since the oil-for-food program began, "Iraq has earned approximately $57 billion in oil revenues, of which it has spent about $23 billion on goods that actually arrived," Gordon concludes. "This comes to about $170 per year per person, which is less than one half the annual per capita income of Haiti, the poorest country in the Western Hemisphere."[34]

As of April 2002, Iraq had paid more—$38 billion—in war reparations than it had actually received in humanitarian relief. This was mainly paid to Kuwait, which was awarded $15.9 billion in September 2000 for compensation for lost oil production and damage to oil reserves and equipment. However, U.S. oil and service companies have also been awarded hundreds of millions for the disruption of their operations in Kuwait during the 1991 Persian Gulf War, including Halliburton, then being run by current Vice President Dick Cheney.[35]

The U.S. charged that Hussein and top officials were hoarding aid, or squandering it on luxuries and palaces. As Von Sponeck and others have pointed out, the problem was not that Hussein and his cronies were living in splendor, the problem was that even under the oil-for-food program, not enough money was coming in to support the population. Even if every single dime earned through permitted oil sales went straight to Iraq's civilians, each one would only have received around $170 a year—roughly 50 cents a day—hardly enough to sustain life.[36]

Von Sponeck and Denis Halliday, his predecessor as UN Humanitarian Coordinator in Iraq, both resigned to protest sanctions and the inadequacy of the oil-for-food program. Von Sponeck scoffed at U.S. charges that humanitarian aid is being diverted by Iraqi authorities. The U.N. humanitarian mission had "roughly 670 international staff and over 1,000 Iraqis who were helping us," he told me. "Out of this international staff, there are about 300 that have no other job but to ply the roads of Iraq...to insure that the items that arrive actually went where they were supposed to go." These inspectors found that humanitarian shipments were indeed arriving at their intended destinations and being used for their intended purposes.[37]

In 2003, the top UN World Food Program official in Iraq called Baghdad's distribution system "the most efficient in the world." The

Washington Post reported, "Torben Due, the senior U.N. World Food Program official here, said his organization, which has conducted more than 1 million inspections of the system since the oil-for-food arrangement was enacted, has uncovered no significant evidence of fraud or favoritism. 'I don't think anybody could do something that is better in terms of accuracy and timely food distribution to the entire population,' he said. 'It's very impressive.'"[38]

Holding and Blocking Reconstruction

Perhaps the most insidious tactic the U.S. employed to cripple Iraq was blocking desperately needed imports under the rubric of disarmament. Former President Clinton claimed that Iraq had "the absolute freedom to spend it [oil revenues] on food and medicine and development," but this was blatantly false.[39]

Under the oil-for-food program, the UN's "661 committee" (after the UN resolution authorizing sanctions) reviewed all proposed contracts for Iraq's imports and determined whether or not they would be allowed to proceed. Any of the 15 countries on the Security Council could veto any proposed contract before the 661 committee without explanation or appeal. It met behind closed doors and its records were off limits to the public.[40]

As of Spring 2002, this committee had placed "holds" on over 1,500 contracts worth between $3 and $5 billion. Over 90 percent of these holds had been placed by the U.S. or Great Britain.[41] The public rationalization was preventing Iraq from acquiring chemical, biological, or nuclear weapons. In reality, Washington was using the process to limit Iraq's ability to rebuild at all, including its civilian infrastructure.

The U.S. often claimed it was blocking "dual use" items—civilian goods with potential military applications. Yet this category was so broad that it could apply to nearly anything an industrial society needs to function. In early 2000, holds had been placed on 90 percent of all telecommunications contracts and many contracts for rebuilding Iraq's petroleum industry. A 2001 UNICEF study found that $500 million in water and sanitation supply contracts were being blocked.[42] In October 2000, 34 percent of the applications to rebuild Iraq's electricity grid were still pending before the sanctions committee.[43]

Truck tires, hospital ventilators, and vaccines have all been blocked at one time or another. So have refrigeration, firefighting and yogurt production equipment. In 1999, a former head of the World Health Organization's cancer program reported that "requested radiotherapy equipment, chemotherapy drugs and analgesics are consistently blocked by the United States and British advisers (to the UN Sanctions Committee)."[44]

In July 2002, when UN weapons experts reviewed many of the items placed on hold by the U.S., they found few which could have any prohibited military use. Gordon reports that in 2001, while suffering from a severe drought, Iraq had contracted for the delivery of water tankers, and UN arms experts did not raise any objections. Yet on the grounds that they might supposedly be used to haul chemical weapons, the U.S. blocked delivery.[45]

In December 2001, the United Nations Office of the Iraq Programme noted:

> The total value of contracts placed on hold by the 661 Committee continued to rise... The 'holds' covered 1,610 contracts for the purchase of various humanitarian supplies and equipment, including 1,072 contracts worth $3.85 billion, for humanitarian supplies and 538 contracts, worth $527 million, for oil industry equipment. During the week, the Committee released from hold 14 contracts, worth $19.8 million. However, it placed on hold 57 new contracts, worth $140.6 million.

In 1999, the Programme's director pointed out, "The absence of a single spare part or item of equipment, as small as it may be, could be sufficient to prevent the completion of an entire water infection project or well completion programme."[46]

Gordon's study of the 661 Committee's records demonstrated that contrary to claims that the U.S. was not targeting Iraqi civilians, "the United States has fought aggressively throughout the last decade to purposefully minimize the humanitarian goods that enter the country.... It has sometimes given a reason for its refusal to approve humanitarian goods, sometimes given no reason at all, and sometimes changed its reason three or four times, in each instance causing a delay of months." U.S. policy, she concluded, has "consistently opposed any form of economic development within Iraq."[47]

When Iraq tried to evade this strangulation by negotiating its own oil and business deals, the U.S. denounced it as "smuggling" and attempted to tighten UN control over the sale, distribution and even pricing of Iraq's oil. In 2002, the U.S. and Britain imposed "retroactive pricing" on Iraqi oil sales—forcing Iraq to sell its oil below the prices it had proposed in order to prevent it from directly earning income through surcharges. "Some $30-50 million in kickbacks were indeed prevented, by UN estimates," according to *Middle East Report*, "but at a cost of $2-3 billion to the humanitarian program...the Iraqi people were made to pay sixty dollars' worth of humanitarian supplies for every dollar that the Iraqi leadership was denied."[48]

"A Rope Around the Neck of Average Iraqis"

The U.S. also tried to deflect the growing condemnation of sanctions through its proposed "smart sanctions" program, which was adopted by the UN Security Council on May 14, 2002. Smart sanctions were advertised as a humanitarian refinement of sanctions: consumer goods would be let through; military-related goods would not. In reality, it was more of the same. Under "smart sanctions," the 661 Committee no longer had veto power over Iraqi imports, but the program would still be based on an extensive list of prohibited imports. This essentially codified what the U.S. had already been doing—blocking many items needed to rebuild Iraq's infrastructure by labeling them "dual use."[49]

The first list of items banned under smart sanctions was drawn up by the U.S. and then approved by the Security Council on December 31, 2002—while the U.S. was building its military forces in the region in preparation for war. The list of prohibited imports included antibiotics such as ciprofloxacin, gentamicin (used to treat urinary tract infections), doxycycline (used to treat cholera and diarrhea), and streptomycin—supposedly because they could be given to Iraqi troops—as well as organophosphate pesticides, activated charcoal, large hydraulic lifts, meteorological equipment, satellite dishes, full-motion flight simulators, and speedboats.[50]

Von Sponeck and Halliday called smart sanctions a "tightening of the rope around the neck of the average Iraqi citizen."[51] In 2001, the *Wall Street Journal* acknowledged that the main purpose of the new sanctions regime was to "deprive Iraq of the propaganda advantage of being the victim of cruel western sanctions."[52] One Iraqi told the *Washington Post* he was afraid that the large tires he sells at a Baghdad bazaar might be restricted under smart sanctions. "This is oppression. They're trying to affect my living. They're trying to destroy the whole economy."[53]

A 9/11 Catastrophe and More—Every 30 Days

No one knows precisely how many Iraqis died or were permanently injured as a result of the 1991 Gulf War and 12 years of sanctions. In 2002, the Iraqi government stated that 1.7 million children had died from disease or malnutrition since the imposition of sanctions in August 1990.[54]

A 1999 survey by UNICEF and Iraq's Ministry of Health found that the rate of infant mortality among children under five living in south and central Iraq (where 85 percent of the population lives) had risen from 56 per 1,000 live births in 1984-1989, to 131 between 1994-1999—and was continuing to rise over time. Thus, Iraqi children under five were dying at over twice the rate they were before the 1991 Gulf War. The survey reported:

> ...if the substantial reduction in the under-five mortality rate during the 1980s had continued through the 1990s, there would have been half a million fewer deaths of children under-five in the country as a whole during the 8-year period 1991 to 1998.[55]

So roughly 5,000 Iraqi children under five were dying each month thanks to U.S. actions. That's more than a World Trade Center catastrophe every 30 days. The editors of the *New York Times* felt this news was only "fit to print" in a fairly small article at the bottom of page six, which never mentioned UNICEF's estimate of the staggering death toll—500,000 or more.[56]

In February 1999, Halliday, the UN Humanitarian Coordinator in Iraq August 1997 until September 1998, described his experience to me: "You do not find bodies all over the streets. You do not find gross malnutrition that you see in photographs we've all seen in Somalia, and so on. But you hear unending stories of families who have sat there and watched a child die. Or families—daughters and sons—who've seen their parents die for lack of relatively simple surgery which would have been very easy many years ago.... And every day people are dying all over the country, in isolation.... A baby here, a baby there, a child here...it pervades the whole country and the attitude and the feeling of the Iraqi people."

Halliday called sanctions "a deliberate, active program—it's not just negligence, it's active—it's a deliberate decision to sustain a program that they know is killing and targeting children and people. Then it's a program of some sort, and I think it's a program of genocide. I just don't have a better word."[57]

Despite scant coverage in the mainstream media of the sanctions issue—they focused instead on the hunt for Iraq's phantom weapons of mass destruction, while ignoring the real destruction visited on Iraq's people and society—policy makers were made well aware of the sanctions' impact in a 1999 analysis published in *Foreign Affairs*. In "Sanctions of Mass Destruction," John and Carl Mueller concluded that all economic sanctions imposed after 1990, the most significant case being Iraq, "may have contributed to more deaths during the post-Cold War era than all weapons of mass destruction throughout history."[58]

What was the United States trying to accomplish through this policy of slaughter by sanction? It aimed to cripple Hussein's Iraq by preventing it from rebuilding its industry, economy, and military, while blocking other global rivals from making strategic inroads in Iraq (explored further in chapters 8 and 10). And it hoped to make life so miserable for the population that Iraqis would rise up (preferably via a military coup) and topple the Hussein regime—shoring up U.S. regional control and demonstrating its power in the process.

In 1996, then-Secretary of State Madeline Albright made it clear that U.S. officials were well aware of the cost, in Iraqi lives and treasure, of pursuing these objectives. She made clear that they had few qualms about doing so in the face of such a staggering human toll. During a CBS 60 *Minutes* interview, host Leslie Stahl asked her about the impact of sanctions: "We have heard that half a million Iraqi children have died. I mean, that's more children than died in Hiroshima. And—and you know, is the price worth it?"

Albright's answer: "I think this is a very hard choice, but the price—we think the price is worth it."[59]

CHAPTER 7

THE GREAT WMD FLIM FLAM

So, what ever became of Iraq's weapons of mass destruction?—the "25,000 liters of anthrax," the "38,000 liters of botulinum toxin," the "29,984 chemical munitions," the "500 tons of sarin, mustard and VX nerve agent," or the "advanced nuclear weapons development program," that George W. Bush claimed Iraq was hiding or had not accounted for—weapons that could "kill several million people," or "subject millions of people to death by respiratory failure"?[1]

During the 12 years after "Operation Desert Storm," Iraq's supposed non-compliance with UN weapons inspections and its alleged pursuit of "weapons of mass destruction" were the primary rationalization for 12 murderous years of U.S.-imposed economic sanctions and near war with Iraq. In 2002-2003, these charges morphed into the Bush II administration's primary justification for preventive war.

Yet in 2003, after the U.S. invaded and then scoured Iraq for banned weapons, lo and behold, none had been found at this writing five months later, and none will likely ever be found. In other words, U.S. charges against Iraq were a deliberate fraud—a concoction of partial-truths, distortions, and bald-faced lies. Welcome to the great WMD flim flam.

Unraveling this decade plus of deception is key to understanding the vast scope of the deceit perpetrated by Washington, what the United States government, under Bush I, Clinton, and Bush II, has really been up to in the Persian Gulf, and why it went to war in 2003.

Arming Friends, Disarming Enemies

Many people may feel that it's eminently reasonable to disarm a tyrant who had recently invaded a neighbor, used chemical weapons against his own people, and was trying to build nuclear weapons. The problem, however, was that the UN inspection and disarmament program instituted against Iraq in the spring of 1991 was not established in a political vacuum. Rather, it was a continuation of the politics that shaped the U.S. war on Iraq in 1991. As such, it was not a step toward creating a world free from the horrors of weapons of mass destruction, but an effort to strengthen the power of the country with the world's largest stockpile of weapons of mass destruction by far and the only country to have ever used nuclear weapons—the United States of America.

It was a program based on the imperial presumption that the U.S. and other big powers have the right to determine who can have arms, and who can't—driven not by the goal of eliminating oppression, injustice and war, but by their own global agendas, agendas which are routinely hidden from view. Specifically, it was an effort to weaken a regime not firmly under U.S. control, and to ensure that America and its allies, Israel in particular, retained total military domination in the region. As Indyk put it, the U.S. wanted an Iraq with a "much lower level of military capability."[2]

This military dominance serves American imperialist dominance of the Middle East, not justice or liberation. Bush II officials, including Colin Powell and Condoleezza Rice, argued that the confrontation between Washington and Baghdad stemmed from Hussein's refusal to make the "strategic decision" to forego chemical, biological and nuclear weapons. However, successive administrations made it clear over 12 years that they would never accept Hussein's rule even if he abandoned all his weapons programs; the U.S. wanted him gone to both tighten their grip on the Persian Gulf and to teach others in the region and the world about the costs and consequences of defying the United States.

Arms inspections would become a prime tool for maintaining sanctions, for spying on and bludgeoning Iraq, and for illegal attempts to remove Hussein from power, even though it is now apparent that Baghdad largely, perhaps overwhelmingly, complied with UN disarmament demands, probably beginning shortly after the 1991 Persian Gulf War.

Resolution 687 of April 3, 1991 placed the disarmament of Iraq in the context of establishing a "nuclear-weapons-free zone in the region" and ridding the Middle East of all weapons of mass destruction. Yet neither the U.S. nor the UN ever intended to rid the region—or the world—of horrific nuclear, chemical and biological weapons. No effort was made to strip Israel of its 200 to 400 nuclear weapons, or the chemical and biological weapons that may well be in its arsenal.

The U.S. continued to flood the region with billions in advanced weapons intended to strengthen clients like Israel, Turkey, Saudi Arabia, and Egypt. Between 1990 and 1997, the U.S. transferred some $42 billion in weapons to its Persian Gulf allies—Saudi Arabia, Kuwait, Bahrain, U.A.E., and Oman alone.[3]

Meanwhile, the U.S. itself has amassed an enormous stockpile of weapons of mass destruction, while simultaneously weakening global arms control treaties. In 1998, the New York Times reported that UN resolutions regarding Iraq have "the toughest inspection language in modern times...much tougher than the Chemical Weapons Convention, which allows countries to protest proposed surprise inspections at sites that aren't on a list prepared by the host country." It also noted that, "In the U.S., Republicans have insisted on a greater measure of secrecy for American installations. Both the Senate and House passed treaty legislation that gives the president the right to deny inspections that 'may pose a threat to the national security interests of the United States.'"[4] The far weaker Iraq would be allowed no such right, even though Hussein's oppressive regime posed far less a threat to far fewer countries than does the U.S.

Defiance and Compliance

UN Security Council Resolution 687 demanded that Iraq destroy its chemical, biological and nuclear weapons, any ballistic missiles with a range greater than 150 kilometers, as well as related "research, development, support and manufacturing facilities;" provide the UN with a complete list of these weapons and programs within 15 days; and foreswear any future development of such weapons.

Iraq did not immediately comply. In the months following the Gulf War, Iraq frustrated the efforts of weapons inspectors from the United Nations Special Commission (UNSCOM) to find, catalogue and destroy Iraq's ballistic missiles and chemical, biological and

nuclear weapons and the technological infrastructure that supported them.

The Ba'ath regime had considered such weapons crucial to its
survival and power. Chemical weapons had helped the regime suppress the Kurds and stalemate Iran in their 1980-1988 war.
Unconventional weapons and missiles were seen as "force multipli-
ers" and a deterrent against more powerful adversaries such as the
U.S. and Israel, as well as regional rivals like Iran. Hussein may have
felt his chemical weapons deterred a U.S. march on Baghdad in
1991,[5] and they increased Iraq's political weight in the Gulf and the
Arab world.

Scott Ritter was a Marine intelligence officer during the 1991
Persian Gulf War, then a chief UN weapons inspector from 1991
until 1998, and finally a critic of U.S. Iraq policy following his 1998
resignation from UNSCOM. Ritter called Iraq's surface-to-surface
missiles "a strategic resource that represented not only a valuable
military asset for Iraq, but also a tremendous source of national pride
and prestige."[6]

UNSCOM would eventually reveal that before the 1991 Gulf
War, Iraq had been working on chemical, biological and nuclear
weapons on a greater and more advanced scale than previously realized, and had produced VX nerve agent and other biological
weapons.[7]

Especially immediately after the Gulf War, the Ba'ath regime
attempted to preserve at least the technical infrastructure for reconstituting its weapons programs, if not the weapons themselves,
through an elaborate and well-organized concealment system.
Critical materials and documents were hidden or moved from place
to place. Inspectors were denied access to key sites. Records turned
over to UN inspectors were inaccurate or incomplete.

However, Iraq soon began caving in to the pressure of inspections, military assaults, and ongoing economic sanctions. By the
summer of 1991, Iraq had admitted it had had a nuclear weapons
program.[8] Within six months of the end of the Gulf War, Iraqi
weapons programs were being discovered and destroyed. In
November 1993, Iraq formally accepted UN resolution 715, enacted by the Security Council two years earlier, which created a permanent arms monitoring system in Iraq.

Inspections plus some high-level defections led to new revelations concerning the scope of Iraq's military programs. The most significant was the August 1995 defection of General Hussein Kamel Majid, Saddam Hussein's son-in-law and head of Iraq's unconventional weapons programs for 10 years. Gen. Kamel's defection compelled Baghdad to disclose more and more about its pre-1991 efforts to develop unconventional weapons efforts in a futile effort to have sanctions lifted.

U.S. officials caricature Iraq's attitude toward UNSCOM as "cheat and retreat," and claim that inspections failed to disarm Iraq. This was yet another deception. In reality, Iraq complied with UN weapons inspectors far more than it defied them, and the inspections did succeed in largely disarming Iraq, something the Bush II regime knew full well before its 2003 war on Iraq.

From 1991 to 1998, UNSCOM sent 500 teams to Iraq staffed by nearly 3,500 inspectors. These teams examined some 3,400 sites, including 900 formerly secret military installations, and destroyed billions of dollars worth of weapons and equipment.[9] UNSCOM had regular access to Iraqi factories and laboratories, used video cameras to monitor Iraqi industrial and military sites 24 hours a day, placed chemical sampling devices around Iraqi labs, monitored the movement of Iraq's industrial equipment, pored over Iraqi documents, and questioned many Iraqi scientists and technicians.

In February 1998, former weapons inspector Raymond Zilinskas stated that "95 percent of [UNSCOM's] work proceeds unhindered."[10] Writing in Foreign Affairs in 1999, University of Vermont Professor F. Gregory Gause III summed up UNSCOM's impact:

> President Clinton has famously and correctly said that UNSCOM destroyed more Iraqi WMD resources than did the Gulf War air campaigns. Since 1991, UNSCOM has demolished 48 Scud missiles, 30 chemical and biological missile warheads, 60 missile launch pads, nearly 40,000 chemical bombs and shells in various stages of production, 690 tons of chemical weapons agent, 3 million tons of chemical weapons precursor materials, and the entire al-Hakum biological weapons production facility.[11]

Ritter argues that inspectors destroyed Iraq's biological arsenal:

> Under the most stringent on-site inspection regime in the history of arms control, Iraq's biological weapons programs were

dismantled, destroyed or rendered harmless during the course of hundreds of no-notice inspections. The major biological weapons production facility—al Hakum, which was responsible for producing Iraq's anthrax—was blown up by high explosive charges and all its equipment destroyed. Other biological facilities met the same fate if it was found that they had, at any time, been used for research and development of biological weapons.... While it was impossible to verify that all of Iraq's biological capability had been destroyed, the UN never once found evidence that Iraq had either retained biological weapons or associated production equipment, or was continuing work in the field.[12]

In October 1998 the International Atomic Energy Agency certified that Iraq had provided it with a "full, final, and complete" account of its nuclear weapons programs, and that the agency had found no evidence of any prohibited nuclear activities since October 1997.[13] A year later the UN Security Council's disarmament panel concluded, "Although important elements still have to be resolved, the bulk of Iraq's proscribed weapons programmes has been eliminated."[14] In 2001, President Clinton's Defense Secretary William Cohen told the incoming Bush administration that "Iraq no longer poses a military threat to its neighbors."[15]

In fact, Iraq may have destroyed all its unconventional weapons shortly after the 1991 Gulf War. After defecting in 1995, Gen. Kamel told his UN and CIA interrogators that, "Iraq destroyed all its chemical and biological weapons stocks and the missiles to deliver them" after the war in order to hide the programs from weapons inspectors. All that was left, he said, were the records of design and engineering details as well as procurement information so that Iraq could some day reconstitute its arsenal. After the 2003 war, other top Iraqi scientists and military personnel painted a similar picture—that Iraq had been hiding records and blueprints (by 1998 Iraq had fine tuned its concealment mechanism and was able to destroy evidence on only 15 minutes notice, and routinely moved sensitive materials and documents around every 30-90 days)—but not weapons.[16]

According to Newsweek, which broke the story in March 2003, these revelations were "hushed up by the U.N. inspectors" in order to "bluff Saddam into disclosing still more" and because Iraq had "never shown the documentation to support Kamel's story."[17]

Perhaps, but other motives also suggest themselves. First, the U.S.-led inspections were designed to strip Iraq of the ability to reconstitute its unconventional weapons programs and thus become an impediment to U.S. dominance in the Gulf, not simply destroy whatever weapons it had at the time. And the UN inspectors may also have kept quiet in order to maintain the political rationalization for the strangling Iraq and undermining Hussein's rule.

So by the end of the 1990s, perhaps even earlier, Iraq had probably been mostly, perhaps entirely, disarmed of its banned weapons. Ritter summed up:

> While we were never able to provide 100 percent certainty regarding the disposition of Iraq's proscribed weaponry, we did ascertain a 90-95 percent level of verified disarmament.... With the exception of mustard agent, all chemical agent produced by Iraq prior to 1990 would have degraded within five years (the jury is still out regarding Iraq's VX nerve agent program—while inspectors have accounted for the laboratories, production equipment and most of the agent produced from 1990-91, major discrepancies in the Iraqi accounting preclude any final disposition at this time). The same holds true for biological agent, which would have been neutralized through natural processes within three years of manufacture.[18]

Ritter concluded: "If the Security Council were to reevaluate Iraq's disarmament obligations along qualitative lines not quantitative, it would be very easy to come up with a finding of compliance."[19]

Coming Up Empty

Ritter's assessment has been borne out by the 2003 war and its aftermath: Iraq did not use unconventional weapons, none had been found at this writing five months later, and most experts had concluded that no WMD would ever be found because Iraq had destroyed them—probably at least a decade earlier.

Immediately after the war, the Pentagon organized a 1,400 member Iraq Survey Group, comprised of scientists, military and intelligence experts and headed by former Reagan official and UN weapons inspector David Kay, to scour Iraq for chemical, biological and nuclear weapons and programs. Four months later, the Survey

Group had come up empty—it found neither weapons nor signs of any active unconventional weapons programs. By August 2003, the *New York Times* concluded, "it now seems virtually certain that Iraq did not have the stocks to provide weapons of mass destruction, despite the Bush administration's repeated contention that it believes it will find them."[20]

Later that month, the *Los Angeles Times* reported that, "weapons hunters have yet to find proof that any chemical or bio-warfare agents were produced after 1991," and that some survey group members who spoke on condition of anonymity:

> said the evidence reviewed so far—including more than 30 million pages of documents—still doesn't support charges that Hussein secretly built chemical and biological weapons after UN inspectors were forced out [sic] of Iraq in 1998, as the Bush administration repeatedly warned.[21]

In September 2003, former head UN arms inspector Hans Blix said he thought Iraq had probably destroyed most, perhaps all, of its unconventional weapons at least 10 years earlier. A number of papers, including London's *Independent* and the *Sunday Times*, reported that the survey group's report, scheduled to be presented in September, might never be released because its findings were so damning to the Bush administration's pre-war claims.[22]

There is speculation that Iraq may have attempted to preserve the scientific and technical infrastructure needed to reconstitute chemical and biological weapons production at some point in the future, but even this is not yet clear.

There will no doubt be further revelations of the depths of U.S. and UN deception on the WMD front over the coming months and years. Yet it is already clear that Iraq largely complied with UN demands, and that the main barrier to any resolution of the weapons issue was Washington's unrelenting hostility toward Baghdad. The U.S. sought regime change, not a negotiated settlement.

After the war, one former Iraqi brigadier general told the *Los Angeles Times* that U.S. forces searching for weapons "will never find anything here. Only oil."[23]

Phony Terror Plots

Banned weapons were one myth originated in the 1990s that was used to justify the war of 2003; Iraq's purported support for anti-U.S. terror and "terrorist" organizations including al Qaeda was another.

In June 1993, the Clinton administration claimed that it had "compelling evidence" that Iraq was behind a plot to assassinate Bush Sr. during a visit to Kuwait two months earlier in April, and launched 23 cruise missiles at Iraq as punishment. (Three of them missed their targets and killed eight civilians, including Layla al-Attar, one of Iraq's most renowned artists.)

A decade later, Bush, Jr. would cite the purported plot as yet another justification for overthrowing the Hussein regime: "After all," he said in September 2002, "this is a guy that tried to kill my dad at one time."[24]

In reality, shortly after the 1993 attack and nine years before Bush, Jr. made his charges, an investigation by the *New Yorker's* Seymour Hersh found that Clinton's "evidence" was "seriously flawed;" there was no empirical evidence linking Baghdad to the men arrested or the bomb produced in Kuwait, and the whole incident may have been concocted by Kuwaiti intelligence.[25]

More importantly, claims that Iraq supported attacks on U.S. personnel or had ties with al Qaeda ignored the fact that during the decade of the 1990s, Baghdad's strategy was to wage a political and economic campaign, sometimes with the support of powers like France and Russia, to win the lifting of sanctions. Links with "terrorist" groups or actions would have undermined that overriding goal. Even the pro-war *Wall Street Journal* admitted as much:

> Repeated efforts by U.S. intelligence agencies to find links between Iraq and the 1993 World Trade Center bombing have come up empty, officials say. Hemmed in by U.N. sanctions, Mr. Hussein has sought to rally international support for easing his international isolation. Any link with international terrorist attacks would have given the U.S. further justification for attacking him and for keeping sanctions in place.[26]

Yet Washington would never acknowledge this reality, because acknowledging it would have punctured a gaping hole in the U.S.-created fable that Iraq was defying the United Nations because it was hell-bent on possessing weapons of mass destruction.

Moving Goalposts

In 2003, after failing to find banned weapons in Iraq, Bush II officials tried, to justify their pre-war claims as perfectly reasonable. Defense Secretary Rumsfeld, appearing on NBC's "Meet the Press" in July 2003, offered this rationale: if Hussein had really destroyed his banned weapons, why didn't he go along with UN inspections? Sanctions would then have been lifted, and billions of dollars in oil revenues would have flowed into his regime's coffers. So it was obvious that he had something to hide.[27]

Actually, it was Rumsfeld and other U.S. officials who have many things to hide. One is that Iraq's compliance with UN inspections got it nowhere, and that Washington made clear that it would never lift sanctions as long as Hussein remained in power—no matter how many UN inspections he went along with and no matter how many weapons he destroyed. Inspections and disarmament were the leading edge of U.S. political and diplomatic efforts against Iraq, but Washington's primary objective was never just stripping Iraq of its unconventional weapons: it was strangulation pending regime change.

This is why the U.S. twisted, misinterpreted, and selectively enforced various UN resolutions. Resolution 687 stated that upon "the completion by Iraq of all actions contemplated" in the paragraphs relating to disarmament, sanctions "shall have no further force or effect." In other words, the only UN authorization for sanctions concerned Iraq's prohibited weapons, not any other issue. Yet U.S. officials repeatedly invoked other sections of Resolution 687, or other Security Council resolutions unrelated to disarmament, to justify continuing the embargo.

In 1995, Madeleine Albright, then U.S. Ambassador to the UN, stated that her government was "determined to oppose any modification of the sanctions regime until Iraq has moved to comply with all its outstanding obligations," including the return of Kuwaiti weaponry and other equipment.[28]

Two years later when she was Clinton's Secretary of State, Albright declared, "We do not agree with the nations who argue that if Iraq complies with its obligations concerning weapons of mass destruction, sanctions should be lifted." Other officials demanded that sanctions could not be lifted until Iraq complied with those resolutions "that deal with human rights issues, those that deal with prisoners of war with Kuwait, those that deal with the treatment of his own people." Clinton himself warned that "sanctions will be there until the end of time or as long as [Hussein] lasts."[29] These positions themselves violated Resolution 687.

Von Sponeck notes that UN resolutions were also "so intangible, so loosely defined" that they were "very open to interpretation and therefore to prolongation of sanctions if you have in mind to keep your thumb on Iraq. And this is what we have seen." The conditions for ending sanctions were left so vague that Iraq was forced to plead with the UN Security Council to make clear exactly what it had to do to end the devastating embargo. It never received a clear reply.[30]

President Bush II employed the same "compliance creep" logic in his September 12, 2002 address to the UN laying the groundwork for a new war on Iraq. He claimed "sanctions were maintained after the war to compel the regime's compliance with Security Council resolutions" (i.e., *not* certain paragraphs of one resolution) and raised a laundry list of conditions Iraq would have to meet beyond disarmament, including accounting for all Kuwaiti prisoners of war, ending domestic repression, and halting all unsanctioned commercial dealings. Then Bush called on the UN to help "build a government that represents all Iraqis"—making clear that the U.S. was determined to overthrow the Hussein regime whether it complied with UN demands or not.[31]

None of this is to say that UN sanctions or disarmament have been just or legitimate. As explained above, these actions and their enforcement did not reflect some sort of universal principles of justice and humanity, but rather the political agendas of the world's dominant powers, the United States in particular. The point here is that Washington violated and pushed beyond even the coercive UN framework. The continuation of sanctions was not "Saddam's fault," as both the Clinton and Bush II administrations have repeatedly claimed. The reality is that no matter what Hussein's government did or didn't do, so long as he remained in power the U.S. was determined to keep the embargo tightly in place.

The Futile Search for a "Quick Fix"

In the decade after the 1991 Persian Gulf War, the U.S. pursued several inter-related but often contradictory efforts in Iraq: sanctions to weaken it and undermine Saddam Hussein's rule, disarmament through UN inspections, and attempted internal coups to overthrow the Hussein regime. By the late 1990s, Iraq had been severely weakened, yet all three legs of U.S. strategy were unraveling. Sanctions had not undermined Hussein's grip on power; several coup plots had collapsed; the U.S. had pulled UN weapons inspectors out of Iraq and Baghdad refused to allow their return; and there was mounting international pressure to lift the embargo.

The U.S. was facing a potential geopolitical setback. Washington strategists feared that Baghdad could emerge from sanctions with Hussein still in charge, his prestige enhanced, and his desire to assert Iraqi interests intact. Global rivals would be better positioned to gain political influence and secure oil and reconstruction contracts in post-sanctions Iraq. U.S. credibility would be damaged at a time when other developments were also posing problems for it in the region. Finally, a growing number of imperial strategists felt that America's post-Soviet global predominance had opened a window for dealing decisively with "problem" states like Iraq, and failing to do so meant failing to capitalize on the opportunity and failing to fully extend America's global reach.

These concerns led to an intense debate within the U.S. establishment over how to handle Iraq, and a concerted campaign by prominent ruling class strategists, including Donald Rumsfeld, Paul Wolfowitz, Richard Perle, Douglas Feith and others who would become top officials in the Bush, Jr. administration, to make regime change Washington's central and immediate goal. These debates, explored in the next chapter, helped shape the Bush, Jr. administration's post-Sept. 11, 2001 decision to wage war on Iraq, as well as its overall grand strategy.

The first element of U.S. strategy to collapse were what some officials called the "quick fix" option—attempting to overthrow Hussein via an internal coup without having to go to war. In March 1995 the Iraqi National Congress (INC) launched an uprising against the Ba'ath regime from the Kurdish north. The CIA had helped create the INC in 1992, and two years later it set up a permanent station in the city of Salahuddin. Three teams of intelligence agents were assigned to work directly with the INC, and anti-Hussein Iraqis saw this as strong encouragement for their planned military offensive against Baghdad.[32]

However, much to the INC's dismay, on the morning the offensive began, the CIA delivered an urgent cable directly from Anthony Lake, Clinton's National Security Advisor. "You are on your own," it said. "The United States will not support this operation militarily or in any other way."[33] The INC went ahead anyway, but their assault collapsed within four weeks. By September 1996, the Iraqi government had driven the entire INC network from northern Iraq, thanks in part to clashes between rival Kurdish organizations (the Kurdish Democratic Party or KDP and the Patriotic Union of Kurdistan or PUK). Many Kurds were killed in the fighting, but the CIA suffered no casualties. Their officers left the country a few days before the Iraqi military moved in.[34]

"Gotcha"

A second conspiracy collapsed ignominiously in June 1996. This fiasco not only represented a major blow to U.S. plans to eliminate Hussein, but also exposed that Washington was deceitfully and illegally using UN weapons inspections to further its coup plots and assassination attempts.

Since its inception, UNSCOM relied on intelligence agencies including the CIA for technical assistance, and shared its findings with them in return (and by the mid-1990s was working with Israeli intelligence as well). This was sometimes done, secretly and directly, by U.S. military personnel working as arms inspectors. It was also illegal—an agreement between the UN and Iraq banned the publication of information collected during inspections. Such intelligence gathering was expanded in the mid-1990s following General Kamal's defection and revelation that Iraq may have been hiding the technical-scientific information it had accumulated for producing banned weapons.[35]

UNSCOM then began to focus on unraveling Iraq's concealment mechanisms, calling the effort their "special collections mission." Israel and the U.S. provided the inspectors with high tech radio scanners and communications equipment. The inspectors would stage provocative or surprise visits to sites the Hussein regime considered sensitive, and then listen to and record encrypted microwave communications between Iraqi officials. It turned out that the elite military units in charge of hiding Iraq's weapons were also in charge of protecting Saddam Hussein. UNSCOM's publicly stated goal may have been finding Iraq's weapons, but it was turning over recordings of these covert monitoring operations to the CIA for deciphering, and the CIA had another objective: overthrowing Hussein.[36]

By 1994, perhaps earlier, the CIA had begun working with the Iraqi National Accord—an anti-Hussein group organized by British intelligence made up of former Iraqi military officers living in exile in Amman, Jordan. As was the case following the 1991 Gulf War, if Hussein were to be overthrown, the U.S. wanted it done by elements in the Iraqi military, not by the Iraqi people. This, the Clinton leadership calculated, was the best way to keep Iraq intact and maintain the regional balance of power.[37]

The U.S. and the INA plotted a coup, and the CIA smuggled special communications equipment into Baghdad under cover of weapons inspections to facilitate it. This equipment wasn't used to hunt for Iraq's weapons; it was used to track Iraqi military movements and communicate with INA contacts in Iraq's armed forces. The *Washington Post* reported that in the mid-1990s, U.S. intelligence agents, posing as technicians in charge of maintaining UNSCOM's remote monitoring system, secretly installed antennas for intercepting the microwave transmissions of the Iraqi military and transmitters for relaying the data back to the U.S. The *Washington Post* noted that the intercepted communications "were of considerable value to U.S. military planners but generally unrelated to UNSCOM's special weapons mandate."[38]

The New York Times reported, "The eavesdropping equipment was brought into Iraq on each inspection mission, and used to listen in as Iraqi security officers, speaking in code and using scrambling devices, worked to conceal weapons and protect President Hussein." CIA agents also debriefed weapons inspectors in hopes of obtaining intelligence useful for their covert operations.[39]

When the plot was in place, the U.S. planned to have

UNSCOM stage provocative inspections and trigger a confrontation with Baghdad. The U.S. would then use this as an excuse to
launch cruise missile attacks in support of an anti-Hussein coup.
Before this could happen, however, Iraqi intelligence uncovered the
CIA operation and rounded up the conspirators, along with some of
their U.S. equipment. "To add insult to injury," ABC News reported, "Iraqi intelligence agents made contact with the CIA using the
captured communications equipment. 'Gotcha,' they said."[40] This
fiasco dealt a major blow to U.S. plans to oust Hussein.

Another Quick Fix Fails

The U.S. tried another "quick fix" in December 1998 by
attempting a cruise missile assassination of Saddam Hussein.

The CIA's 1995 and 1996 intrigues had collapsed, but the
agency continued to use UNSCOM for covert eavesdropping operations. More high tech listening and communications devices were
secreted into Baghdad, and UNSCOM kept staging surprise inspections in order to monitor Iraqi government and military communications.

By 1997, if not earlier, Iraqi authorities were well aware that the
U.S. was using inspections for covert operations. During 1997 and
1998, Iraq resisted by protesting vigorously to the Security Council,
blocking some inspections, and threatening to expel U.S. members
of the inspection team, who then held 37 percent of the sensitive
positions in UNSCOM. The Iraqis were particularly incensed by
UNSCOM inspections of Presidential palaces. These were not carried out, they argued, to search for arms, but rather to gather intelligence and provoke confrontations—the U.S. was trying to demonstrate Iraqi "non-compliance" so that sanctions could be extended
indefinitely. In April 1998, Iraq complained to the Security Council
that it "ignores everything that Iraq had done over the past seven
years" in order to prolong sanctions, and charged that arms inspections were gathering intelligence for U.S. air strikes. Revelations following America's December 1998 "Desert Fox" air assault, detailed
below—as well as the U.S. failure to find any banned weapons following its 2003 invasion including at Presidential sites—confirmed
that Iraq's charges were true.[41]

The month Iraq sent its protest letter, U.S. covert operations moved into higher gear. After several years of close monitoring, its intelligence agencies were finally able to decrypt the Hussein regime's internal communications. "Saddam's most closely protected communications were suddenly pouring into UNSCOM," Hersh wrote in an expose published in the *New Yorker* in April 1999. "For the first time, with the aid of intercepts, Saddam's hour-to-hour whereabouts could conceivably be tracked—and even anticipated."[42]

The CIA soon took exclusive control of these intercepts and cut UNSCOM out of the loop. "Once the American technicians were in control," Hersh writes, "they focussed on Saddam—and not on his missiles and warheads. They eventually found a pattern in Saddam's movements, as tracked by intercepts, which they believed might lead to a successful attempt to eliminate him."

Intelligence gathering efforts were stepped up. In July 1998, Ritter was ordered to bring sophisticated U.S. listening devices into Iraq known as the "black boxes." Disguised to look like an office safe and placed in the inspectors' work space in Baghdad, these black boxes tracked frequencies used by Iraq's Special Security Organization charged with protecting Hussein and whatever may have been left of Iraq's unconventional weapons. The data were transmitted by satellite uplink to the National Security Agency in Ft. Meade, Maryland for processing, with the resulting intelligence controlled solely by U.S. agencies, not the UNSCOM inspectors.[43]

By the winter of 1998, the U.S. thought it had enough intelligence to launch missile strikes on Iraq and kill Hussein. Once again, this covert operation would be carried out under the cover of UN arms inspections.[44]

Richard Butler, an Australian diplomat, had become Executive Chairman of UNSCOM in 1997 (serving until 2000) and began working very closely with U.S. officials. Ritter reports that Butler talked to Clinton National Security Advisor Sandy Berger on a daily basis, coordinating inspections and consulting on his reports to the Security Council concerning UNSCOM's work and Iraq's compliance.[45]

After minimizing provocative inspections during much of 1998, the U.S. and Butler suddenly shifted course and staged a number of confrontational site visits in November and December. These set up

Butler's mid-December report to the Security Council charging that weapons inspectors had made "no progress" during the previous month. However, the body of the report could cite only five incidents—out of 300 inspections—when there had been any controversy.[46]

It turned out that on December 13, Butler had secretly met with Berger to go over his report before submitting it to the Security Council. The *Washington Post* later reported that U.S. officials played "a direct role in shaping Butler's text during multiple conversations with him." Berger and Butler even called Clinton, then in Israel, who instructed them to make the report even tougher on Iraq.[47] Once again, "intelligence" and a supposedly objective evaluation process was shaped to suit American geopolitical objectives in the Gulf. Truth had nothing to do with it.

Ritter concluded, "The controversial inspection with dubious arms-control value provided cover for the release of the Butler report. Given Mr. Butler's close relationship with the U.S. throughout this process, it can be interpreted only as providing a pretext for military action."[48]

On December 15, Peter Burleigh, the U.S. Ambassador to the UN, instructed Butler to pull his inspectors out of Iraq, removing them from harm's way before the Clinton team unleashed its air assault. Butler did so without consulting the Security Council. The next day, as Butler presented his report, the U.S. launched "Operation Desert Fox"—without Security Council authorization. For the next 100 hours, the U.S. lashed Iraq with 415 cruise missiles and 600 laser guided bombs. Defense Secretary William Cohen claimed, "We are concentrating on military targets."[49]

Cohen's half-truth was designed to conceal the fact that the U.S. was also illegally "concentrating" on assassinating Saddam Hussein: Desert Fox's targets included homes where the Iraqi president was thought to spend time with mistresses. According to the *New York Times*, some of the targets were "selected from data gleaned by the American-led espionage" operations utilizing arms inspections.[50]

Former inspector Ritter states, "when the Americans bombed, they went after more than a hundred targets that had nothing to do with weapons of mass destruction or industrial manufacturing, and had everything to do with Saddam Hussein and his security. They attempted to remove Saddam Hussein through a bombing campaign that was empowered by the intelligence information gathered by the weapons inspectors."[51]

Clinton may have timed Desert Fox, in part, to sidetrack impeachment proceedings, which were scheduled to begin in the U.S. House of Representatives on December 17, the day after the attacks began. If so, his ploy didn't succeed. The debate was briefly postponed but went ahead on December 18, and the House voted to impeach him.

U.S. Spies and UNSCOM's Demise

Desert Fox ended in another U.S. setback. The operation didn't kill Saddam Hussein, but it did kill UNSCOM. Tensions had been building in the Security Council over weapons inspections as it became clearer that Iraq was largely, perhaps completely, disarmed.

One UN official told the *Washington Post:* "The secretary general has become aware of the fact that UNSCOM directly facilitated the creation of an intelligence collection system for the United States in violation of its mandate. The United Nations cannot be party to an operation to overthrow one of its member states. In the most fundamental way, that is what's wrong with the UNSCOM operation."[52]

The U.S. had pulled the inspectors out, they had been exposed as spies, and Iraq refused to let them return. The divisions in the Security Council were so sharp it took a full year for it to agree on how to proceed. UNSCOM was disbanded and a new organization called the United Nations Monitoring, Verification, and Inspection Commission, or UNMOVIC, was formed under Security Council Resolution 1284.

Iraq refused to accept UNMOVIC, arguing that UN weapons inspections were designed to create "recurrent and concocted crises to prolong sanctions," a charge that carried more than a little truth. Iraq had little incentive to comply without firm assurances that sanctions would be lifted if it did so, and the U.S. refused to provide such assurances. (Iraq only accepted Resolution 1284 creating

UNMOVIC on September 16, 2002 under threat of a U.S. war.) The embargo, Saddam Hussein concluded, "will not be lifted by Security Council resolution but will corrode by itself."[53]

The U.S. had subverted UNSCOM—and then blamed Iraq. "This is a regime that agreed to international inspections, then kicked out the inspectors," Bush, Jr. charged in his 2001 State of the Union message. "This is a regime that has something to hide from the civilized world."[54]

The myth that Iraq "kicked the inspectors out" has been treated as hard fact in establishment discourse and in 2002-2003 became an important component of the Bush II case for war. In reality, it was the U.S. that pulled the inspectors out, not Iraq. In August 2002, Ritter pointed out:

> The reason why weapons inspectors aren't in Iraq today is because Richard Butler had allowed the inspection process...to be abused by the United States in pursuit of its own unilateral objectives of destabilizing and eliminating Saddam Hussein. And the Iraqis would be damned fools to let such an inspection team back in, and that's why we don't have inspectors right now.[55]

So it was actually the United States government that had "something to hide"—12 years of lies about Iraqi "weapons of mass destruction," which were used to justify 12 years of murderous and crippling sanctions, and 12 years of illegal covert efforts to overthrow Saddam Hussein.

CHAPTER 8

A GROWING CLAMOR FOR REGIME CHANGE

The clamor for regime change in Iraq began, not months, but years before Sept. 11, 2001. For all its bullying—through sanctions, weapons inspections, coup attempts and military attacks—the U.S. was unable to fully get its way in Iraq during the 1990s. Top American officials and policy thinkers, particularly former members of the Reagan and Bush I administrations (including many who would become top figures in the Bush II administration), felt the situation was becoming a major problem for the U.S.—not just in Iraq, but in the Middle East and the world.

This Iraq debate was linked with another bitter struggle within the political establishment over post-Soviet global strategy and how to take full advantage of America's new "primacy" as the world's only imperial superpower. These debates contributed to the ascension of George W. Bush to the presidency, the declaration of a new U.S. global strategy, and the launching of an unbounded "war on terror"—starting in Afghanistan in 2001 and then moving on to Iraq in 2003.

Slip Sliding Away:
Fraying Sanctions, Unraveling Coalitions

By the late 1990s, sanctions and the coalition that sustained them were eroding on a number of fronts. Instead of undermining the Hussein regime, sanctions ended up strengthening its hold on power, because most Iraqis understood that the United States, not Saddam Hussein, was imposing the embargo and its attendant suffering, and that the only thing standing between them and starvation was the Ba'ath regime's very efficient food distribution system.[1]

Disarmament had been the main justification for continuing the embargo, which was the bedrock of U.S. efforts to strangle Iraq and topple its government. UNSCOM's expulsion had fractured that political framework and exposed deep divisions between the major powers. Since 1993, permanent Security Council members France and Russia had favored easing sanctions. After Desert Fox, they, along with China, called for ending the oil embargo, while continuing to enforce Iraq's disarmament.[2]

Neither France nor Russia had the strength to directly challenge America's dominance in the Middle East, yet each had its own agenda and feared that U.S. actions were undermining Western interests in the region. Both also wanted to impose some constraints on U.S. actions globally. In their view, Iraq did not pose an immediate threat to the flow of Gulf oil, and exposure of sanctions' horrendous toll was politically damaging their governments and the UN.

Secondarily, both also had extensive commercial interests in Iraq, which sanctions and U.S. hostility were thwarting. Baghdad tried to exploit these contradictions by commercially rewarding countries that favored the easing of sanctions, while freezing out those—like the United States—that didn't.

Russian firms had helped arm Iraq and develop its oil industry beginning in the 1970s, and Baghdad still owed Moscow some $8 billion from these various endeavors. Beginning in the early 1990s, Russian firms pursued new deals in Iraq's oil sector, and in 1997 Iraq granted Russia most favored nation status, giving it privileged access to Iraqi petroleum. Nearly 20 percent of the first contracts approved under the UN "oil-for-food" program went to Russian companies. A new Iraq/Russian oil joint venture was established to develop the West Qurna oil field in southern Iraq which was expected to produce 4.4 billion barrels of oil over 23 years and generate $80 billion in earnings for Iraq.[3]

France and China were also actively exploring commercial deals with Baghdad. French oil multinational TotalFinaElf SA, which had been active in Iraq for 75 years, negotiated for 10 years to develop and share Iraqi oil production, but could not conclude an agreement with sanctions in place.[4] By 2001, German exports to Iraq had increased four-fold from previous years. These developments mirrored a regional trend: in 2000, U.S. exports to the Middle

East totaled $23 billion (excluding Israel), while European exports were nearly triple that amount—$63.7 billion.[5]

During the 1990s, U.S. petroleum giants openly "worried about being left out" of the oil grab in Iraq, according to the *Wall Street Journal*, which reported that oil executives realized that "Iraq is the biggie," but feared they would wake up one day to find:

> the European companies will have grabbed the best deals.... International politics is creating an uneven playing field for U.S. companies and could lead to a major power shift away from the U.S. oil industry.... Indeed, the companies that win the rights to develop Iraqi fields could be on the road to becoming the most powerful multinationals of the next century.[6]

The Hussein regime also sought to use global currency competition as a wedge against sanctions. Since the early 1970s, the denomination of OPEC oil revenues in dollars and their recycling back to Western financial institutions as so-called petrodollars has helped maintain the U.S. dollar's strength, which in turn is a key element of American global power. In November 2000, Iraq bucked this tradition by insisting on—and receiving—UN approval to receive its oil-for-food revenues in Euros, not dollars. Baghdad probably hoped that its act of defiance would encourage other oil producers, including Iran, Venezuela and Russia, to consider doing likewise, increasing the pressure on Washington to ease the embargo.[7]

So long as sanctions remained in place most ventures could not take effect without UN approval, and the U.S. often blocked proposed deals, in part to prevent others from making commercial inroads in Iraq. Following its 2003 invasion, the U.S. sought aid and investment from other countries to help rebuild Iraq. Yet in 1999, it publicly rejected direct foreign investment in Iraq's oil industry, even though Iraq was unable to produce enough oil to meet its allowed quota. This competition fed U.S. determination to maintain sanctions: ending them could allow competitors to develop Iraq's vast oil resources without U.S. participation.[8]

Washington was not above using the economic leverage provided by sanctions to muster Security Council votes. After Russia vetoed the Bush II administration's "smart sanctions" proposal in July 2001, the U.S. put holds on Russian contracts to develop Iraq's oil, claiming they were imposed for disarmament purposes. Yet when a similar proposal passed in May 2002 with Russian support, holds were removed on $740 million in Russian deals with Iraq. One diplomat, quoted anonymously by London's *Financial Times*, described it as "the boldest move yet by the U.S. to use the holds to buy political agreement."[9]

Reaping a Regional Whirlwind

As Saddam Hussein had predicted, by the late 1990s the embargo was also eroding in the region as Iraq gradually rebuilt its commercial and political ties with its neighbors. Its trade with Jordan, Turkey, Syria, and Egypt grew and had become significant for their economies, thanks in part to discounted prices for Iraqi oil. By 2002, Jordan was receiving all its oil from Iraq–at half the world price.

Many former members of the Gulf War coalition reopened their embassies in Baghdad, and in 1998 Iraqi officials attended their first Arab League meeting in a decade. Turkey remained concerned that removing the Hussein regime would open the door to a Kurdish state. By March 2001, the *New York Times* summed up, "After years as a diplomatic pariah, Iraq once again has friends in foreign capitals."[10]

Professor Fouad Ajami of Johns Hopkins University, who would become a favored advisor to the Bush II administration, wrote:

> Primacy begot its nemesis.... The power secured during Desert Storm was destined not to last. The United States could not indefinitely quarantine Iraq. It was idle to think that the broad coalition cobbled together during an unusually perilous moment in 1990-91 would stand as a permanent arrangement. The demographic and economic weight of Iraq and Iran meant that those countries were bound to reassert themselves... [Hussein] worked his way into the local order of things.... The Iraqi ruler knew well the distress that settled on the region after Pax Americana's swift war. All around Iraq, the region was poorer: oil prices had slumped, and the war had been expensive for the oil states that financed it.[11]

This regional distress was deep and if allowed to go unchecked could threaten U.S. interests. The 1991 Gulf War marked the first time the U.S. had so directly waged war on an Arab country. It spawned anti-U.S. anger across the region, which was amplified over the 1990s by America's cruel assault on the Iraqi people. This smoldering fury intensified deep stresses in a number of pro-U.S. regimes, raising concerns in Washington about their reliability and stability.

Saudi Arabia was a prime case in point. Desert Storm's goals included maintaining the Royal Kingdom as a pillar of U.S. dominance in the Persian Gulf. Yet in significant ways the war had the opposite affect.

For one, it marked a seminal moment in Osama bin Laden's transformation from a CIA asset and friend of the House of Saud into an enemy of both. After Iraq's invasion, bin Laden and his followers were stunned when the Saudis (probably at Washington's behest) rejected their request to lead Islamic "Mujahadeen" fighters from the Afghan campaign against the Soviet Union into battle against Iraq to create an Islamic state ruled from Baghdad. Bin Laden reportedly called it "the most shocking moment of his life." Anger among Saudis grew when the U.S.-led Coalition deployed 500,000 troops in Saudi Arabia. Bin Laden and other Islamists felt that the enormous foreign presence had defiled Islam's most revered sites, that the U.S. sought to dominate Muslim lands, and that Saudi Arabia was complicit in these transgressions. (Bin Laden's rage at the House of Saud may also have been stoked by its expulsion of some 800,000 workers from Yemen, where his family originally hailed from, after Yemen's refusal to support Desert Storm.) So after the Gulf War, they turned their "jihad" on America and its allies, including the Saudi royal family.[12]

Egypt, another U.S. client, also faced a growing Islamist revolt, and between 1992 and 1997 the Mubarak government killed over 1,200 people in an effort to suppress it.[13]

Desert Storm emboldened Israel, and the Palestinian people paid a heavy price. Illegal Israeli settlements in the West Bank and Gaza, land seizures, area closures, house demolitions, and detentions continued in the occupied territories, along with daily violence and humiliations at the hands of settlers and the Israeli military. These intolerable conditions, the collapse of the Oslo "peace process," and Israel's murderous response to the second Palestinian Intifada (launched in September 2000) sparked a new wave of militant

Palestinian resistance along with outrage across the Muslim world and beyond. In 2002, French journalist and diplomat Eric Rouleau described the fallout in Saudi Arabia:

> A major crisis is now brewing in Saudi Arabia.... The deterioration of the Arab-Israeli situation has started to threaten the very stability of the Saudi state in a way many Westerners, particularly Americans, had not anticipated. In particular, outsiders have underestimated the anger roused in the Saudi population by the suffering of the Palestinian people— and the fact that this suffering is blamed less on Israel than on its American protector. Given the privileged nature of relations between Washington and Riyadh, this anger has also started to focus on the House of Saud itself.[14]

Discontent in the region was also stoked by economic decline. In Saudi Arabia, stagnating oil revenues, an estimated $55 billion outlay for the Gulf War, and soaring population growth had combined to produce budget deficits and a staggering reduction in average per capita income, from $28,600 a year in 1981 to just $6,800 in 2001. For the first time, unemployment had become a serious issue in the Kingdom.[15]

The *Los Angeles Times* reports that when Saudi King Fahd vacationed in Spain in 2002, he took with him "50 black Mercedes, 350 attendants and a 234-foot yacht, and had $2,000 worth of flowers and 50 cakes delivered each day." Meanwhile, back in Saudi Arabia:

> The dozen years since the Persian Gulf War have seen slums grow up on the outskirts of Jidda and Riyadh, the capital. Beggars hawk bottles of water at intersections. Penniless women huddle in strips of shade outside their crumbling mud-brick houses, begging for money. Many families in the capital are so poor they can't afford electricity. Raw sewage runs through parts of Jidda.[16]

(A secondary U.S. motive for maintaining sanctions on Iraq may have been propping the Royal Kingdom: reducing Iraq's share of world oil revenues resulted in a $100 billion "windfall" for Saudi Arabia during the 1990s.[17])

In years past, both Saudi Arabia and Kuwait had been stabilizing sources of jobs, income and financial assistance for many non-oil producing countries in the Middle East. However, Kuwait too began running budget deficits after it kicked between $16 and $20 billion into the Desert Storm kitty and was forced to spend another $65 billion rehabilitating its oil industry.[18]

The Gulf War did nothing to relieve the distress of women in the region. In Kuwait, the all-male parliament refused to give women the right to vote, while in Saudi Arabia women can neither vote nor drive, and have few legal rights. The situation is only slightly better in Jordan and Egypt.

Clamoring for Regime Change

By the mid-1990s, the failed anti-Hussein coups, the erosion of sanctions, and increased tensions in the region prompted a growing clamor in the political elite for more drastic action against Iraq, including regime change in Baghdad—both to deal with the situation in the Persian Gulf, and to push forward their agenda of greater U.S. global supremacy.

After the 1996 coup attempt in Iraq collapsed, Paul Wolfowitz, then out of government, wrote:

> Saddam has achieved major gains—in reasserting control over Iraqi territory, in terrorizing his enemies, in demonstrating the increasing weakness of the coalition against him, and in getting the US to reduce its strategic goals.... Iraq is not a sideshow.... It has huge strategic consequences for American credibility in this critical region and beyond.... Now that the US has lost its position in Northern Iraq, it will be much more difficult to go beyond a containment strategy. But it will be no less necessary.[19]

In January 1998, the Project for a New American Century sent President Clinton an open letter warning, "The policy of 'containment' of Saddam Hussein has been steadily eroding," and "we can no longer depend on our partners in the Gulf War coalition to continue to uphold the sanctions." It argued that these developments endanger "our friends and allies like Israel and the moderate Arab states, and a significant portion of the world's supply of oil." The letter, which raised the specter of Iraqi acquisition of "weapons of mass destruction," but made no mention of "terrorism," concluded that the "only acceptable strategy" was "removing Saddam Hussein and his regime from power. That now needs to become the aim of American foreign policy."

Many of the letter's signatories would become top officials in the Bush II administration: Rumsfeld, Wolfowitz, Dov Zakheim, Peter Rodman, William Schneider, Jr. and Richard Perle in the Defense Department; Richard Armitage, Paula Dobriansky, and John Bolton in the State Department; Zalmay Khalilzad and Elliott Abrams in the White House; and U.S. trade representative Robert Zoelick.[20]

Over the next two years, ex-officials, think-tank strategists and right-wing pundits churned out a stream of letters, articles, and books calling for more forceful action against the Hussein regime. These would play a major role in reshaping U.S. policy toward Iraq—and its global strategy.[21] They argued that the continuation of Ba'ath rule in Iraq could undermine U.S. hegemony in the Persian Gulf. None centered on the "terrorist" danger, the threat Iraq purportedly posed to the U.S., or any alleged links between Saddam Hussein and bin Laden's al Qaeda network.

In October 1998 Congress passed the "Iraq Liberation Act of 1998" which declared, "It should be the policy of the United States to support efforts to remove the regime headed by Saddam Hussein from power in Iraq." The next month the Clinton administration adopted regime change as its stated policy.[22]

Following the December 1998 Desert Fox attacks, the U.S. also greatly escalated its air assaults on Iraq, partly out of frustration at its failure to assassinate Hussein and at the collapse of UNSCOM, and partly because the Iraqis were more frequently challenging the illegal American and British incursions into their airspace by firing on their warplanes.

In the eight months following "Desert Fox," U.S. and British airplanes attacked Iraq nearly every day, firing over 1,100 missiles against 359 targets. In the 18 months after the December 1998 attacks, Baghdad said that 300 Iraqis had been killed and more than 800 wounded by these airstrikes, mostly civilians. In 1999, von Sponeck's UN humanitarian mission began tracking the air assaults and found that 144 Iraqis had been killed and 446 wounded in 132 separate incidents in 1999 and 2000. These strikes were generally treated as "business as usual" and rarely given more than brief, passing coverage in the mainstream U.S. press.[23]

By the end of the decade, the U.S. was spending $50 billion a year to maintain and equip its military forces in and around the Persian Gulf and over $1 billion a year on its patrols over Iraq. Besides killing civilians and destroying Iraqis facilities, the attacks also "yielded a wealth of new intelligence and targeting information," according to military analyst William Arkin, which would be put to use in the 2003 war.[24]

Nonetheless, sanctions remained the bedrock of U.S. strategy until after Sept. 11, 2001. In 1998, the Clinton National Security Council concluded that pro-U.S. Iraqi groups like the Iraqi National Congress (INC) were weak. Thus, "short of an invasion, the United States had no good military options on Iraq," so there was no consensus on how regime change could take place. One administration official acknowledged, "Nobody that I know has a strategy that they think will get rid of Saddam in the next six months or year, unless you are willing to put in a large U.S. ground force there."[25]

Even those pushing for more aggressive action focused on beefing up the pro-U.S. Iraqi opposition, not invading and occupying Iraq. Less than $1 million of the $97 million Congress authorized for the Iraqi opposition was dispersed due to serious doubts about the INC's effectiveness and support within Iraq. Meanwhile, fear of the regional repercussions and costs of a U.S. war remained strong. During the 2000 presidential campaign, both George W. Bush and Al Gore supported ousting Hussein. Bush's running mate Cheney, speaking of Iraq, complained: "We have swept that problem under the rug for too long. We have a festering problem there."[26]

Iraq, Impeachment and Grand Strategy

The Iraq debate took place in the context of, and helped shape, a sharp struggle within the bourgeois establishment during the 1990s over U.S. grand strategy in the post-Soviet world. The collapse of the Soviet empire represented a geopolitical earthquake that left the U.S. the world's only imperial superpower, and assessing the dimensions of its "primacy" soon became a staple of think-tank literature. Globally, military spending declined by 50 percent during the past decades, yet America's remained high. The gap in military technology between the U.S. and the rest of the world grew wider and wider, and the U.S. economy remained by far the world's largest, equal to the next three—Japan, Germany and Britain—combined.[27]

After the 1991 Gulf War, the Bush, Sr. administration began to formulate a global strategy to maintain that dominance, which was spelled out in its 1992 "Defense Planning Guidance." Written by Wolfowitz, Lewis Libby and Khalilzad under the leadership of then-Defense Secretary Dick Cheney, the Defense Guidance called for the U.S. to insure, as the *New York Times* reported, "that no rival superpower is allowed to emerge in Western Europe, Asia or the territory of the former Soviet Union." The Defense Guidance called this the:

> dominant consideration underlying the new regional defense strategy and requires that we endeavor to prevent any hostile power from dominating a region whose resources would, under consolidated control, be sufficient to generate global power. These regions include Western Europe, East Asia, the territory of the former Soviet Union, and Southwest Asia.[28]

The Defense Guidance also placed special emphasis on the Persian Gulf: "In the Middle East and Southwest Asia, our overall objective is to remain the predominant outside power in the region and preserve U.S. and Western access to the region's oil."[29]

However, the vision articulated in the Defense Guidance didn't fully take hold. Bush, Sr. had reservations, the paper came in for sharp criticism, and the next year Bill Clinton took office. U.S. military spending still outstripped that of any other country in the world, and Clinton championed Washington's "right" to act unilaterally and shape the global environment by force—"assertive multilateralism" as they called it.[30] U.S. armed interventions continued around the world—in Somalia, Haiti, Bosnia, and Kosovo—and the assault on Iraq never let up. Yet the Clinton team did not fully break with the Cold War's strategic legacy, and envisioned U.S. global power continuing not only through military superiority, but by more traditional alliances and treaties as well.[31]

Meanwhile, U.S. power was facing new challenges around the globe. The Soviet Union had collapsed, but much of the Cold War world order remained in place—there had been no titanic, ground-clearing battle, as had been the case in World War II. The Soviet demise had not led to a new, sustained wave of global economic growth. Japan, much of Asia, and Germany—which had been counted on as engines of economic expansion—were mired in slow-downs, if not crises. Overall, capitalist globalization was running into obstacles and instabilities—while provoking massive popular opposition.

In the eyes of Cheney, Wolfowitz, Khalilzad, and other imperi-al thinkers, things were drifting in the wrong direction, and Clinton and his team were frittering away American preeminence. Power was being wasted on missions in places like Haiti and Somalia which were not critical to seizing global preeminence, while the U.S. was unwilling to boldly and forcefully commit its military might in areas that were—such as Iraq and the Persian Gulf. Bush I Secretary of State James Baker complained that Clinton had "squandered American credibility and undermined our preeminence around the world."[32]

Khalilzad, an Afghan-born American, one-time advisor to the Unocal oil company, and then a top official in the Bush II adminis-tration, has been one of the key players in the campaign for a more aggressive U.S. global posture. In 1995, he warned that the U.S. was confronting a host of new dangers around the world, including the potential for "major regional conflicts, attempts at regional hegemo-ny, and proliferation of weapons of mass destruction," as well as "chaos and fragmentation within states," and possibilities ranging from a "growing number of small wars" to "Russian reimperialization and Chinese expansionism." He complained that, "Despite efforts by both the Bush and Clinton administrations...no grand strategy has yet jelled and there is no consensus on overarching national securi-ty objectives. It appears that the country is still trying to get its strategic bearings."

This lack of consensus stemmed in part from an ongoing shift in global power as the Soviet Union disintegrated. Indeed, in the early 1990s most think-tankers felt the world was moving toward three regional groups, centered around the U.S., Germany, and Japan, not one "unipolar world" of U.S. hegemony. So there was no "unifying concept" in the Clinton global vision, Khalilzad argued, and its strategy "does not deal with some of the tough issues.... It also does not provide a clear sense of priorities." Khalilzad argued that the U.S. should focus on preventing others from having "hegemony over critical regions," including the Persian Gulf.[33] Others in the establishment worried that an historic window of opportunity could close before the U.S. could consolidate and lock in its dominance.

The public face of the Clinton impeachment may have been Monica Lewinski and sex, but issues of much greater moment were being fought out, including how to rule at home and how to best dominate the world abroad.[34]

Plotting a New American Century

Over the decade, these strategists continued to refine and aggressively promote their vision. In 1996, former Reagan officials Kristol and Robert Kagan wrote what would become a seminal article for *Foreign Affairs*—"Toward a Neo-Reaganite Foreign Policy." It called for "benevolent" U.S. global hegemony: "Having defeated the 'evil empire,' the United States enjoys strategic and ideological predominance. The first objective of U.S. foreign policy should be to preserve and enhance that predominance...."[35]

They also applied their vision to the Middle East, which they viewed as key to a new American imperium. In 1996, Perle, Douglas Feith, and David Wurmser—all later top officials in the Bush II administration—and others produced a strategy paper for the Likud Party leadership titled "A Clean Break: A New Strategy for Securing the Realm." It called for radically reshaping the Middle East and targeting Iraq:

> Israel can shape its strategic environment in cooperation with Turkey and Jordan, by weakening, containing and even rolling back Syria. This effort can focus on removing Saddam Hussein from power in Iraq—an important Israeli strategic objective in its own right—as a means of foiling Syria's regional ambitions.[36]

In September 2000, the Project for the New American Century issued a major study expanding on the 1992 Pentagon Guidance's theme of American global dominance. A number of its authors would become top officials under Bush, Jr.: Wolfowitz, Zakheim, Stephen Cambone, and Abram Shulsky in the Pentagon, and Vice President Cheney's chief of staff, Lewis Libby.

Titled "Rebuilding America's Defenses, Strategy, Forces and Resources For a New Century," it asked: "Does the United States have the resolve to shape a new century favorable to American principles and interest?" Its prescription: "At present the United States faces no global rival. America's grand strategy should aim to preserve and extend this advantageous position as far into the future as possible."

"Rebuilding America's Defenses" called for a major military build-up and vast extension of U.S. military deployments around the world. Significantly, it singled out Iran, Iraq and North Korea as immediate targets nearly two years before George W. Bush labeled them an "axis of evil," and criticized previous Pentagon planning for giving "little or no consideration to the force requirements necessary not only to defeat an attack but to remove these regimes from power."[37]

"Rebuilding" concluded that radically recasting U.S. global strategy would take time—barring a dramatic attack on America itself. These crusaders for U.S. global hegemony got their "Pearl Harbor" on Sept. 11, 2001, their grand vision became government policy, and suddenly war on Iraq seemed both feasible and necessary.

CHAPTER 9

OPERATION IRAQI COLONIZATION

Now they put plastic bags on our heads, throw us to the ground, and accuse us of being agents of Saddam Hussein. In other words, if you're not with America, you're with Saddam.... Mr. Bremer, you remind us of Saddam.... We've waited a long time to be free. Now you want us to be slaves.

Bremer is a Baathist.
—*As-Saah* (Iraq) editorial, June 18, 2003[1]

The swift and brutal stroke of war in 2003 was an attempt to resolve the Iraq "problem" that had plagued the United States government throughout the 1990s. Its policy of punitive containment through sanctions, subversion and military strikes was fraying, and the toll it was taking on Iraqis had become, in the words of former CIA analyst and Clinton official Kenneth Pollack, "a major irritant [in] U.S. relations with the Muslim world in general."[2] Meanwhile, as noted in the last chapter, other powers had strengthened their ties with Iraq, and U.S. power and "credibility" in the region were being challenged.

So the problem was not that Iraq "threatened its neighbors," as Bush II charged. The problem was that if sanctions were lifted and the Hussein regime survived, it would have undercut U.S. "credibility" by demonstrating that its power was not infinite. Baghdad might emerge with its regional ambitions intact and possibly enough oil wealth to pursue them. Such an outcome could have left the U.S. weaker in the Persian Gulf than before the 1991 war.

Yet the 2003 war was also a leap beyond past U.S. interventions: it was fought in the context of a new overarching strategy and its objectives went well beyond previous stratagems of balancing

Iran against Iraq, or maintaining the Middle East status quo. It represented a radical leap in direct U.S. intervention, war, and colonization. Unlike the war of 1991, this war of 2003 would not seek to cripple Iraq while preserving Ba'ath rule: its aim was regime change and occupation. The war of 2003 wouldn't end with a refusal to march on Baghdad; it would begin with one.

U.S. strategists saw conquering Iraq as a key step in unfolding their broader global agenda and facilitating a host of objectives in the Middle East and beyond: it would demonstrate U.S. might and determination; it could initiate the political, economic and social reordering of the entire Middle East; and it was part of an ensemble of actions undertaken to solidify U.S. control of the entire arc from Afghanistan through Egypt. These goals in turn were linked to a larger struggle for global energy supremacy and overall dominance, explored in chapter 10. For Bush and the advocates of greater American empire, war wasn't the last resort, it was the first, and a bridge to the brave new world they openly dreamed of creating.

Of course, devising these grand schemes is one thing, while realizing them can be another, as shown by the difficulties the U.S. has already encountered in post-invasion Iraq. "Operation Iraqi Freedom" may not end up creating the new Middle East and world order that Washington strategists envisioned. It could instead end up sucking the U.S. into a quagmire of defeat, with profound domestic and global consequences.

"Now It's Political Shock and Awe"

The war on Iraq was designed to give further impetus to the overall U.S. "war on terror." This explains a major motivation for pumping up the "imminence" of the purported Iraqi threat: Bush II and company wanted war—not disarmament. Any delay past spring 2003 could have dissipated the political momentum created by the Sept. 11 attacks—or even derailed the campaign entirely if UN inspections were shown to be effective, or Iraq was shown to be disarmed.

The U.S. sought to "shock and awe" not only Iraqis, but all Arabs, other imperial rivals, and anti-war protestors across the globe, while emboldening advocates of ongoing war to reshape the planet in U.S. interests. Bush wasted no time: on May 1, 2003 when he declared victory in Iraq from the deck of the aircraft carrier *Abraham Lincoln,* he also emphasized that the "war on terror that began on September the 11th, 2001" was not over, but "still goes on."[3]

The intended message was plain: American might is overwhelming and resistance is futile. Such messages, along with overcoming America's "Vietnam syndrome," were central to Bush I's calculations in the 1991 Persian Gulf war; they were doubly important in Bush II's 2003 war and his more expansive and hegemonic conception of a U.S. dominated "new world order."

U.S. officials extolled the war's regional impact before it even ended. "Some of Mr. Bush's closest aides assert that there is already a 'demonstration effect' in which the American and British forces in command in Baghdad will be able to exert pressure on Iraq's neighbors in ways they could only imagine a few months ago," the *New York Times* reported.[4]

James Schlesinger, formerly head of the Departments of Defense and Energy as well as the CIA, spelled out the message the U.S. political elite wished to impart in an April 2003 *Wall Street Journal* opinion piece appropriately titled "Now It's Political Shock and Awe:"

> The outcome will alter the strategic—and psychological—map of the Middle East. The war has most dramatically conveyed the following realities: 1) The U.S. is a very powerful country. 2) It is ill-advised to arouse this nation by attacking or repeatedly provoking it—or by providing support to terrorism; and 3) Regularly to do so means a price will likely be paid. Far less credence will now be placed in the preachments of Osama bin Laden regarding America's weakness, its unwillingness to accept burdens, and the ease of damaging its vulnerable economy.[5]

However, as explored more fully in chapter 11, Iraqis and others in the region may have been shocked by the sudden fall of the Hussein regime, but so far they seem less in awe than enraged by the U.S. conquest and occupation.

21st Century Colonialism

U.S. officials have repeatedly reassured the world that the 2003 war was fought to "liberate" the Iraqi people. "We come to Iraq with respect for its citizens, for their great civilization and for the religious faiths they practice," Bush II declared the night the war began. "We have no ambition in Iraq, except to remove a threat and restore control of that country to its own people."[6]

This was as big a lie as Washington's now-discredited WMD claims—perhaps even bigger. The top levels of the Ba'ath regime were indeed Washington's first targets, but its war was still aimed at Iraq's people—not only because they have been its main casualties, but because the war was fought to create a pro-U.S. client state and deny Iraqis the chance to determine their own futures.

While the exact shape of a new Iraqi government is still in formation, it is already clear from Washington's planning and actions that it is attempting to create a colonial-client state suited to U.S. interests, a state which would more directly impose American authority over Iraq's people and resources and facilitate broader U.S. objectives in the Middle East and Central Asia. As one Bush II official put it, "To the victor, the spoils, and in this case the spoils are choosing who governs."[7] Many Iraqis sensed this, and protests against the American occupation erupted in Baghdad, Mosul, Najaf and other Iraqi cities within days of Baghdad's fall, and resistance—armed and unarmed—has continued ever since.

Examining the various elements of the U.S. plan for the new Iraq—its relationship to the United Nations, its new government, its military posture, its economic structure, its foreign policy, its educational system, and its political system—makes clear that Bush team's vision of a "liberated" Iraq is simply 21st century neo-colonialism.

The New Internationalism = Exclusive U.S. Control

After the war, the U.S. quickly demanded that UN sanctions be lifted and that it be granted authority to rule the country. The Security Council complied, and on May 22, 2003, passed Security Council Resolution 1483, which granted the "Coalition Provisional Authority" (CPA) a formal mandate to administer Iraq, including its oil revenues. The UN's role was limited to dispatching a special representative to coordinate humanitarian work and to monitor the transition to the formation of a new government. This made clear that other powers—including Russia, Germany and France—would have no substantial decision-making role in the new Iraq.[8]

The U.S. even insisted on sending its own "Iraq Survey Group" of 1,400 scientists, technicians and intelligence analysts chosen by the Bush II administration and headed by former Reagan official and UN arms inspector David Kay, to search for banned weapons, rather than relying on UN weapons inspectors for fear that could have given other countries additional leverage in post-war Iraq.[9]

Continuing turmoil and resistance may force Washington to modify its unilateralist approach and try to involve other countries in the ruling, policing, and rebuilding of Iraq. However, at this writing, the U.S. still insists on virtually total control because one of its primary war aims was precisely to reduce the influence of other powers in Iraq and the Middle East, as well as their voice in global affairs. So ongoing negotiations have so far made little progress, and deep divisions remain between Washington and Paris, Bonn, and Moscow.

Sham Self-Determination

In mid-July 2003, with great fanfare, the U.S. announced the formation of a "Governing Council" of 25 Iraqis. L. Paul Bremer III, the U.S. viceroy (officially, its chief civilian administrator) in Iraq, and the Bush administration hailed this as the first step in creating a new democratic and representative Iraqi government, and promised that the Council would have real power, including the authority to name ministers and ambassadors, to approve the 2004 budget, and to begin work on a new constitution.[10]

In reality, the formation of a "Governing Council" was an effort to deflect rising Iraqi anger toward the occupation and to relieve U.S. forces of some administrative and security duties, while keeping political power firmly in American hands.

For one, naming a small council represented a retreat from earlier U.S. promises to convene a larger assembly where Iraqis could at least debate the form and composition of their first governing council.[11]

Second, Council members were handpicked by Bremer and his team, and any who openly opposed the U.S. occupation were excluded.[12] The Council was also chosen so it would be "dominated by the Iraqi exile leaders and Kurdish chieftains," as the *New York Times* reported. These Kurdish and exile groups—the Iraqi National Congress (INC), the Iraqi National Accord (INA), the Kurdistan Democratic Party, and the Patriotic Union of Kurdistan—have all worked closely with the Pentagon and the CIA for over a decade. The INC and INA, in particular, are essentially creations of U.S. and British intelligence with little support in Iraq, who represent the most subserviently pro-U.S. elements in the country.[13]

Third, final authority and veto power over any Iraqi Council decisions remains with chief U.S. administrator Bremer, who answers directly to the Pentagon, while also advising the White House.[14] Bremer, a Henry Kissinger protégée who was in charge of counter-terrorism in the Reagan administration, was rushed to Iraq in early May to replace U.S. administrator retired General Jay Garner, because the White House feared that Garner was allowing the situation in Iraq to spiral out of control.[15]

Under Coalition Provisional Authority Regulation No. 1, Bremer's word is law, and his decrees take full effect upon his signature. According to the *Washington Post*, elections could be two years away, and in the meantime "Bremer has made clear that he is in charge" and "has warned he will veto any of the council's decisions that 'are fundamentally against coalition interests' or not in the 'better interests of Iraq.'" In fact, the U.S. Provisional Authority has already made many wide-ranging decisions, including revoking import duties, taking over Ba'ath party assets, and assuming telecommunications licensing power, that will shape Iraq's future even before a new government is in place.[16]

When Iraqis have attempted to elect their own local councils, the U.S. military has stepped in and stopped them, putting its own hand-picked choices in power instead—including former members of Hussein's military. Bremer admitted that the elections were suppressed to prevent anti-U.S. forces from winning: "It's often the best-organized who win," he said in June 2003, "and the best-organized right now are the former Ba'athists and to some extent the Islamists." The local councils created by the CPA have neither budgets (they must request money from the occupation authority) nor executive authority.[17]

The *Washington Post* reported that U.S. and British officials orchestrated the formation of the Council "to appear as if it emerged from consultations among Iraqis and not as a creation of the occupation authority," and assessed U.S. objectives in forming it as follows:

> the occupation authority is attempting to appease the country's Shiite Muslim majority and the legions of Iraqis who are suspicious of politicians who lived outside the country during Saddam Hussein's rule. At the same time, occupation forces are trying to create a body that will cooperate with them *and support policies that are generally in line with U.S. interests....* Giving the group a more prominent role in postwar governance is intended to place Iraqis at the receiving end of some of the popular discontent that has been directed at the occupation administration, a strategy that senior officials with the authority said will eventually help to stem attacks on U.S. and British troops....[emphasis added][18]

The largely symbolic nature of the "Governing Council" was illustrated by its first action: while Iraqis were suffering from power outages, water shortages, job losses, and humiliation at the hands of U.S. forces, the Council contented itself with declaring Baghdad's April 9 fall a national holiday and revoking six holidays celebrated by the former regime. Shortly after the Council's formation, thousands of protestors marched in Najaf declaring, "America and the Council are infidels," while even mainstream U.S. journalists reported on the "widely held perception among Iraqis and the rest of the world that the new Governing Council was an American puppet."[19]

In August, one Iraqi advisor to the Governing Council told the *Los Angeles Times*,

> It's just like in the old days under the British mandate. Technically, you had an Iraqi minister. But it was the senior advisor, who was always a Briton, who was running things. If you wanted to get things done, you went and saw the fellow with the blue eyes, not the Iraqi. That is very much the situation as it's perceived today.[20]

Political Power—From the Barrel of a U.S. Gun

Weapons—of mass destruction and otherwise—did factor into the U.S. decision to wage war on Iraq, but not because Iraq possessed unconventional weapons or was a threat to the region, much less to America. Washington's goal was to lock in its Persian Gulf dominance by permanently stripping Iraq of any ability to project military power, assert its interests in the region, or impede U.S. and Israeli military actions. "The Bush administration fears that the acquisition of nuclear weapons by Iraq could change the balance of power in the Persian Gulf," the *New York Times* reported before the war, "by making other Arab states less willing to align themselves with Washington and by limiting the United States' military options."[21] The U.S. solution to this potential has been regime change, followed by downsizing the Iraqi armed forces and removing Ba'ath officials from power.

In April 2003, as the Hussein regime crumbled, Zalmay Khalilzad, U.S. envoy to the Iraqi opposition, presided in Nasiriya over the first meeting of Iraqis hand-picked by the Pentagon to help form a new government. "The United States has no desire to govern Iraq, and I have made that clear in all my discussions here," he wrote. "The Iraqi people should govern their own affairs as soon as possible."[22]

In fact, the Bush administration had been planning how Iraq's affairs should be arranged for over a year, first by the State Department's "Future of Iraq" project, and later by the Pentagon and National Security Council.[23] Speaking in Washington in October 2002, six months before the Nasiriya meeting, Khalilzad had already proscribed Iraqi sovereignty: "Our objective for the long term in Iraq would be to establish a broad-based representative government...that will renounce terror and weapons of mass destruction.... We would eliminate the WMD threat from Iraq. We would decrease the threat that Iraq poses to regional peace and stability...."[24]

After the war, the U.S. quickly carried out this plan. On May 23, 2003, Bremer formally dissolved the Ba'ath government's military and paramilitary forces. At their peak, these forces had included an army of 400,000 soldiers and 2,600 tanks and an air force of over 300 war planes. A month later the U.S. announced that the new Iraqi army would have only 40,000 soldiers and that its duties would be confined to guarding Iraq's border and key facilities. Walter Slocombe, the official in charge, who represents a country that spends more on its armed forces than the rest of the world combined, explained that Iraq had been "grotesquely over-militarized."[25]

Rumsfeld's "Core Principles for a Free Iraq"

The CPA has stated that the "Governing Council" will choose a committee that will organize a constitutional convention, paving the way for a referendum on a new constitution, followed by general elections, perhaps within a year or so. "Once approved, democratic free and fair elections will be held in Iraq for a fully sovereign Iraqi government, and then our job is over," Bremer stated shortly after the interim council was announced. U.S. forces would then supposedly leave the country. "We have no desire to stay a day longer than is necessary," Bremer said, although he has acknowledged that U.S. "security" forces may stay on.[26]

The U.S. is clearly hoping to stage-manage this process in order to create a reliable client state, probably to allow it to withdraw most American military personnel. Elections are being delayed in order to ensure that the most pro-U.S. elements—often exile groups with little popular standing or organization within Iraq (which is why, much to the U.S.'s frustration, they could never topple Hussein via an internal coup, despite a number of attempts during the 1990s)—have the opportunity to gather enough strength to prevail. One tactic to ensure that this takes place was spelled out by Rumsfeld in his "Core Principles for a Free Iraq": "Promote Iraqis who share the goals of a free and moderate Iraq" by "staffing ministries and positioning Iraqis in ways that will increase their influence."[27]

Washington may also seek to strengthen the hand of its most trusted frontmen—the INA and INC—by placing them in charge of the new intelligence and security apparatus. the *New York Times* reported in July 2003 that Ahmad Chalabi of the INC was working with U.S. officials to reconstitute Iraq's intelligence services, including by rehabilitating agents from Hussein's dreaded Mukhabarat in order to help identify and combat anti-U.S. resisters. Chalabi, who is from a wealthy Iraqi family which was close to the pro-British monarchy, has lived outside of Iraq for decades. Charged with bank fraud in Jordan, he has been a key contributor more recently to Washington's WMD intelligence fraud. Chalabi attended the key September 19-20, 2001 Defense Policy Board meeting that helped chart the course for war on Iraq and has been the Pentagon's choice to rule in post-Hussein Iraq.[28]

This is Liberation?

The U.S. hopes to parlay the just popular hatred of the former Hussein regime into acceptance of the new client regime. Meanwhile, the Pentagon is attempting to crush the armed resistance to occupation through search and destroy missions and targeted assassinations, and to put in place mechanisms for suppressing future outbreaks of mass opposition, whether from Ba'ath party loyalists, Shi'a Islamists, or secular nationalists or revolutionaries.

Law, order and "justice" have so far been mainly enforced by the U.S. military, while the CPA tries to reconstitute the Iraqi legal system and police force. The U.S. has imposed draconian and illegal punishments against those who have opposed—or are suspected of opposing—its occupation. In June 2003, after sending a delegation to Iraq, Amnesty International reported:

> The conditions of detention Iraqis are held under at the Camp Cropper Center at Baghdad International Airport—now a US base—and at Abu Ghraib Prison may amount to cruel, inhuman or degrading treatment or punishment, banned by international law... Detainees held in Baghdad have invariably reported that they suffered cruel, inhuman or degrading treatment immediately after arrest, being tightly bound with plastic handcuffs and sometimes denied water and access to a toilet in the first night of arrest. Delegates saw numerous ex-detainees with wrists still scarred by the cuffs a month later.[29]

As of October 2003, the U.S. was holding some 10,000 prisoners, including "security detainees," suspected criminals, foreigners, and members of the former regime.[30]

Any Iraqis who work for the new government are required to sign a statement denouncing the Ba'ath Party and pledging obedience to the U.S.: "I will obey the laws of Iraq and all proclamations, orders and instructions of the Coalition Provisional Authority." In May, the U.S. demanded that Iraqis turn in all automatic and heavy weapons within three weeks.[31]

More than 100 newspapers sprouted in the wake of Hussein's fall, many of them critical, in one way or another, of the U.S. occupation. So in June, Bremer issued an edict "prohibiting the local media from inciting attacks on other Iraqis—and on the coalition forces." Since then, U.S. authorities have closed down at least two newspapers and one radio station for violating Bremer's edict, continued to censor Iraqi TV, and in August appointed a UN official to oversee the media.[32]

Over the summer, the CPA announced it was forming a 7,000-man American-trained militia to "put an Iraqi face on the coalition's postwar security efforts," according to the *New York Times*. However, it has also been reported that the Pentagon is seeking a long-term military relationship with Iraq's new government which would include access to four bases on Iraqi soil: one outside Baghdad, another near Nasariya in the south, a third in the western desert, and the fourth in the Kurdish north. This means that while most U.S. forces might be withdrawn, the U.S. could still redeploy troops in case its new client government proves incapable of controlling the population, much as the Britain's Royal Air Force served as a guarantor for Iraq's pro-British monarchy for over 30 years.[33]

A Cauldron of Ethnic and Religious Tensions

In choosing its first Iraqi "Governing Council," the U.S. paid close attention to creating the appearance of inclusion and fair representation of Iraq's religiously and ethnically diverse population: the council included 13 Shi'as, five Kurds, five Sunnis, one Assyrian Christian and one Turkoman; three of the members were women.

However, this top-down selection provides neither genuine self-determination for Iraq's ethnic minorities, nor insures genuine democracy, and U.S. interests will predominate. For instance, Shi'as make up 60 percent of Iraq's population, yet Rumsfeld quickly ruled out the formation of a Shi'a theocracy in Iraq or an alignment with Iran—regardless of how Iraqis feel about these issues. The U.S. also made a point of picking more secular than religious leaders for the interim Iraqi council.[34]

Nor does the U.S. intend to give Kurds full self-determination, or even control of a share of Kirkuk's oil-wealth—which would strengthen Kurdish independence (potentially emboldening Kurds in Turkey). This is a continuation of imperial policy dating back to the British creation of Iraq in the 1920s. Kurdish leaders Barzani and Talabani, while making clear their willingness to continue working with the U.S., have openly expressed concerns that Kurds forced from Kurdistan during Hussein's rule are not being provided the assistance necessary to return home, and that "aspects" of overall U.S. strategy "remain vague," including whether the new Iraqi state will be organized on a federal basis to ensure Kurdish autonomy.[35]

In September 2003, Secretary of State Colin Powell gave the Iraqi Governing Council six months to finalize a new constitution, but Council members quickly complained the goal was impossible due to what the *Washington Post* called "profound disagreements over the role of Islamic law and the basic contours of a new political system," including relations between Iraq's Shi'as, Sunnis and Kurds. Rather than improving as a result of the U.S. war and occupation, the *Washington Post* reported that Sunni-Shi'a divisions "have widened," and that there were "deepening divisions between Iraq's principal ethnic and religious groups."[36]

So the deep internal tensions that for 80 years led Britain and later the U.S. to support Sunni Arab domination over Iraq's diverse peoples have not been resolved and have the potential to explode into civil war or an uprising against the occupation in the months and years ahead.

Political and Economic Shock, No Awe

The Hussein regime embodied, at least to some extent, the politics of Arab nationalism forged in the anti-colonial upheavals of the 1950s and 1960s. It had nationalized Iraq's oil industry, encouraged domestic industrialization, provided some support to the Palestinian struggle, and attempted to maintain a certain degree of independence from the world's major powers.

The overthrow of that Ba'ath regime is intended to deal a death blow to such Arab aspirations and to reorient Iraq's foreign and economic policies to suit U.S. interests. Shortly after the war ended, Rumsfeld spelled out Washington's plan to turn Iraq into a platform for its regional aims: Iraq, he argued, could become "a new ally in the global war on terror and the struggle for freedom and moderation in the Muslim world."[37]

What this could mean in practice began to come into view shortly after the war when the Pentagon began reconstituting elements of the Hussein regime's intelligence services which had spied on Iran and Syria—both prime targets in the Bush "war on terror."[38]

A gigantic shift in Iraq's orientation toward Israel may also be in the works: shortly after the war one State Department official said that he hoped one of Iraq's first actions would be to extend diplomatic recognition to Israel, and in August 2003, the Israeli paper *Ha'aretz* reported that the U.S. had asked Israel to explore the possibility of pumping oil from Iraq to oil refineries in Haifa, in part as repayment for Israeli support for the war.[39]

Bremer has claimed, "The people of Iraq are now on the road to political and economic independence," that "America has no designs on Iraq and its wealth," and that Iraq's new Governing Council will have the power to set oil and economic policies.[40]

In fact, long before the Governing Council was picked, the Bush team had already made plans to reshape Iraq's economy in U.S. interests. In May 2003, two months before the Council's formation was announced, the *Wall Street Journal* reported that it had obtained a secret 100-page document titled, "Moving The Iraq Economy From Recovery to Sustainable Growth," which laid out a detailed U.S. plan for radically restructuring Iraq's economy after the war:

> The Bush administration has drafted sweeping plans to remake Iraq's economy in the U.S. image. Hoping to establish a free-market economy in Iraq following the fall of Saddam Hussein, the U.S. is calling for the privatization of state-owned industries such as parts of the oil sector, forming a stock market complete with electronic trading and fundamental tax reform.

According to the story, implementation of the plan was being delegated "largely to private American contractors working alongside a smaller team of U.S. officials," and it included mass privatization of Iraq's previously state-dominated economy and revamping Iraq's tax and tariff system. "Officials would spend a year building a consensus for industry privatization," the *Wall Street Journal* reported, "and then transfer assets over the following three years."[41]

Rumsfeld and Bremer have echoed this orientation. Rumsfeld's "Core Principles for a Free Iraq" stipulate: "Decisions will favor market systems.... The coalition will encourage moves to privatize state-owned enterprises."[42] In June, Bremer wrote, "economic growth will depend on the birth of a vibrant private sector. And this will require the wholesale reallocation of resources and people from state control to private enterprise, the promotion of foreign trade, and the mobilization of domestic and foreign capital."[43]

Bremer reportedly plans to enact new laws favoring foreign investment, has bragged about "opening Iraq's borders and bringing modern free-trade policies here," and shepherded an Iraqi delegation to that vanguard of capitalist globalization—the World Economic Forum, which held a summit in Amman, Jordan in June 2003.[44]

U.S. officials justify this drastic restructuring by blaming—who else—Saddam Hussein: "We need to undo the enormous economic damage that has been done here over the last 30 years," Bremer declared in July. "This is a problem we inherited from a regime that for 35 years underinvested in every aspect of this country."[45]

In fact, it was the Ba'ath government's efforts to invest domestically to build up Iraq's economic, technical and military strength (as opposed to other oil-producing Gulf states which invest billions of petrodollars in the West), that helped deepen Washington's animosity toward Saddam Hussein. Of course, Bremer and company never take responsibility for the role played by U.S. bombs and sanctions in devastating Iraq's economy.

Having savaged Iraq, Washington now seeks to revamp its economy to suit American interests and control. U.S. officials frequently compare their current occupation to the rebuilding of Japan and Germany following World War II. There are many differences between these times and these places, but one stands out: Iraq's position in the global economy. It is to remain a Third World country oriented toward, and dependent upon, petroleum production for the world market.

Under Hussein, Iraq practiced a form of capitalism in which major industries were owned by the state, and the country remained dependent on oil sales on the global market for most of its income and on foreign technology for its petroleum and manufacturing sectors. However, it exercised a degree of national control through the state.

Selling off these state-owned industries and opening Iraq up to foreign trade and investment are designed to both help pay for Iraq's reconstruction—although post-war difficulties may be forcing Bush leadership to modify its plans—and more fundamentally to lead to more direct dominance by foreign capital, U.S. capital in particular, and perhaps even direct foreign ownership. Iraq is being used as something of a test lab for privatization and increased globalization in the region—economic "shock and awe." As discussed in chapter 1, such globalization at gunpoint is a core element of the new U.S. National Security Strategy.

In country after country, this kind of shock therapy has led to massive suffering, and the results are already apparent in Iraq. An estimated 500,000 Iraqis may be laid off by the privatization of Iraqi state-run firms and the downsizing of Iraq's military. This means one worker out of every ten could be sacked in a country where unemployment two months after the war stood at 60 percent.[46]

The *San Francisco Chronicle's* Robert Collier writes from Baghdad:

> Almost overnight, it seems, Baghdad has been turned into a vast emporium of imported goods.... It's part of a bold yet risky economic strategy by the U.S. occupation authorities, who have eliminated all import taxes for goods coming to Iraq at the same time they are pumping hundreds of millions of dollars into the economy through cash payments to government workers.... But the boom has come at a high price because it has accelerated the closure of hundreds of factories. After 12 years of economic crisis and strict import regulations under U.N. sanctions, Iraqi manufacturers cannot begin to compete with the price and quality of foreign goods. The closures, in turn, have thrown large numbers of people out of work, increasing social tensions at a time when public dissatisfaction with the U.S. occupation is growing to dangerous levels.[47]

Anti-globalization writer and activist Naomi Klein wonders if Bremer's campaign of removing Ba'ath Party officials from power, or "de-Ba'athification," is actually a cover for "a full-scale assault" on the state:

> Is he working only to get rid of Ba'ath Party members, or is he also working to shrink the public sector as a whole so that hospitals, schools and even the army are primed for privatization by US firms? Just as reconstruction is the guise for privatization, de-Baathification looks a lot like disguised downsizing.[48]

The Bush II regime appears to be ready to shock and ruin Iraqi agriculture as well. Dan Amstutz, formerly a top executive at Cargill, the world's biggest grain exporter, and a trade negotiator for the Reagan administration, has been put in charge of Iraqi agriculture.

Middle East Report notes with alarm:

> Relief groups such as Oxfam worry this means that Iraqi agriculture will be left unprotected from cut-rate US competition, and that Amstutz will try to dump cheap US grain on the potentially lucrative Iraqi market rather than encourage the country to rebuild the agricultural sector.[49]

The U.S. is also moving to reshape Iraq's finances. A new currency—without Saddam's image—is scheduled to debut in October, but as the *New York Times* remarks, "It appears...that American officials may retain veto power over monetary policy and other decisions."[50]

Meanwhile, U.S. banks are lining up for their share of the take. The *Wall Street Journal* reported in June:

> American banks are aggressively seeking what could be a lucrative role in rebuilding Iraq's financial system.... J.P. Morgan Chase & Co., Citigroup Inc. and Bank of America Corp.— three of the nation's top five banks—and several others have conferred with Treasury Department officials in recent weeks about helping the Iraqis with trade finance, payments systems, foreign-currency exchange and the daunting task of building a modern retail banking system.[51]

On September 20, 2003, Bremer enacted a sweeping privatization of the Iraqi economy which, as the *Washington Post* put it, "allows foreign firms to enter and potentially dominate key elements of the economy, from banking to manufacturing." Iraqi petroleum was not included in this initial firesale, but it could soon be on the auction block. Kamil Mubdir Gailani, Iraq's new Finance Minister, announced the new privatization plan at the annual meeting of the IMF and World Bank in Dubai, stating that the new government would "allow up to 100 percent foreign ownership in all sectors except natural resources," that foreigners could now lease land for up to 40 years, that tax rates for the most wealthy would be drastically reduced, and that some foreign banks were already poised to fully take over a number of Iraqi banks.[52]

The whole process has been set up to favor U.S. capital—not its global competitors, not even Iraqis themselves. According to Iraqi contributors to OccupationWatch.org, "Iraqi business people are complaining that U.S. companies are being given preference in the bidding process," while others express concern that Iraqi businesses will be unable to compete with global U.S. behemoths. Paul Krugman of the *New York Times* writes that Middle Eastern entrepreneurs, including some who tried to set up a cellphone network as well as Iraqis with expertise in repairing the country's electrical grid, have so far been prevented from doing business by the CPA.[53]

Klein sums up:

> Iraq looks like every other country that has undergone rapid-fire 'structural adjustments' prescribed by Washington, from Russia's infamous 'shock therapy' in the early 1990s to Argentina's disastrous 'surgery without anesthetic.' Except that Iraq's 'reconstruction' makes those wrenching reforms look like spa treatments.[54]

Re-Education—American Style

The scope of U.S. ambitions is perhaps best illustrated by what has so far been revealed of plans for a radical reshaping of Iraqi education and public opinion. USAID has given the U.S. company Creative Associates International a $62 million contract to revamp the Iraqi educational curriculum, hire teachers, and rewrite Iraq's school textbooks, which now "demonized the U.S. as a fearsome enemy," "touted Iraqi battlefield prowess" and vilified "Israel and the United States." Presumably, such nationalist and anti-colonialist sentiments would be stricken from the new U.S.-government approved texts along with any flattering mention of Saddam Hussein.[55]

U.S. propaganda, in the form of the evening news, is being beamed into Iraq. On April 15, 2003, the day Bush declared the Hussein regime was no more, the *Los Angeles Times* reported:

> Sometime this week, Iraqis with television reception will turn on their sets and see a parade of new faces delivering the evening news: Dan Rather, Tom Brokaw, Peter Jennings, Jim Lehrer and Brit Hume. The news package—which will include nightly programming produced by Arab journalists in Washington and the Middle East—is part of an ambitious effort that White House officials say will show Iraq what a free press looks like in a democracy. 'Iraq and the World,' funded by the U.S. government, will feature nightly contributions from CBS,

NBC, ABC, PBS and Fox News translated into Arabic...[56]

By August, the *New York Times* was reporting that the Pentagon-run "Iraqi Media Network" was "a $5-million-a-month dud. Iraqis do not watch it, having judged its programming to be repetitive and larded with official propaganda...."[57]

In one surreal touch, while touring Iraq in July, Wolfowitz declared, "I think all foreigners should stop interfering in the internal affairs of Iraq." Apparently when the U.S. invades, conquers and occupies a country, then restructures its politics, economics, governance, education and foreign policy, the Pentagon does not consider it foreign interference.[58]

"The Primary Strategic Challenge of Our Time"

Global dominance is impossible without Middle East dominance, not only for its stupendous petroleum reserves, but for its strategic location at the intersection of Africa, Asia and Europe as well.

The U.S. senses both an historic opportunity to deepen its control of this region—and thus its global primacy—in the wake of the Soviet collapse, as well as a compelling necessity to intervene due to the accumulation of rage, conflict, and instability across the region. The Middle East's petroleum wealth is vast, yet per-capita income growth in the 22 Arab League states is lower than anywhere on earth except sub-Saharan Africa. In 1999, these Arab countries produced a total gross domestic product of $531.2 billion—less than Spain's. The 280 million people living in the Arab world earn on average less than one-seventh what people living in industrialized countries do. One in five lives on less than $2 a day, and 65 million are illiterate—two-thirds of them women. The region is dominated by repressive U.S.-backed regimes, from Turkey, to Saudi Arabia, to Egypt.[59]

In his *History of the Modern Middle East*, William Cleveland summarizes the situation in the aftermath of the 1991 Persian Gulf war:

> Popular disaffection with the ruling elites spread throughout the region, whether in Islamic Iran, secular Turkey, or authoritarian Egypt.... It is difficult to recall a period prior to the late 1990s when popular discontent was so widespread, when so many authoritarian rulers in key states had held onto power for

so long and were simultaneously reaching the age when their rule must end, or when a single outside power–the United States—exercised such exclusive domination and aroused such deep—seated resentment.[60]

Raymond Lotta argues that these Middle East tensions and instabilities, and the U.S. response to them, are part of a larger global pattern:

> Economically and socially, there is great and growing instability in much of the Third World—as imperialist globalization, wrenching turns of the world economy, and chaotic urbanization tear at economic structures and the social fabric. Politically, there is a growing crisis of the neocolonial state.... Imperialism's mechanisms of control in the Third World have grown shakier and more unreliable. Under the signboard of the war on terrorism, the U.S. imperialists are seeking to restructure neocolonial rule, to tighten their rule. And they are speaking a more openly *colonial* language. They are talking about global military action and direct and long-term military occupation to bring order, stability, and "civilizing norms" to "failed states" and societies that are "breeding grounds for terrorism."[61]

The Bush regime and its supporters see Iraq as a first step and a test case in dealing with these dangerous problems and to open up new opportunities for the U.S. in the Middle East. Before the war, Khalilzad called conquering Iraq "a key element in a long-term strategy for the transformation of this region as a whole." Afterward, former Clinton administration officials Ronald Asmus and Kenneth Pollack argued that, "A consensus is emerging in Washington that the greater Middle East constitutes the primary strategic challenge of our time."[62]

This restructuring campaign is being carried out under the banners of freedom and democracy. In 2003, Bush II echoed Bush I's 1991 promise that war on Iraq would help resolve the region's deep problems and bring peace and prosperity. "A liberated Iraq can show the power of freedom to transform this vital region by bringing hope and progress into the lives of millions," Bush II told the American Enterprise Institute in February 2003. "A new regime in Iraq would serve as a dramatic and inspiring example of freedom for other nations in the region."[63]

The son's promises will likely prove as empty as the father's. The suffering that grips the Middle East and the anti-U.S. hatred it has spawned are largely the product of decades of Western economic, political, and military domination and suffocation. Now, in response, Washington offers more direct and forceful dominance. "Democracy" and "freedom" serve as rhetorical camouflage for further opening the region up to global capital, and for deeper American penetration and control—as is becoming evident in post-Hussein Iraq. The *Wall Street Journal* acknowledges that Bush's real goal is making the entire Middle East "safer for American interests."[64]

U.S. officials and think-tank strategists have made the brutality and sweep of the Bush administration's designs clear. A July 2002 Rand Corporation briefing at the Pentagon called for reconfiguring the entire region to U.S. specifications with Iraq the "tactical pivot," Saudi Arabia the "strategic pivot," and Egypt "the prize." Journalist Sasha Lilley reported that before the war, British officials were busily discussing the "break-up of Saudi Arabia and Iraq," as well as "the possible partition of Egypt, the Sudan, Syria and Lebanon." Anti-war British MP George Galloway stated that the motive was to "better to ensure the hegemony of the big powers over the natural resources of the Middle East and the safety and security of the vanguard of imperialist interests in the area—the state of Israel."[65]

Influential right-wingers talk of "reforming" the entire Islamic world. After interviewing Bush II officials and Washington strategists prior to the 2003 war, the *New Yorker's* Nicholas Lemann detailed the sweep of their ambitions following war with Iraq:

> After regime change, the United States would persuade Iran to end its nuclear weapons program and its support for terrorists elsewhere in the Middle East, especially Hezbollah. Syria, now surrounded by the pro-American powers of Turkey, the reconfigured Iraq, Jordan, and Israel, and no longer dependent on Saddam for oil, could be pressured to cooperate with efforts to clean out Hamas, Islamic Jihad, and Hezbollah. As Syria moved to a more pro-American stand, so would its client state, Lebanon. That would leave Hezbollah, which has its headquarters in Lebanon, without state support. The Palestinian Authority, with most of its regional allies stripped away, would have no choice but to renounce terrorism categorically. Saudi Arabia would have much less sway over the United States because it would no longer be America's only major source of oil and base of military operations in the region, and so it might

finally be persuaded to stop funding Hamas and Al Qaeda
through Islamic charities.[66]

James Woolsey, former CIA Director and post-9/11 pointman
for regime change in Iraq, echoed these sentiments in even more
blunt and brutal terms: "America and the western world are at war
with 'fascist' Middle East governments and totalitarian Islamists," he
wrote. It is "a war to the death," and like the Cold War, it would last
for "decades."[67]

In an August 2003 speech to the National Association of Black
Journalists, National Security Adviser Condoleezza Rice called for
the U.S. to "go on the offense" and "make a generational commitment to helping the people of the Middle East transform their
region."[68]

The specifics of this ambitious and radical agenda have been
left purposely vague. However, from the actions and policy stances
the Bush team has recently taken, and statements made by this
agenda's leading proponents, it is possible to discern six overarching
and interconnected strategic objectives in the Middle East, explored
below in relation to different countries in the region, in the wake of
regime change in Iraq:

1. To intimidate or overthrow governments whose actions clash
    with U.S. regional designs, including Iran, Syria, Lebanon,
    and Libya;
2. To end the Palestinian struggle on Israeli terms and force the
    Arab states to halt any support for the Palestinians, while
    strengthening Israel and expanding its role as a sub-imperial
    power;
3. To suppress popular struggles against the U.S. and Israel—
    often branded "terrorism" by Washington—and force
    regimes in the region to crackdown on anti-U.S. groups and
    sentiments, including Islamist movements;
4. To restructure vulnerable U.S. clients such as Saudi Arabia;
5. To further open the Middle East to capitalist globalization;
    and
6. To diminish the influence of other world powers in the
    region.

The Bush II regime's top leadership intends to use American
political, economic, and military might to achieve these ambitious

goals, and are planning to extend their "war on terror" for years, if necessary, to realize them.

Pressing On to Damascus or Tehran?

Iran and Syria have been obstacles to American hegemony in the Middle East for over two decades. Both have their own national and regional agendas which have come into conflict with U.S. interests, including over their hostility to Israel, their support for certain Palestinian organizations and Lebanon's Hezbollah (which has put them on the State Department list of countries supporting "terrorism"), and U.S. claims that both are pursuing "weapons of mass destruction." Syria is also at odds with Washington and Tel Aviv over Israel's continued occupation of the Golan Heights, which it seized during the 1967 war, and Syrian influence in Lebanon. Iran's size, oil wealth, strategic location, and recent history of conflict with Washington make it a particular concern, as well as a major strategic prize.

Since the 1990s, the leading architects of a more dominant American empire have been calling for targeting both Damascus and Tehran. The 1996 "Clean Break" paper, whose authors included Perle, Douglas Feith and David Wurmser—all later top officials in the Bush II administration—argued that Israel could be strengthened "by weakening, containing and even rolling back Syria."[69]

In his 1999 book advocating war on Iraq, Wurmser, speculated that regime change in Baghdad could be used to weaken Iran and strip it of its regional militancy: "Liberating the Shi'ite centers in Najaf and Karbala, with their clerics who reject the wilayat al-faqih, could allow Iraqi Shi'ites to challenge and perhaps fatally derail the Iranian revolution." This in turn could weaken Shi'ite forces in Lebanon, he theorizes, and "whittle away at Syria's power."[70]

After Bush's election in 2000, a Presidential Study Group whose Steering Committee included Wolfowitz, published a paper titled "Navigating through Turbulence: America and the Middle East in a New Century" that pointed to Syria and Iraq as the U.S.'s two main adversaries in the region.[71] The drumbeat for attacking Syria and Iran was stepped up after Sept. 11 via such neoconservative organizations as the so-called "Coalition for Democracy in

Iran."[72] Months before the 2003 Iraq War, Israeli Prime Minister Ariel Sharon urged that Tehran be targeted "the day after" the war because it was a "centre of world terror," and Israeli threats against Iran have continued after the war.[73]

During and after the 2003 war, Bush officials have made numerous belligerent statements against both Syria and Iran for allegedly allowing anti-U.S. fighters into Iraq, and the U.S. cut off Syria's oil supply from Iraq. Bush has continued to charge that Tehran and Damascus "harbor and assist terrorists," and warned, "This behavior is completely unacceptable, and states that support terror will be held accountable."[74]

The U.S. has demanded that Syria end its support for Lebanon's Hezbollah, shut down the offices of Palestinian guerrilla organizations in the country, deport their leaders and refuse to allow them to hold press interviews.[75] Bush has spoken in support of anti-regime demonstrators in Iran, warned Tehran against meddling in post-Hussein Iraq, intensified his campaign against its alleged pursuit of weapons of mass destruction, and for the first time warned the Islamic Republic that he would "not tolerate the construction of a nuclear weapon."[76]

Just how to handle Iran and Syria has been the subject of intense debate within the Bush team. In April 2003, Britain's *Guardian* reported that Defense Secretary Rumsfeld had ordered contingency plans be drawn up for war on Syria, but they were tabled by the Bush administration.[77]

In early summer, the Pentagon was also reportedly advocating a "massive covert action program" to topple the Islamic Republic, and that the U.S. was considering a preemptive strike on Iran's nuclear facilities.[78] There has also been a campaign underway to push Bush to adopt "regime change" as official policy, arguing that the war to reshape the Middle East can't be stopped half-way: "We're riding a horse and we're in the middle of the stream," said Sen. Sam Brownback of Kansas, who has pushed for a congressional resolution mandating the overthrow of the Islamic Republic. "We've got to press on to the other side."[79]

As of this writing in fall 2003, however, it appears that the U.S. will not immediately extend its "war on terror" to Iran or Syria, partly due to its mounting difficulties in Iraq and partly because it had no sure military options. The U.S. hopes that its assault on Iraq will intimidate Iran and Syria into capitulation or collapse, short of war. As Undersecretary of State Bolton warned as the Iraq war was winding down, "We are hopeful that a number of regimes will draw the appropriate lesson from Iraq that the pursuit of weapons of mass destruction is not in their national interest." The *New York Times* speculated that, "the administration would far prefer that Iraq proved to be the catalyst for velvet revolutions across the Middle East and beyond."[80]

So the Bush team is attempting to achieve its far-reaching regional objectives, step-by-step and flexibly without getting bogged down or overextended, while maintaining the momentum of its "war on terror." These contradictory pulls and tensions are inherent in their global strategy, whose magnitude and brutality are already greatly intensifying them.

The U.S. and Israel: A Deepening Convergence

The 2003 Iraq War and the broader U.S. regional agenda are also intended to strengthen Israel as a forward base of American influence and military power, including by ending the Palestinian struggle on terms favorable to American and Israeli interests. This has become more urgent to Bush and company in light of their larger objectives in the region: reshaping Middle East politics, suppressing anti-U.S. resistance, and solidifying the America's hold on the region and its petroleum wealth demands an increasing military presence, a readiness to use force, and loyal regional allies to help carry it out. In all these respects, Israel fills the bill.

The Palestinian struggle for national self-determination graphically embodies the clash between foreign domination and Arab self-determination—in part because Israel's colonialization of historic Palestinian is a blatant throw-back to a previous era of imperialist sponsored settler-states. The courage of the Palestinian resistance in the face of vastly superior military force reverberates profoundly across the Middle East, fueling anti-U.S. anger, creating major difficulties for pro-U.S. regimes (including preventing them from openly supporting America's 2003 Iraq war "coalition"), and posing a serious obstacle to American dominance. Israel has never been accepted or fully integrated into the Middle East, but has instead existed in a near constant state of conflict with the Palestinians and neighboring states.

The attack-Iraq caucus has always viewed regime change in Baghdad and the "war on terror," in part, as the means to forcibly resolve these issues—not through recognizing the just demands of the Palestinian people, but by demoralizing them, removing any regional allies, and forcing them to submit to Israeli terms. This brutal approach was repeatedly spelled out prior to the war by its most vocal advocates. For instance, the *Wall Street Journal* editorialized that the creation of a "democratic pro-western Iraq" would "do more for peace in Palestine than 100 trips by Colin Powell."[81]

In a speech to the American Enterprise Institute on the eve of war, Bush echoed these themes:

> Success in Iraq could also begin a new stage for Middle Eastern peace and set in motion progress towards a truly democratic Palestinian state. The passing of Saddam Hussein's regime will deprive terrorist networks of a wealthy patron that pays for terrorist training and offers rewards to families of suicide bombers. And other regimes will be given a clear warning that support for terror will not be tolerated.... And the Arab states will be expected to meet their responsibilities to oppose terrorism, to support the emergence of a peaceful and democratic Palestine, and state clearly they will live in peace with Israel.[82]

The U.S. and Israeli governments are increasingly close, even incestuous; many top officials in the Bush II administration, in particular those who were at the forefront of pushing for war on Iraq—Wolfowitz, Perle, Wurmser, and company—are closely linked to the Israeli right-wing. The point is not that these officials are beholden to Israel or are being controlled by the "Jewish lobby." The point is that there is a growing confluence between the U.S. and Israeli agendas in the region. As Stanford professor Joel Beinin notes, "The interests of the pro-Israel lobby and the attack-Iraq caucus of the second Bush administration have converged, and are to a significant degree represented by the same people."[83]

Writing in the *London Review of Books*, Anatol Lieven of the Carnegie Endowment for International Peace concludes, "From the point of view of the Arab-Israeli conflict, war with Iraq also has some of the character of a *Flucht nach vorn*—an 'escape forwards'—

on the part of the U.S. Administration." In many ways, this is an apt description of the entire U.S. "war on terror" as well—an attempt to escape the contradictions gripping its empire, by brutally grasping for greater empire.[84]

Much has been made of the so-called U.S. roadmap to peace—officially "A Performance-Based Road Map to a Permanent Two-State Solution to the Israeli-Palestinian Conflict"—and its promise to lead to the "emergence of an independent, democratic, and viable Palestinian state."[85]

It should be recalled that Bush I made similar promises leading up to the first Gulf War and that these promises did not bring justice, but resulted in the intensification of Israel's illegal settlement activity, forced closures and destruction of the Palestinian economy, and of the daily humiliation and abuse Palestinians face in their historic homeland.

Bush II's promises will likely prove as hollow, as evidenced by his actions since taking office and by the nature of the U.S. "roadmap." When Palestinian anger exploded in 2000 in the second Intifada, the Bush II administration increased its support of Israeli brutality, calling its war on the Palestinian Authority "self defense," while basically labeling the Palestinian people's desperate struggle for national survival "terrorism." The Bush II regime has refused to seriously demand even minor concessions from Israel or force it to end its ongoing and illegal settlement activities in the occupied territories—which Rumsfeld and Perle have even called legitimate spoils of war. No wonder Israeli Prime Minister Sharon stated, "we never had such a cooperation in everything as we have with the current administration."[86]

The "roadmap" is a continuation of these politics. It lays out three phases before a final settlement by 2005. The first phase centers on "security," focusing not on ending Israeli violence, but on ending the Palestinian resistance. Professor Rashid Khalidi notes that phase one's discussion, "concentrates on Palestinian violence and how to combat it—as if it came out of nowhere, and as if, were it to be halted, the situation of occupation and settlement would be normal." The goal was spelled out by Israel's army chief of staff, Lieut. Gen. Moshe Ya'alon: "The Palestinians must be made to understand in the deepest recesses of their consciousness that they are a defeated people."[87]

The core issues for Palestinians are put off until the final stage: the fate of Israeli settlements now covering over 40 percent of the occupied territories; the status of Palestine's historic capital of Jerusalem; the right of return for the estimated 4.5 million Palestinians now living in exile in Jordan, Lebanon, Syria and other countries, often in squalid refugees camps; and the actual content of Palestinian "sovereignty."

In all likelihood, Israel will be allowed to annex large swaths of the West Bank, leaving Palestinians living in disconnected cantons encircled by Israeli walls, roads, settlements and checkpoints. In previous negotiations, Israel has insisted that it retain control of Palestine's borders, aquifers, airspace, and most if not all of Jerusalem, while refusing any right of return for Palestinian refugees. All this guarantees that any future Palestinian state created by the U.S. and Israel—if indeed one is ever created—would be little more than an Israeli-controlled Bantustan, to be exploited as a pool of cheap labor.

The roadmap is, in short, an attempt to force the victims to give up their struggle for justice with no guarantee that their demands will ever be met, while attempting to reward the aggressors with illegally occupied land and social "peace."

Restructuring Wobbly Clients

Washington's post-war regional agenda also includes propping up and restructuring wobbly clients. Saudi Arabia, a long-time pillar of American oil dominance and regional power, is a particular focus. In 1991, the U.S. waged war on Iraq in part to defend Saudi Arabia. In 2003, it waged war in part to transform Saudi Arabia.

Sept. 11 triggered a barrage of criticism of the House of Saud because 15 of the 19 reputed hijackers were Saudis, and the operation was allegedly organized and inspired by Osama bin Laden, who grew up in the Kingdom and reportedly received extensive financial support from prominent Saudis. And there have been a number of attacks on American forces in the Royal Kingdom over the past decade. A July 2003 House and Senate intelligence committees report on the Sept. 11 attacks concluded that the Saudi government had impeded U.S. efforts against al Qaeda and may have given the hijackers monetary and logistical support, charges vehemently denied by Saudi officials.[88]

The Summer 2002 Rand Pentagon briefing, mentioned above, was even harsher. It labeled Saudi Arabia an "enemy" of the U.S., "active at every level of the terror chain" and recommended that the U.S. "demand that Saudi Arabia stop all anti-U.S., anti-Israel, and anti-western rhetoric in the region; dismantle and ban the kingdom's `Islamic charities' and confiscate their assets; and prosecute those involved in terrorism." If Saudi Arabia didn't comply, the briefer recommended the U.S. "target" Saudi oil fields along with its assets in the U.S. There has even been talk on the think-tank circuit of overturning the Saudi regime or partitioning the Royal Kingdom into several small states, with American forces occupying the oilfields in the eastern provinces, while placing the holy cities of Mecca and Medina under separate administration without an inflammatory U.S. presence.

There are a number of factors at work here. Some of this talk was intended to strong-arm the Saudi royal family into more closely supporting the war on Iraq and to crack down harder on anti-U.S. forces within the Kingdom. And the Saudis have apparently done both. The Kingdom quietly assisted the U.S. during the Iraq war. The Israeli newspaper *Ha'aretz* reported, "Saudi Arabia is the hidden player in the American war on Iraq...the American public would be surprised to discover just how critical was the Saudi contribution to the American war effort." It has also been reported that the Saudi government, under pressure from Washington, is stepping up its cooperation with U.S. law enforcement and cracking down harder on anti-U.S. political forces in the Kingdom.[89]

The U.S. has deep and long-standing ties with Saudi Arabia, which remains a key American asset, and the White House is not prepared to toss that relationship overboard and invite greater regional instability just yet. Hence its refusal in late July 2003 to declassify the portions of a Congressional report on security lapses leading up to Sept. 11 which discussed—and apparently harshly criticized—Saudi government culpability.[90]

However, U.S. concerns about Saudi Arabia go well beyond Sept. 11 and bin Laden. Deep tensions have built within the

Kingdom following the 1991 Persian Gulf War (discussed in chapter 6), and Washington fears that the corrupt, autocratic monarchy it has supported for 60 years may not be viable for the long term. The 2001 Baker report warned that if Saudi Arabia and other Gulf states "cannot deliver a better standard of living for rapidly increasing populations, social upheaval could result, and anti-Western elements could gain power." British MP Galloway says, "The United States is afraid that one day they'll wake up and a Khomeini type—or be it Wahhabi Sunni Khomeini—revolution would have occurred, and they would have lost everything in the country."[91]

Army Gen. Joseph P. Hoar, commander of U.S. Middle East forces between 1991 and 1994, has stated that one of the 2003 war's "unstated goals" was to shrink the U.S. military footprint in Saudi Arabia, thereby reducing the political opposition their presence generated.[92] Hussein's overthrow means that the U.S. will no longer need to keep thousands of troops and hundreds of aircraft in Turkey and Saudi Arabia to enforce "no-fly" zones over northern and southern Iraq. Even before Bush declared major combat over in May, the U.S. announced that it would withdraw all its combat forces from Saudi Arabia within several months.[93]

A longer-term goal is to "reform" countries like Saudi Arabia and Egypt by further opening them to global trade and investment. This is intended to both create greater opportunities for U.S. capital, including in Saudi Arabia and Kuwait's oil sectors as mentioned above, but also to try and stimulate economic growth and, Washington hopes, increase political stability. In 2002, Secretary of State Powell raised these concerns during a speech at the Heritage Foundation:

> The countries of the Middle East are also largely absent from world markets. They generate barely one percent of the world's non-oil exports. Only ten Middle Eastern countries belong to the World Trade Organization. The region's governments are now recognizing, as Egypt's President Hosni Mubarak has warned, that 'giving a boost to exports is a matter of life or death.' A shortage of economic opportunities is a ticket to despair. Combined with rigid political systems, it is a dangerous brew indeed.[94]

The *Los Angeles Times* reports that a main objective of the Bush regional strategy is to "foster economic reform based roughly on the East Asian model, with economic prosperity followed by government moves to open up politically. Malaysia, a major Islamic country in Southeast Asia, is often cited as an example."[95]

There is much debate within the U.S. establishment over how far and how fast to push Saudi Arabia to clamp down internally and open up externally. Shortly after the war, the *Wall Street Journal* bluntly editorialized:

> In the best case, the Saudi royals will learn from the fall of Saddam that they should introduce economic reforms in their country and move in a more democratic direction. At least they won't be able to use the excuse of U.S. forces anymore if they refuse to do so.[96]

* * *

Setting up a neo-colonial client state in Iraq, striking down troublesome regimes in the region, strengthening Israel, quelling anti-U.S. opposition, restructuring even loyal allies, and further opening up the whole Middle East to the depredations of foreign investment and trade—this is the sweeping and unprecedented mission the United States is embarking on.

What accounts for Washington's determination to push forward—in the face of potentially enormous costs and dangerous consequences, already visible in Iraq? The next chapter explores some of the economic and political roots of this new global agenda.

CHAPTER 10

OIL, POWER & EMPIRE

The U.S. government has mustered a dizzying and often shifting assortment of "reasons" for invading and occupying Iraq. At one time or another—sometimes in the next breath—it cited weapons of mass destruction and imminent threats to America, links to terrorism and al Qaeda, liberating the Iraqi people, and transforming the entire Middle East. Yet, as it was going on *ad nauseam* about such nonexistent threats, phantom connections, and hollow promises, there was one *real* issue that the Bush team adamantly refused to discuss at all: oil. Before the war, Rumsfeld even told CBS News that the U.S. conflict with Iraq "has nothing to do with oil, literally nothing to do with oil."[1]

Bush II officials studiously avoided even mentioning the "o-word." At one White House briefing on October 9, 2002, a reporter asked press spokesman Ari Fleischer, "how much does oil have to do with the assessment of the threat from Saddam Hussein? President Bush didn't mention it." Fleischer first claimed not to "follow" the question, then said it was "not a factor." He wouldn't even utter the word "oil" in the back-and-forth. Two days later, the *New York Times* reported that the Pentagon had plans to occupy Iraq and take control of its oil fields.[2]

Behind closed doors, Bush was giving top U.S. corporate heads and financiers a different message: according to Bob Woodward's recent book *Bush At War*, in October 2001, on the eve of war with Afghanistan and as planning was beginning for invading Iraq, he told a private New York meeting of business leaders, "I truly believe that out of this will come more order in the world—real progress to peace in the Middle East, stability with oil-producing regions." In his paean to his former boss, Bush speech writer David Frum laid it out more directly: America's new global "war on terror," he wrote, was designed to "bring new freedom and new stability to the most vicious and violent quadrant of the earth—and new prosperity to us all, by securing the world's largest pool of oil."[3]

Overthrowing Saddam Hussein, creating a client state in Iraq, and opening up Iraq's economy are key components of a much larger, multi-faceted global agenda in which energy resources play a crucial role. The point is not that the Bush inner circle waged war simply to secure Iraq's oil for American profit or consumption. Yet petroleum *was* a central and major objective—if understood in the larger context of global empire. Most broadly, the 2003 invasion and occupation were designed to solidify American political/military domination of the energy heart of world—the Middle East/Central Asian region, and are part of broader efforts to secure control of global energy sources and use that control to ensure the smooth functioning of U.S. capitalism, strengthen its competitive position in world markets, and increase U.S. leverage against potential rivals. In short, oil is a powerful instrument of hegemony, which is what the new Bush II National Security Strategy is all about.

Controlling Persian Gulf oil and dominating world energy markets has been a prime U.S. strategic objective for over 60 years, as examined in previous chapters. However, the global energy picture does not remain constant: the tension between supply and demand evolves, and new dynamics and problems arise. Two trends stand out today: the precarious nature of the global economy and the possibility that growing energy demand will outstrip the global capacity to meet it.

A look at these concerns and how the capitalist political elite is approaching them opens a window on some of the deep compulsions and potential opportunities that drove the 2003 war on Iraq and continue to drive the Bush II global agenda.

U.S. Strategists Declare: "It's the Oil, Stupid!"

A key element of the new Bush doctrine is leveraging current U.S. military supremacy into economic supremacy and dealing with various difficulties confronting the global economy. Oil and natural gas play an important part in this grand design.[4]

The 1991 collapse of the Soviet Union was a geopolitical earthquake, but it did not lead to U.S. economic dominance. In his 1995 brief for global supremacy, current Bush II official Zalmay Khalilzad worried that rivals were gaining ground: "economic growth under way in Asia...will produce important changes in relative economic power—with important potential geopolitical and military implications" and "intensified international economic competition."[5]

Nor did the fall of the Soviet empire usher in an era of sustained economic growth; instead, the global economy has remained fragile. "The world economy is in trouble," wrote Jeffrey Garten, a former government official and now dean of the Yale School of Management, in early 2003. "Corporate investment and trade are slowing, factories are producing more than they can sell, and deflation is threatening many regions. The two potential economic engines besides the United States—Germany and Japan—are stagnating. Big emerging markets, from Indonesia to Brazil, are in deep trouble."[6]

The new National Security Strategy promises to ignite "a new era of global economic growth through free markets and free trade," and to use American preeminence to promote an "efficient allocation of resources, and regional integration." In other words, the U.S. seeks to use its military power to secure favored access to markets, raw materials, and human labor across the planet.

Joseph Nye, dean of the Kennedy School of Government at Harvard, compares the Bush II strategy to a three-dimensional chessboard: "The top board is the military and we can do pretty much what we want. The middle board is economics, and is not a world America controls." Cheney and Rumsfeld are focusing on the "top board," he argues, in order to parlay U.S. military power into greater economic and political power. Nye's "bottom level" consists of factors beyond Washington's control—anti-U.S. movements, weapons proliferation, the spread of infectious disease, etc. He warns, "The Cheney-Rumsfeld focus on the top board may win in the short run, but will cause lots of problems in the long run."[7]

This is where oil ties in: global capitalism remains dependent on a steady flow of low-priced petroleum, making oil both vital to the health of the world economy and key to the competitive position of rival nations. "The single best cyclical indicator for the world economy is the price of oil," one economist told the *New York Times*, "Nothing moves in the world economy without oil in there somewhere."[8]

Despite a shift from manufacturing to services and increases in energy efficiency, the U.S. still relies on petroleum products for 40 percent of its energy needs and remains the world's biggest energy glutton, devouring 19 million barrels of oil a day. With a mere three percent of the world's population, it consumes over 25 percent of the global output of crude.[9] "The price shocks from a serious disruption in oil supplies would course through every quarter of the United States economy," the *New York Times* notes. "The drain on people's incomes and companies' revenue would further sap a weakened economy." One Goldman-Sachs analyst told *Forbes* magazine, "Any [oil] price increase has devastating effects on the U.S. economy."[10]

On the other hand, in 1991 economics lecturer Alan Freeman estimated that each $1 fall in the price of a barrel of oil transferred roughly $5 billion a year from Third World producing countries to North America, and the difference between oil at $20 and oil at $25 a barrel meant the transfer of $70 to $100 billion from the impoverished south to the industrialized north.[11] Today, these figures are no doubt even more staggering given the rise in world oil consumption.

Former Clinton official Kenneth Pollack, echoing Kissinger's words from two decades earlier, is blunt about the oil connection:

> It's the Oil, Stupid—The reason the United States has a legitimate and critical interest in seeing that Persian Gulf oil continues to flow copiously and relatively cheaply is simply that the global economy built over the last 50 years rests on a foundation of inexpensive, plentiful oil, and if that foundation were removed, the global economy would collapse.[12]

Supply versus Demand

World oil markets have become increasingly tight and volatile, and this has become a major potential problem.[13] Several trends are responsible: global supplies have not been growing as fast as demand, key energy-producing regions are highly unstable, and there is heated competition for control of oil and natural gas sources.

The demand for energy has been rising by some 2.5 percent a year as industrialization spreads around the world. In 2003, global consumption stood at 77 million barrels of oil a day; by 2010, if these trends continue, it could rise to over 90 million barrels a day, a 17 percent increase.

However, petroleum output—and especially production capacity—are not growing nearly as fast. (Of course, immediate demand for petroleum oscillates with the ups and downs of the global economy; here we are focusing on longer-term trends in capacity and demand.) An April 2001 report by the U.S. Council on Foreign Relations and the Baker Institute for Public Policy, two high profile establishment think-tanks run by former government officials, was commissioned by Vice President Dick Cheney to help shape a new U.S. energy strategy. Their report, "Strategic Energy Policy Challenges For The 21st Century" (hereafter the "Baker Report"), singled out the lack of spare production capacity as a key concern:

> Perhaps the most significant difference between now and a decade ago is the extraordinarily rapid erosion of spare capacities at critical segments of energy chains. Today, shortfalls appear to be endemic. Among the most extraordinary of these losses in spare capacity is in the oil arena.[14]

The Baker Report noted that in 1985, OPEC spare production capacity stood at 25 percent of global demand, but in 1990 it had fallen to eight percent, and by 2001 was a mere two percent. Without an adequate cushion of spare capacity, shortages could occur and prices could spike:

> the world is currently precariously close to utilizing all of its available global oil production capacity, raising the chances of an oil supply crisis with more substantial consequences than seen in three decades.[15]

A related problem is that energy sources are concentrated in some of the most tumultuous areas in the world. According to energy forecasts, by 2050 the Persian Gulf/Caspian Sea region will account for more than 80 percent of world oil and natural gas production. The region's reserves are estimated to be 800 billion barrels of oil and an energy equivalent amount in natural gas. Meanwhile, total oil reserves in the Americas and Europe are less than 160 billion barrels and will be exhausted in the next 25 years.[16]

Former Carter official Zbigniew Brzezinski calls the Persian Gulf/Central Asian region "the global zone of percolating violence" and warns that it will likely be "a major battlefield, both for wars among nation-states and, more likely, for protracted ethnic and religious violence." In his book *Jihad vs. McWorld*, Benjamin Barber calculates that 69 percent of the total world production of oil and 92 percent of the world's proven oil reserves are "in nations that are at a high and moderate risk for current or future ethnic conflicts"— located mainly in this same region.[17] Pentagon officials talk of an "arc of instability" running from the Andes in South America through North Africa, the Middle East, into Southeast Asia.[18]

This volatility, which results from many factors including resistance to oppressive U.S.-backed regimes, presents a number of challenges to U.S. power. First, America faces difficulties maintaining its hold on the Middle East, which remains the world's premiere oil-producing region. Second, another center of world energy production has opened up in the former Soviet Republics of Central Asia. The region's geopolitical "tectonic plates" are in motion and its future economic and political orientation is now being fought out. Third, these and other developments have impeded investment in oil and natural gas production and hindered their expansion. The Baker Report points to political difficulties and under-investment in oil-producing countries as prime culprits in a crisis of energy production growth:

> [T]he US government has operated under the assumption that the national oil companies of these countries would make the investments needed to maintain enough surplus capacity to form a cushion against disruptions elsewhere. For several years, these assumptions appeared justified.
>
> But recently, things have changed. These Gulf allies are finding their domestic and foreign policy interests increasingly at odds with US strategic considerations, especially as Arab-Israeli tensions flare. They have become less inclined to lower oil prices in exchange for security of markets, and evidence suggests that investment is not being made in a timely enough manner to increase production capacity in line with growing global needs. A trend toward anti-Americanism could affect regional leaders' ability to cooperate with the United States in the energy area.[19]

The Baker Report argued that these problems "highlight the concentration of resources in the Middle East Gulf region and the vulnerability of the global economy to domestic conditions in the key producer countries."[20] The U.S. agenda includes reshaping these "domestic conditions"—by force if need be.

The world's major energy multinationals are blocked from investing in many of the world's richest producing countries—mainly by the nationally-owned oil companies which were a product of the anti-colonial upsurges of the 1950s and 1960s. In February 2003, the chairman of ExxonMobil stated that his company's output was not keeping up with demand: "When we consider, that as demand increases, our existing base production declines, we come squarely to the magnitude of the task before us. About half the oil and gas volume needed to meet demand 10 years from now is not in production today." the New York Times concluded that ExxonMobil's problems stem from "flat" production, the decline of its existing fields in North America and the North Sea, and the fact that "more than 90 percent of the world's proven oil reserves are owned by countries, national oil companies and the Russian oil companies"—many of which are closed to direct foreign investment. "As competition in the oil industry gets tighter, the challenge is accessing the reserves in the new areas, and every issue counts," one energy company executive commented.[21]

In Iraq, non-Arab foreign investment was outlawed by the Ba'ath regime, and in 2000, investment in the Middle East accounted for only 70 cents of every $100 spent by U.S. companies for oil and gas exploration and development.[22]

Feeding America's Petro-Dependence

The U.S. government has made clear that it is incapable of dealing with these mounting problems through conservation, ending the petro-dependence of the U.S. economy, or energy self-reliance. In May 2001, the Bush administration issued a "National Energy Policy," often referred to as the Cheney report, which emphatically declared that the U.S. economy would continue to consume a grossly disproportionate share of the planet's natural resources: "Our prosperity and way of life are sustained by energy use."[23]

A year later, the Environmental Protection Agency reported that average fuel economy for U.S. cars and trucks fell to its lowest level in 22 years.[24]

The Cheney report made no bones about the fact that domestic oil production won't come close to meeting U.S. consumption, even if the Arctic wilderness was exploited. The same will soon be true for natural gas, so the U.S. will have to import more and more of each. "Over the next twenty years, U.S. oil consumption will increase by 33 percent, natural gas consumption by well over 50 percent, and demand for electricity will rise by 45 percent. If America's energy production grows at the same rate as it did in the 1990s, we will face an ever-increasing gap," the report states, noting that the U.S. produces "39 percent less oil today than we did in 1970." It concludes that if current trends continue, the U.S. will be importing two-thirds of its oil within 20 years—up from 37 percent in 1980.[25]

The U.S. Energy Information Administration (EIA) predicts that natural gas imports will more than double between 2001 and 2025, and imports of liquefied natural gas, much of it from Third World countries, will increase more than tenfold. Shortly after the 2003 war, the director of Rice University's energy program told the *New York Times*, "We're on the verge of discovering that natural gas is almost as important as oil for our energy supplies.... Once we wake up to this, we'll have to deal with the geopolitical implications of importing natural gas from some of the more unsavory parts of the world."[26]

The Cheney report's solution is to gain access, leverage, and control of energy sources across the planet, from Colombia and Venezuela—where the U.S. has been maneuvering against guerrilla insurgents and a nationalist-oriented government—to the Middle East, the Caspian Basin and east Asia. The report argues that "energy security must be a priority of U.S. trade and foreign policy."[27]

The new National Security Strategy echoes this orientation. It calls enhancing "energy security," a major goal and commits the U.S. to "expand the sources and types of global energy supplied, especially in the Western Hemisphere, Africa, Central Asia, and the Caspian region."[28]

Energy and Hegemony

When U.S. officials discuss energy issues publicly, they speak in terms of domestic consumption or "energy independence," as Bush put it in his 2003 State of the Union address.

But U.S. strategy is not being guided simply by filling the tanks of the nation's growing fleet of SUVs. It is guided by the needs of global dominance and empire, which entails having its hand on the world's energy spigot in order to control others and to successfully compete in the global economy. These facets of energy politics are rarely discussed, but central to U.S. calculations.

There are many aspects to the global struggle for energy supremacy, including its impact on the economic strength of competing nations. Oil analyst Daniel Yergin has criticized the notion that the Iraq war was simply fought to obtain petroleum contracts for U.S. firms, but does acknowledge this larger oil connection:

> By the year 2010, world oil demand, driven by countries such as China and India, could be almost 90 million barrels a day.... And where will that oil come from?.... One can already see the beginning of a larger contest. On one side are Russia and the Caspian countries, primarily Kazakhstan and Azerbaijan; on the other side, the Middle East, including Iraq...the prize of this larger race to meet growing world demand is very tangible—by 2010, an additional $100 billion or more a year in oil revenues flowing into national treasuries.[29]

National income is not the only thing at stake—so is the global balance of power and leverage over those who depend on imported oil. Vice President Dick Cheney once remarked that the country that controls Middle East oil can exercise a "stranglehold" over the global economy.[30]

Pollack bluntly spells out these larger calculations of empire:

> [T]he United States is not simply concerned with keeping oil flowing out of the Persian Gulf; it also has an interest in preventing any potentially hostile state from gaining control over the region and its resources and *using such control to amass vast power or blackmail the world*." [emphasis added][31]

U.S. blackmail, it seems, is fine with Pollack and the rest of the political elite. As detailed in previous chapters, the U.S. has wielded its control over Persian Gulf oil to maintain its "leadership"—i.e., dominance—of its Western allies for some 60 years, as well as in its Cold War rivalry with the former Soviet Union. Although Japan and Europe have attempted to diversify their sources of petroleum, Persian Gulf oil remains critical to both. In 1983, 60 percent of

Japan's oil came from the Persian Gulf; by 2000 this dependence had risen to 73 percent. And roughly 22 percent of Western Europe's oil still comes from the Gulf, a dependence which will probably increase as production from Britain's North Sea oil fields declines over time. (In contrast, while American imports of Gulf oil have increased—from 2.9 percent of consumption in 1983 to 12.5 percent in 2000—the U.S. remains less directly dependent on the region than its rivals—a situation Washington is striving to preserve.)[32]

With energy markets tightening, new potential sources of petroleum and natural gas opening up, Russia rising as an oil power, and turmoil deepening across the Middle East and Central Asia, a contest is underway for energy advantage and dominance. After detailing this growing competition, the Baker Report makes clear that the U.S. bourgeoisie has no intention of relinquishing its energy supremacy: "unless the United States assumes a leadership role in the formation of new rules of the game, it will not simply forfeit such a role, which others will assume. It will rather become reactive to initiatives put forth by other governments which, if agreed by others, could leave U.S. firms, U.S. consumers, and the U.S. government in a weaker position than is warranted." The conclusion within this framework is inescapable: as the Baker Report puts it, the U.S. must seize the "strategic initiative."[33]

The 2003 Iraq war was—in part—a high stakes move to strengthen America's global energy position for the coming decades by strengthening its political-military control of the Persian Gulf and Central Asian regions, undercutting the influence of rivals and further opening these areas up to new U.S. energy investment. Iraq and its oil are important components of this broader power play.

Eyeing Iraqi Oil—Months Before War

The U.S. has bent over backward to assure the world, the Arab world in particular, that its war has not been motivated by controlling Iraq's oil, which Bush officials say is the "patrimony of the Iraqi people." U.S. actions before and after the war, however, make clear that this disclaimer is no more credible than the other now-discredited pretexts Bush II and company marshaled to justify conquering Iraq.

The post-Hussein structure of Iraq's industry is in formation, yet there is much evidence that the Bush administration intends to reshape Iraq's petroleum sector to America's advantage—even if Iraq's oil is formally owned and controlled by Iraqis—and planning for this began well before "Operation Iraqi Freedom."

The Bush leadership has vigorously resisted releasing any information about the Energy Task Force headed by Vice President Cheney that formulated the new U.S. energy policy in May 2001. After two years of legal action via the Freedom of Information Act and when the 2003 war was over, the government watchdog organization Judicial Watch was finally able to obtain some of these documents. They included maps of Middle East and Iraqi oilfields, pipelines, refineries and terminals, and charts of Iraq's dealings with foreign petroleum concerns.[34]

In October 2002, six months before the war, *Oil and Gas International* reported that U.S. planning was already underway to reorganize Iraq's oil and business relationships:

> The Bush administration wants to have a working group of 12 to 20 people focused on Iraqi oil and gas to be able to recommend to an interim government ways of restoring the petroleum sector following a military attack in order to increase oil exports to partially pay for a possible U.S. military occupation government...the working group will not only prepare recommendations for the rehabilitation of the Iraqi petroleum sector post-Hussein, but will address questions regarding the country's continued membership in OPEC [Organization of Petroleum Exporting Countries] and whether it should be allowed to produce as much as possible or be limited by an OPEC quota, and it will consider whether to honor contracts made between the Hussein government and foreign oil companies, including the $3.5 billion project to be carried out by Russian interests to redevelop Iraq's oilfields.[35]

A month later, London's *Observer* stated that "planning for Iraq's post-Saddam oil industry is being driven by a coalition of neo-conservatives in Washington think-tanks with close links to the Bush administration"—the same neo-conservatives pushing for war on Iraq and greater U.S. global hegemony.[36]

In January 2003, the *Wall Street Journal* reported:

> Executives of U.S. oil companies are conferring with officials from the White House, the Department of Defense and the

State Department to figure out how best to jump-start Iraq's oil industry following a war, industry officials say. With oil reserves second only to Saudi Arabia's, Iraq would offer the oil industry enormous opportunity should a war topple Saddam Hussein.... Industry experts say that with...serious investment,...[Iraq] could be producing six million barrels a day within five years.... The Bush administration is eager to secure Iraq's oil fields and rehabilitate them, industry officials say. They say Mr. Cheney's staff hosted an informational meeting with industry executives in October, with Exxon Mobil Corp., ChevronTexaco Corp., ConocoPhillips and Halliburton among the companies represented.[37]

The *Wall Street Journal* noted that Bush officials and the oil companies both denied that such a meeting took place, yet seizing and protecting Iraq's oil fields was a top U.S. war aim, even while other ministries were being looted and sacked: before the fighting had ended, Halliburton subsidiary Kellogg Brown & Root was on the ground in Iraq shutting down and securing its oil fields.[38]

Exploiting Iraq's Untapped Wealth

The conquest of Iraq was designed to open up new avenues for the U.S. to economically, politically and strategically exploit the country's petroleum wealth—although the ongoing guerrilla resistance could turn these schemes to ashes. Washington hoped to use Iraqi oil revenues to pay for the cost of rebuilding its oil and economic infrastructure, which had been devastated by two U.S. wars and 13 years of sanctions, and to make their new client state economically viable, without the need for infusions of aid from Washington. Soon after the war, Bremer stated that Iraq's first post-Saddam budget will depend "almost exclusively on oil revenues," which he hoped would rise to $13 to $14 billion annually by the end of 2004.[39]

Before the war, some U.S. officials, including one former Energy Department official went further, arguing that under international law, "The actual costs of supporting the occupying army could also be paid."[40] In other words, Iraq's wealth would be used to pay for its conquest and subordination. By the summer of 2003, however, Iraq was not yet selling enough oil to pay for occupation and reconstruction—and may not for some time to come.

Overthrowing Saddam Hussein's Ba'ath Party also removed a regime that had used its oil as a political tool (to generate international pressure for lifting sanctions or for a more pro-Arab stance on Israel-Palestine, for instance), which sometimes disrupted global oil markets. The Baker Report complained about Hussein's oil leverage:

> [T]ight markets have increased US and global vulnerability to disruption and provided adversaries undue potential influence over the price of oil. Iraq has become a key 'swing' producer, posing a difficult situation for the US government..... Iraq remains a de-stabilizing influence to...the flow of oil to international markets from the Middle East. Saddam Hussein has also demonstrated a willingness to threaten to use the oil weapon and to use his own export programme to manipulate oil markets.[41]

This leverage is one reason, among many, that the U.S. government was never willing to simply lift sanctions and allow an increase in Iraqi oil production with Hussein still in power. Significantly, the Baker Report concluded that the U.S. should immediately review its Iraq policy, including its *military* options.

Most importantly, the U.S. hopes to ramp up Iraqi oil production in order to increase global supplies and help alleviate disruptions, spare capacity shortages and possible price spikes. This would be enormously beneficial to U.S. capital even if no Iraqi oil is imported (although the Bush team may hope Iraq could become a secure long-term supplier to the U.S. itself). As that reliable barometer of Bush II thinking, the *Wall Street Journal,* enthused in September 2002: "If war with Iraq comes, President Bush's goal will be to change the regime in Baghdad. But the war would also change the economics of the oil world. And oil could get cheaper and more plentiful."[42]

Overthrowing the Hussein regime paved the way for the May 2003 lifting of UN sanctions, which the Baker report noted "had a severe effect on potential Iraqi production." The report estimated that Iraq's production had declined by 20 percent during the 1990s and contributed to global "spare capacity dips."[43] Washington hopes that regime change and the ending of sanctions could open Iraq up to U.S.-led foreign investment to raise its petroleum output.

Iraq may have more oil potential than any other place on earth. Thanks to the policy of holding down Iraq's oil production pursued for nearly 50 years by the British and U.S.-owned Iraq Petroleum

Company, and then a decade of war and sanctions in the 1990s, Iraq has not had access to the latest advances in oil technology, and it remains relatively unexplored and untapped. There are varying estimates of Iraq's oil reserves, but by all counts they are enormous. The EIA estimates that in addition to its 112 billion in proven reserves—which are five times U.S. reserves—it probably has another 100 (and possibly as much as 220) billion barrels in unexplored areas. One Iraqi oil official told the *Guardian* that his country's oil reserves would "exceed 300 billion barrels when all Iraq's regions are explored"—equal to one-quarter of total world reserves.[44]

In comparison, the U.S., Mexico, and Canada have a mere 64 billion barrels between them, oil giants Venezuela and Russia have 78 billion and 65 billion barrels respectively, all of Africa contains 77 billion barrels, and the entire Asia-Pacific region only 44 billion.[45]

Iraq also contains 110 trillion cubic feet (Tcf) of proven natural gas reserves, along with roughly 150 Tcf in probable reserves—enough to supply the entire U.S. for ten years.[46]

Iraq may be one place where oil production can most quickly be boosted. In early 2002, only 15 of 73 Iraqi oil fields were operating, producing some 2.65 million barrels a day (mbd). While there is considerable debate about how far and how fast Iraqi production can be increased, some analysts feel it could rise to 3.5 mbd, and ultimately reach 6 mbd. Former Iraqi oil minister Issam Chalabi claims, "Iraq has the potential to produce 4.7 million barrels a day more oil from discovered fields that are ready to be developed," and with further investment, Iraq could produce six million barrels a day by 2010.[47] Other analysts argue that Iraq could be pumping 10 mbd within five years.[48] Of course all these projections are contingent on the political situation on the ground.

So, the global economy remains fragile, and the potential for a new "energy crisis" remains real should energy demand outstrip production capacity. Meanwhile, the United States is attempting to take control of a vast sea of oil in Iraq. The facts are not unconnected. Control of Iraq's energy resources is designed to give the U.S. greater power to control these worrisome trends. Given this context, it's small wonder that Washington went after Iraq. That Hussein's regime had neither weapons of mass destruction nor links to Osama bin Laden was irrelevant to those in charge of the empire. For them, global power and greater hegemony were in play.

Privatization, Expansion & Petroleum Leverage

Developments in Iraq's petroleum sector are also intended to reverberate among the region's oil producers and eventually increase their production as well. Washington is planning to use Iraq as a test run for privatization in the region and a lever to force other oil-producers to open up to greater foreign investment. The lack of access to oilfields, even in pro-Western states like Saudi Arabia and Kuwait, has become a sore point for U.S. business. The Baker Report blames it for declining Middle East crude oil production: "the Persian Gulf's output has grown only slightly, with the result that its output has declined to less than 30 percent of total world output."[49]

Echoing this theme, the *New York Times* notes:

> [D]espite years of negotiations, deals to develop natural gas fields in Saudi Arabia and oil fields in Kuwait remain distant. Such limited access to the world's best new fields has meant that the global oil giants find it harder every year to increase their production substantially.... For global oil companies, the true prize would be working on large new fields—and Iraq promises plenty of those.[50]

Robert Dreyfuss reports that this drumbeat for privatization and opening up the Middle East was a theme among the strategists shaping the Bush agenda prior to the war on Iraq:

> Today, a growing number of Washington strategists are advocating a direct U.S. challenge to state-owned petroleum industries in oil-producing countries, especially the Persian Gulf. Think tanks such as the American Enterprise Institute, the Heritage Foundation, and CSIS [Center for Strategic and International Studies] are conducting discussions about privatizing Iraq's oil industry. Some of them have put forward detailed plans outlining how Iraq, Saudi Arabia, and other nations could be forced to open up their oil and gas industries to foreign investment. The Bush administration itself has been careful not to say much about what might happen to Iraq's oil. But State Department officials have had preliminary talks about the oil industry with Iraqi exiles.... 'One of the major problems with the Persian Gulf is that the means of production are in the hands of

the state,' Rob Sobhani, an oil-industry consultant, told an American Enterprise Institute conference last fall in Washington. Already, he noted, several U.S. oil companies are studying the possibility of privatization in the Gulf.[51]

After the 2003 war, both Rumsfeld and Bremer make clear that U.S. plans to privatize Iraq's economy and open it up to foreign investment, discussed in chapter 9, included its petroleum industry.

Iraqi Ownership and U.S. Control

U.S. officials have repeatedly claimed that they were not out to steal Iraq's oil, but according to New York Times columnist Paul Krugman, before the war—and behind closed doors—the Bush leadership was calling Iraq's oil the "spoils of war." The Wall Street Journal brashly called the 2003 invasion "one of the most audacious hostile takeovers ever: the seizure and rejuvenation of Iraq's huge but decrepit state-run petroleum industry" and admitted that "the U.S. will have unprecedented influence over the oil fields in the short term."[52]

Months before combat, both the Pentagon and the State Department set up working groups to study Iraq's oil industry and to make recommendations for "reviving" it in harmony with U.S. long-term interests. After the war, the Pentagon hand-picked the Iraqis it wanted to run the oil industry, many of whom had been working closely with these Pentagon and State Department teams.

The Pentagon also appointed an advisory board, made up largely of U.S. officials and oil industry veterans, to oversee the Iraqis formally in charge. Philip Carroll, previously the top executive at Shell Oil Co., the U.S. subsidiary of the global petroleum giant Royal Dutch/Shell, and Fluor Daniel, a U.S. construction multi-national, was chosen to head the board. It will mark the first time that foreigners are directly in charge of running Iraq's oil industry since the nationalization of 1972.[53]

The State Department's Future of Iraq oil working group, which included both Iraqi exiles and U.S. officials, recommended that Iraqi production be increased by restructuring its National Oil Company along Western lines and by guaranteeing foreign multinationals a sizeable share of oil profits—well before any new Iraqi government was in place. According to the *Wall Street Journal*, the Iraqis the Pentagon has put in charge of oil have "embraced the idea of eventually seeking foreign help in exploration and development."[54] In August 2003, the U.S. occupation authorities announced they had abandoned plans to form an international corporate-style advisory board to run Iraq's oil industry, in part because of reluctance of Iraqis and foreign oil experts to join the board for fear of being branded "agents of a U.S.-orchestrated takeover of the Iraqi industry," as the *Los Angeles Times* reported, and souring future business dealings with Iraq. Iraq's oil sector would instead be run by Iraqis, albeit Iraqis hand-picked by the hand-picked U.S. Governing Council.[55]

There are a variety of ways to structure deals between global oil corporations and producing countries, but given the nature of the war and the recommendations coming out of the Pentagon and State Department, it is highly likely that the U.S. government and American oil multinationals will attempt to dominate Iraq's oil industry, including pricing, production, and development decisions, although the oil giants may move carefully to avoid the appearance of direct colonial-style control that could spark anger and protest in Iraq as well as other Third World producing countries.[56]

On May 22, 2003, Bush secretly tried to accelerate U.S. corporate investment—and profiteering—in Iraq's oil sector by signing Executive Order 13303. This Order gave American petroleum giants blanket immunity from criminal prosecution or civil lawsuits for any actions they undertook in relation to exploiting or selling Iraqi oil—including bribery, damaging the environment, violating human rights, labor practices, or international treaties, or breaking business contracts.[57]

For instance, production-sharing agreements can give multinationals at least part ownership of oil fields or a share of the oil produced, as well as hefty tax breaks and concessions. These agreements, increasingly pushed by the global oil giants, are "among the most lucrative in the oil industry," the *San Francisco Chronicle* reports, adding that "Companies often take home 30 percent of the oil produced."[58]

Washington is using the vast debt, destruction, and war reparations that it helped visit upon Iraq as a club to force it to open up its petroleum sector to foreign exploitation. Iraq's external debt is an estimated $60 to $130 billion, and it faces compensation claims of over $200 billion, including from Iran and Kuwait. Since it will take an estimated $40 billion to restore Iraq's savaged oil sector, what choice does it have—the State Department/Pentagon/oil company argument goes—but to turn to foreign capital for help—petroleum potential and hat in hand.[59]

A plan was even in the works shortly after the war, backed by the U.S. Export-Import Bank and American corporations, to pledge a share of Iraq's future oil and natural gas production in return for post-war loans to rebuild Iraq—an approach Congressional Republicans also demanded following Bush's September 2003 demand for another $87 billion to police and reconstruct Iraq and Afghanistan. This would basically force Iraq into debt peonage and give global capital a whip hand over the country's economics and politics—again, stripping any new Iraqi government of sovereign decision-making before it has even been put into office.[60]

Another component of this imperialist approach is increasing Iraq's technological dependence on U.S. technology and know-how. *Middle East Report's* "Reconstruction Tracker" notes that, "The U.S. and Britain have created a reconstruction structure almost solely of foreign expertise, ignoring the Iraqis who rebuilt their oil industry with no international assistance under sanctions and the idea that local expertise may offer ingenious low-budget strategies to outside experts."[61]

Opting Out of OPEC?

Taking over Iraq could increase American political leverage in the Middle East, as well as its petroleum leverage in world energy markets. It could make the U.S. less reliant on Saudi oil, which accounted for 15 percent of U.S. imports in 2001, and thus better positioned to demand changes in Saudi policies. Control of Iraq could also provide a hedge against instability in the Kingdom. Some Saudi leaders are already nervous. Before the war, one Saudi oil executive worried, "If the United States takes over Iraq and Iraqi production rises dramatically, Saudi Arabia will lose position in the market and political influence with the United States."[62]

After the 2003 war, these fears apparently prompted the Saudi government to move quickly to increase its energy production by concluding long-stalled negotiations with two foreign oil giants, even guaranteeing them a 20 percent annual return. *Business Week* reported:

> If you want to see how the overthrow of Saddam Hussein in Iraq may be changing the Middle East, you need look no further than the breakthrough gas deal signed by Royal Dutch/Shell Group and Total Group in Saudi Arabia. The accord is the first to allow foreign companies to explore and produce gas since the industry was nationalized in the mid-1970s.[63]

Occupying Iraq could also give the U.S. enormous clout in OPEC, perhaps the ability to cripple it and drive down world oil prices. OPEC's share of world oil production has fallen from over 55 percent in 1973 to 35-40 percent in 2003, but will likely rise again as non-OPEC fields decline, potentially making it a greater impediment to U.S. energy interests.

Leon Feurth, Vice President Al Gore's former national security advisor, writes that by taking over Iraq, the U.S. has become "a virtual member of OPEC, and one of the most powerful at that. So immense military power will be united with an equally impressive form of economic power."[64] Both Carroll and the Iraqis picked by the U.S. to run Iraq's new oil industry have warned that Iraq may need to exceed its OPEC production quota and perhaps even leave the cartel.[65]

Such sweeping changes and radical restructuring—all in the interests of U.S. capital and global dominance—illustrate what is meant by the new National Security Strategy's call for the "efficient allocation of resources, and regional integration."[66]

A Crude Bonanza

Oil and reconstruction contracts for U.S. corporations were not the primary motivations for the 2003 war, but they were certainly part of the foul war-of-conquest mix.

Oil and energy companies began hovering over Iraq like so many vultures months before the war began, hashing over post-war rebuilding with the Pentagon, the State Department and various Iraqi exiles. One closed-door meeting of oilmen, imperialist strategists and pro-U.S. Iraqis was held in London in October 2002 and called "Invading Iraq: Dangers and Opportunities for the Energy Sector." The *Guardian* reported, "One delegate said the entire day could be summarized as: 'Who gets the oil?'" The paper concluded that once Hussein was overthrown, Iraq's 1972 oil nationalization could be reversed: "We could see three of the world's largest public companies—BP, Shell, and ExxonMobil—fighting for their old IPC [Iraq Petroleum Company] possessions."[67]

All this was done with encouragement from the Bush II administration, which has made handing out war spoils to U.S. multinationals a "core principal," as Rumsfeld put it, for the new Iraq: "Whenever possible, contracts for work in Iraq will go to those who will use Iraqi workers and to countries that supported the Iraqi people's liberation."[68]

The process of dividing spoils began weeks before the war started: between January 31 and March 4, 2003, according to *Middle East Report*, the Bush administration issued nine requests for reconstruction proposals, awarding its first contract two days after Colin Powell's February 5, 2003 show-and-tell deception at the United Nations, which aimed to show that the U.S. would go the last mile for peace.[69]

On March 24, while fighting still raged, the Army Corps of Engineers awarded Haliburton subsidiary Kellogg Brown & Root a no-bid contract to put out oil fires and then basically run Iraqi's oil fields. This contract could be worth $7 billion over the next two years; between 1995 and 2000, Halliburton was run by now-Vice President Cheney. The U.S. Agency for International Development (USAID) next awarded Bechtel National, Inc. a contract worth as much as $680 million to restore and rebuild Iraq's infrastructure, roads, airports, sewage and irrigation systems, and power plants. In July 2003, Bechtel announced it would be hiring some 25,000 Iraqis to carry out these projects (which is over half as large as its entire worldwide staff), making it one of the biggest employers in Iraq. The *New York Times* noted, "The reconstruction effort could cost up to $100 billion and become one of the most lucrative building programs in decades."[70]

The oil payoff may be much larger, and Iraq could become, in the *Washington Post's* words, "a bonanza for American oil compa-

nies" and other U.S. firms.[71] Oil giants have been salivating over
Iraq because, according to the EIA, "Iraq's oil production costs are
among the lowest in the world," giving it a huge profit potential. Oil
experts estimate that production costs could be as low as 97 cents a
barrel. Britain's *Guardian* estimates that Iraq could be producing
eight million barrels a day within a decade; at $30 a barrel that could
generate over $87 billion a year.

One oil executive told the *New York Times*, "We estimate we
will only have to spend between $2,200 and $2,700 for every barrel
of capacity" (compared with $5,000 to $20,000 a barrel in other
countries). 'That's why people are interested—it's the cheapest oil in
the world."[72]

During the Vietnam War, one U.S. officer infamously remarked
that his troops had to "destroy the village to save it." In Iraq, it seems
that the U.S. has destroyed the country, in part, to rebuild and
exploit it.

Oil Deals and Global Rivalries

Profits for U.S. corporations are not all that's at stake in awarding contracts in post-Hussein Iraq; hard-edged competition between
rival nations is also being played out. The behind-the-scenes
intrigue over Iraqi contracts and oil provides a glimpse into how this
broader global competition factored into the 2003 Iraq war, as well
as some of the Bush cabal's broader aims in the Middle East/Central
Asia region.

During the 1990s, the former Ba'ath regime had held out the
promise of lucrative oil contracts to industrialized countries which
favored the easing or lifting of sanctions, particularly Russia and
France. Most of the biggest such offerings never came to fruition due
to sanctions and Baghdad's withdrawal of various offers (to Paris and
Moscow) over what it felt was their half-hearted support for Iraq
internationally. However, if the contracts signed by the Hussein
regime were to be honored by a new Iraqi government, the French
oil firm TotalFinaElf could end up with one of the largest positions
in Iraq, with exclusive rights to develop fields in the Majnoon and
Bin Umar regions. This deal was valued at some $7 billion and could
double Total's global reserves and increase its production by an esti-

mated 400,000 barrels a day.[73]

(French companies also exported some $3.5 billion worth of goods to Iraq between 1996 and 2002, including $650 million in 2001 alone. French firms supplied Iraq with an estimated $25 billion in arms during the 1980s and 1990s, and were still owed money on these transactions when the Hussein regime fell.[74])

Roughly 300 Russian companies also did business in Hussein's Iraq, which owed Moscow some $8 billion for their work. One of the biggest was a consortium led by LukOil, which signed deals to develop the massive West Qurna oilfields in southern Iraq. Calculations of their ultimate size vary, but the *New York Times* has reported that the contracts could come to more than 70 billion barrels of oil— over half of Iraq's reserves. One oil executive said the volume of these deals was "huge"—a "colossal amount."[75]

Russia and France insist their contracts remain valid, but in reality they've been thrown up for grabs by the U.S. conquest of Iraq. There will no doubt be intense negotiations and struggle between the world's industrialized countries over just which contracts get honored and which don't, and which "quids" are exchanged for which "pro quos," but Washington has long been concerned about the possibility of other countries gaining the upper hand in Iraq, as was discussed in chapter 8. Among documents from his Energy Task Force that Cheney sought to withhold from the public were two charts detailing various Iraqi oil and gas projects and a March 2001 list of "Foreign Suitors for Iraqi Oilfield Contracts," which includes the status of their efforts.[76]

There are many indications that Washington intended to ruthlessly use its military conquest to weaken French and Russian influence, as well as that of other rivals, in post-Hussein Iraq and more broadly. The *Washington Post* reported that Hussein's overthrow could lead to "scuttling oil deals between Baghdad and Russia, France and other countries, and reshuffling world petroleum markets." Pentagon acolyte Ahmad Chalabi warned that after the coming war he would favor American companies and that French and Russian contracts could be null and void. One oil analyst exuded: "If you turn up and it's your tanks that dislodged the regime and you have 50,000 troops in the country and they're in your tanks, then you're going to get the best deals."[77]

The Bush administration may have used this threat to secure French and Russian support for the November 2002 UN Resolution 1441 authorizing the resumption of intrusive UN weapons inspections. That month, the *Washington Post* reported that during negotiations over the resolution, Washington and Moscow reached a "gentleman's agreement" on Russian economic interests in post-Saddam Iraq and on an acceptable floor for world oil prices—$21 a barrel—in the event of a post-Saddam "Iraqi oil boom."[78] Russia was so concerned that its Iraqi interests would be quashed that it held secret talks with the Iraqi National Congress—the Pentagon's choice to rule Iraq—in the months before the war.[79]

However, now that the U.S. has inflicted "regime change" on Iraq, both Carroll and the Iraqis put in titular charge of their country's oil have stated that all contracts signed by the Hussein regime would be up for review and could either be voided or renegotiated.[80]

Should the U.S. succeed in invalidating Russia's contracts, increasing Iraqi oil output and driving down world oil prices, or crippling OPEC, the damage to Russia's economy would be severe. Oil accounts directly and indirectly for 60 percent of Russia's state income and 40 percent of its export revenues, and oil profits are key to reviving the Russian economy. One study by the Center for Strategic and International Studies, a Washington think-tank, estimated that a $6 a barrel fall in oil prices would cut Russia's economic growth in half, and a $13 a barrel fall would render most Russian oil firms unprofitable. One official in Moscow stated flatly that if the prices of oil dropped significantly, "Our budget will collapse."[81]

At present, the U.S. seems to be playing a double game with Russia on the oil front. On one hand, the rise of Russian oil production has helped maintain global supplies and weaken prices, benefiting the U.S. So there has been talk of a U.S.-Russia energy "partnership."[82] On the other hand, Washington does not want Russia's energy leverage or oil income to grow so much that it could reemerge as a serious global challenger. In that struggle, Iraqi oil is a hammer over Moscow's head.

So beneath the surface of cordial relations, there are deep tensions between American and Russian imperial interests. During the war, the *Wall Street Journal* noted, "The rift between Russia and the U.S. over the war in Iraq has exposed the weak foundation underly-

ing a much-ballyhooed friendship between George W. Bush and
Vladimir Putin." One Russian official worried that if the U.S.
attacked countries with whom his nation had extensive ties, such as
Iran and North Korea, "the fragile Russian-American partnership
will fall apart for good."[83]

As of May 2003, all post-war reconstruction contracts had been
awarded—not by Iraq's interim "Governing Council," but by the
U.S. Agency for International Development, the U.S. Army Corps
of Engineers, or the State Department. All had gone to U.S. firms,
often without competing bids. However, after being awarded its massive contract, Bechtel announced that "subcontracting" opportunities would be open to all.[84] In some ways, this is an apt metaphor for
the new world Bush II hopes to create: other global powers will
henceforth be reduced to "subcontractors" for the U.S. empire.

Water Power

Iraq's natural resources don't end with oil—it is also rich in
water. Worldwide, water use has more than tripled since 1950 and
may become even more precious—and contentious—than oil.[85] In
the Middle East, water is a particularly scarce and valued resource.
For instance, Israel's seizure and occupation of the Palestinian West
Bank is aimed in part at seizing underground aquifers to supply
Israeli water needs.[86]

Stephen Pelletiere, a CIA analyst during the Iran-Iraq War,
calls Iraq's historic waterways key to U.S. regional dominance:

> We are constantly reminded that Iraq has perhaps the
> world's largest reserves of oil. But in a regional and perhaps even
> geopolitical sense, it may be more important that Iraq has the
> most extensive river system in the Middle East. In addition to
> the Tigris and Euphrates, there are the Greater Zab and Lesser
> Zab rivers in the north of the country. Thus America could alter
> the destiny of the Middle East in a way that probably could not
> be challenged for decades—not solely by controlling Iraq's oil,
> but by controlling its water.[87]

Strategic Positioning in the New "Great Game"

It is no accident that Afghanistan and Iraq were the first two

stops in America's new global war. Both are strategically located in
Eurasia, which Brzezinski argues is America's "chief geopolitical
prize":

> Eurasia is the globe's largest continent and is geopolitical-
> ly axial. A power that dominates Eurasia would control two of
> the world's three most advanced and economically productive
> regions. A mere glance at the map also suggests that control
> over Eurasia would almost automatically entail Africa's subordi-
> nation.... About 75 percent of the world's people live in Eurasia,
> and most of the world's physical wealth is there as well, both in
> its enterprises and underneath its soil. Eurasia accounts for
> about 60 percent of the world's GNP and about three-fourths of
> the world's known energy resources.[88]

Russia, France, Germany, and Japan, as well as rising regional
powers like China, were not the immediate targets of the 2003 war
on Iraq, and the U.S. is trying to enlist them one way or another in
crusades against—and the exploitation of—the Third World. In
Afghanistan, for example, French and German troops now make up
the bulk of foreign military forces. Yet in many ways, the war on Iraq
was directed at these rivals and potential rivals—indeed the rest of
the world. Relegating other powers to a more subordinate status and
preventing the emergence of any new challengers are key aspects of
current U.S. grand strategy.

This is the key reason that France, Germany, and Russia would
not go along with a UN resolution authorizing a U.S. war, despite
Washington's intense arm-twisting, and why deep divisions remain
over how political power is apportioned in post-Hussein Iraq. The
depth of these tensions was reflected in a September 2003 column
by the pro-war *New York Times* columnist Thomas Friedman entitled
"Our War With France." Friedman complained, "France is not just
our annoying ally. It is not just our jealous rival. France is becoming
our enemy.... France wants America to fail in Iraq."[89]

Washington's posture toward Russia and China also illustrate
these larger objectives, which were an integral part of the strategic
calculus for the 2003 Iraq war. There has been much talk that the
U.S. and Russia have "moved from confrontation to cooperation" as
the NSS put it, but one of Washington's main objectives, dating
back to the 1992 Defense Planning Guidance, has been "preventing...the reemergence of a new rival, either on the territory of the

former Soviet Union or elsewhere."[90]

China's emergence as a regional power has also drawn the attention of Bush II strategists. Khalilzad called it "the most likely candidate" to become America's main global rival. Washington perceives potential danger, not so much from China alone, but in combination with others. Khalilzad argued: "Over the longer term—the next twenty years—there is a real possibility of efforts by China or Russia or a coalition of states to balance the power of the United States and its allies." The Project for a New American Century's "Rebuilding America's Defenses" focused heavily on "coping with the rise of China to great-power status" by increasing the U.S. military presence in Asia.[91]

The strategic interests of the world's global powers and many regional players clash sharply in the Middle East/Central Asia region—over energy, trade, markets, and overall political and military dominance. For example, two-thirds of the Gulf's oil is now exported to Western industrial nations. By 2015, according to a CIA study, three-quarters will go to Asia, mainly China; by 2030 China may be forced to import as much petroleum as the U.S. did in 2003. This growing dependence on foreign energy has prompted China to seek contracts to secure oil and gas in the Persian Gulf and Central Asia—including with the former Hussein regime in Iraq. "They have different political interests in the Gulf than we do," one U.S. analyst said. "Is it to our advantage to have another competitor for oil in the Persian Gulf?"[92]

The U.S. seeks to gain the upper hand by expanding its military presence and increasing its control of the region's oil and natural gas, while Russia, China and others are pursuing their own counter strategies. Michael Klare writes:

> Russia, which once dominated the Caspian area through its central role in the former Soviet Union, has continuing aspirations to control the region and its massive energy supplies. And China, which is running out of domestic oil and fears Islamic unrest in its extreme western provinces, is determined to become a major Caspian and Central Asian power.[93]

Over the past decade, a contest has developed over building and controlling the oil and gas pipelines that link newly developed Caspian Sea energy fields to the world market. The 2001 war on

Afghanistan, and the establishment of bases in Uzbekistan, Tajikistan and Kyrgyzstan to support the war, could give the U.S. greater freedom to construct a pipeline from Turkmenistan across Afghanistan to Pakistan and the Arabian Sea, a route some oil strategists favor in order to bypass both Iran and Russia and link Central Asia directly to Western corporations and markets.[94] These new Central Asian bases are also intended to put American forces in close proximity to the new Baku-Ceyhan pipeline, running from the Caspian Sea through Georgia and Turkey to the Mediterranean, which oil analyst Yergin calls "one of the linchpins of world supply and energy security in the years ahead."[95]

"The most radical redeployment of American forces since the end of the Cold War"

The 2003 Iraq war took place against the backdrop of a dramatic leap in direct American military presence across an arc stretching from North Africa to China's western borders. The *Wall Street Journal* called this buildup, in conjunction with the reduction of U.S. forces in Europe, "the most radical redeployment of American forces since the end of the Cold War."[96]

The *New York Times* described these efforts—and the Pentagon's decision to seek four permanent bases in post-Hussein Iraq—as part of "a strategic revolution now playing out across the Middle East and Southwest Asia, from the Mediterranean to the Indian Ocean." This aggressive military deployment, underway since the late 1990s, accelerated following Sept. 11, in what the *New York Times* called "a concerted diplomatic and military effort to win permission for United States forces to operate from the formerly Communist nations of Eastern Europe, across the Mediterranean, throughout the Middle East and the Horn of Africa, and across Central Asia, from the periphery of Russia to Pakistan's ports on the Indian Ocean."[97]

In recent years, the Pentagon has sought or established bases in this arc of countries and beyond, including in Afghanistan, Azerbaijan, Qatar, Oman, Djibouti, Kenya, Singapore, Philippines, Mali, Bulgaria, Romania, and Hungary. Military officials explain that often, "permanent access is all that is required, not permanent basing." This orientation flows from Rumsfeld's goal of transforming the military into what he has called an "agile, flexible and adaptable" force, not tied down but ready for rapid deployment to theaters around the world.[98]

As of July 2003, the Pentagon had 370,000 Army troops deployed in 120 countries, including some 150,000 in Iraq (out of a total active-duty force of 491,000), prompting worries in Washington that U.S. forces were stretched thin and calls in Congress for building an even larger military.[99]

These steps have placed U.S. military forces near the world's largest oil and gas fields, at the major naval chokepoints for global oil traffic, and surrounding the flanks of Russia and China. The *Wall Street Journal* acknowledged that Pentagon moves are being "driven by the increasing importance that the U.S. is placing on protecting key oil reserves in Africa and the Caucasus region near the Caspian Sea, as well as addressing concerns about combating terrorism." General Charles Wald, deputy commander of U.S. European Command, candidly admitted, "In the Caspian Sea you have large mineral reserves.... We want to be able to assure the long-term viability of those resources." Pentagon strategic assessments emphasize that "in the coming years, energy and resource issues will continue to shape international security."[100]

One think-tank study concluded, "the U.S. military presence will help ensure that a majority of oil and gas from the Caspian basin will go westward," bypassing Russia and China. And a recent Brookings Institution paper noted that, "U.S. strategic domination over the entire region, including the whole lane of sea communications from the Strait of Hormuz, will be perceived as the primary vulnerability of China's energy supply."[101]

Big Lies and Bigger Lies

In July 2003, polls reportedly showed that more and more Britons and Americans were waking up to the fact that their governments lied about the threat from Iraq to drag them to war. According to columnist Krugman, most apparently still didn't believe their governments did so "knowingly." [102]

However, dissecting their real war aims and agenda—that

heady combination of subduing a troublesome regime, solidifying the U.S. hold on world energy sources, reducing the power of rivals and potential rivals, and reigning supreme for decades to come—demonstrates that it was a knowing lie. Indeed, the claim that the war was fought to "liberate" Iraq is as big a lie as anything said about Baghdad's purported weapons of mass destruction or ties to al Qaeda.

The 2003 conquest of Iraq was an opening salvo in this grand agenda, and the ongoing war planned to realize it could make the Iraq war pale in scope, violence, and human suffering.

CHAPTER 11

THE BITTER FRUITS OF UNJUST WAR

They hate our freedoms; our freedom of religion, our freedom of speech," Bush declared on September 20, 2001, "our freedom to vote and assemble and disagree with each other."

This self-serving vilification of any who oppose American actions in the Middle East, no matter their ideology or politics, and blanket justification for U.S. assaults was hollow long before Sept. 11 and the 2003 Iraq War. When I traveled to Iran in 1979 and again in 1980, Iranians—whether leftists, liberals, or Islamists—never complained about America's "freedoms." They described what it meant to live under an American-backed dictator and torturer—the Shah. When I traveled to Palestine in 1988, people in Gaza and the West Bank didn't rail against "freedom of religion" in the USA. They pointed to tear gas canisters and rubber bullets littering the ground marked "Made in the USA" (and today they would be pointing to U.S.-made Apache helicopters, and tanks and missiles). And when I traveled to Iraq shortly after the 1991 Gulf War, I wasn't mobbed in the streets because I was from the U.S. Iraqis, like most people I met in the region, understood the distinction between rulers and ruled, and treated me with great hospitality. Then they showed me bombed-out electrical generation plants and took me to hospitals where infants lay wasting away thanks to American bombs and sanctions.

In August 2003, Bush repeated his "hate our freedoms" mantra to the American Legion. Coming five months after an American aggression that may have killed anywhere from 10,000 to 50,000 Iraqi soldiers and civilians, wounded countless more, and plunged the country into near-anarchy and economic ruin, it simply demonstrated the absurdity and transparency of official propaganda. Iraqis now have many more bitter stories to tell, and some are speaking through resistance to an unjust U.S. occupation.

The notion that a government that supported Iraq's oppressive British-created monarchy, conspired against its 1958 revolution, covertly supported Saddam's Ba'ath Party, repeatedly manipulated and betrayed the Kurds, fueled the Iran-Iraq slaughter, savaged Iraq in the 1991 Gulf War, and then strangled and starved it for 12 years afterward could transform itself an agent for "liberating" the Iraqi people was ludicrous on the face of it. Instead, Washington's 2003 invasion and conquest of Iraq represented a quantum leap in both aspects of the sordid history of U.S. depredations in the region: in its efforts to brutally and directly control events on one hand, and in the potential for such interventions to backfire or spin out of control on the other.

How the Cakewalk Crumbled

For all its death and destruction, the most striking thing about the 2003 war was not how quickly U.S. forces overran Iraq. It was clear beforehand that the Hussein regime had been severely weakened by two decades of war and sanctions—which is precisely why Bush, Cheney, Rumsfeld, et. al. considered it such an inviting target of opportunity. And they understood quite well that the Ba'ath regime was based on repression, not broad popular support, and so was incapable of rallying the Iraqi population for the kind of heroic, self-sacrificing, grass-roots war of resistance that could have seriously challenged the American juggernaut.

Rather, what was most striking was how quickly Washington's audacious aggression ran into difficulty. As British reporter Robert Fisk put it in a mid-April dispatch from Baghdad: "It's going wrong, faster than anyone could have imagined."[1]

Leading up to the war, the Bush cabal predicted that Iraq would be a cakewalk: the Iraqi people would rise against the Ba'ath regime and welcome American troops as liberators. Four days before the assault began, Vice President Cheney told NBC that he had been talking with "a lot of Iraqis"—even had some over to the White House—and he believed "we will, in fact, be greeted as liberators."[2]

According to the Bush script, Iraqi exiles, hand-picked and airlifted into the country by the Pentagon, would quickly take over the state and establish a new pro-U.S. Iraq. This "plug-and-play" conquest would enable U.S. forces to quickly depart and proceed merrily on their way to their next "war on terror" target. According to the *Washington Post*, the Pentagon envisioned: "Within weeks, if all went well, Iraqis would begin taking control of their own affairs and the exit of U.S. troops would be well underway."[3] Consequently, the pre-war talk was all of "liberation," never "occupation."

Iraq's oil wealth was supposed to pay for the whole operation—"We are dealing with a country that can really finance its own reconstruction, and relatively soon," Deputy Defense Secretary Paul Wolfowitz told Congress in March 2003. He derisively dismissed Gen. Eric Shinseki's prediction that the U.S. would need hundreds of thousands of troops to occupy and stabilize Iraq.[4]

These claims were a combination of deliberate lies aimed at undercutting public fears of a long, costly war, and the miscalculations of arrogant empire-builders who, in a rush to conquer the world, neither understood nor respected those they sought to conquer and subjugate.

Shortly after Bush (in a moment of premature triumphalism) declared victory on May 1, 2003, the cakewalk began to crumble. By mid-July, Gen. Tommy Franks acknowledged that U.S. forces were being hit by 10 to 25 attacks a day.[5] Iraqi resistance forced the Pentagon to extend tours of duty to a full year and to maintain its roughly 150,000 troop level "for the foreseeable future."[6]

By July, U.S. combat fatalities reached 149, surpassing the total killed in the 1991 Gulf War. By late August, American forces registered their 141st post-war fatality—surpassing the number killed during the war itself—and bringing total U.S. dead to 277. By September, 10 per day were being wounded in action (over 1,124 total since the war began), and some 6,000 troops had been evacuated for medical reasons. Because it's Pentagon policy to only announce casualties when a fatality occurs during the incident, the actual number of wounded may be even higher.[7]

In July, the Pentagon dispatched a group of civilians to assess the post-war situation in Iraq. They reported back that the U.S. had a "closing window" in which to stabilize the country or risk alienating the broader population.[8] The *Washington Post* echoed their warning:

> [I]n military terms, the postwar situation is getting worse
> rather than better...the militants pose a clear strategic threat to
> the U.S. mission.... The danger is that they will succeed in trig-
> gering a broader guerrilla war against U.S. troops fed not just by
> loyalty to the Ba'ath Party but also by popular discontent with
> American occupation—a war that could destabilize Iraq and the
> region around it.[9]

This warning was brought home in dramatic fashion by the subsequent bombings of the Jordanian embassy, the UN compound
(twice), and the street outside the shrine of Ali in Najaf, which
killed Ayatollah Mohammed Bakr al-Hakim, one of the most
prominent Shi'a clerics supporting the U.S. occupation, along with
over 90 others.

In early summer, Britain's *Mirror* reported: "This is Basra three
months after British tanks rolled in to a rapturous welcome. Instead
of jubilation there is frustration. In the broiling summer heat this is
a city waiting to explode." A member of a Christian Peacemaker
observer delegation to Iraq wrote: "At the end of June, I returned
from 15 days in Iraq. What I saw is this: The country is on the verge
of a firestorm, one that could engulf the entire Middle East."[10]

The Brutality of War and Occupation

In spite of these mushrooming difficulties, the Bush administration has insisted it will stay the course and press ahead with its
plans for Iraq, the region, and the world: "There will be no retreat,"
Bush belligerently declared in August 2003. "Our only goal, our only
option, is total victory in the war on terror."[11]

The potential exists, however, for America's quick victory over
the Ba'ath regime to turn into a morass and possibly even a defeat;
instead of strengthening the U.S. grip on the Middle East, it could
end up eroding or undermining it; and instead of solving the
empire's manifold challenges, it could end up exacerbating them.

Webster's Third New International Dictionary defines quagmire
as, "A complex or precarious position where disengagement is difficult." What makes the occupation particularly precarious for the
U.S. and disengagement particularly difficult is that its mounting
difficulties are not mainly the product of poor planning or easily cor-
rectable errors, but are instead deeply "embedded" in the unjust and

predatory character of the war and occupation themselves, as well as the broader global agenda they serve.

To begin with, the invasion and conquest resulted in thousands of dead and wounded. Bush officials continue to claim they did everything they could to avoid civilian casualties, but their military strategy relied on overwhelming firepower and extreme speed and brutality to rapidly crush Iraq's defenses and score a quick, decisive victory. A post-war Air Force assessment acknowledged that a third of U.S. bombs were old-fashioned "dumb" bombs, not "precision" weapons, and that more than 240,000 anti-personnel cluster bombs were dropped on Iraq. The U.S. also dropped at minimum dozens of "Mark 77 firebombs"—i.e., napalm—on Iraqi troops during the march toward Baghdad. All told, it is estimated that between 10,000 and 45,000 Iraqi troops may have been killed during the fighting.[12]

Civilians suffered heavily as well. Some neighborhoods were reduced to rubble, Iraqi hospitals were filled to overflowing during the war, and thousands were killed or wounded. As during the 1991 Persian Gulf War, the Pentagon has refused to tally Iraqi deaths, but independent and media investigations paint a grim picture, and no doubt more will emerge as time goes on as it did following the 1991 war.

A *Los Angeles Times* survey of Baghdad's hospitals found that "at least 1,700 Iraqi civilians died and more than 8,000 were injured in the battle for the Iraqi capital." An Associated Press investigation concluded that at least 3,240 civilians had been killed between March 20 and April 20, including 1,896 in Baghdad. AP warned that "the count is still fragmentary, and the complete toll—if it is ever tallied—is sure to be significantly higher."

By late August, the Iraq Body Count website put the minimum number of civilian dead at 6,113, the maximum at 7,830, and the wounded between 16,439 and 19,733.[13]

The *Christian Science Monitor*'s estimate runs even higher—between 5,000 and 10,000 civilian deaths. Haidar Taie, the head of the tracing department for the Iraqi Red Crescent in Baghdad told the *Monitor*: "It is a big disaster. Thousands are dead, thousands are missing, thousands are captured." Researchers for Human Rights Watch say they have found evidence of "massive use of cluster bombs in densely populated areas."[14]

War-time casualties are rarely mentioned in mainstream discussions of the roots of anti-U.S. resistance in Iraq, but eyewitnesses describe how these deaths ripple throughout Iraqi society. Jodie Evans, an environmental activist who traveled to Iraq in February and again in July 2003 with the anti-war group "Code Pink," told the *Revolutionary Worker*:

> There wasn't anybody I met that hadn't in some way been personally affected. Like somebody they knew had been taken prisoner at the airport, or somebody was dead, or somebody got killed in the war, or somebody's house got bombed. Everybody had some story to tell you about what was happening, or somebody who couldn't work. Everybody felt the effects of this. There isn't an Iraqi you meet who doesn't feel that they're being disrespected, that this is being done on purpose. It's made them hate the American government, hate it. They just think it's stupid and cruel and mean and thoughtless and everything you can think of.[15]

One Iraqi described the mood in Baghdad's al Adhamiya neighborhood to the *Miami Herald*:

> A year ago, on these streets, we would have yawned if someone had mentioned America to us. Now, look what they have done to us. Everyone feels this pain. Everyone here now wants to kill. Everyone here now wants to kill Americans.[16]

100 Days of Suffering

A second major cause of anger, protest, and resistance has been the collapse of Iraq's government, economy, and social order. This too is rooted in U.S. wars—past and present.

The seeds of this rapid collapse were sown by the 1991 Gulf War and 13 years of punishing sanctions, designed to cripple if not destroy Iraq's economy and governing structures, as discussed in chapter 6. One of the most galling instances of U.S. media and government hypocrisy has been their collective refusal to even mention the part played by sanctions in the destruction of what had previously been one of the most developed economies in the Middle East.

When reporters first entered Basra, they seemed astonished to discover that people there were without adequate water supplies, but never explored the U.S. role in creating this horror. Apologists for the empire and its Middle East aggressions, such as Thomas Friedman of the *New York Times*, now act as if sanctions never existed and instead blame Iraq's economic difficulties on "how poor and rundown Saddam had made it." ABC's "Evening News" of August 27 repeated this revisionist history: it blamed current power shortages on Saddam's "neglect" of Iraq's electrical grid, as if U.S. bombs had never savaged it; and it reported that U.S. occupation authorities were now spending 26 times as much on health care as the Ba'ath regime, as if sanctions never crippled Iraq's once-extensive health care system.[17]

Further, it was not surprising that a population that had been squeezed and impoverished for over a decade would try to grab what it could—by looting if need be—when given half a chance.[18]

The post-war chaos, destruction and suffering were part and parcel of a war aimed at destroying a troublesome regime—it's leading edge, after all, was "shock and awe"—not freeing the Iraqi people. This too flowed from the military strategy guiding the war and the larger global "war on terror," in particular the need to fight wars quickly and in succession, not entangle large numbers of U.S. troops in extensive "nation-building." The idea was to come, conquer, and move on. One senior U.S. occupation official told the *Washington Post* that the Pentagon "wanted 'occupation-lite.' They never thought they would actually have to alight in Iraq, just pass through."[19]

In this case, however, these calculations seem to have backfired. Instead of all going as planned, the Ba'ath regime fell, and pent-up Iraqi anger, desperation, and resistance erupted much more quickly than expected, creating what the *Washington Post* called a "security crisis," which then led to "a cascade of other crises."[20] When he arrived in Baghdad, Garner discovered that 17 of Iraq's 21 governmental ministries had "evaporated."[21]

Iraq used to be one of the most crime-free countries on earth, so Iraqis rightly hold the United States responsible for the current crime and chaos. One outraged shop owner told the *New York Times*, "Don't talk to me about Saddam Hussein. The Americans are in charge of everything here. They could have brought generators in here within 24 hours."[22]

In August, the White House issued a pollyannaish, 24-page

report titled "Results in Iraq: 100 Days Toward Security and Freedom," cataloguing "highlights of the successes." On August 8, Bush claimed that "The liberation of Iraq has improved the lives of the Iraqi people and the safety and security of the world."[23]

Meanwhile, journalists and human rights workers on the ground reported that the situation had deteriorated during the intense heat of summer. In early July, CARE reported that the security situation in Iraq is getting worse, not better," and Johanna Bjorken of Human Rights Watch told *Salon* that the electricity situation had also gotten worse in June.[24]

The United Nations Children's Fund (UNICEF) has reported that the incidence of diseases such as diarrhea, cholera, dysentery and typhoid was 2.5 times higher in May 2003 than May 2002.[25] In August, the *Washington Post* noted that while there had been improvements in some areas, "Electricity production still is well below prewar levels. The unemployment rate is 60 percent. Fuel is in short supply, causing hours-long waits at gas stations. Murders, carjackings and other violent crimes are rampant."[26]

"Conditions have never been worse," one American-educated tribal sheik who initially welcomed the U.S. invasion, told the *New York Times* in July. "We've never been through such a long bad period."[27]

Beshar Latif, an unemployed electrical engineer, complained bitterly to the *San Francisco Chronicle* about his treatment by U.S. occupation authorities:

> I have a family, and they are offering very little. It's only $150 per month. They make us wait and wait, and tell us to come back tomorrow, and nothing happens, and then they yell at us and treat us like animals. At my home there is no electricity now—there is no water. There is no safety. This is our country. They're stealing our oil. Who are they to give us orders?[28]

Occupation Logic 101

Post-war U.S. assaults have also fueled Iraqi resistance, perhaps even more than the death and destruction during the war itself. The U.S. has responded to anti-occupation guerrilla attacks as foreign colonial occupiers do: with a combination of brutal search-and-destroy missions, sweeping round-ups, and indiscriminate house-to-house searches. "Accidental" killings are inevitable when nervous, fearful soldiers have few, if any, real ties to the local population and cannot tell friends from enemies. Such tactics generally end up fueling resistance, not crushing it.

In July, ABC News showed some rare footage of U.S. troops on one such operation in a village in central Iraq. Soldiers were screaming at Iraqis in English in an effort to enforce a curfew that many villagers didn't even know existed. GIs forced Iraqis onto the ground, blindfolded and handcuffed them, and then threw them into trucks. One soldier loudly warned the locals that if they didn't help finger resisters, the U.S. would "come back with our tanks and drive through your fields and your homes," and that "this town will be punished."[29]

In early August, the *San Francisco Chronicle* reported that such U.S. assaults were backfiring:

> Iraqis say that the regularity of deaths in their own civilian population has drastically affected feelings regarding the U.S. occupation. In numerous interviews, they warn that more than other factors—like widespread unemployment, fuel shortages and electricity blackouts—civilian casualties have hardened bitterness against U.S. soldiers, and could prolong or widen the armed resistance against them. "It has increased our hate against Americans," said Ali Hatem, 23, a computer science student at the University of Baghdad. "It also increases the violence against them. In Iraq we are tribal people. When someone loses their son, they want revenge."[30]

This grim reality has been largely hidden from Americans because the media rarely covers the full impact of such U.S. assaults, and because those monitoring the occupation in Washington refuse to tally Iraqi casualties. "They don't count. They are not important," one Pentagon official explained to long-time Associated Press reporter Helen Thomas when she asked if the Pentagon was tabulating Iraqi deaths as carefully as American deaths. "If the Iraqis laid down their arms there was no problem," he told her. "But if we have to go in by force to kill them, the numbers don't make a difference. It's not something we are concerned with."[31]

"Bring 'Em On"

Through Summer 2003, U.S. officials argued that those resisting the occupation were either "dead-end" Hussein loyalists or outside agitators, rather "terrorists," and that many Iraqis weren't supporting the U.S. only because they still lived in fear of Saddam Hussein. These were yet further deceptions, designed to obscure past history and current realities.

These claims imply that Iraqis have either never suffered from past U.S. assaults on their country, are ignorant or blithely unaware of them, or simply don't care. They also ignore at least 80 years of Iraqi resistance to foreign domination, assume that nationalism is no longer a potent political force, and attempt to conflate Iraqi national dignity and pride with support for Saddam Hussein.

Many reports, however, make it clear that anti-U.S. resistance is diverse, growing, and probably more rooted in the occupation present than the Ba'ath past. To begin with, many Iraqis who welcomed the fall of the Hussein regime have made clear that they would not welcome an extended American occupation. Their sentiment, reported in many news accounts, is basically, "thank you for toppling Hussein, now please leave."

Ahmed Hashim, a professor of strategic studies at the U.S. Naval War College, divides the Iraqi opposition into three broad categories: regime loyalists, nationalist and patriotic individuals, and Islamists—and details the numerous and distinct organizations that exist within each of these trends.[32]

The assassination of Saddam Hussein's two sons—with the U.S. acting as judge, jury, and executioner—did not halt the attacks on occupation forces as promised, but rather inflamed Iraqi anger. Some observers feel that their deaths—and even the death of Saddam himself—might actually spur broader resistance by those who don't want their actions construed as support for the *ancienne regime* or taken advantage of by regime loyalists.

At this writing, most of the armed attacks on U.S. occupation forces have occurred in the so-called "Sunni triangle" of central Iraq. However, in July 2003, Robert Collier of the *San Francisco Chronicle* reported that deep anger extends even to Shi'a areas which have generally been calm because many top Shi'a religious leaders are so far cooperating with the occupiers:

Abdul Aziz al-Hakim, a Shiite cleric who represents the Supreme Council for the Islamic Revolution of Iraq and is pressing for an elected government to quickly replace the U.S.-backed council. "We should get rid of the occupation." If Islamic groups give in to growing pressures from their grass roots to take a more militant stance, the guerrilla resistance to U.S. forces could grow quickly. Even now, some appear ready to bolt. "We completely reject the council," said Mustafa Jaffar, spokesman for Moqtada al-Sadr, a 30-year-old radical cleric... "Is it a legislative council if the Americans can simply reject anything it does? What is the point?"[33]

In July, Sadr denounced the Iraqi Governing Council as an "illegitimate" group of American "lackeys," and announced plans to form an independent "Islamic army," a step that U.S. forces have stated they would not tolerate.[34]

In September, the *New York Times* reported that new U.S. intelligence assessments warned that the American occupation's most "formidable foe" was not Ba'ath loyalists, but "the resentment of ordinary Iraqis increasingly hostile to the American military occupation." The *Times* also noted that there were indications of "significant levels of hostility to the American presence," and that such hostility "extended well beyond the Sunni heartland of Iraq."[35]

In sum, a series of sharp jolts hit Iraqis in rapid succession: the devastation of war, the fall of the old regime, and the collapse of services, safety, and the economy; rising expectations fueled by the overnight opening of Iraq's political space; and a humiliating foreign occupation and intrusive and deadly U.S. counter-insurgency operations. It seems that the Iraqi people have been shocked—but not awed—by U.S. power. Instead many have become enraged, and the conditions for a deep-rooted popular insurgency against the U.S. occupiers could be in the making.

Evaporating Pretexts

The cakewalk isn't the only thing that's crumbled for the U.S. government; so have its pretexts for going to war: no banned weapons have been found, Iraq was shown to be weak, not dangerous, there was no Al Qaeda connection—except possibly the one created in the wake of the U.S. overthrow of Iraq's government—and no proof has emerged that Hussein was connected to Sept. 11.

Someday the Bush leadership's many statements, speeches, and pronouncements on Iraq and Saddam Hussein will be on display in a future library of preposterous imperialist propaganda, where visitors will scratch their heads in disbelief, and children will ask their parents how anyone could have fallen for it.

Yet in our present reality, Bush continues to chant the same lies, albiet in somewhat modified form, long after they've been discredited. In his September 8, 2003 address to the country, he raised the same old canards—terror and WMD: "we acted in Iraq, where the former regime sponsored terror, possessed and used weapons of mass destruction and for 12 years defied the clear demands of the United Nations Security Council." Like prosecutors attempting to justify having executed the wrong person, the Bush administration is parsing its language and revising its case in a desperate effort to make its charges fit the now-clear evidence. Thus, Bush states that Saddam *"possessed and used"*—past tense—banned weapons, as if this had been his argument all along, when in fact he had argued before the war that Iraq was a "grave and growing" danger which possessed chemical, biological and nuclear weapons.[36]

Bush also used variations on the word "terror" 28 times in his 15-minute speech, attempting to stoke the fear his administration hopes is a trump card. A week or so later, both he and Rumsfeld were forced to admit that there was no evidence linking Saddam Hussein to September 11.[37]

War supporters in and out of government have also attempted to spin the Kay Report—which actually demolished their pre-war claims—in much the same way. On October 2, 2003, David Kay, a Bush loyalist and the head of the CIA's Iraq Survey Group, reported that after searching Iraq for over four months, his team had found neither chemical, biological, nor nuclear weapons. The *New York Times* called it an "astonishing admission," which demonstrated that Iraq's unconventional weapons programs "barely existed and posed no immediate threat to the global community."[38]

Joseph Cirincione of the Carnegie Endowment for International Peace points out that Kay tried to bury these "bombshells" deep in his report to Congress:

> In the middle of a paragraph halfway through his testimony, Kay presents what should have been his lead finding:

"Information found to date suggests that Iraq's large-scale capability to develop, produce, and fill new CW munitions was reduced—if not entirely destroyed—during Operations Desert Storm and Desert Fox, 13 years of UN sanctions and UN inspections." Similarly, three paragraphs into Kay's description of Saddam's intention to develop nuclear weapons, he says: "to date we have not uncovered evidence that Iraq undertook significant post-1998 steps to actually build nuclear weapons or produce fissile material."

It is understandable that Mr. Kay did not wish to highlight these findings. They are not mentioned in his concluding points, nor in his opening summary. They directly refute the two main charges of administration officials before the war as well as the claim that UN inspections were not working.[39]

Another Kay revelation that received scant attention was his admission to Fox News that his team had found no evidence of any links between Iraq's WMD programs and al-Qaeda. In other words, there was no evidence whatsoever to support the U.S. government's pre-war claim that Iraq could be handing off biological, chemical or nuclear weapons to al-Qaeda.[40]

The White House spin-meisters have tried to shift attention away from these central and damning exposures, and onto Kay's as yet unsubstantiated and politically-motivated claims to have found bits and pieces of unconventional programs, including papers, materials and equipment. Kay emphasized, "we have discovered dozens of WMD-related program activities and significant amounts of equipment that Iraq concealed from the United Nations during the inspections that began in late 2002." Bush seized on these claims to argue that Kay's report validated his decision to wage war: "It states that Saddam Hussein's regime had a clandestine network of biological laboratories. They had a live strain of deadly agent called botulinum. And he had sophisticated concealment efforts. In other words, he's hiding his program."[41]

The bulk of Kay's 200-page report remains classified—only a 13-page summary has so far been made public—and even UN weapons inspectors have been prevented from examining its entire contents. One former weapons inspector told Britain's *Guardian* that Kay's team had been "under huge pressure to come up with whatever" to paint Iraq as a threat. So this secrecy is undoubtedly motivated by the Bush administration's fear that making the full report public would expose more gaping holes in the public case it presented for war.[42]

Yet even the limited claims that Kay has so far trumpeted are extremely thin. The "live strain of deadly agent called botulinum" that Kay turned up and which Bush has pointed to, turned out to be a single vial that had been kept in one scientist's home refrigerator for 10 years—hardly the stuff of active and dangerous biological weapons program. Kay himself admitted that Iraq had only "the very most rudimentary" nuclear research program, and could only vaguely speculate that Hussein may have intended to "continue production at some point in time."[43]

Former chief UN weapons inspector Hans Blix told the *Los Angeles Times* that Kay's report showed only "some fairly minor items that should have been declared" and that most of the materials or equipment Kay cited "don't seem very big, and some may be legitimate dual-use items" permitted under UN resolutions due to their civilian applications. Blix concluded: "In many cases, Kay's report says they may be suitable for this or suitable for that. Well, a butcher's knife is also suitable for murder."[44]

In short, even Kay's limited claims have probably been "sexed-up," and further exposure of the bankruptcy of the Bush case for war will emerge over time. As Maureen Dowd of the *New York Times* sardonically noted, in reference to botulinum's different uses, "we know now that our first pre-emptive war was launched basically because Iraq had...a vial of Botox?"[45]

Kay's failure to find an Iraqi "smoking gun" is so politically damaging that government officials have even concocted the convoluted "theory" that Saddam Hussein is to blame for deceiving U.S. and British intelligence for years by pretending to have banned weapons. In fact for over a decade, Iraq had been pleading to the UN and anyone else who would listen that it no longer had chemical, biological or nuclear weapons, and therefore sanctions should be lifted.[46]

(Scott Ritter raised the provocative question: if the U.S. was so intent on finding WMD, why didn't its troops secure the most extensive repository of documentation on Iraq's unconventional weapons programs—the Iraqi National Monitoring Directorate in Baghdad—instead of allowing it to be sacked and looted during the invasion?[47])

At this juncture, whether "weapons of mass destruction" turn up in Iraq or not is in many ways beside the point. The U.S. went to war on the claim that it had clear, compelling and specific evidence that Iraq possessed and was actively developing chemical, biological and nuclear weapons and therefore posed a threat to the region and the world. These charges were raised repeatedly by Bush officials including in Bush's September 12, 2002 speech to the UN, his October 7, 2002 speech in Cincinnati, his Januray 2003 State of the Union message, Colin Powell's February 5, 2003 UN presentation, and innumerable talks and media appearances by administration officials, as detailed in the appendix. This propaganda barrage included both very specific "evidence"—satellite photos, tape recordings, alleged documents—as to the exact nature and location of Iraqi weapons, as well as the most dire of warnings. For instance, on March 16, 2003, Vice President Cheney declared on NBC's "Meet The Press" that, "We believe he (Saddam) has, in fact, reconstituted nuclear weapons." On October 7, 2002, Bush warned that the U.S. had to wage war and could not "wait for the final proof, the smoking gun, that could come in the form of a mushroom cloud."[48]

Months of searching and the Kay Report have now made clear that the U.S. had no such incontrivertible evidence—in fact mountains of evidence amassed during a decade of UN inspections and again when UN inspectors returned to Iraq in late 2002 showed that Iraq had been stripped of its unconventional weapons—and that U.S. officials were deliberately exaggerating and deliberately lying about Iraq's intentions and capabilities. It is worth repeating that these deceptions not only formed the core of the Bush administration's case for war in 2003, they were also the central rationalization for 12 murderous years of U.S. enforced sanctions and economic strangulation against Iraq.

There is a method to this surreal yet deadly madness. The Bush regime continues to repeat its lies for fear that admitting too much at once could collapse its entore propaganda house-of-cards. And there is a more sinister side to the Bush team's continued manipulation and deceit: it is a belligerent declaration that they're determined to press ahead with their unbounded war for greater empire, whether the world likes or believes their excuses—or not.

The Politics of Plunging GI Morale

The fallout from the evaporation of the government's pretexts for war is potentially enormous, and is already being felt among U.S. troops in Iraq; the lies they were told going into the war—that they were "liberating" Iraq and that their quickest route home lay through Baghdad—have begun coming home to roost. Some are turning against the war, many are reportedly deeply worried and frustrated. In Summer 2003, Tim Predmore, stationed near Mosul with the 101st Airborne, wrote: "For the last six months I have participated in what I believe to be the great modern lie: Operation Iraqi Freedom.... From the moment the first shot was fired in this so-called war of liberation and freedom, hypocrisy reigned.... At least to me, oil seems to be the reason for our presence."[49]

U.S. troops understand neither the culture, nor the history, nor the language of the country they are attempting to rule—most can't even read street signs or communicate their orders. In July, an officer from the Army's 3rd Infantry Division told the *Christian Science Monitor*, "Make no mistake, the level of morale for most soldiers that I've seen has hit rock bottom."[50]

Unease, anxiety and frustration have grown among military families, and some have spoken out against the war. In July, the *New York Times* reported that frustrations were running so high at Fort Stewart, Georgia that, "a colonel, meeting with 800 seething spouses, most of them wives, had to be escorted from the session." Military families have created websites such as "Military Families Speak Out," and in August, parents of children stationed in Iraq initiated a campaign to end their deployment called "Bring Them Home Now."[51]

Occupation Fiscal Shock

Before the war, the Bush administration said little about how much it would cost, except to hint that it would be covered by the spoils of war—Iraq's oil—as well as selling off Iraqi industries to private investors. Instead, much of Iraq's petroleum infrastructure, which had been savaged by the 1991 war and subsequent sanctions, was looted in the chaos of 2003, and then targeted by those resisting the U.S. occupation. So it could be many years and billions in investment before oil exports rise to the levels predicted in rosy Pentagon and Iraqi exile forecasts; and with attacks on occupation troops continuing, it may be a long time before foreign investors consider sinking serious capital into Iraq.

Growing Iraqi resistance has necessitated extending tours of duty, which means rising military costs. In July, Defense Secretary Rumsfeld admitted costs were running at $3.9 billion a month— double the Pentagon's April projection. That same month, Paul Bremer, the U.S. administrator of Iraq, acknowledged that "getting the country up and running again" could cost $100 billion and take three years. Other non-governmental analyses have concluded that military and rebuilding costs in Iraq could reach $600 billion.[52]

In September 2003, the Bush administration began taking drastic steps to deal with these fiscal shocks from Iraq. First, Bush asked for an additional $87 billion in funding. Coming on top of an earlier $79 billion appropriation for the war, it meant that the U.S. would be spending $166 billion on Iraq (mainly) and Afghanistan in 2003 and 2004. That's 25 times more than the U.S. spent in 1991 on Desert Storm, when U.S. allies coughed up $60 billion ($84 billion in today's dollars). Most—78 percent, or $65.6 billion of the new request—would go to the military, with only $15 billion going toward rebuilding Iraq.[53]

Second, the U.S. has stepped up efforts to strong-arm or entice other countries to bail it out with money and troops. Finally, the U.S. hurriedly put Iraqi businesses and industry—except its oil industry—on the market to raise funds for occupation and reconstruction. On September 22, Britain's *Guardian* noted sardonically, "Iraq was effectively put up for sale yesterday, when the US-backed administration unveiled a sweeping overhaul of the economy, giving foreign companies unprecedented access to Iraqi firms which are to be sold off in a privatization windfall."[54]

In requesting an additional $87 billion, Bush declared that the U.S. must be willing to pay whatever price is needed to achieve its goals in Iraq. Yet these mounting costs are taking place in the context of an uncertain global economy, rapidly ballooning government deficits (in August the Congressional Budget Office projected that the federal budget deficit would reach a record $401 billion for 2003, soar to $480 billion in 2004, and could total $5 trillion over the next decade—without taking into account the cost of the Iraq war and occupation), and worsening U.S. external financial balances. All could give rise to further complications and difficulties.[55]

The U.S. Agenda at Risk?

Confronted with these difficulties in Iraq and the region (including the escalation of the Israeli-Palestinian struggle and the fracturing of the so-called "roadmap to peace"), the Bush administration has been forced to tack and maneuver, adjust its plans, and modify its timetables. At this writing, the Bush team is still scrambling to get control of the situation, including by trying to enlist international support via the UN. So far, the effort has not gone far because of American unwillingness to share the political and economic spoils of war, because such sharing would represent a defeat of one of Washington's war aims—increasing U.S. leverage over other global powers.[56]

As argued in this book, dominating the Middle East and its vast oil reserves has been a key link in the chain of empire that has been pursued by Republicans and Democrats alike for over 60 years, and has become even more crucial to U.S. global power today. That was the message of Bush's September 8, 2003 declaration that in the war on terror, "Iraq is now the central front. Enemies of freedom are making a desperate stand there, and there they must be defeated. This will take time and require sacrifice. Yet we will do what is necessary, we will spend what is necessary, to achieve this essential victory in the war on terror...for America, there will be no going back to the era before September the 11th, 2001."

Democrats and Republicans alike say that the U.S. cannot afford to lose in Iraq. In September 2003, in a show of ruling class solidarity, the Democrats announced they were dropping plans to investigate the Bush administration's prewar claims concerning Iraqi WMD because, "We're past that."[57]

Robert Baer, a former CIA agent in the Middle East, spells out the imperialist case for "staying the course" in Iraq, along with the impact on U.S. global dominance of not doing so:

> Leaving Iraq now, in a state of anarchy, would lead to civil war. And then almost anything could happen, from pulling in

Iran to spreading chaos to the Arab sheikdoms of the Gulf—
which, by the way, control something like 60 percent of the
world's oil reserves. No matter how tough things get, we cannot
leave Iraq until it is mended.[58]

Robert Kagan and William Kristol, writing in the neoconservative *Weekly Standard*, argue that the stakes in Iraq are global:

[T]he president's vision will, in the coming months, either
be launched successfully in Iraq, or it will die in Iraq. Indeed,
there is more at stake in Iraq than even this vision of a better,
safer middle east. The future course of American foreign policy,
American world leadership and American security is at stake.
Failure in Iraq would be a devastating blow to everything the
United States hopes to accomplish, and must accomplish, in the
decades ahead."[59]

A Cauldron of Contradictions

The U.S. rulers still have considerable initiative in their drive
for greater empire, but their juggernaut is fraught with complex and
dangerous tensions. "There is the potential at any given point—and
especially as they roll down the road with this," Bob Avakian argues,
"for this to get wildly out of control...the imperialists have set things
in motion that can't be easily reversed, and may not be easily controlled." He describes this situation as "a cauldron of contradictions."[60]

These dynamics and potentials are already evident. Many
countries—such as industrialized imperial powers like Russia and
France—are reacting to America's widening military dominance and
its aggressive post-Sept. 11 agenda by accelerating their own military
buildups. This heightens the possibility that global rivalries could
intensify and new coalitions of countries arrayed against the U.S.
could emerge, and even that at some point global military conflict
could once again loom over the planet. Meanwhile, the U.S. military is stretched thin and in danger of becoming overextended, with
roughly one-third of its combat forces tied down in Iraq.

In the Middle East and Central Asian regions, the U.S. has, for
decades, mainly exerted its control indirectly, through proxies, limited interventions, and sometimes war. American power faced limits
and impediments, but its forces weren't generally on the front lines

or directly ruling local populations. Consequently, the U.S. often wasn't seen as their immediate enemy. Now, America has marched directly into this volatile region at a time when anti-U.S. anger is rising.

The resistance in Iraq is overwhelmingly home-grown, and the U.S. may be exaggerating the involvement of foreign fighters to bolster its now-discredited claim that Saddam Hussein had links with Al Qaeda. Yet, there are numerous reports that foreign fighters may be coming into Iraq to confront U.S. forces.

Washington's Iraq war may have created the very hot-bed of anti-U.S. resistance it was supposed to destroy—not simply in Iraq, but across the region. In September 2002, Ahmed Rashid, author of *The Taliban*, warned that, "Across Central and South Asia...the aftermath of the war in Afghanistan has led to growing instability and domestic political crises in every country."[61]

Rashid's prediction is already coming to pass in Afghanistan, which may be a chronicle of Iraq's future foretold. On August 13, 2003, nearly two years after the U.S. "liberated" the country, the *New York Times* reported that Afghanistan had experienced its "most violent day" in nearly a year. The *Los Angeles Times* painted an even more damning picture: "As opium production and banditry soar, the country is at risk of anarchy."[62] So the net results of the U.S. wars of terror could include falling client dominoes, greater support for Islamist movements like al Qaeda, or simply uncontrollable chaos.

These, however, are not the only possibilities. The yearning for genuine liberation runs deep across the region, and the shocks of Washington's wars and interventions could also create conditions for the development and further development of secular anti-imperialist and revolutionary political movements—movements that strive for genuine equality for women, freedom from oil-dependence and the crushing dynamics of global capitalism, and uprooting feudal bondage, tradition, and land-tenure. Such movements would give lie to the claim by Bush and other U.S. apologists that the only choice today is between McWorld and Jihad, between predatory imperialism on one hand and backward looking and oppressive religious movements on the other.

War Without End? Not In Our Name

Shortly after Sept. 11, Bush promised, "We will rally the world" in support of America's new war without end. He did rally the world—against it. On February 15, 2003 alone, some 10-15 million people marched against the coming war on Iraq in hundreds of actions across the planet, constituting an unprecedented global outpouring. One *New York Times* dispatch called it evidence of the existence of two superpowers—the U.S. and world public opinion. Another noted:

> The breadth and magnitude of the demonstrations opened a rift between ruler and the ruled, convincing many that street protest had overtaken conventional democracy in expressing the popular will.[63]

The protests, unfortunately, did not stop the war, but they did have an enormous impact and offered a glimpse of the potential for global resistance from below. At a time when the institutions of the established order—the press, the major political parties, international and government institutions, big business—were largely silent, complicit or supportive of the coming war, millions of ordinary people altered the world's political dynamics by speaking out, taking to the streets, and making their voices heard.

Suddenly, there was a global dialogue and shared sense of outrage, unity, and purpose; suddenly the terms of the debate shifted as anti-war voices forced their way into the media discourse. The massive outpouring clearly demonstrated to people around the world, the Middle East in particular, that Bush did not speak for all Americans, and that he could not wage his wars in their name. Deep-seated and diverse resistance also prevented many governments—most notably Turkey's—from going along with the Iraq war, and played a major part in preventing the United Nations from officially sanctioning it. The ripples and ramifications from those protests continue to be felt. The lesson is not that protest doesn't work, but that it must become even broader, even deeper, and even more determined.

For this to happen, many more need to come to grips with the realities of U.S. interventions and wars—their real goals, devastating impacts, and the deeper forces driving them. Many more need to break with the basic premise of government and media discourse—

that the U.S. has the unquestioned right to shape the destinies of peoples and countries across the globe and the only issue up for discussion is how Washington can best do so.

Many more need to reject the official rationale for the so-called "war on terror," which is based on demonizing the peoples of the Middle East and Central Asia and their various resistance struggles on the one hand, and the false and chauvinist claim that the war's mission is "protecting Americans" on the other.

One does not have to subscribe to all the ideologies, political agendas, strategies, or tactics of the complex and various anti-U.S. forces across the region to understand that the Bush's "they hate us because..." charge is a lie that sweeps 60 years of United States interventions, aggressions, and support for tyranny and oppression under the rug, and constitutes a racist caricature of the thinking and aspirations of millions of Arabs, Muslims, Persians, and others in the region. In reality, what Bush and the U.S. political elite call a "clash of civilizations" is at root a sharpening clash between the world's haves and have-nots, between the industrialized countries and the Third World. At heart, this complex battle pits the 100-plus year struggle of oppressed nations for self-determination and liberation against the demands of global capital for deeper penetration, greater exploitation, and tighter control, although of course culture and religion are part of the mix.

"They hate us because..." is designed to allow the U.S. to vilify resistance to its aggressions, whatever the political agenda at work, as "terrorism" and give Washington a blank check for the unlimited use of state violence, anywhere on earth. Today, even Iraqis fighting the unjust occupation of their own country by a foreign power which resulted from an illegal war, are labeled "terrorists." "The surest way to avoid attacks on our own people is to engage the enemy where he lives and plans," Bush declares—both trying to spin the unexpected results of his Iraq adventure and to establish a rationalization for ongoing intervention around the world.[64]

As much as they bandy about the term, Bush and company publicly avoid defining what constitutes "terrorism." But at one December 2001 hearing before the Senate Judiciary Committee, Attorney General John Ashcroft did just that: "Since 1983 the

United States government has defined terrorists as those who perpetuate premeditated, politically motivated violence against non-
combatant targets."[65] One can understand the U.S. government's
reticence on this point. By its own definition, and taking into
account all its wars and interventions over the past 50 plus years
including those in Iraq described here, the United States government could legitimately be described as the largest and most violent
terrorist organization on earth.

The Bush administration has claimed its unjust global war for
greater empire is driven by a desire to protect Americans, to save
American lives, even as its actions increase hatred for the United
States and put Americans in harms way. This is not surprising—the
U.S. establishment is driven by concerns of world power and empire,
not the needs and aspirations of the people living under its rule—
including those in the USA itself.

And why should American lives be worth any more than others? What kind of society feigns great concern for its own fallen,
while adamantly refusing to even estimate the numbers it kills in
combat—"We don't do body counts," Gen. Tommy Franks
declared—let alone allow us to know them, their stories, their his-
tories? Where are the newspaper pages devoted to individually iden-
tifying the Iraqis killed by the United States, during or after official
combat, detailing their families ties and their suffering? Instead, the
American people have been deliberately isolated from the world's
peoples, and deliberately lied to about the impact of U.S. global
actions. As the Iraq Body Count website recently put it, "The
maimed civilians of Iraq have been brushed under the carpet." The
U.S. government is attempting to scare and threaten us into accepting a foul, Faustian, and ultimately phony bargain: it will supposedly protect us in exchange for our acquiescence in whatever killings,
interventions, or wars it decides to wage, wherever and whenever.

It is heartening that millions in the United States have rejected such a bargain, along with official efforts to stoke fear and narrow
chauvinism, along with the murderous imperial logic of its "war on
terror." Many have instead reached out to others around the world,
including those targeted by America's new war, whether in street
protests, letters to the editors, prayer vigils, web postings, paid ads,
or simply discussions with neighbors.

Many of these best sentiments are captured in the "Not In Our Name" Statement of Conscience, signed by over 30,000 people, including prominent actors, academics, artists, writers, and public figures, and published in dozens of newspapers and magazines around the world.

"We believe that peoples and nations have the right to determine their own destiny, free from military coercion by great powers," it declares, and calls upon us not to allow the government to act in our names:

> We believe that people of conscience must take responsibility for what their own governments do—we must first of all oppose the injustice that is done in our own name. Thus we call on all Americans to RESIST the war and repression that has been loosed on the world by the Bush administration. It is unjust, immoral, and illegitimate. We choose to make common cause with the people of the world.[66]

Appendix

"A Bodyguard of Lies"

Dissecting U.S. Pretexts for War

> Of course, this conjures up Winston Churchill's famous phrase when he said—don't quote me on this, okay? I don't want to be quoted on this, so don't quote me. He said 'sometimes the truth is so precious it must be accompanied by a bodyguard of lies.'
>
> —Donald Rumsfeld, US Department of Defense Briefing, September 25, 2001[1]

> "To build its case for war with Iraq, the Bush administration argued that Saddam Hussein had weapons of mass destruction, but some officials now privately acknowledge the White House had another reason for war—a global show of American power and democracy.
>
> Officials inside government and advisers outside told ABC News the administration emphasized the danger of Saddam's weapons to gain the legal justification for war from the United Nations and to stress the danger at home to Americans.
>
> "We were not lying," said one official. "but it was just a matter of emphasis."
>
> —ABC News, April 25, 2003[2]

In fact, they were lying. Following the September 11, 2001 attacks, the U.S. government relentlessly created pretexts to wage war against Iraq. Charges were featured daily on the front pages of newspapers and as lead stories on TV. As the truth leaked out before the war, it was buried, downplayed, or barely reported. No wonder a USA Today poll reported that over 50 percent of Americans believed there was a direct link between the Sept. 11 attacks and Saddam Hussein,[3] even though there was no evidence of such a connection.

The main pretexts that the U.S. used to argue for war on Iraq were that:

1. Iraq possessed weapons of mass destruction in violation of

UN resolutions;

2.   with such weapons, Iraq posed a significant threat to the U.S. and neighboring countries; and

3.   Iraq was linked to alleged terrorist organizations, such as al Qaeda.

Yet, as of this writing, no "weapons of mass destruction" have been found in Iraq, more than half a year after the U.S. invasion, and it seems very unlikely that the U.S. will ever find anything resembling the quantities alleged to justify the invasion. In addition, no credible link had been established between the Iraqi government and al Qaeda, the Ansar al-Islam group, September 11th, or any attack against the U.S. in at least ten years. What emerges is a portrait of a big power willing to use any fig leaf, no matter how flimsy, to cover its naked imperialist motives for waging war on Iraq.

In fact, by the end of the summer 2003, in the face of the failure to find any weapons of mass destruction and some exposure of the "intelligence" relied upon by the White House, the Bush administration began to revise its reasons for invading Iraq, downplaying the WMD pretext. Rather than charge that Iraq actually had weapons of mass destruction, the administration began to claim only that Iraq had a WMD "program," that the invasion was intended to "liberate" the people of Iraq, and that it was part of an overall effort to transform the Middle East. The *Washington Post* noted, "As the search for weapons in Iraq continues without success, the Bush administration has moved to emphasize a different rationale for the war against Saddam Hussein: using Iraq as the 'linchpin' to transform the Middle East and thereby reduce the terrorist threat to the United States. President Bush, who has stopped talking about Iraq's weapons, said...that 'the rise of a free and peaceful Iraq is critical to the stability of the Middle East, and a stable Middle East is critical to the security of the American people.'"[4] Deputy Defense Secretary Wolfowitz, after a trip to Iraq, said flat out, "I'm not concerned about weapons of mass destruction.... I'm concerned about getting Iraq on its feet. I didn't come [to Iraq] on a search for weapons of mass destruction."[5]

The following discussion examines some of the charges that were raised to justify the attack on Iraq. It also examines government statements during and after the war related to weapons of mass destruction and Iraq's alleged links to terrorism.

ALLEGED IRAQI LINKS TO AL QAEDA, ANSAR AL-ISLAM, AND TERRORISM

Alleged Iraqi Links to al Qaeda

Assertion:

The New York Times, September 27, 2002:

> Defense Secretary Donald H. Rumsfeld said today that American intelligence had "bulletproof" evidence of links between Al Qaeda and the government of President Saddam Hussein of Iraq.
>
> Mr. Rumsfeld said that recently declassified intelligence reports about suspected ties between Al Qaeda and the Iraqi government, including the presence of senior members of Al Qaeda in Baghdad in "recent periods," were "factual" and "exactly accurate."[6]

The Facts:

- No evidence has emerged of Iraqi involvement in the September 11 attacks or of links between Iraq and Al Qaeda.
- Shortly after the September 11th attacks, even the *Wall Street Journal* noted that "few U.S. officials believe that any real alliance between Iraq and Al-Qaeda ever emerged... The two groups share few aims and have very different motivations..."[7]
- According to the *New York Times*, intelligence officials from Jordan, Israel and Saudi Arabia do not believe there is any serious Hussein-bin Laden connection.[8]
- Former UNSCOM inspector Scott Ritter says with regard to the alleged Iraq/al Qaeda link: "This one is patently absurd. He has spent the last thirty years declaring war against Islamic fundamentalism, crushing it.... Osama bin Laden has a history of hating Saddam Hussein."[9] In fact, Ritter thinks a more likely scenario is that if al Qaeda obtained a nuclear device the group would use it against Saddam Hussein.
- The State Department's own report on terrorism, released in April 2001, stated that Iraq had not attempted an anti-

Western attack since 1993.[10]

- "At the Federal Bureau of Investigation, some investigators said they were baffled by the Bush administration's insistence on a solid link between Iraq and Osama bin Laden's network. "We've been looking at this hard for more than a year and you know what, we just don't think it's there," a government official said…. Mr. Bush asserted in his State of the Union address this week that Iraq was protecting and aiding Qaeda operatives, but American intelligence and law enforcement officials said the evidence was fragmentary and inconclusive… "It's more than just skepticism," said one official, describing the feelings of some analysts in the intelligence agencies. "I think there is also a sense of disappointment with the community's leadership that they are not standing up for them at a time when the intelligence is obviously being politicized."[11]

- British intelligence also said there was no Iraq al Qaeda link. As reported by the BBC: "There are no current links between the Iraqi regime and the al-Qaeda network, according to an official British intelligence report seen by BBC News. The classified document, written by defense intelligence staff 3 weeks ago, says there has been contact between the 2 in the past… The defense intelligence staff document, seen by BBC defense correspondent Andrew Gilligan, is classified Top Secret and was sent to UK Prime Minister Tony Blair and other senior members of the government. It says al-Qaeda leader Osama Bin Laden views Iraq's ruling Ba'ath party as running contrary to his religion, calling it an 'apostate regime'."[12]

- Greg Thielman, the director of the strategic, proliferation, and military affairs division at the State Department's Bureau of Intelligence and Research until September 2002, says "Based on the terrorism experts I met with during my period of government, I never heard anyone make the claim that there was a significant tie between Al Qaeda and Saddam Hussein." He added, "The Bush administration…was 'misleading the public in implying there was a close connection.'"[13]

- On August 1, 2003, Deputy Defense Secretary Wolfowitz, was asked on The Laura Ingraham Show when he started to think that Iraq had something to do with the September 11, 2001 attacks. In what was believed to be the first such admission by the Bush administration by that date, Wolfowitz conceded that "I'm not sure even now that perhaps Iraq had something to do with it."[14]

* Former U.S. intelligence officials also doubt the alleged connection between Iraq and Al Qaeda. A Pentagon unit, the Office of Special Plans, had been formed to try to find links between Iraq and Al Qaeda, but was disbanded late in 2002. "About a dozen former CIA intelligence officials have been quoted as saying that the Office of Special Plans cherry-picked intelligence, much of which was gathered by unreliable Iraqi defectors, to make a stronger case for war and delivered directly to Vice President Dick Cheney's office and National Security Advisor Condoleezza Rice without first being vetted by the CIA."[15]

The Alleged Meeting in Prague Between Iraqi Intelligence and Mohammed Atta

Assertion:

Shortly after the September 11 attack, former CIA chief James Woolsey was dispatched to London "on a mission," according to the *New York Times*, "to gather evidence linking Mr. Hussein to the Sept. 11 attacks."[16] Woolsey began raising various charges against Iraq. One of the charges, first floated by Woolsey in London, was a purported meeting in Prague, the capital of the Czech Republic, between Mohammed Atta and an Iraqi intelligence agent in April 2001.

CNN report one month after Sept. 11: "U.S. officials revealed Thursday that Mohammed Atta—one of the suspected suicide hijackers—had two meetings, not one, with Iraqi intelligence officers in Prague, Czech Republic.

"The first meeting was in June 2000 and the second one was in April 2001, sources said. In both cases Atta met in Prague with Iraqi intelligence officers operating under cover as diplomats.

"Officials declined to identify the Iraqis, except to say *Newsweek* magazine was incorrect in reporting that one of them was Farouk Hijazi, Iraq's ambassador to Turkey."[17]

The Facts:

* The reports of a meeting between Mohammed Atta and Iraqi

intelligence have been completely discredited.

- Nearly a year after this story was planted in the media, it completely fell apart. On October 21, 2002, the New York Times reported "The Czech President, Vaclav Havel, has quietly told the White House he has concluded that there is no evidence to confirm earlier reports that Mohammed Atta, the leader of the Sept. 11 attacks, met with an Iraqi intelligence officer in Prague just months before the attacks on New York and Washington, according to Czech officials." "Today, Czech officials say they have no evidence that Mr. Atta was even in the country in April in 2001. In fact, American records indicate he was in Virginia Beach, Va. in early April." The article adds that "Over the years, Czech security officials also say that they have never seen any other evidence that Iraqi intelligence officers stationed in Prague were involved in terrorist activities."18

The Alleged Iraqi Connection with Al-Zarqawi and with Ansar al-Islam

Assertions:

U.S. Secretary of State Colin Powell at the UN, February 5, 2003:

> Iraq today harbors a deadly terrorist network headed by Abu Musab Al-Zarqawi, an associate and collaborator of Osama bin Laden and his Al Qaeda lieutenants.
>
> Zarqawi, a Palestinian born in Jordan, fought in the Afghan war more than a decade ago. Returning to Afghanistan in 2000, he oversaw a terrorist training camp. One of his specialties and one of the specialties of this camp is poisons. When our coalition ousted the Taliban, the Zarqawi network helped establish another poison and explosive training center camp. And this camp is located in northeastern Iraq.
>
> The network is teaching its operatives how to produce ricin and other poisons. Let me remind you how ricin works. Less than a pinch—imagine a pinch of salt—less than a pinch of ricin, eating just this amount in your food, would cause shock followed by circulatory failure. Death comes within 72 hours and there is no antidote, there is no cure. It is fatal.
>
> Those helping to run this camp are Zarqawi lieutenants operating in northern Kurdish areas outside Saddam Hussein's controlled Iraq. But Baghdad has an agent in the most senior levels of the radical organization, Ansar al-Islam, that controls this corner of Iraq. In 2000 this agent offered Al Qaeda safe haven in the region. After we swept Al Qaeda from Afghanistan, some of its members

accepted this safe haven. They remain there today.[19]

On March 27, 2003 U.S. forces destroyed the camp in northern Iraq belonging to Ansar al-Islam. Chairman of the Joint Chiefs of Staff General Richard Myers said on March 30: "It's from this site where people were trained and where poisons were developed that migrated into Europe."[20] In London on March 31, 2003 two newspapers, the *Mirror* and the *Sun* reported that the American finds at the Ansar al-Islam site offered proof that Iraq had weapons of mass destruction.[21]

The Facts:

- Powell misled the public about a link between al-Zarqawi and al-Qaeda. In February 2003, the *Washington Post* reported: "Senior administration officials said that, although Zarqawi has ties to bin Laden's group, he is not under al Qaeda control or direction. 'They have common goals,' one intelligence analyst said, 'but he [Zarqawi] is outside bin Laden's circle. He is not sworn al Qaeda.'"[22]

- *New York Times* editorial (February 14, 2003): "Mr. Zarqawi, a Palestinian, fought along side Qaeda forces in Afghanistan. But Washington has yet to establish publicly that he is an important figure in Al Qaeda or maintains links with Mr. bin Laden."[23]

- There is no hard evidence of any link between Zarqawi and Iraq. The *Washington Post* reported that "U.S. intelligence officials acknowledged that the terrorist, Abu Musab Zarqawi, was no longer in Iraq and that there was no hard evidence Hussein's government knew he was there or had contact with him." In any case, this person was removed from Iraq by authorities within days of being told he was there.[24]

- *Chicago Tribune* (February 11, 2003): "A former Al Qaeda recruit told German authorities last year that Abu Musab al-Zarqawi, portrayed by the Bush administration as the critical link between Osama bin Laden's group and Iraqi leader Saddam Hussein, was actually opposed to Al Qaeda. In voluminous statements given to German federal police after his April arrest, Shadi Abdallah, a 26-year-old Jordanian who claims to have served briefly as a bin Laden bodyguard, maintained that Zarqawi was allied instead with Iraq's enemy, the fundamentalist Islamic government of Iran."[25]

- Senior U.S. officials told the *Washington Post* that although the Iraqi government is aware of the [Zarqawi] group's activity, it does not operate, control or sponsor it.[26]

- Al-Zarqawi had close ties with and support from members of the Qatari royal family. Washington officials acknowledge that al-Zarqawi had support from a member of the Qatari Royal family, Abdul Karim al-Thani, who hosted him in Qatar. However, Washington officials do not claim that, as with Iraq, these facts show that the Qatari court is also connected to al Qaeda—particularly since the United States depends on Qatar to provide staging support for the U.S. Central Command.[27]

- The leader of Ansar al-Islam said Saddam Hussein is his enemy. Mullah Krekar told the Guardian newspaper of London that he has no links with Iraqi leaders. "I am against Saddam Hussein. I want (Iraq) to change into an Islamic regime."[28]

- Powell's claim that said Baghdad had an "agent" in "the most senior levels" of Ansar, implying a special relationship with the Hussein government, was not true. The *Washington Post*: "A senior government official said U.S. intelligence has no direct knowledge of what the "agent" does. "He may be spying on the Ansar group. He may be a liaison with Baghdad," the official said. "Saddam Hussein likes to keep an eye on such groups."[29]

- The head of Ansar threatened to produce evidence of extensive contacts—with *Washington*. Mullah Krekar : "I had a meeting with a CIA representative and someone from the American army in the town of Sulaymaniya (Iraqi Kurdistan) at the end of 2000. They asked us to collaborate with them...but we refused to do so," he said.[30]

- A description of the Ansar "base" by reporters two days after Powell's speech was of a site that was clearly no threat to the U.S. or neighboring countries, and showed no evidence of "poison" production. "A remote site in the mountains of northern Iraq identified by U.S. officials as a crude laboratory where al-Qaeda terrorists concoct poisons is a muddy, decrepit, refuse-strewn compound devoid of any signs of deadly substances.

Ansar al Islam, a Kurdish militant group accused by U.S. and Kurdish officials of harboring al-Qaeda fugitives from Afghanistan, on Saturday took foreign journalists on a tour of the site and denied it had a poison-making facility."

"There were no sign of chemicals, mixing vessels, running water or other things associated with the production of deadly substances. The only sharp odor at the compound came from rotting food overflowing from a trash container. The site is in Sargat, an impoverished hamlet of scattered hovels high up steep slopes that crest in snow-crowned peaks of the Iranian border."

"The satellite photograph presented to the Security Council gave the compound's location as Khurmal, a town about 4 miles away that is not controlled by Ansar. Khurmal is the headquarters of a more moderate Kurdish Islamic faction, Komal Islami. While some of Komal fighters are said to sympathize with Ansar, Komal's leaders cooperate with Ansar's rival, the Patriotic Union of Kurdistan."

"The cinderblock and concrete dwellings were empty except for discarded shoes, sandals and clothing, old pots and pans, worn blankets, and broken cupboards. The grounds were littered with garbage. Inside the main building were a TV studio, computers and a digital scanner."[31]

- No chemical or biological weapons or evidence linking the camp with Baghdad were found in the Ansar camp. A *Los Angeles Times* reporter, who visited the camp after it had been destroyed during the 2003 war, said that some manuals were found including some that described how to make various chemical weapons. The *Times* reported that some conventional weapons were found in the camp but no chemical or biological weapons. The *Times* also reported that the documents and statements by now-imprisoned Ansar guerrillas produced no evidence of connections to Baghdad. According to the *Times*, "the group was a dedicated but fledgling Al-Qaeda surrogate lacking the capability to muster a serious threat beyond its mountain borders."[32]

Iraq and the Anthrax Letters

<u>Assertion:</u>

On October 15, 2001 Senator Tom Daschle announced that his office had received a letter laced with "weapons grade" anthrax. On October 18, the *Wall Street Journal* featured three articles blaming Iraq: a front-page article accused Iraq of being "at the top of [the] suspect list"; the lead editorial said that "by far the likeliest supplier [of the anthrax in the letter to Daschle] is Saddam Hussein"; and an opinion piece by CIA chief James Woolsey, titled "The Iraq Connection," which claimed, "There are substantial and growing indications that a state may, behind the scene, be involved in the attacks."[33]

Washington Post columnist Richard Cohen screamed, "Saddam and his bloody bugs have to go."[34]

Two days later, two top senators, McCain and Lieberman, advocated attacking Iraq.

<u>The Facts:</u>

- The anthrax mailed to Senator Daschle was most likely "Made in the USA." When the anthrax spores in the Daschle letter and other samples were analyzed, they turned out to be the "Ames" strain—the strain of anthrax bacteria developed in the U.S., which the U.S. military tried to "weaponize" in the 1960s. It is not the vollum strain that Iraq had been working with (after buying it from American Type Culture Collection, a Maryland company which sells biological material such as anthrax worldwide).

- Researchers also discovered silica in the anthrax in the Daschle letter. Silica is the agent that U.S. weapons makers mixed with anthrax so that it could more easily disperse through the air. Iraq reportedly used bentonite, which was not found.[35]

- A U.S. government official admitted that the "evidence at hand—involving not just the coatings, but also genetic analysis of the bacteria and other intelligence—suggested that it was unlikely that the spores were originally produced in the former Soviet Union or Iraq."[36]

WEAPONS OF MASS DESTRUCTION

Nuclear Weapons

Iraq Six Months Away from Developing a Nuclear Weapon

Assertion:

> I would remind you that when the inspectors first went into Iraq and were denied, finally denied access, a report came out of the IAEA [International Atomic Energy Agency] that they were six months away from developing a weapon. I don't know what more evidence we need."[37]
>
> —George W. Bush, September 7, 2002

The Facts:

- The IAEA denied ever issuing such a report.[38] The IAEA did issue a report in 1998, around the time weapons inspectors were denied access to Iraq for the final time, but the report made no such assertion. It declared: "...based on all credible information to date...the IAEA has found no indication of Iraq having achieved its program goal of producing nuclear weapons or of Iraq having retained a physical capability for the production of weapon-useable nuclear material or having clandestinely obtained such material."[39]
- In his first major report to Congress on the status of the U.S. effort to find weapons of mass destruction, in October 2003, David Kay, the Bush administration's chief inspector for the Iraq Survey Group (ISG), had to concede "that Iraq's nuclear program was in only 'the very most rudimentary state.'"[40] The report (Kay Report) also stated "...to date we have not uncovered evidence that Iraq undertook significant post-1998 steps to actually build nuclear weapons or produce fissile material."[41]

Satellite Evidence that Iraq Is Rebuilding Nuclear Facilities

Assertion:

> The evidence indicates that Iraq is reconstituting its

nuclear weapons program.... Satellite photographs reveal that
Iraq is rebuilding facilities at sites that have been part of his
nuclear program in the past.[42]

—George W. Bush, October 7, 2002

The Facts:

- Analysts believe that the facility Bush is referring to is Iraq's former nuclear complex at Tuwaitha. However, the IAEA, which repeatedly inspected the site—presumably with a greater degree of accuracy than a satellite photo—said that Tuwaitha "now conducts civilian research in the non-nuclear field."[43]
- In February 2003, prior to the invasion, "UN sources have told CBS News that American tips have lead to one dead end after another. Example: satellite photographs purporting to show new research buildings at Iraqi nuclear sites. When the UN went in to the new buildings they found 'nothing.'" "So frustrated have the inspectors become that one source has referred to the U.S. intelligence they've been getting as 'garbage after garbage after garbage.' In fact, [reporter Mark] Phillips says the source used another cruder word."[44]

The "High-Ranking" Nuclear Engineer

Assertion:

In 1998,

> information from a high-ranking Iraqi nuclear engineer
> who had defected revealed that despite his public promises,
> Saddam Hussein had ordered his nuclear program to continue.[45]

—George W. Bush, October 7, 2002

The Facts:

- Bush's statement about the Iraqi nuclear defector, implying such information was current in 1998, was a reference to Khidhir Hamza. But Hamza, though he spoke publicly about his information in 1998, retired from Iraq's nuclear program in 1991, fled to the Iraqi north in 1994 and left the country in 1995. Hamza had no knowledge of Iraq's nuclear program after 1995, at the latest.[46]

Aluminum Tubes to Be Used to Enrich Uranium For a Nuclear Weapon

Assertion:

Powell at the UN: "Saddam Hussein is determined to get his hands on a nuclear bomb. He is so determined that he has made repeated covert attempts to acquire high-specification aluminum tubes from 11 different countries, even after inspections resumed... These tubes are manufactured to a tolerance that far exceeds U.S. requirements for comparable rockets."[47]

The Facts:

- While the matter is still under investigation and further verification is foreseen, the I.A.E.A.'s analysis to date indicates that the specifications of the aluminum tubes sought by Iraq in 2001 and 2002 appear to be consistent with reverse engineering of rockets. While it would be possible to modify such tubes for the manufacture of centrifuges, they are not directly suitable for it.[48]
  —Dr. Mohammed El Baradei in IAEA report, quoted in the New York Times, January 10, 2003

- A source close to the inspectors said the US military uses similar tubes for a rocket known as the Hydra 70.[49]
  —Dan Stober, San Jose Mercury News, March 18, 2003

- In February 2003, prior to the invasion, "UN sources have told CBS News that American tips have lead to one dead end after another. Example: Interviews with scientists about the aluminum tubes the U.S. says Iraq has imported for enriching uranium, but which the Iraqis say are for making rockets. Given the size and specifications of the tubes, the U.N. calls the 'Iraqi alibi air tight.'"[50]

Iraqi Uranium Purchase from Niger

Assertion:

As a result of the intelligence we judge that Iraq has...sought significant quantities of uranium from Africa, despite having no active civil nuclear programme that could require it...[51]

—September 2002 "Blair Dossier"

The British government has learned that Saddam Hussein recently sought significant quantities of uranium from Africa.... Saddam Hussein has not credibly explained these activities. He clearly has much to hide.[52]

—George W. Bush, State of the Union Address,
January 28, 2003

The Facts:

- UN Weapons Inspector Hans Blix on the supposed purchase of uranium from Niger:

    Consider the case of the production of contracts for a presumed Iraqi purchase of enriched uranium from Niger. This was a crude lie. All false. The information was provided to the international Atomic Energy Agency by the U.S. intelligence services.... When one sees the things that the United States tried to do to show that the Iraqis had nuclear arms, one does have many questions.[53]

- Mohamed El Baradei, head of the International Atomic Energy Agency: El Baradei charged that:

    documents provided by unidentified states may have been faked to suggest that the African country of Niger sold uranium to Iraq between 1999 and 2001. He said inspectors concluded that the documents were "not authentic" after scrutinizing "the form, format, contents, and signatures...of the alleged procurement-related documentation."[54]

- The CIA had expressed doubts about this claim to the White House months earlier than the State of the Union Address. "The CIA sent two memos to the White House in October [2002] voicing strong doubts about a claim President Bush made three months later in the State of the Union address that Iraq was trying to buy nuclear material in Africa, White House officials said yesterday." "The acknowledgment of the memos, which were sent on the eve of a major presidential speech in Cincinnati about Iraq, comes four days after the White House said the CIA objected only to technical specifics of the Africa charge, not its general accuracy."[55]

- Former diplomat Joseph Wilson had reported to the CIA nearly a year earlier, in February 2002, that the alleged Iraqi purchase was highly unlikely. After spending eight days in Niger investigating this claim at the request of the CIA, retired diplomat Joseph Wilson "made an oral report" back to the Agency that the "Iraqi uranium purchase was 'highly unlikely.'"[56] The report was quietly forgotten until reported in the *Washington Post* on June 12, 2003, setting off a firestorm of controversy about the validity of the claim.

- Wilson then became the object of a White House smear campaign. "Wilson says his family is the subject of a smear campaign" telling "NBC News the White House deliberately leaked his wife's identity as a covert CIA operative, damaging her career and compromising past missions..."[57]

- Others had also warned the Administration that the claim didn't check out. "...Ambassador to Niger Barbro Owens-Fitzpatrick reported it was false in February 2002. So did four-star Marine Gen. Carlton Fulford two months later."[58]

- The U.S. then warned Niger to stay out of the controversy. "America has warned the Niger government to keep out of the row over claims that Saddam Hussein sought to buy uranium for his nuclear weapons programme from the impoverished West African state." Mr. Hama Hamadou told the British newspaper The Telegraph that "...the Niger government had never had discussions with Iraq about uranium and called on Tony Blair to produce the 'evidence' he claims to have to confirm that Iraq sought uranium from Niger in the 1990s."[59]

- Officials repeated the same allegation both before and after the State of the Union speech. The allegation of the uranium purchase was made not just in the Bush State of the Union speech, but several times. "...[In] the days before and after the State of the Union address, the allegation was repeated by national security advisor Condoleezza Rice, Secretary of State Colin L. Powell, Defense Secretary Donald H. Rumsfeld, Deputy Secretary of Defense Paul D. Wolfowitz, and in at least two documents sent out by the White House."[60]

Cheney On the Peril of a Nuclear Iraq

Assertion:
The *New York Times*:

Vice President Dick Cheney today presented the administration's most forceful and comprehensive rationale yet for attacking Iraq, warning that Saddam Hussein would "fairly soon" have nuclear weapons. "…What he wants is time, and more time to husband his resources to invest in his ongoing chemical and biological weapons program, and to gain possession of nuclear weapons," Mr. Cheney said. "The risks of inaction, he said, "are far greater than the risk of action."[61]

The Facts:

- IAEA Director General Dr. Mohamed El Baradei on Iraq's Nuclear Program:

There is no indication of resumed nuclear activities in those buildings that were identified through the use of satellite imagery as being reconstructed or newly erected since 1998, nor any indication of nuclear-related prohibited activities at any inspected sites.

There is no indication that Iraq has attempted to import uranium since 1990.

There is no indication that Iraq has attempted to import aluminum tubes for use in centrifuge enrichment. Moreover, even had Iraq pursued such a plan, it would have encountered practical difficulties in manufacturing centrifuges out of the aluminum tubes in question.

Although we are still reviewing issues related to magnets and magnet production, there is no indication to date that Iraq imported magnets for use in a centrifuge enrichment programme.

After three months of intrusive inspections, we have to date found no evidence or plausible indication of the revival of a nuclear weapons programme in Iraq. We intend to continue our inspection activities, making use of all the additional rights granted to us by resolution 1441 and all additional tools that might be available to us, including reconnaissance platforms and all relevant technologies. We also hope to continue to receive from States actionable information relevant to our mandate. I should note that, in the past three weeks, possibly as a result of ever-increasing pressure by the international community, Iraq has been forthcoming in its co-operation, particularly with regard to the conduct of private interviews and in making available evidence that could contribute to the resolution of matters of IAEA concern. I do hope that Iraq will continue to expand the scope and accelerate the pace of its cooperation.[62]

Chemical and Biological Weapons
Iraq's Chemical and Biological Weapons Program and Inventory

Assertion:

George Bush, January 28, 2003: "Our intelligence officials estimate that Saddam Hussein had the materials to produce as much as 500 tons of sarin, mustard, and VX nerve agent...upward of 30,000 munitions capable of delivering chemical agents...materials sufficient to produce more than 38,000 liters of botulinum toxin."[63]

At the Geneva biological weapons conference the U.S. claimed, "Iraq has taken advantage of three years of no UN inspections to improve all phases of its offensive biological weapons program... The existence of Iraq's program is beyond dispute."[64]

The Facts:

- The charges related to Iraq's WMD inventory were largely based on Iraq's inability to definitively "verify" the destruction of certain stocks to UN inspectors in the 1990s. As Scott Ritter has discussed in his book with William Rivers Pitt, *War on Iraq*, simply because UNSCOM did not verify that all the chemical weapons (CW) inventory had been destroyed did not mean Iraq still maintained that inventory. In addition, CW agents have a "shelf life" after which they are no longer useful. Ritter explained that, by 2003, virtually all of the CW agents that may have existed even as late as 1998 had likely degraded and were no longer useful.[65]
- Secretary of State Colin Powell in February 2001 "told reporters during a trip to Egypt" that Saddam Hussein "'has not developed any significant capability with respect to weapons of mass destruction. He is unable to project conventional power against his neighbors.'"[66]
- The Pentagon's own intelligence group said it had no reliable information on Iraqi chemical weapons. It wasn't until June 2003, after the U.S. invasion, that the existence of a second intelligence report was revealed, a report that contradicted the earlier, highly publicized CIA Report on chemical weapons. In November 2002, the Pentagon's Defense Intelligence Agency (DIA) "issued a report stating that there was 'no reliable infor-

mation' showing that Iraq was actually producing or stockpiling chemical weapons…" In fact, the DIA's assessment in November "mirrors a September [2002] analysis that the agency made on the same subject." The DIA report is titled "Iraq's Nuclear, Biological, and Chemical Weapon and Missile Program: Progress, Prospects, and Potential Vulnerabilities". Specifically, the DIA report says, "No reliable information indicates whether Iraq is producing or stockpiling chemical weapons or where the country has or will establish its chemical agent production facility."[67]

- After the 2003 war had begun, no weapons were found at the top sites identified by U.S. intelligence. After searching more than 80 of the top 100 sites that U.S. intelligence had labeled as possible Iraqi hiding places for chemical and biological weapons, no stockpiles have been found and the search teams said they were setting aside their "intelligence" reports for the time being.[68]

- After the 2003 U.S. invasion, reports of discoveries of chemical or biological weapons in each case turned out to be false. For example:

  - On April 7, 2003, at an Iraqi military camp near Karbala, U.S. troops discovered two dozen drums that allegedly tested positive for sarin and mustard gas.[69] Later, the U.S. military determined the chemicals were ordinary pesticides.

  - MSNBC/NBC News, reported on May 11, 2003 that military teams searching for biological and chemical weapons in Iraq found three trailers believed to be mobile biological weapons laboratories capable of producing deadly germs for weapons."[70] Later, the Defense Intelligence Agency determined that hydrogen for weather balloons was made in the trailers, not biological weapons. "Engineering experts from the Defense Intelligence Agency have come to believe that the most likely use for two mysterious trailers found in Iraq was to produce hydrogen for weather balloons rather than to make biological weapons, government officials say. The classified findings by a majority of the engineering experts differ from the view put forward in a white paper made public on May 28, 2003 by the CIA and Defense Intelligence

Agency, which said that the trailers were for making biological weapons."[71]

- On April 27, 2003, AP reported out of Baiji, Iraq: "U.S. troops found about a dozen 55-gallon drums in an open field near this northern Iraqi town, and initial tests indicated one of them contained a mixture of a nerve agent and mustard gas, an American officer said Sunday." "A chemical team checked the drums, one of which tested positive for cyclosarin, a nerve agent, and a blister agent which could have been mustard gas," a U.S. military officer said.[72] However, the material in the drums turned out to be rocket fuel.[73]

- As of October 2003, no chemical or biological weapons had been found in Iraq. In October 2003, the Kay Report admitted that the ISG had "not yet found stocks of weapons." The Kay Report also acknowledged that "information found to date suggests that Iraq's large-scale capability to develop, produce and fill new CW munitions was reduced—if not entirely destroyed—during Operations Desert Storm and Desert Fox, 13 years of UN sanctions and UN inspections.[74]

Amiriyah Serum and Vaccine Institution

Assertion:

A CIA Report, "Iraq's Weapons of Mass Destruction Programs," released in October 2002, and which received extensive media coverage, states as evidence of Iraq's biological weapons capabilities that "Iraq has the capabilities to convert quickly legitimate vaccine and biopesticide plants to biological warfare production and may have already done so....The Amiriyah Serum and Vaccine Institution is an ideal cover location for biological weapons research, testing, production and storage."[75]

The Facts:

- The U.S. routinely placed "holds" on Iraqi purchases of vaccines under the sanctions program, saying that Iraq could develop biological weapons with the live cultures in the vaccines. In an exposure of the sanctions program, Joy Gordon noted in *Harpers* that, "UNICEF and UN health agencies...objected strenuously. European biological weapons experts maintained that such a feat was in fact flatly impossible. At the same time, with massive epidemics ravaging the country, and skyrocketing child mortality, it was quite certain that preventing child vaccines from entering Iraq would result in large numbers of child and infant deaths."[76]

- Another plant that the CIA report cites as a factory that could produce chemical weapons is the Fallujah II facility. This is a "dual use" facility that could produce these chemicals for civilian or military use. What the CIA report doesn't say is that the plant produces chlorine that is desperately needed in Iraq for water treatment facilities that were decimated by the U.S. in the Persian Gulf War.

al-Dawrah Foot and Mouth Disease Vaccine Facility

Assertion:

The October 2002 CIA Report also asserted that in 2001 Iraq announced it was going to begin renovating the al-Dawrah Foot and Mouth Disease Vaccine Facility. The Report's "Key Judgments," i.e., the sound bites that hit the news, were that Iraq had largely rebuilt and was expanding its biological weapons facilities "under the cover of civilian production."[77]

The Facts:
- In fact, the CIA Report admitted that UNSCOM could not prove the facility was connected to biological weapons work.
- As part of the renewed UN inspections that restarted in November 2002, the al-Dawrah facility was inspected by UN inspectors who had "raced up to the gates" of the facility. After looking around for four hours, the inspectors "concluded that the plant was no longer operational—not for the production of toxins, and not for animal vaccines either. Reporters who were allowed to wander around the plant after the inspectors left found the place largely in ruins," according to a report in the *San Francisco Chronicle*.[78]

Satellite Evidence of Weapons at the Taji Facility

Assertion:

Let's look at one. This one is about a weapons munition facility, a facility that holds ammunition at a place called Taji. This is one of about 65 such facilities in Iraq. We know that this one has housed chemical munitions. In fact, this is where the Iraqis recently came up with the additional four chemical weapon shells. Here, you see 15 munitions bunkers in yellow and red outlines. The four that are in red squares represent active chemical munitions bunkers. How do I know that? How can I say that? Let me give you a closer look. Look at the image on the left. On the left is a close-up of one of the four chemical bunkers. The two arrows indicate the presence of sure signs that the bunkers are storing chemical munitions. The arrow at the top that says security points to a facility that is the signature item for this kind of bunker. Inside that facility are special guards and special equipment to monitor any leakage that might come out of the bunker. The truck you also see is a signature item. It's a decontamination vehicle in case something goes wrong. This is characteristic of those four bunkers. The special security facility and the decontamination vehicle will be in the area, if not at any one of them or one of the other, it is moving around those four, and it moves as it needed to move, as people are working in the different bunkers. Now look at the picture on the right. You are now looking at two of those sanitized bunkers. The signature vehicles are gone, the tents are gone, it's been cleaned up, and it was done on the 22nd of December, as the U.N. inspection team is arriving, and you can see the inspection vehicles arriving in the lower portion of the picture on the right."[79]

—Colin Powell at the UN, February 5, 2003

The Facts:

*   *The New York Times* reported:

Both sides agree that American satellites photographed what American analysts said were Iraqi clean-up crews operating at a suspected chemical weapons site they had identified within 48 hours after the information about the site was shared with Unmovic. But the diplomats say inspectors concluded that the site was an old ammunition storage area often frequented by Iraqi trucks, and that there was no reason to believe it was involved in weapons activities. "It was a wild goose chase," one diplomat said.[80]

- Hans Blix, Briefing at the Security Council, February 14, 2003:

> The presentation of intelligence information by the U.S. Secretary of State suggested that Iraq had prepared for inspections by cleaning up sites and removing evidence of proscribed weapons programmes. I would like to comment only on one case, which we are familiar with, namely, the trucks identified by analysts as being for chemical decontamination at a munitions depot. This was a declared site, and it was certainly one of the sites Iraq would have expected us to inspect. We have noted that the two satellite images of the site were taken several weeks apart. The reported movement of munitions at the site could just as easily have been a routine activity as a movement of proscribed munitions in anticipation of imminent inspection. Our reservation on this point does not detract from our appreciation of the briefing.[81]

Mobile Biological Weapons Laboratories

Assertion:

> Let me take you inside that intelligence file and share with you what we know from eye witness accounts. We have firsthand descriptions of biological weapons factories on wheels and on rails.
>
> The trucks and train cars are easily moved and are designed to evade detection by inspectors. In a matter of months, they can produce a quantity of biological poison equal to the entire amount that Iraq claimed to have produced in the years prior to the Gulf War.[82]
>
> —Colin Powell at UN, February 5, 2003

The Facts:

- Powell attributed his information on the mobile laboratories to Iraqi defectors. What Powell didn't report is that the claims of these defectors, including one of a secret biological laboratory beneath the Saddam Hussein Hospital in central Baghdad, had repeatedly been disproved by UN inspectors.[83]

> Mr. Blix took issue with what he said were Secretary of State Colin L. Powell's claims that the inspectors had found that Iraqi officials were hiding and moving illicit materials within and outside of Iraq to prevent their discovery. He said that the inspectors had reported no such incidents.[84]
>
> —The New York Times, January 31, 2003

- Raymond Zilinskas, a microbiologist and former UN weapons inspector, told the *Washington Post* that the 24-hour production cycle Powell reported was insufficient for creating significant amounts of pathogens such as anthrax:

  > "You normally would require 36 to 48 hours just to do the fermentation," said Zilinskas, director of the Chemical and Biological Weapons Nonproliferation Program at the Monterey Institute of International Studies. "The short processing time seems suspicious to me."
  >
  > Zilinskas and other experts said the drawing presented by Powell as an example of Iraq's mobile labs did not deal with big problems such as how to dispose of large quantities of highly toxic waste. "This strikes me as a bit far-fetched," Zilinskas told the *Post*.[85]

- The Kay Report of October 2003 stated "We have not yet been able to corroborate the existence of a mobile BW [biological weapons] production effort.[86]

Scud Missiles

Assertion:

> While inspectors destroyed most of the prohibited ballistic missiles, numerous intelligence reports over the past decade, from sources inside Iraq, indicate that Saddam Hussein retains a covert force of up to a few dozen Scud variant ballistic missiles. These are missiles with a range of 650 to 900 kilometers.[87]
> —Colin Powell at UN, February 5, 2003

The Facts:

- No scud missiles were used during the war and none were found since.[88]
- On day one of the war, March 20, 2003 military spokesmen for the U.S. and UK announce that "Scud-type" missiles have been fired into Kuwait. This was significant because Iraq was banned from having Scuds or other missiles of a similar range under UN resolutions. Three days later U.S. General Stanley McChrystal reports: "So far there have been no Scuds launched."[89]
- The Kay Report of October 2003 stated "...one high-level detainee has recently claimed that Iraq retained a small quan-

tity of Scud-variant missiles until at least 2001, although he subsequently recanted these claims..."[90]

Sources of Information for Weapons of Mass Destruction

Powell's Claims of Solid Evidence

Assertion:

> My colleagues, every statement I make today is backed up by sources, solid sources. These are not assertions. What we're giving you are facts and conclusions based on solid intelligence. I will cite some examples, and these are from human sources.[91]
> —Colin Powell at UN, February 5, 2003

The Facts:

- Analysts believe that much of U.S. information on WMDs has come from Ahmed Chalabi's Iraqi National Congress (INC) which received Pentagon money for intelligence gathering. "The INC saw the demand and provided what was needed," an analyst told the *Independent* newspaper in the UK. "The implication is that they polluted the whole U.S. intelligence effort."[92]
- Another human source that Powell cites are detainees being held in Guantanamo, who are being held in horrific conditions, denied access to attorneys or the media, and who are threatened with torture (if not actually being tortured).

Iraq's Failure to Allow UN Unrestricted Access to Scientists

Assertion:

> You know the basic facts. Iraq has not complied with its obligation to allow immediate, unimpeded, unrestricted and private access to all officials and other persons as required by Resolution 1441.
>
> The regime only allows interviews with inspectors in the presence of an Iraqi official, a minder. The official Iraqi organization charged with facilitating inspections announced, announced publicly and announced ominously that, quote, "Nobody is ready to leave Iraq to be interviewed.
>
> Iraqi Vice President Ramadan accused the inspectors of conducting espionage, a veiled threat that anyone cooperating with UN inspectors was committing treason.[93]
> —Colin Powell at UN, February 5, 2003

The Facts:

- Once Saddam Hussein was removed, according to U.S. logic, the scientists and others would feel free to reveal the secrets about Iraq's suspected hidden arsenal. But few have come forward. And U.S. officials say that those in custody are sticking to their stories—that Iraq hadn't had a chemical, biological or nuclear weapons program in years.[94]
- In fact the scientists' denials come despite the pressure that the U.S is putting on them. Rumsfeld announced that the US will pay a reward to anyone providing evidence of Iraqi weapons of mass destruction and he has threatened Iraqi scientists that if they don't cooperate they would be taken to a detention facility for interrogation and ultimately could be charged with war crimes.[95]

British Intelligence Documents

Assertion:

> I would call my colleagues attention to the fine paper that United Kingdom distributed yesterday, which describes in exquisite detail Iraqi deception activities.[96]
> —Colin Powell at UN, February 5, 2003

The Facts:

- It turns out that the British report plagiarized from two earlier sources. Britain's intelligence document entitled "Iraq: It's Infrastructure of Concealment Deception and Intimidation" plagiarized from articles from the military magazine *Jane's Intelligence Review* and from a school thesis by a post graduate student in California. The author of the articles from *Jane's* said, "I don't like to think that anything I wrote has been used as an argument for war. I am concerned because I am against the war." The student, Ibrahim al-Marashi said, "this is wholesale deception. How can the British public trust the government if it is up to these sort of tricks? People will treat any other information they publish with a lot of skepticism from now on." Both of the authors said that their figures had been altered in the British document.[97]

- The BBC reported that the British government exaggerated claims of Iraqi weapons, which then hounded the BBC to reveal its source. In late May/early June 2003, the BBC quoted an unnamed government official alleging the British government wanted the "Blair Dossier" "'sexed up' with a reference to Saddam Hussein's ability to launch a biological or chemical attack within 45 minutes." The British government subsequently hounded the BBC about its source for the statement and demanded that the BBC confirm or deny that Dr. David Kelly was the source. Ten days later, Kelly was found dead, an apparent suicide.[98]

Powell's Audio Tapes

Assertion:

During his February 5, 2003 speech before the UN, Powell played what he said were intercepted conversations between Iraqi officers who were discussing ways to conceal prohibited materials from UN inspectors.

The Facts:

- None of the three recordings, if real, amounted to a "smoking gun." If they were real, they could be incriminating in a certain context, but they could also have been taken out of a context in which they were entirely innocent.
- Or they could have been faked. New York's *Village Voice* newspaper reported late last year how, during the 1990s, a Harvard graduate student celebrated for his convincing impersonation of Saddam Hussein was hired by the high-powered, US government-linked public relations firm, the Rendon Group, to make fake propaganda broadcasts of Saddam's voice to Iraq.[99]

Iraq's Disclosure Statement

Assertion:

My colleagues, operative paragraph four of U.N. Resolution 1441, which we lingered over so long last fall, clearly states that false statements and omissions in the declaration and a failure by Iraq at any time to comply with and cooperate fully in the implementation of this resolution shall constitute—the facts speak for themselves—shall constitute a further material breach of its obligation.

We wrote it this way to give Iraq an early test—to give Iraq an early test. Would they give an honest declaration and would they early on indicate a willingness to cooperate with the inspectors? It was designed to be an early test. They failed that test. By this standard, the standard of this operative paragraph, I believe that Iraq is now in further material breach of its obligations. I believe this conclusion is irrefutable and undeniable.[100]

—Colin Powell at UN, February 5, 2003

The Facts:

* The United States edited out more than 8,000 crucial pages of Iraq's 11,800 page dossier on weapons before passing on a sanitized version to the 10 non-permanent members of the United Nations Security Council.
* A UN source in New York said: "The question being asked is valid. What did the U.S. take out? And if weapons inspectors are supposed to be checking against the dossier's content, how can any future claim be verified? In effect the US was saying trust us and there are many who will not."
* Current and former UN diplomats are said to be "livid" at what some have called the "theft" of the Iraqi documents by the U.S. Hans von Sponeck, the former assistant secretary general of the UN and the UN's humanitarian coordinator in Iraq until 2000 said: "This is an outrageous attempt by the US to mislead."[101]

Weapons Inspections

Assertion:

National Security Adviser Condoleezza Rice: "I don't understand how anyone can say the inspections are working."[102]

The Facts:

* IAEA Director General Dr. Mohamed ElBaradei:

In the past three months they have conducted over 200 inspections at more than 140 locations, entering without prior notice into Iraqi industrial facilities, munitions factories, military establishments, private residences, and presidential palaces, following up on inspection leads provided by other States, confiscating nuclear related Iraqi documents for further scrutiny, interviewing scientists and engineers known to have played a key role in Iraq's past nuclear weapons programme, lowering themselves by rope into abandoned underground reactor chambers, and—taking advantage of the "signature" of radioactive materials—conducting radiation surveys over thousands of kilometres of Iraqi roads and collecting samples of soil, air, water, and vegetation and particulate matter from key locations in Iraq for laboratory analysis.

In short, the nuclear inspectors in Iraq have been far from idle, and their efforts far from futile. The IAEA's inspectors have systematically examined the contents and operations of all Iraqi buildings and facilities that were identified, through satellite surveillance, as having been modified or newly constructed since December 1998, when inspections were brought to a halt. They have determined the whereabouts and functionality of Iraq's known "dual-use" equipment—that is, equipment that has legitimate industrial uses, such as precision machining, but that could also be used for the high-precision manufacture of components relevant to a nuclear weapons programme...

Nuclear weapons inspections in Iraq are making marked progress. To date, we have found no substantiated evidence of the revival in Iraq of a nuclear weapons programme—the most lethal of the weapons of mass destruction.... The IAEA should be able, in the near future, to provide the Security Council with credible assurance regarding the presence or absence of a nuclear weapons programme in Iraq.[103]

• Hans Blix, February 14, 2003:

The eight helicopters are fully operational. With the resolution of the problems raised by Iraq for the transportation of minders into the no-fly zones, our mobility in these zones has improved. We expect to increase utilization of the helicopters.

Since we arrived in Iraq, we have conducted more than 400 inspections covering more than 300 sites. All inspections were performed without notice, and access was almost always provided promptly. In no case have we seen convincing evidence that the Iraqi side knew in advance that the inspectors were coming.

The inspections have taken place throughout Iraq at industrial sites, ammunition depots, research centres, universities, presidential sites, mobile laboratories, private houses, missile production facilities, military camps and agricultural sites. At all sites which had been inspected before 1998, re-baselining activities were performed. This included the identification of the function and contents of each building, new or old, at a site. It also included verification of previously tagged equipment, application of seals and tags, taking samples and discussions with the site personnel regarding past and present activities. At certain sites, ground-penetrating radar was used to look for underground structures or buried equipment.

Through the inspections conducted so far, we have obtained a good knowledge of the industrial and scientific landscape of Iraq, as well as of its missile capability but, as before, we do not know every cave and corner. Inspections are effectively helping to bridge the gap in knowledge that arose due to the absence of inspections between December 1998 and November 2002.

More than 200 chemical and more than 100 biological samples have been collected at different sites. Three-quarters of these have been screened using our own analytical laboratory capabilities at the Baghdad Centre (BOMVIC). The results to date have been consistent with Iraq's declarations."

The total number of staff in Iraq now exceeds 250 from 60 countries. This includes about 100 UNMOVIC inspectors, 15 IAEA inspectors, 50 aircrew, and 65 support staff.[104]

IRAQ CHRONOLOGY

8000-7000 B.C.	First settled human communities emerge in the Fertile Crescent
3000 B.C.	Earliest form of writing developed in Mesopotamia
1792-1750 B.C.	Hammurabi, author of world's first legal code, rules in Baghdad
322 B.C.	Alexander the Great dies in Babylon
632 A.D.	Death of Mohammed, founder of Islam; Muslim conquest of Mesopotamia.
632-681	Battle over successor to Mohammed leads to the schism between Sunni and Shi'a branches of Islam
749-1258	Abbasid caliphs lead Islamic world from Baghdad
1634	Ottoman Empire rules Iraq

THE EUROPEAN CONQUEST

1901	Englishman William D'Arcy purchases 60-year, 500,000 square mile oil concession in Iran, establishes Anglo-Persian Oil
1914-1918	World War I: Britain invades Iraq, occupies Basra (November 1914), Baghdad (March 1917), and Mosul (November 1918); collapse of Ottoman Empire

1916	Sykes-Picot Agreement divides up Middle East between Russia, Britain, and France
1920	League of Nations San Remo Conference upholds Sykes-Picot, condemns Arab independence, gives Britain a mandate to rule Iraq, and grants the UK a vitural monopoly over Middle East oil
	Iraqi revolt against British occupation crushed by air and gas attacks
1921	Faisal chosen new king of Iraq at British-run Cairo Conference
1922	Percy Cox, Britain's High Commissioner for Iraq, delineates borders between Iraq, Saudi Arabia, and Kuwait
1922, 1924	Kurdish revolts in Iraq crushed by British
1925	Britain forces King Faisal to sign a 75-year concession granting foreign-owned Iraqi Petroleum Company all rights to Iraqi oil in return for small royalties
	League of Nations incorporates Mosul region into Iraq
1927	Oil struck near Kirkuk
1928	Red Line Agreement divides Middle East oil between American, British, Dutch, and French companies, and gives U.S. and French firms shares of Iraqi petroleum
1932	Iraq gains independence, but British armed forces and control remain

1937	Saddam Hussein born outside of Tikrit
1941	British invade and overthrow Rashid Ali al-Kailani government
1943-45	Iraqi Kurds revolt against monarchy
1944	Ba'ath Party formed in Syria

THE POST-WORLD WAR II PERIOD

1948	"The Leap"—mass anti-government demonstrations after Iraq's monarch extends British military presence
1949	Iraqi branch of Ba'ath Party established
1950	Middle East proven oil reserves equal rest of the world's combined
1952	Massive Iraqi street protests against Britain and the monarchy
1953	CIA organized coup overthrows Iran's Prime Minister Mossadeq and puts Shah Reza Pahlevi back on throne
1955	Baghdad Pact creates U.S./British military alliance with countries on Soviet border, including Iran, Iraq, Turkey, and Pakistan
1958	Iraqi monarchy overthrown in revolution led by Abd al-Karim Qasim; U.S. begins conspiring to undermine the new government
1960	Organization of Petroleum Exporting

Countries (OPEC) founded in Baghdad

1963   Coup by Ba'athist and Arab nationalist officers overthrows Qasim; CIA-supplied list
used in massacre of communists and other
leftists and nationalists

1966   Saddam Hussein appointed Deputy Secretary
General of Ba'ath Party

1967   Six-Day Arab-Israeli War

Iraq breaks relations with the U.S.

1968   After series of coups, Ba'ath party consoli-
dates power

1972   Iraq and Soviet Union sign Treaty of
Friendship and Cooperation

Iraqi Petroleum Company nationalized

Nixon, Kissinger and the Shah of Iran conspire to weaken Iraq through support for the
Kurdish insurgency

1973   Arab-Israeli "Yom Kippur" war

OPEC embargoes oil to the U.S., prices skyrocket

1975   Treaty of Algiers settles (temporarily) Iran-
Iraq border disputes; U.S. and Iran withdraw
support for Iraqi Kurdish insurgency

1977-78   Several hundred Iraqi Kurdish villages along
the frontiers with Turkey, Iran, and Syria are
systematically destroyed or depopulated

IRAN-IRAQ WAR

1979	**February** Iranian revolution topples the pro-U.S. Shah
	June Saddam Hussein becomes President of Iraq
	July Hussein purges Ba'th Party
	July U.S. initiates covert campaign to destabilize Afghanistan's pro-Soviet government
	November Iranian students seize American embassy in Iran, hold it and U.S. personnel for 444 days
	December Soviet Union invades Afghanistan
1980	**January** President Carter articulates "Carter Doctrine," declaring U.S. would go to war to defend its "interests" in the Persian Gulf
	September Iraq invades Iran, beginning 8-year Iran-Iraq War
1981	**January** President Reagan inaugurated; Iran releases U.S. hostages the same day
1982	Reagan issues secret National Security Directive (NSD) to aid Iraq and prevent its defeat by Iran
	Iraq removed from State Department's list of alleged sponsors of terrorism
1983 & 1984	Donald Rumsfeld travels to Baghdad, assures

Hussein of U.S. support

1984   Iraq begins using chemical weapons against Iran

     U.S. restores diplomatic relations with Iraq

1985   Reagan administration begins secretly shipping arms to Iran

1986   **November** "Iran-Contra" arms-for-hostages deal exposed

1988   **February** Iraq launches "Al-anfal" campaign against Iraqi Kurds

     March 5,000 Kurds die in Iraqi gas attack at Halabja

     July U.S. warship *Vincennes* shoots down unarmed Iranian civilian airliner; Iran accepts UN cease fire resolution ending Iran-Iraq War in August

1989   President Bush, Sr. signs NSD-26: relations with Hussein's Iraq serve U.S. interests and no support would be extended to Iraq's Kurds

1991 PERSIAN GULF WAR

1990   **July 25** Saddam Hussein meets with U.S. Ambassador April Glaspie

1990   **August 2** Iraq invades Kuwait

1990   **August 6** UN Security Council Resolution 661 imposes economic sanctions on Iraq

1990   **November 29** UN Resolution 678 authorizes
                       "all necessary means" to force Iraq from of
                       Kuwait

1991   **January 16** U.S.-led "Operation Desert
                       Storm" begins with massive air bombard-
                       ment of Iraq

                       February 24 U.S. launches ground war
                       against Iraqi forces

                       February 26 Iraq accepts any terms U.S.
                       dictates

                       February 27 Ground war ends

                       February 28 Iraq agrees to cease-fire terms
                       with the U.S.-led coalition

                       March Anti-regime uprisings in northern
                       and southern Iraq collapse by April after
                       U.S. allows Hussein's forces to counter-
                       attack; some 2 million Kurds flee to moun-
                       tains

POST-GULF WAR: SANCTIONS, WEAPONS INSPECTIONS & COUP ATTEMPTS

1991   **April 3** UN Resolution 687 imposes harsh
                       conditions on Iraq in return for a permanent
                       cease-fire, including continued economic
                       sanctions, reparations to Kuwait and perma-
                       nent disarmament

                       April U.S. and Britain unilaterally establish
                       no-fly zone in northern Iraq

August Collapse of the Soviet Union

1992   Pentagon Defense Policy Guidance calls for U.S. global hegemony

               August U.S. and Britain unilaterally establish no-fly zone in southern Iraq

1993   Bill Clinton inaugurated

1995   **March** Iraqi National Congress launches "uprising" against Hussein regime; it quickly collapses after Clinton administration withdraws CIA support

1996   UN "oil-for-food" program begins

               May Secretary of State Madeline Albright says on national television that the deaths of a half million Iraqi children is an acceptable price to pay to achieve U.S. goals in Iraq

               June CIA plots coup against Hussein regime via Iraqi National Accord, using intelligence obtained through UNSCOM inspections; Iraqi intelligence uncovers and dismantles the covert operation

1997   **March** Albright states that sanctions will not end until Hussein removed from power

1998   **January** Project for New American Century letter to President Clinton calling for "regime change" in Iraq

               October International Atomic Energy Agency certifies that Iraq had provided a "full, final, and complete" account of its nuclear weapons program

Congressional "Iraq Liberation Act" calls for overthrow of Saddam Hussein

December Operation Desert Fox bombing attacks aimed at assassinating Saddam Hussein; UNSCOM inspectors withdrawn in advance by U.S.

1999   UNICEF study finds that some 500,000 Iraqi children under 5-years old had been killed due to sanctions

2000   **September** Project for New American Century's "Rebuilding America's Defenses, Strategies, Forces, and Resources for a New Century"

IRAQ WAR OF 2003

2001   **January** George W. Bush inaugurated; half of his first national security meeting devoted to Iraq and the Persian Gulf

April Pentagon seeks to link Hussein regime and al Qaeda

"Strategic Energy Policy Challenges for the 21st Century" (Baker Report)

May National Energy Policy (Cheney report) issued

September 11 Hijacked airliners crash into

World Trade Center Towers and Pentagon, killing nearly 3,000

September 12 Bush administration discusses war on Iraq

Mid-September Bush approves "Worldwide Attack Matrix" mandating covert counterinsurgency operations in 80 countries

October Anthrax scare; government and media allege Iraqi involvement

October 7 U.S. initiates conquest and occupation of Afghanistan

November Bush leadership decides on regime change in Iraq

December Initial military planning for war on Iraq

2002   **January** Bush labels Iraq part of "axis of evil," along with Iran and North Korea

February New U.S. "Nuclear Posture Review" leaked to press

April Military planning for war on Iraq accelerates

July Rand briefing at Pentagon calls for reconfiguring the entire Middle East

September New National Security Strategy issued

President Bush, Jr. signs secret Presidential

Directive 17, reserves right to use nuclear weapons in response to use of weapons of mass destruction

British dossier alleges Iraq has weapons of mass destruction, and attempted to purchase "significant quantities" of uranium in Africa

September 12 Bush condemns Iraq before UN, calling it a "grave and gathering danger"

October In Cincinnati, Bush accuses Iraq of possessing weapons of mass destruction

CIA issues "Iraq's Weapons of Mass Destruction Programs" report, charging, among other things, that Iraq was expanding its biological weapons programs

October 10 U.S. Congress approves joint resolution authorizing use of force against Iraq

2002

November UN Resolution 1441 demands Iraq fully disclosure all weapons programs and that UN weapons inspectors return to Iraq

December U.S. "National Strategy to Combat Weapons of Mass Destruction" issued which threatens "first strikes," possibly with nuclear weapons, against countries thought to be developing advanced weapons

Iraq releases 12,000 page report detailing its destruction of WMD programs

2003

January Pentagon drafts "National Military Strategic Plan for the War on Terrorism" calling for 20-30 years of war

February Secretary of State Powell tells the UN that the U.S. has hard evidence that Iraq possesses banned weapons and links to "terrorist" organizations

March U.S. fails to secure new UN resolution authorizing war

March 20 U.S. launches war on Iraq, attacking in the air and invading on the ground

April 9 Baghdad taken by U.S. forces

May 1 Bush declares victory on aircraft carrier USS *Abraham Lincoln*, saying "major combat in Iraq have ended," but the "war on terror" continues

May U.S. dissolves Iraq's Ba'ath Party

UN Security Council Resolution 1483 grants the U.S.'s "Coalition Provisional Authority" a mandate to administer Iraq

NOTES

CHAPTER ONE
"GO MASSIVE. SWEEP IT ALL UP."

1   www.newamericancentury.org/RebuildingAmericasDefenses.pdf, 51

2   Dan Balz and Bob Woodward, "America's Chaotic Road to War—Bush's Global Strategy Began to Take Shape in First Frantic Hours After Attack," *Washington Post*, January 27, 2002, A01

3   Charles Feldman and Stan Wilson, "Ex-CIA direct: U.S. faces 'World War IV,'" CNN.com, April 4, 2003

4   "Transcript of President Bush's address," CNN.com, September 20, 2001 (www.cnn.com/2001/US/09/20/gen.bush.transcript)

5   "Full Text: Bush Speech Aboard the USS Abraham Lincoln," FDCH E-Media, May 1, 2003

6   Carl Von Clausewitz, On War (New York: Penguin Books, 1968) 106, 119

7   Patrick E. Tyler, "U.S. Strategy Plan Calls for Insuring No Rivals Develop," *New York Times*, March 8, 1992

8   Tyler, *New York Times*, March 8, 1992; Steven R. Weisman, "Pre-emption: Idea With a Lineage Whose Time Has Come," *New York Times*, March 23, 2003

9   Zalmay M. Khalilzad, From Containment to Global Leadership, (Santa Monica, CA: RAND, 1995); William Kristol and Robert Kagan, "Toward a Neo-Reaganite Foreign Policy," *Foreign Affairs*, July/August 1996; Institute for Advanced Strategic and Political Studies, "A Clean Break: A New Strategy for Securing the Realm," (no date); Paul Wolfowitz, "Clinton's Bay of Pigs," *Wall Street Journal*, September 27, 1996. See also, Robert Blecher, "Intellectuals, Democracy and American Empire," *Middle East Report*, March 2003; "Review & Outlook: Beyond the Bombing," *Wall Street Journal*, February 20, 2001

10   Other right-wing luminaries who contributed to the September 2000 study included Stephen Cambone (a member of Bush II's Defense Department), Eliot Cohen, Donald Kagan, Robert Kagan, William Kristol, Abram Shulsky, Michael Vickers, and Dov Zakheim.

11   See Weisman, *New York Times*, March 23, 2003; Todd S. Purdum, "The Brains Behind Bush's War," *New York Times*, February 1, 2003; David Carr, "White House Listens When Weekly Speaks," *New York Times*, March 11, 2003

12   R. W. Apple, Jr., "Bush's Peril: Shifting Sand and Fickle Opinion," *New York Times*, March 30, 2003

13   Eric Schmitt and James Dao, "Iraq is Focal Point as Bush Meets With Joint Chiefs," *New York Times*, January 11, 2001, A20

14   "Outside the Box," *Wall Street Journal*, December 5, 2000

15   Bob Woodward and Dan Balz, "At Camp David, Advise and Dissent—Bush, Aides Grapple With War Plan," *Washington Post*, January 31, 2002, A01

16   Nicholas Lemann, "The Iraq Factor," *New Yorker*, January 22, 2001

17   Raymond Bonner, "Experts Doubt Iraq Had Role in Latest Terror Attacks," *New York Times*, October 11, 2001; David S. Cloud, "Bush's Efforts to Link Hussein To al Qaeda Lack Clear Evidence," *Wall Street Journal*, October 23, 2002

18   Cloud, *Wall Street Journal*, October 23, 2002

19   "Review & Outlook: Smarting Over Iraq," *Wall Street Journal*, July 5, 2001

20   Neil King Jr., "Powell's Plan for New Sanctions On Iraq Runs Aground at U.N.," *Wall Street Journal*, July 3, 2001

21   Jane Perlez, "Allies Bomb Iraqi Air Defenses in Biggest Attack in 6 Months," *New York Times*, August 11, 2001

22   Woodward and Balz, *Washington Post*, January 31, 2002

23   Woodward and Balz, *Washington Post*, January 27, 2002

24   "Plans For Iraq Attack Began On 9/11," CBS TV, Evening News, September 4, 2002. It is beyond the scope of this book to evaluate what intelligence U.S. agencies may, or may not, have had concerning the attacks prior to Sept. 11.

25   Woodward and Balz, *Washington Post*, January 27, 2002

26   Woodward and Balz, *Washington Post*, January 27, 2002

27   Christopher Layne, "The Power Paradox," *Los Angeles Times*, October 6, 2002

28   Woodward and Balz, *Washington Post*, January 28, 2002

29   April 2002 speech at the Johns Hopkins School of Advanced International Studies cited in Frances FitzGerald, "George Bush & the World," *New York Review of Books*, September 26, 2002

30   Woodward and Balz, *Washington Post*, January 27, 2002; Bob Woodward and Dan Balz, "'We Will Rally the World'—Bush and His Advisers Set Objectives, but Struggled With How to Achieve Them," *Washington Post*, January 28, 2002, A1

31   Nicholas Lemann, "Next World Order," *New Yorker*, April 1, 2002

32   Woodward and Balz, *Washington Post*, January 28, 2002

33   After listing a series of belligerent demands he stated, "These demands are not open to negotiation or discussion. The Taliban must act and act immediately. They will hand over the terrorists or they will share in their fate." "Transcript of President Bush's address," CNN.com, September 20, 2001 (www.cnn.com/2001/US/09/20/-gen.bush.transcript)

34   Woodward and Balz, *Washington Post,* January 31, 2002

35   Woodward and Balz, *Washington Post*, January 28, 2002; Bonner, *New York Times*, October 11, 2001

36   Woodward and Balz, *Washington Post*, January 31, 2002

37   Woodward and Balz, *Washington Post*, January 31, 2002

38   John Diamond, Judy Keen, Dave Moniz, Susan Page and Barbara Slavin, "Iraq course set from tight White House circle," *USA Today*, September 11, 2002

39   Woodward and Balz, *Washington Post*, January 31, 2002

40   Elaine Sciolino and Patrick E. Tyler, "Some Pentagon Officials and Advisers Seek to Oust Iraq's Leader in War's Next Phase," *New York Times*, October 12, 2001, B6. The Defense Policy Board is a group of some 30 former officials and establishment analysts who advise the Pentagon on strategic matters. Under Rumsfeld it had become, as one reporter put it, "hawk central." Its Chairman, Richard Perle, was a Defense Department official under President Reagan. In 2001, the Board included Bush Sr.'s Vice President Dan Quayle, one-time House Speaker Newt Gingrich, ex-CIA head James Schlesinger, Henry Kissinger, former head of the Justice Department William Bennett, and Reagan's UN Ambassador Jeanne Kirkpatrick. A number of Board members became highly visible and vocal advocates for war on Iraq.

41   See Appendix, p. 310.

42   Other high level groups were formed to push for war on Iraq and more aggressive global action, including the "Committee for the Liberation of Iraq" (created in 2002) and "Americans for Victory Over Terrorism." For more on this PR campaign for war and empire, see: Sheldon Rampton and John Stauber, Weapons of Mass Deception: The Uses of Propaganda in Bush's War on Iraq (New York: Penguin, 2003); Tom Barry and Jim Lobe, "The People," in John Fedder, ed., Power Trip: U.S. Unilateralism and Global Strategy After September 11 (New York: Seven Stories Press, 2003), 39-49; and "Empire builders—Neoconservatives and their blueprint for US power," *Christian Science Monitor*, August 28, 2003

43   William Kristol, et al., "Open Letter to the President," September 20, 2001 (www.newamericancentury.org/Bushletter.htm)

44   Carla Anne Robbins and Jeanne Cummings, "How Bush Decided That Hussein Must Be Ousted From Atop Iraq," *Wall Street Journal*, June 14, 2002; David Frum, The Right Man: The Surprise Presidency of George W. Bush (New York: Random House, 2003), 195

45   Jeanne Cummings and Greg Hitt, "In Iraq Drama, Cheney Emerges As President's War Counselor," *Wall Street Journal*, March 17, 2003; Glenn Kessler and Peter Slevin, "Cheney Is Fulcrum of Foreign Policy," *Washington Post*, October 13, 2002, A1

46   Lawrence F. Kaplan, "Phase Two," *New Republic*, December 10, 2001

47   Diamond, et al., *USA Today*, September 11, 2002

48   Glenn Kessler, "U.S. Decision on Iraq Has Puzzling Past," *Washington Post*, January 12, 2003

49   Diamond, et al, *USA Today*, September 11, 2002

50   Bob Woodward, "President Broadens Anti-Hussein Order: CIA Gets More Tools to Oust Iraqi Leader," *Washington Post*, June 16, 2002, A1

51   Kessler, *Washington Post*, January 12, 2003; Michael Elliott and James Carney, "First Stop, Iraq," *Time*, March 23, 2003

52   "Watergate Plus 30: Shadow of History," PBS, July 30, 2003

53   "Text of President Bush's State of the Union address," Associated Press, January 30, 2002

54   James Risen, "Terror Acts by Baghdad Have Waned, U.S. Aides Say," *New York Times*, February 6, 2002

55   "Commissioner: Bush Deliberately Delayed Inquiry Report Until After Iraq War," *UPI*, July 26, 2003

56   Dana Milbank and Claudia Deane, "Hussein Link to 9/11 Lingers in Many Minds," *Washington*

Post, September 6, 2003, A1

57   "Rumsfeld Sees No Link Between Iraq, 9/11," Associated Press, September 16, 2003; Dana
       Milbank, "Bush Disavows Hussein-Sept. 11 Link," Washington Post, September 18, 2003, A18

58   "Bush's State of the Union speech," CNN.com, January 29, 2003

59   Bryan Bender, "Spy report saw no proof of Iraq arms," Boston Globe, June 7, 2003

60   Joseph C. Wilson, "What I Didn't Find in Africa," New York Times, July 6, 2003

61   "Text of Iraqi Letter On U.N. Resolution," Wall Street Journal, November 13, 2002

62   Douglas Jehl and Judith Miller, "Draft Report Said to Cite No Success in Iraq Arms Hunt,"
       New York Times, September 25, 2003

63   Jason Leopold, "Wolfowitz: Iraq Not Involved in 9-11, No Ties to Al Qaeda," Antiwar.com,
       August 7, 2003; Jason Leopold, "CIA Probe Finds Secret Pentagon Group Manipulated
       Intelligence on Iraqi Threat," Antiwar.com, July 25, 2003; Julian Borger, "The spies who
       pushed for war," Guardian (UK), July 17, 2003

64   Walter Pincus and Dana Priest, "Some Iraq Analysts Felt Pressure From Cheney Visits,"
       Washington Post, June 5, 2003, A1

65   Michael R. Gordon, "In Bush's Axis of Evil: Why Iraq Stands Out," New York Times, September
       9, 2002

66   Diamond, et al., USA Today, September 11, 2002

67   Diamond, et al., USA Today, September 11, 2002

68   Kaplan, New Republic, December 10, 2001

69   Kessler, Washington Post, January 12, 2003; Thom Shanker and David E. Sanger, "U.S.
       Envisions Blueprint on Iraq Including Big Invasion Next Year," New York Times, April 28, 2002;
       Eric Schmitt, "U.S. Plan for Iraq Is Said to Include Attack on 3 Sides," New York Times, July 5,
       2002

70   Robert Burns, Associated Press, "Bush Has Pentagon's Plans for Iraq," Washington Post,
       September 21, 2002

71   Bob Woodward, "A Struggle for the President's Heart and Mind: Powell Journeyed From
       Isolation to Winning the Argument on Iraq," Washington Post, November 17, 2002, A1

72   "Dance of Saddam's Seven Veils," Wall Street Journal, December 6, 2002

73   Paul Gilfeather, "War, Whatever: Bush Aide: Inspections or Not, We'll Attack Iraq," Daily
       Mirror (UK), November 22, 2002

74   "Hans Blix: War Planned 'Long in Advance,'" News24.com, April 9, 2003

75   Bob Avakian, "The New Situation and the Great Challenges," Revolutionary Worker, March 17,
       2002. See also, Fatima Resolucao, "Dangers and Opportunities: America's Global Rampage and
       the   People's   Resistance,"   A   World   To   Win,   No.   28,   2002
       (www.awtw.org/back_issues/28_Global_Rampage.htm)

76   The White House, "The National Security Strategy of the United States of America,"
       September 2002

77   Donald Rumsfeld, "Transforming the Military," Foreign Affairs, May/June 2002, 27, 29

78   James Webb, "Heading for Trouble: Do we really want to occupy Iraq for the next 30 years?"
       Washington Post, September 4, 2002, A21

79   Eric Schmitt, "Pentagon Draws Up a 20-to-30-Year Anti-Terror Plan," New York Times, January
       17, 2003

80   Associated Press, "Bush Signs $355 Billion Military Spending Bill," New York Times, October
       23, 2002; Tony Judt, "Its Own Worst Enemy," New York Review of Books, August 15, 2002;
       Fareed Zakaria, "The Arrogant Empire," Newsweek, March 24, 2003

81   It should be noted here that the war plan for Iraq settled on within the Bush administration,
       after much internal debate, was shaped by both the Pentagon's assessment of the forces needed
       to remove the Hussein regime, but also by the broader objectives of the new NSS and the need
       to be able to strike at or wage war against a number of targets at the same time or in quick suc-
       cession. These broader calculations may have played a role in reducing the size of the force ini-
       tially deployed to Iraq.

82   The review had been underway since September 2000, and was made public after it was leaked
       to the Los Angeles Times in February 2002. Paul Richter, "U.S. Works Up Plan for Using
       Nuclear Arms," Los Angeles Times, March 9, 2002

83   Jonathan Schell, "The Case Against the War," The Nation, March 3, 2003

84   "National Strategy to Combat Weapons of Mass Destruction," December 2002; David E.
       Sanger, "U.S. Issues Warning to Foes in Arms Plan," New York Times, December 11, 2002; Mike

Allen and Barton Gellman, "Preemptive Strikes Part Of U.S. Strategic Doctrine," *Washington Post*, December 11, 2002, A1

85   Rumsfeld, *Foreign Affairs*, May/June 2002, 31
86   Paul Richter, "U.S. Weighs Tactical Nuclear Strike on Iraq" *Los Angeles Times*, January 25, 2003
87   Zakaria, *Newsweek*, March 24, 2003
88   Henry A. Kissinger, "Iraq 'regime change' is a revolutionary strategy," *San Francisco Chronicle*, August 9, 2002
89   Robert Kagan, "Power and Weakness," *Policy Review*, No. 113 June/July 2002
90   Glenn Kessler and Walter Pincus, "Fear of U.S. Power Shapes Iraq Debate—As U.N. Considers War Resolution, a Distrust of American Policy Emerges," *Washington Post*, October 30, 2002, A1
91   Richard A. Oppel, Jr. with Julia Preston, "Administration seeking to build support in Congress on Iraq issue," *New York Times*, August 30, 2002; Keith B. Richburg, "French See Iraq Crisis Imperiling Rule of Law, Concern Focuses on Future of International Order," *Washington Post*, March 6, 2003, A19; Kessler and Pincus, *Washington Post*, October 30, 2002
92   National Security Strategy, 17, 19
93   Arundhati Roy, "Come September," speech at Lensic Performing Arts Center, September 29, 2002
94   For more on civil liberties post-Sept. 11, see "Bad Moon Rising—The War on Civil Liberties: An Emerging Police State in the U.S.?" *Revolutionary Worker* special issue, July 6, 2003 (www.rwor.org)
95   Jason Vest, "Beyond Osama: The Pentagon's Battle With Powell Heats Up, *Village Voice*, November 20, 2001
96   Max Boot, "Doctrine Of the 'Big Enchilada,'" *Washington Post*, October 14, 2002, A29: For a discussion of the growing body of establishment literature openly justifying empire, see "Behind the invasion of Iraq," *Aspects of India's Economy*, Nos. 33 and 34, December 2002 (www.rupe-india.org/34/pillar.html) and The Editors, "U.S. Imperial Ambitions and Iraq," *Monthly Review*, December 2002
97   "Saddam Hussein Has Made The Case Against Himself," prepared text of President Bush's speech, *Wall Street Journal*, September 12, 2002
98   Jay Bookman, "The president's real goal in Iraq," *Atlanta Journal-Constitution*, September 29, 2002
99   Kissinger, *San Francisco Chronicle*, August 9, 2002
100   Bush, *Wall Street Journal*, September 12, 2002
101   Paul Wolfowitz, "United on the Risks of a War With Iraq," *Washington Post*, December 23, 2002, A19
102   Michael Ignatieff, "Nation-Building Lite," *New York Times Magazine*, July 28, 2002, 28. See also, John Bellamy Foster, "The Rediscovery of Imperialism," *Monthly Review*, November 2002
103   State Department Policy Planning Study, February 23, 1948 cited in Noam Chomsky, *On Power and Ideology: The Managua Lectures* (Boston: South End Press, 1987), 15-16
104   "Remarks by the President to AFL-CIO Biennial Convention," Pittsburgh, Pa. September 24, 1997, cited in Joseph Gerson, "Continuity and Change In the Aftermath of September 11," American Friends Service Committee, July 26, 2002 (www.afsc.org/pes.htm)
105   Thomas Friedman, The Lexus and the Olive Tree: Understanding Globalization (New York: Farrar, Strauss, and Giroux, 1999), 464
106   Energy Information Administration (EIA), "Persian Gulf Oil and Gas Exports Fact Sheet," April 2003, http://www.eia.doe.gov/emeu/cabs/pgulf.html

CHAPTER TWO
IRAQIS—NOT PRESENT AT THE CREATION

1   Robert Fisk, "Library books, letters and priceless documents are set ablaze in final chapter of the sacking of Baghdad," *Independent* (UK), April 15, 2003; William Booth, "Most Iraqi Treasures Recovered," *Washington Post*, June 8, 2003, A22; Martin Gottlieb, "U.S. Archaeologists Paint a Mixed Picture of Looting Damage," *New York Times*, June 11, 2003
2   Jared Diamond, Guns, Germs, and Steel (New York: W.W. Norton, 1999), 125-27
3   Jared Diamond, "The Erosion of Civilization," *Los Angeles Times*, June 15, 2003

4   Ashton Hawkins and Maxwell L. Anderson, "Preserving Iraq's Past," *Washington Post*, November 29, 2002, A43

5   Geoff Simons, Iraq: From Sumer to Saddam, 2nd ed. (New York: St. Martin's Press, 1994), 122

6   The term Shi'a derives from Shi'at Ali or follower of Ali. (Shi'as refers to the group as a whole; individuals or groups of individuals are often called Shi'ites.)

7   John M. Blair, The Control of Oil (New York: Vintage Books, 1978), 29-31

8   Daniel Yergin, The Prize (New York: Simon & Schuster, 1992), 183

9   Simons, 189

10   Hugh Pope and Peter Waldman, "Past Mideast Invasions Faced Unexpected Perils," *Wall Street Journal*, March 19, 2003

11   Simons, 195

12   Dilip Hiro, Dictionary of the Middle East (New York: St. Martin's Press, 1996), 308

13   Phillip Knightly, "Imperial Legacy," in The Gulf War Reader, eds. Micah L. Sifry and Christopher Cerf (New York: Times Books, 1991), 11

14   Noam Chomsky, The Fateful Triangle: The United States, Israel & The Palestinians (Boston: South End Press, 1983), 90

15   Simons, 201

16   Knightly, 12

17   Simons, 213

18   David Blair, "Meddling in Mesopotamia was always risky," *Telegraph* (UK), March 18, 2003

19   Simons, 212, 214, Charles Trip, A History of Iraq (Cambridge, UK: Cambridge University Press, 2000), 44; Jonathan Glancey, "Our last occupation—Gas, chemicals, bombs: Britain has used them all before in Iraq," *Guardian* (UK), April 19, 2003

20   Trip, 47; Simons, 203

21   Simon Henderson, Instant Empire: Saddam Hussein's Ambitions for Iraq (San Francisco: Mercury House, 1991), 10

22   Simons, 202-203

23   Simons, 205; Knightly 13

24   William L. Cleveland, A History of the Modern Middle East, 2nd edition, (Boulder, CO: Westview Press, 2000), 203

25   Simons, 199, 203-204; Knightly 13; Hiro, Dictionary, 152-53

26   Marion Farouk-Sluglett and Peter Sluglett, Iraq Since 1958: From Revolution to Dictatorship (New York: I. B. Tauris, 1990), 30-31

27   Tripp, 77

28   E.M. Earle, Turkey, the Great Powers, and the Baghdad Railway: A Study in Imperialism (New York: Russell & Russell, 1966), 15, cited in Berch Berberoglu, Turmoil in the Middle East: Imperialism, War, and Political Instability (Albany, NY: State University of New York Press, 1999), 12

29   Cleveland, 204; Tripp, x. The foreign-owned Iraq Petroleum Company (IPC) had originally been formed in 1914 as the Turkish Petroleum Company as a means of ending the rivalry between British and Dutch groups.

30   Cleveland, 448-449; Frankel, 17

31   Bishara A. Bahbah, "The Crisis in the Gulf: Why Iraq Invaded Kuwait," in Beyond the Storm, a Gulf Crisis Reader, eds. Phyllis Bennis and Michel Moushabeck (Brooklyn, NY: Olive Branch Press, 1991), 50; Cleveland, 463-464

32   Glenn Frankel, "Lines in the Sand," The Gulf War Reader, 18

33   John Bulloch and Harvey Morris, No Friends but the Mountains: the Tragic History of the Kurds (New York: Oxford University Press, 1992), 73

34   Simons, 297

35   Gerard Chaliand, ed., People Without A Country: The Kurds and Kurdistan (London: Zed Press, 1980), 12

36   Peter Sluglett, "The Kurds," in Saddam's Iraq: Revolution or Reaction?, Committee Against Repression and for Democratic Rights in Iraq, 2nd ed., (London: Zed Books, 1989), 179

37   Chaliand, People Without A Country, 235; Sluglett, 179-80

38   Richard Boundreau, "Nameless Kurds of Turkey," *Los Angeles Times*, January 30, 2003

39   Vanly, 159

40   Middle East Watch, Human Rights in Iraq (New Haven, CT: Yale University Press, 1990), 71

41   Middle East Watch, 72

42   Middle East Watch, 72
43   Cleveland, 201
44   Simons, 217
45   Neela Banerjee, "Arabs Have a Litmus Test for U.S. Handling of Iraqi Oil," *New York Times*, April 6, 2003
46   Blair, 49
47   Simons, 186
48   Simons, 186
49   Blair, 32
50   Simons writes that at the time, there were reports that the U.S. helped fund the 1920 anti-British uprising in southern Iraq. (Simons, 186-187)
51   Blair, 32-33
52   Blair, 32
53   Simons, 187
54   Blair, 34
55   Blair, 34
56   Simons, 184
57   Blair, 31
58   Simons, 214
59   Michael T. Klare, "High-Death Weapons of the Gulf War," *The Nation*, June 3, 1991
60   Greg Jaffe, "New Battle Theory Would Be Tested In an Iraq Invasion," *Wall Street Journal*, November 27, 2002, A1; Rowan Scarborough, "U.S. ready to unleash weapons," *Washington Times*, December 26, 2002; Michael Evans, "Why any war with Iraq will be over in a flash," *Times of London*, December 24, 2002; Matt Kelley (Associated Press), "Rumsfeld: U.S. Used New Missile in Iraq," *Washington Post*, May 14, 2003; James W. Crawley, "Officials confirm dropping firebombs on Iraqi troops," *San Diego Union-Tribune*, August 5, 2003

CHAPTER THREE
SADDAM HUSSEIN'S AMERICAN TRAIN

1   Gabriel Kolko, The Roots of American Foreign Policy (Boston: Beacon Press, 1969), 52
2   Yergin, The Prize, 395
3   Howard Zinn, A People's History of the United States (New York: Harper & Row, 1980), 404
4   Yergin, The Prize, 396; Carl Solberg, Oil Power: The Rise and Imminent Fall of an American Empire (New York: New American Library, 1976), 200; Gabriel Kolko, Confronting the Third World: United States Foreign Policy 1945-1980 (New York: Pantheon Books, 1988), 69
5   Yergin, The Prize, 13
6   Solberg, 186
7   Solberg, 187
8   Noam Chomsky, "After the Cold War: U.S. Middle East Policy," in Beyond the Storm, 77
9   Yergin, 480, 491
10   Joe Stork and Ann M. Lesch, "Why War," *Middle East Report*, November-December 1990, cited in James Ridgeway, ed., The March to War (New York: Four Walls Eight Windows, 1991), 5
11   Joe, Stork, "Middle East Oil and the Energy Crisis: Part 1," *MERIP Reports #20*, 1973, 14-15
12   Blair, 49-50
13   Yergin, 13, emphasis in original.
14   Raymond Lotta with Frank Shannon, America in Decline: An Analysis of the Developments Toward War and Revolution, in the U.S. and Worldwide, in the 1980s (Chicago: Banner Press, 1984), 98; Henry Kissinger, Years of Upheaval (Boston: Little, Brown, 1982), 862
15   Yergin, 401
16   Harry Magdoff, The Age of Imperialism (New York: Monthly Review, 1969), 43
17   In November 1948 a new "Group Agreement" was drawn up between the Western oil powers to replace the previous Red Line Agreement. This new agreement gave the U.S. firms Exxon, Mobil, Socal, and Texaco exclusive access to Saudi oil, soon the world's largest producer. The U.S. also supported a 50-50 revenue split between ARAMCO (Arabian American Oil Company) and the Saudi government, with the aim of encouraging similar moves by the governments of Iraq and Iran, further undercutting Britain's position in the region. Yergin, The Prize, 413-416

18   Mostafa T. Zahrani, "The Coup That Changed the Middle East—Mossadeq v. The CIA in Retrospect," *World Policy Journal*, Summer 2002, 94

19   Solberg, 195-97; Blair, 78-80

20   Solberg, 197

21   Kissinger notes: "On November 29, 1956, the U.S. government, hailing the recent Baghdad Pact summit...declared: 'a threat to the territorial integrity or political independence of the members would be viewed by the United States with the utmost gravity.' It was the diplomats' way of saying that the United States would undertake the defense of the Baghdad pact states, a role for which Great Britain was now too weak and too discredited." Henry Kissinger, Diplomacy (New York: Simon & Schuster, 1994), 548-49

22   Shibley Telhami, "Shrinking Our Presence in Saudi Arabia," *New York Times*, January 29, 2000

23   Chomsky, "After the Cold War," 81

24   "U.S. Financial Aid To Israel: Figures, Facts, and Impact Summary," Washington Report on Middle East Affairs, January 15, 2003 (http://www.wrmea.com)

25   Cleveland, 317-18; Farouk-Sluglett and Sluglett, 31-34

26   Farouk-Sluglett and Sluglett, 34, 36; Richard Becker, "The U.S. and Iraq In Historical Perspective," International Action Center, 2003 (www.iacenter.org)

27   Tripp, 128, 138; www.odssa.com/Eagle/eagle10.htm

28   Blair, 83-84

29   Blair, 86

30   Farouk-Sluglett and Sluglett, 40

31   Tripp, 131

32   On May 2, 1958, Radio Cairo broadcast this call to Iraq: "Arise, my brethren on the police force and in its army in Iraq! Stand side by side with your brothers and your people against your enemies! The freedom of Iraq is in your hands." David Wise and Thomas B. Ross, The Invisible Government (New York: Vintage Books, 1974), 318. The Slugletts report that "Nasser's passionate speeches over Cairo Radio were reaching an eager and appreciative audience in Iraq." Farouk-Sluglett and Sluglett, 44

33   Farouk-Sluglett and Sluglett, 49

34   Michel Moushabeck, "Iraq: Years of Turbulence," in Beyond the Storm, 29

35   Farouk-Sluglett and Sluglett, 78. The U.S. State Department's legal office acknowledged that under Iraq's December 1961 Public Law No. 80, which took away drilling rights, "IPC's property as such has not been taken, and in fact IPC's operations have continued substantially unimpeded. What IPC has been deprived of is mineral rights granted in a number of concessions awarded by the government of Iraq." Blair, 85

36   Blair 81, 85; Frankel, 19

37   Saïd K. Aburish, Saddam Hussein: The Politics of Revenge (New York: Bloomsbury, 2000), 71

38   Micah L. Sifry, "U.S. Intervention in the Middle East: A Case Study," in The Gulf War Reader, 28

39   William Blum, Killing Hope: U.S. Military and CIA Interventions Since World War II (Monroe, ME: Common Courage, 1995), 89

40   Blum, Killing Hope, 90-94; Kolko, Confronting the Third World, 85

41   Blum, Killing Hope, 93. See also, Wise and Ross, 315-320 on clandestine CIA broadcasts directed against the Nasser government.

42   Sifry, 27, 30; Blum, Killing Hope, 97

43   Sifry, 30; Barry M. Blechman and Stephen S. Kaplan, Force Without War (Washington: Brookings Institution, 1978), 238, 256, cited in Daniel Ellsberg, "Introduction: Call to Mutiny," in Protest and Survive, eds. E.P. Thompson and Dan Smith (New York: Monthly Review Press, 1981), v-vi

44   Michael Tanzer, "Oil and the Gulf Crisis," in Beyond the Storm, 263; Sifry, 30-31, emphasis in original

45   Sifry, 28. According to Blum, the U.S. may also draw up a secret plan for a joint U.S.-Turkish invasion of Iraq shortly after the 1958 revolution. William Blum, Rogue State: A Guide to the World's Only Superpower (Monroe, ME: Common Courage, 2000), 134

46   Sifry, 30

47   *New York Times*, April 29, 1959, cited in Blum, Rogue State, 133

48   Roger Morris, "A Tyrant 40 Years in the Making," *New York Times*, March 14, 2003

49   Tanzer, 263

50   Sifry, 32
51   Morris, *New York Times*, March 14, 2003
52   Blair, 86-87
53   Blum, Rogue State, 134; Lee F. Dinsmore, "Regrets for a Minor American Role in a Major Kurdish Disaster," *Washington Report on Middle East Affairs*, May/June 1991, 9
54   Morris, *New York Times*, March 14, 2003
55   Farouk-Sluglett and Sluglett, 89; al-Khalil, 226
56   Tripp, 153-54; Blum, Rogue State, 133-34
57   U. Zaher, "Political Developments in Iraq 1963-1980," in Saddam's Iraq, 32; Moushabeck, 29
58   Cleveland, 395
59   Aburish, 54-55
60   Morris, *New York Times*, March 14, 2003
61   Aburish, 57
62   Zaher, 32. Zaher writes that "the French Service de Documentation Exterieure et de Contre-Espionnage also helped to overthrow Qasim and harass the Communists."
63   Farouk-Sluglett and Sluglett, 86
64   Aburish, 58
65   Zaher, 32
66   Farouk-Sluglett and Sluglett, 86
67   Tanzer, 263; Blum, Rogue State, 134; Aburish, 55-56
68   Morris, *New York Times*, March 14, 2003; Aburish, 59
69   Blum, Rogue State, 134; Frankel, 19
70   Aburish, 59; Morris, *New York Times*, March 14, 2003
71   Yousef, 58
72   Morris, *New York Times*, March 14, 2003; Simons, 276-77; Aburish, 64-66, 74
73   Aburish, 74
74   Aburish, 73-74
75   Farouk-Sluglett and Sluglett, 118
76   Cleveland, 396
77   Samir al-Khalil, Republic of Fear (New York: Pantheon, 1989), xvii
78   Henry Kissinger, White House Years (Boston: Little, Brown, 1979), 344
79   It is my view that by the 1960s, the once-socialist Soviet Union had embraced a form of state capitalism, and like other capitalist states, it was compelled to expand its global reach, including in the Middle East.
80   Mark Phythian, Arming Iraq (Boston: Northeastern University Press, 1997), 11
81   Ismet Sheriff Vanly, "Kurdistan in Iraq," in People Without A Country, 183
82   Robert Engler, The Brotherhood of Oil (New York: New American Library, 1977), 18-19; Blair, 52
83   Blair, 90
84   Kolko, Confronting the Third World, 230
85   Henderson, 37, 46
86   Kolko, Confronting the Third World, 230.
87   Engler, 124
88   Cleveland, 400-402. During the 1970s, it expanded its land reform program, enacted a mass literacy campaign, built a nationwide health care system, and broadened women's rights. Forced marriage was outlawed and women were given greater access to education. By 1982, 30 percent of Iraq's university students were women. Working women were given paid maternity leave, equal pay for equal work, and had access to childcare.
89   Kissinger, Years of Upheaval, 863
90   Kissinger, Years of Upheaval, 888
91   Robert Dreyfuss, "The Thirty Year Itch,"*Mother Jones*, March/April 2003, 42
92   Kissinger, Years of Upheaval, 863
93   Kissinger, Years of Upheaval, 674-75
94   Kissinger, Years of Upheaval, 669
95   Phythian, 10-12; Kissinger, Years of Upheaval, 669
96   Joe Stork and Martha Wenger, "From Rapid Deployment to Massive Deployment," in The Gulf War Reader, 36
97   Bush, *Wall Street Journal*, September 12, 2002

98   Seymour M. Hersh, The Price of Power: Kissinger in the Nixon White House (New York: Summit Books, 1983), 542

99   Kissinger, Years of Upheaval, 674-75

100   Middle East Watch, 70

101   Tripp, 200-201

102   Dinsmore, Washington Report on Middle East Affairs, May/June 1991; Washington Post, June 22, 1973 cited in Simons, 302

103   Bulloch and Morris, No Friends But the Mountains, 138-39

104   CIA: The Pike Report (United Kingdom: Spokesman Books, 1977), 211. Extensive excerpts from the Select Committee on Intelligence, or Pike report, were also published in the New York Times and the Village Voice. "The CIA Report the President Doesn't Want You to Read," Village Voice, February 16, 1976; "House Committee Finds Intelligence Agencies Generally Go Unchecked" and "Intelligence Report Leaks Denounced by White House," articles by Nicholas M. Horrock and John M. Crewdson, New York Times, January 26 and 27, 1976

105   Pike Report, 214

106   Vanly, 187

107   Bulloch and Morris, No Friends But the Mountains, 140

108   Pike Report, 197

109   Dilip Hiro, The Longest War (New York: Routledge, 1991),16; Simons, 303

110   Vanly, 186

111   Vanly, 187

112   Pike Report, 197-98; Cleveland, 398-99; Vanly, 189

113   Pike Report, 198, 217

114   Pike Report, 197

115   Cleveland, 398-99

116   Pike Report, 198

117   Otis Pike, "We've Given Them False Hope Before," San Francisco Examiner, April 10, 1991; Daniel Schorr, "1975 Background to Betrayal," Washington Post, April 7, 1991, D3; Christopher Hitchens, "Minority Report," The Nation, May 6, 1991, 58; all cited in Tony Murphy, "Encouraging Rebellion: The Cynical Use of the Kurds and the Shiites," in "High Crimes and Misdemeanors: U.S. War Crimes in the Persian Gulf," Research Committee of the San Francisco Commission of Inquiry of the International War Crimes Tribunal, 1991

118   Kissinger, Years of Upheaval, 885-86

119   Kissinger, Years of Upheaval, 854

120   Howard Teicher and Gayle Radley Teicher, Twin Pillars to Desert Storm (New York: William Morrow, 1993), 24

CHAPTER FOUR
ARMING IRAQ

1   Associated Press, "Text of State of Union Address," New York Times, January 30, 2002

2   "Inside the Den of Spies in Tehran," Revolutionary Worker, July 18, 1980

3   Hiro, Iran Under the Ayatollahs, 284

4   Zbigniew Brzezinski, Power and Principle (New York: Farrar-Straus-Giroux, 1983), 444. The Saudis needed assistance from foreign troops to dislodge the militants.

5   Teicher and Teicher, 27

6   "How Jimmy Carter and I Started the Mujahadeen," Le Nouvel Observateur (France), January 15-21, 1998, 76, cited in Blum, Rogue State, 4-5

7   Teicher and Teicher, 141-44

8   Brzezinski, 457

9   Brzezinski, 443; Stork and Wenger, 35; Teicher and Teicher, 145-46

10   Brzezinski, 452-54

11   Christopher Hitchens, "Realpolitik in the Gulf: A Game Gone Tilt," in The Gulf War Reader, 112

12   Dilip Hiro, Iran Under the Ayatollahs (London: Routledge & Kegan Paul, 1985), 318

13   Jimmy Carter, Keeping Faith (New York: Bantam Books, 1982), 518

14   Brzezinski, 489

15   Brzezinski, 489

16 John K. Cooley, "US keeping an eye on Soviet tactics as Iran crisis unfolds," *Christian Science Monitor*, November 28, 1979, A10; Hiro, Iran Under the Ayatollahs, 282. In November 1979, Khomeini abrogated the military assistance provisions of the 1921 Soviet-Iranian friendship treaty, but the Soviets refused to accept his declaration. Hiro, Iran Under the Ayatollahs, 286

17 Hiro, Iran Under the Ayatollahs, 285; Kevin Klose, "Soviets, in Scathing Attack, Call Iran Mission 'Madness,'" *Washington Post*, April 26, 1980, A18

18 Jack Anderson, "Iran invasion plan reported, denied," *Chicago Sun-Times*, August 16, 1980, A4

19 Former Carter official Sick claims there was no invasion plan, but admits Anderson's revelations "bore at least some resemblance to the plan for the second rescue [of the hostages] mission." Sick argues that Anderson was being fed misinformation by "national security officials who opposed Carter" and "worked from the inside of the administration to attempt to sabotage it and assist in a Reagan victory." Gary Sick, October Surprise: America's Hostages in Iran and the Election of Ronald Reagan (New York: Times Books, 1991), 25-26

20 Brzezinski, 451-452; Richard Halloran, *New York Times*, September 2, 1986; Benjamin F. Schemmer, "Was the U.S. Ready to Resort to Nuclear Weapons for the Persian Gulf in 1980?" *Armed Forces Journal International*, September 1986. Halloran and Schemmer are cited in an unpublished paper by Daniel Ellsberg.

21 Brzezinski, 453

22 Hiro, Iran Under the Ayatollahs, 325-26

23 Brzezinski, 500

24 Iraq abrogated the Agreement on September 17, 1980—five days before attacking Iran. Cleveland, 403

25 Cleveland, 399

26 Tripp, xiii, 220-21; See also, Ofra Bengio, "Shi'is and Politics in Ba'thi Iraq," *Middle Eastern Studies*, January 1985, 1-14

27 Teicher and Teicher, 98

28 Hiro, The Longest War, 39

29 Teicher and Teicher, 62

30 Teicher and Teicher, 61; Brzezinski, 504

31 Teicher and Teicher, 62

32 Hiro, Iran Under the Ayatollahs, 320

33 Abol Hassan Bani-Sadr, My Turn to Speak (McLean, VA: Brassey's, 1991), 13, 94

34 Kenneth Timmermann, The Death Lobby: How the West Armed Iraq (New York: Houghton Mifflin, 1991), 112; Aburish, 187

35 Robert Parry, "October Surprise X-Files (Part 5): Saddam's 'Green Light,'" *The Consortium*, January 31, 1996 (online at: www.consortiumnews.com/archive-/xfile5.html)

36 Carter administration officials, not surprisingly, vehemently deny that they gave Iraq a "green light" for its September 22, 1980 attack on Iran. In his autobiography, the former President claims the U.S. "had no previous knowledge of nor influence over" Iraq's plans to attack Iraq, and that when war broke out, he "preferred a cease-fire." Carter, Keeping Faith, 506, 559. Brzezinski has also denied any U.S. encouragement for the Iraqi attack. Sick, 254

37 Teicher and Teicher, 103; Hitchens, 112

38 Bruce W. Jentleson, With Friends Like These: Reagan, Bush, and Saddam, 1982-1990 (New York: W.W. Norton, 1994), 35

39 Iraq claimed the war began on September 4, when Iran again shelled Iraqi border towns.

40 See, for example, Stephen Engelberg, "Iran and Iraq Got 'Doctored' Data, U.S. Officials Say— Given Disinformation—Motive Described as Keeping Either Side From Winning the Persian Gulf War," *New York Times*, January 12, 1987, A1

41 Hiro, Iran Under the Ayatollahs, 168; Hiro, The Longest War, 42, 72

42 Sick, 10-12; for a view from within the Khomeini government, see Bani-Sadr, 32-39

43 Hiro, The Longest War, 250

44 Ditmars, *San Francisco Chronicle*, February 1, 2002

45 Hiro, The Longest War, 251

46 Hiro, The Longest War, 121

47 Estimates of the amount of secret Israeli shipments of U.S. arms to Iran in the early 1980s range from $100-$200 million to several billion dollars. Jentleson, 57; Phythian, 32

48 Bernard Gwertzman, "U.S. Views Defeat of Iraqis By Iran As a Major Danger," *New York Times*, May 26, 1982, A1

49   Michael Dobbs, "U.S. Had Key Role in Iraq Buildup: Trade in Chemical Arms Allowed Despite Their Use on Iranians, Kurds," *Washington Post*, December 30, 2002, A1; "Declaration of Howard Teicher," January 31, 1995, in United States of America v. Carlos Cardoen, et. al. (United States District Court, Southern District of Florida, 93-241-CR-HIGHSMITH), available online at www. RealHistory-Archives.com. See also, Dean Baquet, "U.S. Supplied Arms to Iraq, Ex-Aide Says," *New York Times*, February 5, 1995, A4. Teicher stated that Reagan signed a National Security Directive in June 1982, but NSDD 114 was dated November 26, 1983. However, it seems clear that Reagan initiated the tilt toward Iraq in the summer of 1982. Also, after attacking Teicher's affidavit, the U.S. government convinced the court to seal it on national security grounds. Robert Parry, "Britain's Iraq Accounting & the U.S. Dodge," *The Consortium*, March 14, 1996

50   Teicher affidavit

51   Jentleson, 52

52   Murray Waas, "What Washington Gave Saddam for Christmas," in The Gulf War Reader, 85-95

53   Phythian, 27

54   Cleveland, 404; Phythian, 35-36; Douglas Frantz and Murray Waas, "Bush Secret Effort Helped Iraq Build Its War Machine," *Los Angeles Times*, February 23, 1992, A1

55   Hiro, Iran Under the Ayatollahs, 329

56   Teicher affidavit

57   William Blum, "Chemical Weapons, the US and Iraq: What the New York Times Left Out," *Counterpunch*, August 20, 2002 (www.ccmep.org/2002_articles/-Iraq/082002_Chemical_weapons.htm); citing "U.S. Chemical and Biological Warfare-Related Dual Use Exports to Iraq and their Possible Impact on the Health Consequences of the Persian Gulf War," Senate Committee on Banking, Housing and Urban Affairs with Respect to Export Administration, reports of May 25, 1994 and October 7, 1994

58   "What Iraq Admitted About its Chemical Weapons Program, *New York Times*, April 13, 2003

59   Waas, The Gulf War Reader, 90-91; Nathaniel Hurd with Glen Rangwala, "U.S. Diplomatic and Commercial Relationships with Iraq, 1980-2 August 1990," December 12, 2001 update (www.cam.ac.uk/societies/casi/info/usdocs/usiraq80s90s-.html)

60   Dobbs, *Washington Post*, December 30, 2002

61   Hurd, "U.S. Diplomatic and Commercial Relationships with Iraq"

62   Patrick E. Tyler, "Officers Say U.S. Aided Iraq in War Despite Use of Gas," *New York Times*, August 18, 2002, A1

63   "Iraqgate: Saddam Hussein, U.S. Policy and the Prelude to the Persian Gulf War, 1980-1994," Digital National Security Archive, September 1, 2002 (http://-nsarchive.chadwyck.com/-iges-sayx.htm); Jentleson, 48-49

64   Tyler, *New York Times*, August 18, 2002

65   Bob Woodward, "CIA Aiding Iraq in Gulf War," *Washington Post*, December 15, 1986; Middle East Watch, 81-82; Elaine Sciolino, "Iraq Chemical Arms Condemned, but West Once Looked the Other Way," *New York Times*, February 13, 2003

66   Dilip Hiro, "Iraq and Poison Gas," *The Nation*, August 28, 2002 (online edition)

67   Tyler, *New York Times*, August 18, 2002

68   Hurd, "U.S. Diplomatic and Commercial Relationships with Iraq," section on 1988

69   "President Bush's Speech on the Use of Force," *New York Times*, October 8, 2002

70   See, for instance, David Remnick, "Comment: Making a Case," *The New Yorker*, February 3, 2003, 31-32

71   Teicher and Teicher, 287

72   Jeremy Scahill, "The Saddam in Rumsfeld's Closet," ZNET, August 4, 2002 (www.zmag.org)

73   Cleveland, 404

74   *Middle East Watch*, 103

75   Dobbs, *Washington Post*, December 30, 2002

76   William M. Arkin, "Why a War With Iraq Is Inevitable," *Los Angeles Times*, September 15, 2002

77   Ridgeway, 13-14; Phythian, 37

78   Robert Novak, "A Little U.S.-Iraqi History," CNN.com, September 26, 2002

79   Teicher and Teicher, 287

80   John Tower, Edmund Muskie, Brent Scowcroft, et. al.,The Tower Commission Report: Full

Text of the President's Special Review Board, (New York: Times Books and Bantam Books, 1987), 112-13

81 Murray Waas and Craig Unger, "Annals of Government: How the U.S. Armed Iraq," *New Yorker,* November 2, 1992

82 Teicher and Teicher, 330. The Soviets had initially cutoff arms shipments to Iraq, fearing the war would play into U.S. hands, while trying to gain influence in Tehran with offers of arms, economic assistance, and transhipment routes. But by 1983 these overtures stalled, when Iran cracked down on the pro-Soviet Tudeh Party and expelled a number of Soviet diplomats. The Islamic Republic was deeply suspicious of the Soviet Union due to its long-time support for Iraq and its invasion of Afghanistan. Iran's military and economy had been built by and remained dependent on the West. And there was a deep ideological chasm between the Islamists in power in Tehran and the "godless" Soviet leadership. Meanwhile, Iraq, their long-time ally, was on the brink of defeat, a prospect which the Soviets feared would further undercut their standing in the region. So they resumed aid, offering Baghdad $4.5 billion in new arms and $2 billion in loans in return for Iraqi oil. Jentleson, 47

83 Jentleson, 47

84 See, Teicher and Teicher, 325-32; Jentleson, 47-52; Report of the Congressional Committees Investigating the Iran-Contra Affair, 100th Congress, 1st Session, H. Rept. No. 100-433; S. Rept. No. 100-216 (Washington, D.C.: U.S. Government Printing Office, 1987), 165-66

85 The White House, "U.S. Policy Toward Iran," Draft National Security Decision Directive, June 17, 1985, National Security Archive Electronic Briefing Book No. 21, www.gw.uedu/~nsarchiv

86 Bob Woodward, Veil: The Secret Wars of the CIA 1981-1987 (New York: Pocket Books, 1987), 501

87 Woodward, Veil, 475, 501, 506

88 "Iraq Ascribes a Key Defeat in '86 to Misinformation From the U.S.," *New York Times,* January 19, 1987, A1

89 Stephen Engelberg, "Iran and Iraq Got 'Doctored' Data, U.S. Officials Say—Given Disinformation—Motive Described as Keeping Either Side From Winning the Persian Gulf War," *New York Times,* January 12, 1987, A1

90 Congressional Report on Iran-Contra, 253; Woodward, Veil, 556

91 Woodward, Veil, 556; Teicher affidavit

92 Congressional Report on Iran-Contra, 255

93 Engelberg, *New York Times,* January 12, 1987

94 Engelberg, *New York Times,* January 12, 1987

95 Phythian, 36

96 Woodward, Veil, 507

97 "The No-Win Goal in the Gulf," *New York Times,* May 22, 1984

98 "Iranians remain convinced that they would have won the war but for the U.S. military's downing of an Iranian passenger jet in the summer of 1988, which they interpreted as a sign to back down." Hadani Ditmars, "An unlikely alliance of 'evil': U.S. threats give Iraq, Iran new reason to inch toward rapprochement," *San Francisco Chronicle,* February 1, 2002

99 Tripp, 243

100 Tripp, 243

101 Bulloch and Morris, No Friends but the Mountains, 142

102 Bulloch and Morris, No Friends but the Mountains, 142

103 Scahill, ZNET, August 4, 2003

104 Jonathan Wright (Reuters), "Powell Visits Mass Grave of Hussein's Victims," *Washington Post,* September 15, 2003

105 Cleveland, 506; Noam Chomsky, "Prospects for Peace in the Middle East," speech at the University of Toledo, March 4, 2001 (www.matrixmasters.com/wtc/chomsky); *Middle East Watch,* 79-80. In 1982, Iraq signed an agreement with Turkey authorizing Turkish forces to enter Iraq in pursuit of Kurdish rebels from Turkey, or to conduct joint operations with Iraqi forces against Iraqi Kurds. This agreement helped Iraq deploy more forces against Iran. Clark, 6

106 Phil Donahue Show, January 13, 2003, MSNBC

107 Jentleson, 104, emphasis in original

108 Phythian, 42. It also urged that the U.S. "should pursue and seek to facilitate, opportunities for US firms to participate in the reconstruction of the Iraqi economy, particularly in the energy

area, where they do not conflict with our non-proliferation and other significant objectives," foreshadowing the 2002-2003 discussion of U.S. control of Iraq's petroleum industry following "regime change" in Baghdad.

109   Jentleson, 69

110   Ridgeway, 13-14; Teicher and Teicher, 393

111   Congressional Report on Iran-Contra, 277

112   Bradley Graham and Peter Slevin, "Meeting With Iran-Contra Arms Dealer Confirmed," *Washington Post*, August 9, 2003, A1

113   Phythian, 45. A year earlier, during the summer of 1989, an "Iraqgate" scandal briefly flared after the FBI raided the Atlanta branch of the Banca Nazionale del Lavoro (BNL). BNL was one of Italy's largest banks, owned primarily by the Italian government. It handled billions in U.S. agricultural credit guarantees for Iraq and funneled $1.155 billion in loans to Iraq's Ministry of Industry and Military Production, the agency heading Iraq's effort to build up its military capabilities, including in chemical, biological, and nuclear weapons and missiles. A full investigation of BNL's activities was impeded by top Bush officials, and indictments were not handed down until February 27, 1991, hours after Desert Storm ended. U.S. authorities ended up blaming the bank's dealings with Iraq on one BNL official who, they claimed, acted on his own. "Iraqgate" was quickly buried and never became a major issue. See Russ W. Baker, "Iraqgate: The Big One That (Almost) Got Away," *Columbia Journalism Review*, March/April 1993; Jack Colhoun, "Bush Administration Uses CIA To Stonewall Iraqgate Investigation," *Covert Action Quarterly*, Fall 1992, 40-41; "Iraqgate," Digital National Security Archive, September 1, 2002

114   James Cusick and Felicity Arbuthnot, "White House Tore Out 8000 Pages of Iraq Report," *Sunday Herald* (UK), December 22, 2002; Philip Shenon, "Declaration Lists Companies That Sold Chemicals to Iraq," *New York Times*, December 21, 2002

115   Andreas Zumach, Die Tageszeitung, December 17, 2002; "Top-secret Iraq Report Reveals U.S. Corporations, Gov't Agencies and Nuclear Labs Helped Illegally Arm Iraq," Democracy Now, 12/19/02 (www.democracynow.org); Michael Albert, "Znet Update: U.S. Corps implicated in Iraq," December 19, 2002; "Leaked Report Says German and US Firms Supplied Arms to Saddam," Tony Paterson, *The Independent* (UK) 18 December, 2002

116   "'Moral Case' for deposing Saddam," BBC News, August 15, 2002; Bush, *Wall Street Journal*, September 12, 2002

CHAPTER FIVE
"We Have to Have a War"

1   Appendix B: "The Glaspie-Hussein Transcript," in Beyond the Storm, 392-93; George H.W. Bush, "In Defense of Saudi Arabia," in The Gulf War Reader, 197; George W. Bush, "Saddam Hussein Has Made The Case Against Himself," *Wall Street Journal*, September 12, 2002

2   Phythian, 51; Cleveland, 406

3   Cleveland, 406-407; Sami Yousif, "The Iraqi-US War: A Conspiracy Theory," in The Gulf War and the New World Order, Haim Bresheeth and Nira Yuval-Davis, eds. (London: Zed Books, 1991), 53

4   Yousif, 54

5   Phythian, 28; Cleveland, 407; Hiro, Iraq in the Eye of the Storm, 32

6   John Bulloch and Harvey Morris, Saddam's War (London: Faber and Faber, 1991), 100

7   Dilip Hiro, Iraq in the Eye of the Storm (New York: Thunder's Mouth Press, 2002), 33-34; "Glaspie-Hussein Transcript," Beyond the Storm, 392

8   Teicher and Teicher, 99

9   Cleveland, 464

10   Hiro, Iraq in the Eye of the Storm, 33-34

11   Hiro, Iraq in the Eye of the Storm, 224-25; Simons, 342-43

12   Karen Elliott House, "Iraqi President Hussein Sees New Mideast War Unless America Acts," *Wall Street Journal*, June 28, 1990, A1; Cleveland, 463

13   House, *Wall Street Journal*, June 28, 1990; Beyond the Storm, 362

14   House, *Wall Street Journal*

15   House, *Wall Street Journal*

16   Bob Woodward, The Commanders (New York: Simon & Schuster, 1991), 207

17   Novak, CNN.com, September 26, 2002
18   Brian Urquhart, "The Prospect of War," *New York Review of Books*, December 19, 2002; Henderson, 187
19   Beyond the Storm, 362; Woodward, Commanders, 201-202
20   Pythian, 291
21   George Bush and Brent Scowcroft, A World Transformed (New York: Vintage Books, 1998), 307, 311
22   Thomas Friedman, "Envoy to Iraq, Faulted in Crisis, Says She Warned Hussein Sternly," *New York Times*, March 21, 1991, cited in Clark, 250-51; Elaine Sciolino, "Envoy's Testimony On Iraq Is Assailed," *New York Times*, July 13, 1991, A1; "U.S. Messages on the July Meeting of Saddam Hussein and American Envoy," *New York Times*, July 13, 1991, A4
23   All quotes from "Glaspie-Hussein Transcript," Beyond the Storm, 391-96
24   Elaine Sciolino, "Envoy's Testimony On Iraq Is Assailed," *New York Times*, July 13, 1991, A1
25   Beyond the Storm, 364
26   Bulloch and Morris, Saddam's War, 14
27   Beyond the Storm, 364
28   Beyond the Storm, 363-64; Hiro, Iraq in the Eye of the Storm, 34; Woodward, Commanders, 211
29   Phythian, 291
30   Ramsey Clark, The Fire this Time, U.S. War Crimes in the Gulf (New York: Thunder's Mouth Press, 1992), 3; Yousif, 63, 67
31   Beyond the Storm, 392
32   Frankel, 17
33   Joseph C. Wilson, "A 'Big Cat' With Nothing to Lose," *Los Angeles Times*, February 6, 2003; Bush and Scowcroft, 337
34   Frankel, 19
35   Beyond the Storm, 393; Wilson, *Los Angeles Times*, February 6, 2003
36   Victor Marshall, "The Lies We Are Told About Iraq," *Los Angeles Times*, January 5, 2003
37   Bush and Scowcroft, 317
38   Bush, Gulf War Reader, 199
39   Colin Powell, My American Journey, (New York: Random House, 1995), 485
40   Woodward, Commanders, 236-37
41   Beyond the Storm, 365, 367
42   Woodward, Commanders, 252, 262
43   National Security Directive 45, "U.S. Policy in Response to the Iraqi Invasion of Kuwait," August 20, 1990; National Security Directive 54, "Responding to Iraqi Aggression in the Gulf," January 15, 1991, National Security Archive (www.gwu.edu/~nsarchiv)
44   Energy Information Administration, "Persian Gulf Oil and Gas Exports Fact Sheet," April 2003, (www.eia.gov/emeu/cabs/pgulf.html). While the precise figure has varied over the years, according to the EIA, Persian Gulf countries (mainly Saudi Arabia) maintain an "overwhelming share (around 90%)" of the world's excess oil production capacity.
45   Kenneth M. Pollack, "Securing the Gulf, *Foreign Affairs*, July/August 2003, 4
46   Edward L. Morse and James Richard, "The Battle for Energy Dominance," *Foreign Affairs*, March/April 2002, 29, 20
47   Klare, *The Nation*, November 5, 2001
48   Cleveland, 468
49   Woodward, Commanders, 226-27
50   Bush and Scowcroft, 383
51   Bush and Scowcroft, 354-55
52   Bush and Scowcroft, 327
53   Bush and Scowcroft, 400
54   Bush and Scowcroft, 400
55   Bush and Scowcroft, 323
56   Bush and Scowcroft, 383
57   Simons, 362-364; see also, Michael Emery, "How the U.S. Avoided Peace," *Village Voice*, March 5, 1991
58   Jean Heller, "Photos Don't Show Buildup," *St. Petersburg Times*, January 6, 1991, 1A, cited in Stephen Zunes, Tinderbox: U.S. Middle East Policy and the Roots of Terrorism (Monroe, ME:

Common Courage Press, 2003), 77

59   Zunes, 77; Marshall, *Los Angeles Times*, January 5, 2003

60   *New York Times*, March 3, 1991, cited in Beyond the Storm, 369; George Bush, "The Need for an Offensive Military Option" (Speech of November 8, 1990), Gulf War Reader, 228-29

61   Bob Woodward, Shadow: Five Presidents and the Legacy of Watergate (New York: Simon & Schuster, 1999), 186

62   Scott Ritter, Endgame: Solving the Iraq Problem Once and For All (New York: Simon & Schuster, 1999), 43; Edward Epstein, "Strategists point to succession of blunders by Hussein," *San Francisco Chronicle*, April 9, 2003

63   Bush and Scowcroft, 399-400

64   John R. MacArthur, "Remember Nayirah, Witness for Kuwait?" *New York Times*, January 6, 1992, A15 (story found false in march 1991)

65   See, Lucy Komisar, "Truth in the Crossfire: 'Live From Baghdad' Peddles Lie," *Pacific News Service*, December 2, 2002

66   Ridgeway, 3; Dilip Hiro, A Few of Our Favorite Kings," in Gulf War Reader, 409

67   Bush and Scowcroft, 491

68   For the text of UN resolutions during the crisis see Beyond the Storm, 376-91

69   Kissinger, Diplomacy, 250

70   Beyond the Storm, 372

71   Bush and Scowcroft, 317

72   Thalif Deen, "UN Credibility at Stake Over Iraq, War Diplomats," *Inter Press Service News Agency*, October 1, 2002

73   Bush and Scowcroft, 416

74   William A. Arkin, Damian Durrant, and Marianne Cherni, On Impact: Modern War and the Environment: A Case Study of the Gulf War (London: Greenpeace, May 1991), 5

75   Woodward, Commanders, 344

76   George Bush, "The Liberation of Kuwait Has Begun" (Speech of January 16, 1991), Gulf War Reader, 313; Arkin, et. al., On Impact, 26

77   Powell, 485-86

78   William M. Arkin, "Think About the Unthinkable: U.S. Nukes In the Gulf," *The Nation*, December 31, 1990, 834-35

79   Baker reportedly warned Aziz, "If the conflict involves your use of chemical or biological weapons against our forces, the American people will demand vengeance. We have the means to exact it. This is not a threat. It is a promise." Ann Devroy, "Former State chief tells all," *San Francisco Examiner*, September 24, 1995, C14

80   Wilson, *Los Angeles Times*, February 6, 2003

81   Kenneth M. Pollack, The Threatening Storm: The Case for Invading Iraq (New York: Random House, 2002), 173-77; Urquhart, *New York Review of Books*, December 19, 2002; Barbara Crossette, "Iraqis Set Target of '01 For A-Bomb," *New York Times*, August 26, 1995, A1; Barbara Crossette, "Experts Doubt Iraq's Claims On A-Bomb," *New York Times*, August 30, 1995, A4

82   Arkin, et. al., On Impact, 78-79; DoD News Briefing, March 15, 1991 with Pete Williams (Public Affairs) and General "Tony" McPeak (U.S. Air Force); Department of the Air Force, "White Paper: Air Force Performance in Desert Storm," April 1991; "Greenpeace Report Estimates More Than 200,000 Killed in Gulf War," *Greenpeace News*, May 29, 1991

83   Bush and Scowcroft, 477

84   Bush, Gulf War Reader, 313

85   Eric Rouleau, "America's Unyielding Policy Toward Iraq," *Foreign Affairs*, January/February 1995

86   Barton Gellman, "Allied Air War Struck Broadly in Iraq: Officials Acknowledge Strategy Went Beyond Purely Military Targets," *Washington Post*, June 23, 1991, A1

87   Lee Hockstader, "Baghdad Residents Face Health Crisis," *Washington Post*, March 4, 1991, A1, cited in Arkin, et. al., On Impact, 58; WHO/UNICEF Special Mission to Iraq, "Joint WHO/UNICEF Team Report: A Visit to Iraq, February 16-21 1991," February 1991, 12; "Harvard Study Team Report: Public Health In Iraq After the Gulf War," May 1991, 17

88   Gellman, *Washington Post*, June 23, 1991

89   Gellman, *Washington Post*, June 23, 1991

90   Gellman, *Washington Post*, June 23, 1991

91   Gellman, *Washington Post*, June 23, 1991

92   Patrick J Sloyan, "War without death: The Pentagon promotes a vision of combat as bloodless & antiseptic," *San Francisco Chronicle*, November 17, 2002, D1

93   "Greenpeace Releases New Gulf War Casualty Estimates," *Greenpeace News*, July 23, 1991

94   Sloyan, *San Francisco Chronicle*, November 17, 2002; Arkin, et. al., On Impact, 80; "The Damage Was Not Collateral," *New York Times*, March 24, 1991

95   Arkin, et. al., On Impact, 79; Barton Gellman, "U.S. Bombs Missed 70% of the Time," *Washington Post*, March 16, 1991, A1, cited in Clark, 59; For more on the U.S. bombing, see Clark, The Fire This Time, 59-75.

96   "The Damage Was Not Collateral," *New York Times*, March 24, 1991; "The Ahtisaari Report," Beyond the Storm, 399

97   Estimates of the number of casualties at the Amiriya shelter differ; this comes from Ian Fisher, "Bombing Site Fuels Politics of Bitterness," *New York Times*, February 17, 2003

98   Gellman, *Washington Post*, June 23, 1991

99   Woodward, Shadow, 185

100   Bush and Scowcroft, 463

101   Bush and Scowcroft, 464, 475, 477

102   Bush and Scowcroft, 482-83

103   Bush and Scowcroft, 459

104   Bush and Scowcroft, 461

105   Bush and Scowcroft, 471

106   George Bush, "A Cruel Hoax" (Speech of February 15, 1991), Gulf War Reader, 343

107   Bush and Scowcroft, 473

108   Powell, 516-17

109   Bush and Scowcroft, 478

110   Bush and Scowcroft, 480

111   Bush and Scowcroft, 481-83; Beyond the Storm, 372

112   Beyond the Storm, 372

113   Hiro, Iraq in the Eye of the Storm, 38-39

114   Arkin, et. al., On Impact, 131; Hiro, Iraq in the Eye of the Storm, 39; Cleveland, 469

115   Zunes, 82; Joyce Chediac, "The Massacre of Withdrawing Soldiers on 'The Highway of Death,' in War Crimes: A Report on United States War Crimes against Iraq, eds. Ramsey Clark and Others (Washington, DC: Maisonneuve Press, 1992), 91

116   Sloyan, *San Francisco Chronicle*, November 17, 2002

117   Sloyan, *San Francisco Chronicle*, November 17, 2002; Jason DeParle, "17 News Executives Criticize U.S. For 'Censorship' of Gulf Coverage," *New York Times*, July 3, 1991

118   Sloyan, *San Francisco Chronicle*, November 17, 2002

119   Seymour M Hersh, "Annals of War: Overwhelming Force," *New Yorker*, May 22, 2000

120   Michael R. Gordon, "Report Revives Criticism of General's Attack on Iraqis in '91," *New York Times*, May 15, 2000, A11; Barry R. McCaffrey, "The New Yorker's Revisionist History," *Wall Street Journal*, May 22, 2000

121   Arkin, et. al., On Impact, 10

122   Caryle Murphy, "Iraqi death toll remains clouded," *Washington Post*, June 23, 1991, A1; Patrick E. Tyler, "Iraq's War Toll Estimated By U.S.," *New York Times*, June 5, 1991

123   Arkin, et. al., On Impact, 5, 15, 42, 45, 46

124   Thomas Ginsberg, "War's toll: 158,000 Iraqis and a researcher's position," *Philadelphia Inquirer*, January 5, 2003. One reporter who investigated the number of Iraqi casualties several years after the war writes that one "well-placed Hussein family member" told her that he thought as many as 300,000 civilians had died in the war. Patricia Axelrod, "Baghdad's Terrible Secret," *San Francisco Chronicle*, August 20, 1995

125   Gellman, *Washington Post*, June 23, 1991

126   Suzanne Gamboa, "New study on gulf war illnesses," *San Francisco Chronicle*, December 23, 2002. Gamboa reports that some 130,000 U.S. troops in southern Iraq may have been exposed to low levels of sarin gas following the U.S. destruction of an Iraqi weapons depot at Khamisiyah. Neela Banerjee, "Oil teams recall Kuwait and fear Iraq may be worse," *New York Times*, January 24, 2003

127   Clark, 103; "Gulf War Veterans Association Questions Who Started the Oil Well Fires in Kuwait," Press Release, American Gulf War Veterans Association, February 19, 2003,

(www.gulfwarvets.com/news13.htm)

128   Saul Bloom, John M. Miller, James Warner and Philippa Winkler, eds., Hidden Casualties: Environmental, Health and Political Consequences of the Persian Gulf War (Berkeley, CA: North Atlantic Books, 1994), 82-83, 97; John Horgan, "Science and the Citizen: Up in Flames" and "U.S. Gags Discussion of War's Environmental Effects," *Scientific American*, May 1991, 17-24, cited in Clark, 103

129   Robert Collier, "Iraq links cancers to uranium weapons," *San Francisco Chronicle*, January 13, 2003; Scott Peterson, "A 'silver bullet's' toxic legacy," *Christian Science Monitor*, November 20, 2002

130   Dr. James C. Warf, "On Depleted Uranium," email correspondence

131   Collier, *San Francisco Chronicle*, January 13, 2003; Peterson, *Christian Science Monitor*, December 20, 2002; Scott Peterson, "Remains of toxic bullets litter Iraq," *Christian Science Monitor*, May 15, 2003

132   Collier, *San Francisco Chronicle*, January 13, 2003

133   John Pilger, The New Rulers of the World (London: Verso, 2002), 48. Some leading scientists, including Warf, while recognizing the dangers of depleted uranium, argue that the label "weapons of mass destruction" should be applied only to atomic warheads because their destructive power is many magnitudes greater than depleted uranium and most chemical and biological weapons.

134   Dave Parks, "U.S. to do study on Gulf War vets," *San Francisco Chronicle*, November 2, 2002; Rita Rubin, "Studies tie Lou Gehrig's disease to Gulf War Vets," *USA Today*, September 22, 2003. See also Dennis Bernstein, "Gulf War Syndrome Covered Up," *Covert Action Quarterly* #53, Summer 1995

135   Chalmers Johnson, "Dirty Weapons: Casualties from Iraq War Will Mount," *Pacific News Service*, May 5, 2003

136   Arkin, et. al, On Impact, 133, A-4; "Greenpeace Report Estimates More Than 200,000 Killed in Gulf War," *Greenpeace News*, May 29, 1991; "In the Crosshairs of an Unjust War," *Revolutionary Worker*, February 2, 2003

137   Eugene Carroll and Rachel Stohl, "Another war, another round of land mines?" *Christian Science Monitor*, February 18, 2003

138   Bush, "A Cruel Hoax," Gulf War Reader, 343

139   Bush and Scowcroft, 472; Walter Pincus, "Bush's Father Feared Expanded Role in Iraq," *Washington Post*, September 8, 2002, A28

140   Tony Horwitz, "Forgotten Rebels: After Heeding Calls To Turn on Saddam, Shiites Feel Betrayed," *Wall Street Journal*, December 26, 1991, A1

141   National Security Directive 54, January 15, 1991

142   Gellman, *Washington Post*, June 23, 1991; Bush and Scowcroft, 463-64

143   Michael Wines, "Kurd Gives Account Of Broadcasts to Iraq Linked to the CIA," *New York Times*, April 6, 1991, A1; Horwitz, *Wall Street Journal*, December 26, 1991

144   Brandon Sprague, "Broken Promises—How the United States Failed the Iraqi Resistance," *San Francisco Chronicle*, February 16, 2003

145   Bush and Scowcroft, 490

146   Arkin, et. al., On Impact, 15; Hiro, Iraq in the Eye of the Storm, 43-44; Murphy, *Washington Post*, June 23, 1991

147   Arkin, et. al., On Impact, 15, 48-49; Sprague, *San Francisco Chronicle*, February 16, 2003; Cleveland, 470

148   Bush and Scowcroft, 489

149   Andrew Cockburn and Patrick Cockburn, Out of the Ashes: The Resurrection of Saddam Hussein (New York: Harper Collins, 1999), 37

150   Bush and Scowcroft, 472

151   Horwitz, *Wall Street Journal*, December 26, 1991

·152   Sprague, *San Francisco Chronicle*, February 16, 2003, A1

153   Michael R. Gordon, "A Decade Beyond the Gulf War," *New York Times*, February 18, 2001, A10; "Former President Bush: 'I Hate Saddam,'" CNN.com, September 18, 2002; Bob Drogin, "91 Iraq Toxics Plan Reported," *Los Angeles Times*, March 10, 2003

154   Bush and Scowcroft, 489

155   Bush and Scowcroft, 370, September 11, 1990

156   Cleveland, 480

157   See, for instance, Youssef M. Ibrahim, "Saudi Tradition: Edicts From Koran Produce Curbs on Women," *New York Times*, November 7, 1990, A6

158   Alain Gresh, "The Legacy of Desert Storm: A European Perspective," *Journal of Palestine Studies* 26/4 (Summer 1997), cited in "'Free People Will Set the Course of History,' Intellectuals, Democracy and American Empire," Robert Blecher, *Middle East Report*, March 2003

159   Cleveland, 508; "Turkey Lifts Restrictions Long Imposed In Kurds' Area," *New York Times*, December 1, 2002, A4

160   Rashid I. Khalidi, "Road Map or Road Kill?" *The Nation*, June 9, 2003. For more on the Oslo process, see Marwan Bishara, Palestine/Israel: Peace or Apartheid (London: Zed Books, 2001); Nicholas Guyatt, The Absence of Peace: Understanding the Israeli-Palestinian Conflict (London: Zed Books, 1998); Edward W. Said, Peace and Its Discontents (New York: Vintage Books, 1996); and The New Intifada: Resisting Israel's Apartheid, ed. Roane Carey (New York: Verso, 2001)

161   Ilene R. Prusher, "Turkey braces for refugee flood," *Christian Science Monitor*, January 29, 2003. Says 450,000 flooded into Turkey in 1991.

162   Bill Frelick, "Operation Provide Comfort: False Promises to the Kurds," in A People Without A Country, Gerard Chaliand (Brooklyn, NY: Olive Branch Press, 1993), 234, 237. See also Leo Sarkisian, ed., "The Kurds, Turkey & the Gulf War: A Record of Turkish Mistreatment of Kurdish Refugees During the Gulf War" (Watertown, MA: Armenian National Committee Eastern United States, 1992)

163   Bush and Scowcroft, 564

164   Bush and Scowcroft, 486, 491

CHAPTER SIX
GERM WARFARE

1   Bush and Scowcroft, 487

2   Hiro, Neighbors Not Friends, 69. In 1996 the U.S. imposed sanctions on foreign companies investing more than $40 million in Iran; however, these sanctions were far less stringent—in their substance and enforcement—than those on Iraq. See Stephen Hubbell, "The Containment Myth: US Middle East Policy in Theory and Practice," *Middle East Report*, Fall 1998

3   As regards Kuwait, Resolution 687 demanded that Iraq return Kuwaiti property taken during the war, pay compensation for war damage, and accept a final resolution of its border with Kuwait by the UN.

4   FAIR (Fairness & Accuracy in Reporting) Action Alert: "Common Myths in Iraq coverage," November 27, 2002 (www.fair.org/activism/iraq-myths.html)

5   Hiro, Neighbors Not Friends, 52, 70

6   Daniel Pearl and Robert Greenberger, "U.S. Maneuvers to Keep Military in Gulf," *Wall Street Journal*, July 1, 1996; Edward Cody, "In Iraqi Countryside, Allies' Forgotten War Inflicting Deep Wounds," *San Francisco Chronicle*, June 23, 2000; ABC World News Tonight, November 20, 2002

7   Eric Rouleau, "Trouble in the Kingdom," Foreign Affairs, July/August 2002, 64; Phythian, 37; Per Oskar Klevnas, *Middle East Report Online*, March 4, 2002

8   Ahtisaari Report, Beyond the Storm, 397

9   "Don't Ease the Squeeze on Iraq," *New York Times*, July 24, 1991

10   *Los Angeles Times*, May 9, 1991, cited in Zunes, 61

11   Joy Gordon, "Cool War: Economic Sanctions as a Weapon of Mass Destruction," *Harper's*, November 2002, 43

12   Sadruddin Aga Khan, et. al., "Report to the Secretary-General dated 15 July 1991 on humanitarian needs in Iraq" (Security Council document S/22799), 18-20; Althassiri Report, Beyond the Storm, 398

13   Althassiri Report, Beyond the Storm, 398

14   Gordon, 47-48, citing "Status of the Water and Sanitation Sector in South/Center Iraq," UNICEF, September 2001

15   A.C. Maturin, "Report of the Quaker Peace & Service Aotearoa/New Zealand delegate to Iraq," April 2002

16   Thomas Nagy, "The Secret Behind the Sanctions: How the U.S. Intentionally Destroyed Iraq's

Water Supply," *The Progressive*, September 2001

17   Gellman, *Washington Post*, June 23, 1991

18   Gordon, 44, 47-48

19   Peter Slevin and Vernon Loeb, "Bremer: Iraq Effort to Cost Tens of Billions," *Washington Post*, August 27, 2003, A1

20   Les Donison, "U.N. Sanctions Keep Iraqis Poor, Hopeless," *San Francisco Chronicle*, January 16, 2001

21   George Capaccio, "Sanctions: Killing a Country and a People" in Iraq Under Siege: The Deadly Impact of Sanctions and War, Anthony Arnove, ed. (Boston: South End Press, 2000), 145; Neil King, Jr., "For One Small Education Company, Iraqi Schools Are a Huge Challenge," *Wall Street Journal*, April 14, 2003

22   Donison, *San Francisco Chronicle*, January 16, 2001

23   Ridgeway, 13-14

24   Harvard Study Team, "Environmental and Agricultural Survey," October 1991, 2

25   Dr. Peter L. Pellett, "Sanctions, Food, Nutrition, and Health in Iraq," in Iraq Under Siege, 153; Capaccio, 140

26   Peter Baker, "Iraq's Shortage of Medicine May Grow More Severe," *Washington Post*, December 19, 2002, A24

27   Christopher S. Wren, "Iraq Poverty Said to Undermine Food Program," *New York Times*, October 20, 2000

28   Amy Goodman, Interview with Bill Clinton, Democracy Now, November 9, 2000

29   Bush, *Wall Street Journal*, September 12, 2002

30   Neela Banerjee, "Iraq Is a Strategic Issue for Oil Giants, Too," *New York Times*, February 22, 2003; Alix M. Freedman and Bhushan Bahree, "Iraq Is Shipping Large Cargoes of Crude, Violating U.N. Rules," *Wall Street Journal*, February 21, 2003

31   Energy Information Administration, "Iraq Energy Chronology: 1980-2002" (www.eia.doe.gov/cabs/iraqchron.html) (hereafter, "EIA Chronology")

32   Larry Everest, "Hans von Sponeck: The Inside Story of U.S. Sanctions on Iraq," *Revolutionary Worker*, December 23, 2001

33   Pellett, 157

34   Gordon, 45

35   Anglican Observer Office at the UN, Arab Commission for Human Rights, Center for Development of International Law, Fellowship of Reconciliation, Global Policy Forum, New Internationalism Project, Institute for Policy Studies, Mennonite Central Committee, Middle East and Europe Office of Global Ministries of the United Church of Christ and the Christian Church (Disciples of Christ), Quaker UN Office-New York, United Church of Christ UN Office, World Economy, Ecology & Development Association (WEED) in association with Save the Children UK, "Iraq Sanctions: Humanitarian Implications and Options for the Future" August 6, 2002 (hereafter Anglican Observer Office, et al.), 27-28; EIA Chronology, see July 12, 1999

36   Edmund L. Andrews, "Walk on the Supply Side of a New Iraq," *New York Times*, April 13, 2003

37   Everest, *Revolutionary Worker*, December 23, 2001

38   Chandrasekaran, *Washington Post*, February 3, 2003

39   Goodman, Democracy Now, November 9, 2000

40   Gordon managed to obtain some of the 661 Committee's records from various sources on the condition that they remain anonymous. Gordon, 43-44

41   Sarah Graham-Brown, "Sanctions Renewed on Iraq," *Middle East Report*, Press Information Note 96, May 14, 2002; Alan Sipress, "U.S. Plan refocuses Sanctions on Iraq," *San Francisco Chronicle*, March 26, 2001

42   Gordon, 46, 48

43   Wren, *New York Times*, October 20, 2000

44   Gordon, 46-47; John Pilger, "Not in our name," *Daily Mirror* (London), April 5, 2002

45   Gordon, 47

46   Anglican Observer Office, et. al., 24-25

47   Gordon, 44, 46

48   Klevnas, *Middle East Report Online*, March 4, 2002

49   Graham-Brown, *Middle East Report*, May 14, 2002

50   Baker, *Washington Post*, December 19, 2002

51   Hans von Sponeck and Denis Halliday, "A 'New' Iraq Policy: What About International Law
      and Compassion?" May 29, 2001 (www.scn.org/ccpi/sponeck-halliday.html)
52   "Smarting Over Iraq," *Wall Street Journal*, July 5, 2001
53   Baker, *Washington Post*, December 19, 2002
54   Baker, *Washington Post*, December 19, 2002
55   UNICEF and Government of Iraq Ministry of Health, "Child and Maternal Mortality Survey
      1999: Preliminary Report," July 1999 (www.unicef.org)
56   Barbara Crossette, "Children's Death Rates Rising In Iraqi Lands, Unicef Reports," *New York
      Times*, August 13, 1999, A6
57   Larry Everest, "U.S. Genocide in Iraq: A Conversation with Denis Halliday," *Revolutionary
      Worker*, March 28, 1999
58   John Mueller and Karl Mueller, "Sanctions of Mass Destruction," *Foreign Affairs*, May/June
      1999, 43
59   "Punishing Saddam," CBS, *60 Minutes*, May 12, 1996 cited in Blum, Rogue State, 5-6

CHAPTER SEVEN
THE GREAT WMD FLIM FLAM

1   "Bush's State of the Union speech," CNN.com, January 29, 2003
2   Hiro, Neighbors Not Friends, 69
3   Greenpeace Briefing, "Iraq is not the only country in the region with weapons of mass destruc-
      tion (WMD)," February 2003; Klare, Resource Wars, 66
4   Daniel Pearl, "U.N. Weapon Inspectors Gave Briefings on Iraq," *New York Times*, February 11,
      1998
5   William Shawcross, "Why Saddam will never disarm," *The Observer* (UK), February 23, 2003
6   Ritter, Endgame, 42
7   Cleveland, 473; Cockburn and Cockburn, 265
8   Paul Lewis, "Iraq Now Admits a Secret Program to Enrich Uranium," *New York Times*, July 9,
      1991, A1
9   William Polk, "The Bush Doctrine and Its Implications for US Foreign Policy," Lecture at The
      Centre For Lebanese Studies, November 18, 2002; John Burns, "Iraq's Thwarted Ambitions
      Litter an Old Nuclear Plant," *New York Times*, December 27, 2002
10   Jim Lehrer, interview with Raymond Zilinskas, PBS Newshour, February 16, 1998
11   F. Gregory Gause III, "Getting It Backward on Iraq," *Foreign Affairs*, May/June 1999, 57 (Note;
      for consistency I changed Gause's spelling of "al-Hakam" to al-Hakum)
12   Scott Ritter, "Don't blame Saddam for this one," *Guardian* (UK), October 19, 2001
13   Barbara Crossette, "Clean Bill for Iraqis on A-Arms? Experts Upset," *New York Times*, April 19,
      1998
14   FAIR Media Advisory, "Iraq's Hidden Weapons: From Allegation to Fact," February 4, 2003
      (www.fair.org/press-releases/iraq-weapons.html)
15   Von Sponeck and Halliday, May 29, 2001
16   John Barry, "The Defector's Secrets," *Newsweek*, March 3, 2003; David Kelly, "Regime's Priority
      Was Blueprints, Not Arsenal, Defector Told U.N.," *Los Angeles Times*, April 26, 2003; Bob
      Drogin, "Iraq Had Secret Labs, Officer Says," *Los Angeles Times*, June 8, 2003; Hiro, Iraq in the
      Eye of the Storm, 119. Kamel returned to Iraq in February 1996 and was assassinated shortly
      after a quick divorce from Hussein's daughter.
17   Barry, *Newsweek*, March 3, 2003
18   Scott Ritter, "Is Iraq a True Threat to the US?" *Boston Globe*, July 20, 2002
19   Education for Peace in Iraq Center (EPIC), "Transcript of Scott Ritter's Testimony for the May
      3, 2000 Congressional Briefing" (www.nonviolence.org/vitw/old_site-/Ritter%20Test.html)
20   Michael Gordon, "Weapons of Mass Confusion," *New York Times*, August 1, 2003
21   Bob Drogin, "U.S. Suspects It Received False Iraq Arms Tips," *Los Angeles Times*, August 28,
      2003
22   "Blix Says Iraq Probably Destroyed WMDs," *Los Angeles Times*, September 17, 2003; Andy
      McSmith, Raymond Whitaker and Geoffrey Lean, "Britain and US Will Back Down Over
      WMDs," *Independent* (UK), September 7, 2003; "Indefinite Delay on Weapons Report," *The
      London Advertiser*," September 15, 2003
23   Drogin, *Los Angeles Times*, June 8, 2003; John J. Lumpkin, "Top Iraqi prisoners all denying

Saddam had weapons of mass destruction," *San Francisco Chronicle*, April 29, 2003

24   Thomas M. DeFrank, "Bush's war is personal," *New York Daily News*, September 28, 2002

25   Seymour M. Hersh, "A Case Not Closed," *New Yorker*, November 1, 1993, 80-92

26   David S. Cloud, "Bush's Efforts to Link Hussein To al Qaeda Lack Clear Evidence," *Wall Street Journal*, October 23, 2002

27   "Meet the Press," NBC, July 13, 2003

28   Reuters, January 12, 1995, cited in Institute for Public Accuracy, "Autopsy of a Disaster: The U.S. Sanctions Policy on Iraq," November 13, 1998 (www.accuracy.org/iraq.htm)

29   Cited in Institute for Institute for Public Accuracy, November 13, 1998, chronology for March 26, 1997 and December 9, 1997; Hiro, *Iraq in the Eye of the Storm*, 112

30   Everest, *Revolutionary Worker*, December 23, 2001; see, "Questions Submitted by Iraqi Foreign Minister Naji Sabri to UN Secretary-General Kofi Annan, March 7, 2002," in Hiro, Iraq in the Eye of the Storm, 261-64

31   Bush, *Wall Street Journal*, September 12, 2002

32   Seymour M. Hersh, "Saddam's Best Friend: How the C.I.A. made it a lot easier for the Iraqi leader to rearm," *New Yorker*, April 5, 1999, 36; "CIA Plots in Iraq," *Revolutionary Worker*, February 22, 1998; Ritter, Endgame, 132

33   ABC's "Saturday Night," February 7, 1998, cited in *Revolutionary Worker*, February 22, 1998

34   *Revolutionary Worker*, February 22, 1998

35   Hiro, Iraq in the Eye of the Storm, 125-26; Ritter, Endgame, 135; Hersh, New Yorker, April 5, 1999, 36; Philip Shenon, "C.I.A. Was With U.N. in Iraq For Years, Ex-Inspector Says," *New York Times*, February 23, 1999, A1; Cockburn and Cockburn, 282

36   Hersh, *New Yorker*, April 5, 1999, 34-41

37   Ritter, Endgame, 144; ABC's "Saturday Night" cited in *Revolutionary Worker*, February 22, 1998

38   Barton Gellman, "There's Information-Gathering and There's Spying, "*Washington Post Weekly*, March 8, 1999, 16

39   Tim Weiner, "U.S. Used U.N. Team to Place Spy Device in Iraq, Aides Say," *New York Times*, January 8, 1999, A1

40   Ritter, Endgame, 143-44; *Revolutionary Worker*, February 22, 1998

41   Hiro, Iraq in the Eye of the Storm, 111, 126

42   Hersh, *New Yorker*, April 5, 1999, 32, 35

43   Stephen J. Hedges, "U.S. bug in Baghdad eavesdropped on Hussein," *San Francisco Examiner*, January 10, 1999, A24 (from *Chicago Tribune*)

44   Hersh, *New Yorker*, April 5, 1999, 35

45   Ritter, Endgame, 195-96

46   Milan Rai, War Plan Iraq: 10 Reasons Against War on Iraq (London: Verso, 2002), 52

47   Hiro, Iraq in the Eye of the Storm, 128-29

48   Scott Ritter, "The US Hands Saddam a Victory," *Wall Street Journal*, December 28, 1998

49   Hiro, Iraq in the Eye of the Storm, 129-30; Ritter, Endgame, 196; Hersh, *New Yorker*, April 5, 1999, 32; FAIR, November 27, 2002, citing *Washington Post*, December 18, 1998

50   Weiner, *New York Times*, January 8, 1999

51   Scott Ritter, interview with Dennis Bernstein, Flashpoints, KPFA Radio, Berkeley, CA, August 23, 2002 (www.flashpoints.net)

52   Barton Gellman, "Did the UNSCOM Inspectors Eavesdrop?" *Washington Post Weekly*, January 11, 1999, 15

53   Hiro, Iraq in the Eye of the Storm, 134, 247

54   "Text of State of Union Address," *New York Times*, January 30, 2002

55   Ritter, KPFA, August 23, 2002

CHAPTER EIGHT
A GROWING CLAMOR FOR REGIME CHANGE

1   Chandrasekaran, *Washington Post*, February 3, 2003

2   Craig R. Whitney, "France seeks New U.N. System for Monitoring Iraqi Weapons," *New York Times*, December 23, 1998, A10; Barbara Crossette, "France, in Break with US, Urges End to Iraq Embargo," *New York Times*, January 14, 1999; John Goshko, "Russia Also Pushes Proposal to End Iraqi Oil Embargo," *San Francisco Chronicle*, January 16, 1999

3   EIA Chronology, March 18 and April 14, 1997; see also, Raad Alkadiri, "The Iraqi Klondike:

Oil and Regional Trade," *Middle East Report* 220, Fall 2001

4   Robert J. McCartney, "French oil firm sees future in Iraq," *Washington Post*, February 21, 2003, E1

5   Georg Weishaupt, "German Exports To Iraq Increased Fourfold In 2001," *Dow Jones Newswires*, January 4, 2002; Bill Powell, "How a war with Iraq will change the world," *Fortune*, July 8, 2002

6   Anne Reifenberg and James Tanner, "Left in the Dust? U.S. Oil Companies Fret Over Losing Out On Any Jobs in Iraq," *Wall Street Journal*, April 17, 1995, A1

7   "Super Euro," David Fairlamb, *Business Week*, February 17, 2003, cited in Peter Dale Scott. "Bush's Deep Reasons For War on Iraq: Oil, Petrodollars, and the OPEC Euro Question" (www.ratical.org/ratville/CAH/RRiraqWar.html)

8   See Anglican Observer Office, et. al., "Commercial Interests and Oil Politics," 19-21. Meanwhile, the U.S. was buying one-third of Iraq's exported oil, and U.S. firms were bidding on UN-approved contracts. Hiro, Iraq in the Eye of the Storm, 165

9   *Financial Times*, April 3, 2002, cited in Gordon, 49

10   John F. Burns, "Why Saddam Hussein Is Back Onstage," *New York Times*, March 4, 2001

11   Fouad Ajami, "The Sentry's Solitude," *Foreign Affairs*, November/December 2001, 2, 10, 11

12   Rouleau, *Foreign Affairs*, July/August 2002, 80; Zunes, 78

13   Martin Indyk, "Back to the Bazaar," *Foreign Affairs*, January/February 2002, 82

14   Rouleau, *Foreign Affairs*, July/August 2002, 75-76; see also, Larry Everest and Leonard Innes, "U.S. War Plans & The Saudi Arabia Debate," *Z Magazine*, December 2002

15   Cleveland, 477; Rouleau, 85

16   Kim Murphy, "Saudis' Quicksand of Poverty," *Los Angeles Times*, May 16, 2003

17   Hubbell, *Middle East Report*, Fall 1998

18   Cleveland, 476

19   Paul Wolfowitz, "Clinton's Bay of Pigs," *Wall Street Journal*, September 27, 1996

20   Project for the New American Century, www.newamericancentury.org/iraqclintonletter.htm. Under Bush II, Rumsfeld would become Secretary of Defense; Wolfowitz his top assistant; Rodman, Assistant Secretary of Defense for International Security Affairs; Zakheim, Under Secretary of Defense (Comptroller); Schneider, Chairman of the Pentagon's Defense Science Board; Perle, Chair of the Defense Policy Board; Armitage, Deputy Secretary of State; Dobriansky, Under Secretary of State for Global Affairs; Bolton, Under Secretary of State for Arms Control and International Security; Khalilzad, Special Assistant to the President for Near East, South West Asian, and North African Affairs; and Abrams, National Security Council and presidential adviser for the Middle East. Other ex-officials and right-wing pundits who signed the letter included former Reagan administration officials William J. Bennett, Robert Kagan, and William Kristol; Francis Fukuyama from the Bush, Sr. administration; and Woolsey, head of the CIA from 1993-1995 under Clinton.

21   Other such publications included: Daniel L. Byman and Matthew C. Waxman, Confronting Iraq: U.S. Policy and the Use of Force Singe the Gulf War (Santa Monica, CA: RAND, 2000); David Wurmser, Tyranny's Ally: America's Failure to Defeat Saddam Hussein (American Enterprise Institute, 1999); Patrick L. Clawson, ed., Iraq Strategy Review (Washington, D.C.: Washington Institute for Near East Policy, 1998); and Robert Chandler with Ronald J. Trees, Tomorrow's War, Today's Decisions: Iraqi Weapons of Mass Destruction and the Implications of WMD-Armed Adversaries for Future U.S. Military Strategy (McLean, VA: AMCODA Press, 1996)

22   "Iraq Liberation Act of 1998," October 31, 1998; Jane Perlez, "Albright Introduces a New Phrase to Promote Hussein's Ouster," *New York Times*, January 29, 1999, A3

23   Steven Lee Myers, "In Intense but Little-Noticed Fight, Allies Have Bombed Iraq All Year," *New York Times*, August 13, 1999, A1; Cody, *San Francisco Chronicle*, June 23, 2000; Graf Hans von Sponeck, "'It is an outrage that you repeat fabricated disinformation,'" *The Guardian* (UK), January 4, 2001

24   Hubbell, *Middle East Report*, Fall 1998; Myers, *New York Times*, August 13, 1999; William M. Arkin, "Will 'Shock and Awe' Be Sufficient?" *Los Angeles Times*, March 16, 2003

25   Michael Hirsh and John Barry, "A Plan for Saddam," *Newsweek*, November 16, 1998; James Risen, "Defining the Goal in Iraq," *New York Times*, December 23, 1998, A1. For the debate over U.S. military options, see, Daniel Byman, Kenneth Pollack, and Gideon Rose, "The Rollback Fantasy," *Foreign Affairs*, January/February 1999

26   Elliott and Carney, *Time*, March 23, 2003

27   Vernon Loeb, "The Trouble With Dominance," *Washington Post*, February 24, 2003; Stephen G. Brooks and William C. Wohlforth, "American Primacy in Perspective," *Foreign Affairs*, July/August 2002, 21-22

28   Patrick E. Tyler, "U.S. Strategy Plan Calls for Insuring No Rivals Develop," *New York Times*, March 8, 1992; "Excerpts From Pentagon's Plan: 'Prevent the Re-Emergence of a New Rival,'" *New York Times*, March 8, 1992; Steven R. Weisman, "Pre-emption: Idea With a Lineage Whose Time Has Come," *New York Times*, March 23, 2003

29   "Excerpts From Pentagon's Plan," *New York Times*, March 8, 1992

30   Sonni Efron and Carol J. Williams, "Plan Likely to Further Isolate U.S.," *Los Angeles Times*, September 21, 2002

31   See Efron and Williams, *Los Angeles Times*, September 21, 2002; John Lewis Gaddis, "A Grand Strategy of Transformation," *Foreign Policy*, November/December 2002; "Changes in Strategy for National Security," *New York Times*, September 20, 2002; David E. Sanger, "Bush Outlines Doctrine of Striking Foes First," *New York Times*, September 20, 2002

32   E. J. Dionne Jr., "Having Dished It Out...," *Washington Post*, August 12, 2003, A13

33   Zalmay M. Khalilzad, From Containment to Global Leadership (Santa Monica, CA: RAND, 1995), 6-11, 22; Fareed Zakaria, "Our Way," *New Yorker*, October 14-21, 2002, 74

34   For an in-depth analysis of the Clinton impeachment, see "The Truth About Right-Wing Conspiracy.... And Why Clinton and the Democrats Are No Answer," *Revolutionary Worker*, November 22, 1998 (www.rwor.org/a/v20/980-89/983/-truth.htm)

35   William Kristol and Robert Kagan, "Toward a Neo-Reaganite Foreign Policy," *Foreign Affairs*, July/August 1996

36   Institute for Advanced Strategic and Political Studies, "A Clean Break: A New Strategy for Securing the Realm," (no date). Under Bush II, Feith would become Under Secretary of Defense for Policy and Wurmser a top assistant to Under Secretary of State for Arms Control and International Security, John R. Bolton.

37   "Rebuilding America's Defenses," 2, 8, 16, 22, 51. Under Bush II, Cambone would become Undersecretary of Defense for Intelligence and Shulsky the Director of Pentagon's Office of Special Plans—which helped create the phony "intelligence" used to rationalize the 2003 war on Iraq. Kagan, Kristol and other right-wing luminaries also contributed to the study.

CHAPTER NINE
Operation Iraqi Colonization

1   Ilene R. Prusher, "In volatile Iraq, US curbs press," *Christian Science Monitor*, June 19, 2003. In mid-July, the U.S. shut down the Arabic newspaper *Al Mustaqilla* and took its office manager into custody for reportedly publishing an article stating, "death to all...who cooperate with the United States," and warning it would publish a list of those working with the Coalition Authority. Ann Scott Tyson, "Coalition curbs wild Iraqi press," *Christian Science Monitor*, July 23, 2003

2   Kenneth Pollack, "Next Stop Baghdad," *Foreign Affairs*, March/April 2002, 43

3   Bush, FDCH E-Media, May 1, 2003

4   David E. Sanger and Steven R. Weisman, "Bush's Aides Envision New Influence in Region," *New York Times*, April 10, 2003

5   James Schlesinger, "Now It's Political Shock and Awe," *Wall Street Journal*, April 17, 2003

6   "Transcript of Bush's Remarks On Start of Assault on Iraq," *Wall Street Journal*, March 19, 2003

7   Jane Perlez, "U.S. Team Arrives in Iraq to Establish Postwar Base," *New York Times*, April 9, 2003

8   Colum Lynch, "Security Council Votes to Lift Iraq Sanctions," *Washington Post*, May 22, 2003; Paul Richter and Esther Schrader, "U.S. May Seek U.N. Assistance in Volatile Iraq," *Los Angeles Times*, July 17, 2003

9   John J. Fialka, "U.S. Readies a Different Army to Search for Weapons in Iraq," *Wall Street Journal*, April 17, 2003

10   Rajiv Chandrasekaran, "Appointed Iraqi Council Assumes Limited Role," *Washington Post*, July 14, 2003, A1. The following list the Governing Council members was taken from BBC News, "Iraqi Governing Council members," July 14, 2003 (news.bbc.co.uk/go/pr/fr/-/2/hi/middle_east/3062897.stm): Samir Shakir Mahmoud, al-Sumaidy clan, writer and entreneur (Sunni); Sondul Chapouk, one of three women, an engineer and teacher (Turkmen);

Ahmed Chalabi, Iraqi National Congress, living outside Iraq for 45 years (Shia); Naseer al-Chaderchi, National Democratic Party (Sunni); Adnan Pachachi, foreign minister before Ba'ath Party took power (Sunni); Mohammed Bahr al-Ulloum, religious scholar from Najaf (Shia); Massoud Barzani, head of the Kurdistan Democratic Party (Sunni Kurd); Jalal Talabani, leader of the Patriotic Union of Kurdistan (Sunni Kurd); Abdel-Aziz al-Hakim, second highest leader of the Supreme Council for the Islamic Revolution (Shia); Ahmed al-Barak, human rights activist (Shia); Ibrahim al-Jaafari, spokesman Daawa Islamic Party, one of the oldest of the Shia Islamist movements (Shia); Raja Habib al-Khuzaai, southern tribal leader (Shia); Aquila al-Hashimi, former diplomat in Hussein regime (Shia): Younadem Kana, Assyrian Democratic Movement (Assyrian Christian); Salaheddine Bahaaeddin, General Secretary of Kurdistan Islamic Union (Sunni Kurd); Mahmoud Othman, Kurdistan Socialist Party (Sunni Kurd); Hamid Majid Mousa, Communist Party (Shia); Ghazi Mashal Ajil al-Yawer, northern tribal figure (Sunni); Ezzedine Salim, head of the Daawa Islamic Party and based in Basra (Shia); Mohsen Abdel Hamid, General Secretary of the Iraqi Islamic Party—the Iraqi branch of the Muslim Brotherhood (Sunni); Iyad Allawi, Iraqi National Accord (Shia); Wael Abdul Latif, Basra governor and judge (Shia); Mouwafak al-Rabii (Shia—British-educated doctor); Dara Noor Alzin, judge; Abdel-Karim Mahoud al-Mohammedawi, Hezbollah resistance movement, Amara (Shia).

11   Rajiv Chandrasekaran, "U.S. to Appoint Council in Iraq: Officials Decide Not to Allow Large Assembly to Pick Interim Leaders," *Washington Post*, June 2, 2003, A1

12   Rajiv Chandrasekaran, "Plan Gives Iraqi Council Larger Governing Role: Occupation Authority to Shape Membership," *Washington Post*, July 11, 2003, A1

13   Patrick E. Tyler, "New Iraqi Governing Council to Meet for First Time," *New York Times*, July 13, 2003

14   Robin Wright, "Naming of Iraq Overseer Spotlights Internal Dispute," *Los Angeles Times*, May 7, 2003

15   Karen DeYoung, "U.S. Sped Bremer to Iraq Post," *Washington Post*, May 24, 2003, A1

16   Hector Tobar, "Interim City Council to Debut in Baghdad," *Los Angeles Times*, July 7, 2003; Rajiv Chandrasekaran, "The Final Word on Iraq's Future: Bremer Consults and Cajoles, but in the End, He's the Boss," *Washington Post*, June 18, 2003, A1

17   William Booth and Rajiv Chandrasekaran, "Occupation Forces Halt Elections Throughout Iraq," *Washington Post*, June 28, 2003; Page A20; "Tiny steps in the dance," *The Economist*, July 10, 2003

18   Chandrasekaran, *Washington Post*, July 11, 2003

19   Associated Press, "New Iraqi council declares holiday," MSNBC.com, July 13, 2003; Rajiv Chandrasekaran, "U.N. Chief Backs New Iraqi Council," *Washington Post*, July 21, 2003, A1; Steven R. Hurst, "Iraq Council Fails to Choose President," *Associated Press/Washington Post*, July 19, 2003

20   Warren Vieth, "Iraqi Exiles Say They're Excluded From Rebuilding," *Los Angeles Times*, August 10, 2003

21   Michael R. Gordon, "In Bush's 'Axis of Evil,' Why Iraq Stands Out," *New York Times*, September 9, 2002; David E. Sanger and Eric Schmitt, "U.S. Has a Plan to Occupy Iraq, Officials Report," *New York Times*, October 11, 2002

22   Zalmay Khalilzad, "A Free Country Run By Free People," *Wall Street Journal*, April 17, 2003

23   Mark Fineman, Robin Wright and Doyle McManus, "Preparing for War, Stumbling to Peace," *Los Angeles Times*, July 18, 2003

24   Zalmay Khalilzad, "The Future of Iraq Policy," Remarks at The Washington Institute's 2002 Weinberg Founders Conference, October 5, 2002 (www.washingtoninstitute.org-/pubs/speakers/khalilzad100502.htm); Sanger and Schmitt, *New York Times*, October 11, 2002

25   Patrick E. Tyler, "U.S. to Form New Iraqi Army and Pay Soldiers of Old One," *New York Times*, June 23, 2003

26   John Daniszewski, "Bremer Says U.S. Role Ends After Iraq Elections," *Los Angeles Times*, July 16, 2003; Interview on NewsHour with Jim Lehrer, July 21, 2003

27   Donald H. Rumsfeld, "Core Principles for a Free Iraq," *Wall Street Journal*, May 27, 2003

28   Neela Banerjee with Douglas Jehl, "U.S. Said to Seek Help of Ex-Iraqi Spies on Iran," *New York Times*, July 22, 2003; Anthony Shadid and Daniel Williams, "U.S. Recruiting Hussein's Spies," *Washington Post*, August 24, 2003, A1; Daniel Williams, "Iraqi Council Completes Cabinet," *Washington Post*, September 1, 2003, A18

29   Amnesty International, "Press Release: Iraq: The US must ensure humane treatment and access to justice for Iraqi detainees," June 30, 2003

30   "US admits holding 10,000 Iraqi prisoners," *ABC Online*, September 17, 2003

31   Michael Slackman, "Iraqis Voice Fear of Signing Away Their Identity," *Los Angeles Times*, June 18, 2003; Nadim Ladki, "U.S. Sets Deadline for Iraqis to Hand in Weapons" (Reuters), *Washington Post*, May 24, 2003

32   Saul Hudson, "New Iraqi TV Complains of U.S. Censorship," *Reuters*, May 13, 2003; Daniel Williams, "U.S. Taps Media Chief for Iraq," *Washington Post*, August 19, 2003, A14

33   Eric Schmitt, "U.S. to Create Security Force of 7,000 Iraqis in 45 Days," *New York Times*, July 20, 2003; Thom Shanker and Eric Schmitt, "Pentagon Expects Long-Term Access to Four Key Bases in Iraq," *New York Times*, April 20, 2003

34   Associated Press, "Rumsfeld: Iraq Should Not Be Theocracy," *Guardian* (UK), April 22, 2003; Chandrasekaran, *Washington Post*, July 11, 2003

35   "Bush aides wary of autonomy for Iraq," *The International News* (Pakistan), April 18, 2003 (www.jang.com.pk); Peter S. Goodman, "Kurds' Bid for Stake in Oil Firms Rebuffed," *Washington Post*, May 14, 2003, A18; Jalal Talabani and Massoud Barzani, "What Iraq Needs Now," *New York Times*, July 9, 2003

36   Rajiv Chandrasekaran and Anthony Shadid, "Postwar Tremors Deepen Fissures in Iraqi Society," Washington Post, September 29, 2003, A1; Rajiv Chandrasekaran, "Iraq's Constitution Deadline Will Not Be Met, Iraqis Say," Washington Post, September 29, 2003

37   Rumsfeld, *Wall Street Journal*, May 27, 2003

38   Banerjee with Jehl, *New York Times*, July 22, 2003

39   Thomas Carothers, "Messy Democracy," *Washington Post*, April 8, 2003, A33; Banerjee with Jehl, *New York Times*, July 22, 2003; Amiram Cohen, "U.S. Checking Possibility of Pumping Oil from Northern Iraq to Haifa, via Jordan," *Haartez*, August 25, 2003

40   L. Paul Bremer III, "The Road Ahead in Iraq and How to Navigate It," *New York Times*, July 13, 2003; Patrick E. Tyler, "Iraqis Will Join Governing Council U.S. Is Setting Up," *New York Times*, July 8, 2003

41   Neil King Jr., "Bush Officials Devise a Broad Plan for Free-market Economy in Iraq," *Wall Street Journal*, May 1, 2003, A1

42   Rumsfeld, *Wall Street Journal*, May 27, 2003

43   L. Paul Bremer III, "Operation Iraqi Prosperity," *Wall Street Journal*, June 20, 2003

44   Edmund L. Andrews, "Overseer in Iraq Vows to Sell Off Government-Owned Companies," *New York Times*, June 23, 2003, A13; Robert Collier, "Imports inundate Iraq under new U.S. policy," *San Francisco Chronicle*, July 10, 2003; King Jr., *Wall Street Journal*, May 1, 2003

45   *Associated Press*, "Bremer: Length of U.S. Stay Up to Iraqi People," July 15, 2003

46   Warren Vieth, "U.S. to Lay Off 500,000 in Iraq," *Los Angeles Times*, June 3, 2003; Alexei Barrionuevo, "Bremer Says Iraq Will Depend On Oil to Finance New Budget," *Wall Street Journal*, July 9, 2003

47   Collier, *San Francisco Chronicle*, July 10, 2003

48   Naomi Klein, "Downsizing in Disguise," *The Nation*, June 23, 2003

49   Elizabeth Rosenberg, Adam Horowitz and Anthony Alessandrini, "Iraq Reconstruction Tracker," *Middle East Report*, Summer 2003, 28

50   Patrick E. Tyler, "Iraqis Will Join Governing Council U.S. Is Setting Up," *New York Times*, July 8, 2003

51   Mitchell Pacelle, "U.S. Banks Are Vying for Work Renewing Iraqi Finance System," *Wall Street Journal*, June 12, 2003, A1

52   Rajiv Chandrasekaran, "Economic Overhaul for Iraq," *Washington Post*, September 22, 2003, A1; Fareed Yasseen, "We Don't Want Oligarchs in Iraq," *Wall Street Journal*, September 30, 2003

53   An Iraqi Woman, "Myths, Truth And U.S. Re-Construction," Baghdad Burning Blog, www.occupationwatch.org, September 4, 2003;"Iraq rows back on reform plans," BBC News, September 24, 2003; Paul Krugman, "Who's Sordid Now?" *New York Times*, September 30, 2003

54   Klein, *The Nation*, June 23, 2003

55   David B. Ottaway and Joe Stephens, "In Bid to Shape a Postwar Iraq, U.S. Goes by the Schoolbook," *Washington Post*, April 6, 2003; Neil King Jr., "For One Small Education Company, Iraqi Schools Are a Huge Challenge," *Wall Street Journal*, April 14, 2003; David R.

Baker, "Educators Edit Lessons of Hussein from Textbooks," *San Francisco Chronicle*, August 15, 2003

56   Josh Getlin, "U.S. Nightly News Shows to Make Their Iraqi Television Debut," *Los Angeles Times*, April 15, 2003

57   "America's Television Flop in Iraq," *New York Times*, August 9, 2003

58   Reuters, "Wolfowitz Warns Iraq's Neighbors Not to Interfere," *Yahoo! News*, July 21, 2003

59   "Executive Summary," Arab Human Development Report 2002, United Nations Development Programme, Arab Fund for Economic and Social Development, United Nations Publications, New York 2002, 1-4

60   Cleveland, 525

61   Raymond Lotta, "Dissecting the Bush Doctrine: U.S. Imperialism's Crusade for One World Empire," *Revolutionary Worker*, February 16, 2003

62   Khalilzad, "The Future of Iraq Policy," October 5, 2002; Ronald D. Asmus and Kenneth M. Pollack, "The Neoliberal Take on the Middle East," *Washington Post*, July 22, 2003, A17

63   "Text of Bush's Speech Wednesday Night," *New York Times*, February 26, 2003

64   Robert S. Greenberger and Karby Leggett, "Bush Dreams of Changing Not Just Regime but Region," *Wall Street Journal*, March 21, 2003

65   Jack Shafer, "The PowerPoint That Rocked the Pentagon," Slate.com, August 7, 2002; Everest and Innes, *Z Magazine*, December 2002; Sasha Lilley, "A New Age of Empire in the Middle East, Courtesy of the US and UK," *Dissident Voice*, November 12, 2002

66   Nicholas Lemann, "After Iraq: The plan to remake the Middle East," *New Yorker*, February 17-24, 2003

67   James Woolsey, "At war for freedom," *The Observer* (UK), July 20, 2003

68   FDCH E-Media, "National Security Adviser Condolezza Rice Delivers Remarks at National Association of Black Journalists Convention," *Washington Post*, August 7, 2003

69   Institute for Advanced Strategic and Political Studies, "A Clean Break: A New Strategy for Securing the Realm"

70   David Wurmser, Tyranny's Ally: America's Failure to Defeat Saddam Hussein (Washington, D.C.: American Enterprise Institute, 1999), 78, 110; see, for instance, Reuel Marc Gerecht, "Why We Need a Democratic Iraq," *Weekly Standard*, March 24, 2003

71   Charles Glass, "Is Syria next?" *London Review of Books*, July 24, 2003

72   The Coalition was organized by, among others, American Enterprise Institute fellow Michael Ledeen. Michael Dobbs, "Pressure Builds for President to Declare Strategy on Iran," *Washington Post*, June 15, 2003, A20

73   Stephen Farrell, Robert Thomson and Danielle Haas, "Attack Iran the day Iraq war ends, demands Israel," *London Times*, November 5, 2002

74   David Stout, "Bush Again Accuses Iran and Syria of Harboring Terrorists," *New York Times*, July 21, 2003

75   Glass, *London Review of Books*, July 24, 2003

76   David E. Sanger, "Bush Warns Iran on Building Nuclear Arms," *New York Times*, June 19, 2003

77   Julian Borger, Michael White, Ewen MacAskill, Nicholas Watt, "Bush vetoes Syria war plan," *Guardian* (UK), April 15, 2003

78   Robert Fox, "Special Forces 'Prepare for Iran Attack,'" *The Evening Standard*, June 17, 2003; "Pentagon Eyes Massive Covert Attack on Iran," ABC News.com, May 29, 2003

79   Guy Dinmore, "Bush pressed to pursue 'regime change' in Iran," *Financial Times*, June 17 2003; Robin Wright and Doyle McManus, "U.S. Split Over How Hard to Push Against Iran," *Los Angeles Times*, May 30, 2003

80   Victor L. Simpson, "U.S. Official: Iraq a Lesson for Others," *Associated Press*, April 9, 2003; "Aftermath: The Bush Doctrine," *New York Times*, April 13, 2003

81   "Bush Bends," *Wall Street Journal*, April 5, 2002

82   "Text of Bush's Speech," *New York Times*, February 26, 2003

83   Joel Beinin, "Pro-Israel Hawks and the Second Gulf War," *Middle East Report Online*, April 6, 2003

84   Anatol Lieven, "The Push for War: The Threat from America," *London Review of Books*, October 3, 2002

85   "Text of Proposed 'Road Map' for Mideast Peace," *Los Angeles Times*, April 30, 2003

86   Robert G. Kaiser, "Bush and Sharon Nearly Identical On Mideast Policy," *Washington Post*, February 9, 2003, A1; *Washington Post*, October 17, 2002, cited in Marc Lynch, "Using and

Abusing the UN, Redux," *Middle East Report* 225, Winter 2002

87   Khalidi, *The Nation*, June 9, 2003

88   Josh Meyer, "Report Is Wary of Saudi Actions," *Los Angeles Times*, July 25, 2003

89   Nathan Guttman, "Background: AIPAC and the Iraqi opposition," *Ha'aretz*, April 7, 2003; Don Van Natta Jr. and Timothy L. O'Brien, "Saudis Promising Action on Terror," *New York Times*, September 14, 2003

90   David Johnston, "Saudi Ambassador Assails U.S. Report on Terror Attacks," *New York Times*, July 25, 2003

91   Baker, 71; Lilley, *Dissident Voice*, November 12, 2002

92   "Rumsfeld: No Discussions of U.S. Bases in Iraq," *Reuters*, April 21, 2003; Esther Schrader, "Retreat Is Part of U.S. Strategy," *Los Angeles Times*, April 20, 2003

93   Eric Schmitt, "U.S. to Withdraw All Combat Forces From Saudi Arabia," *New York Times*, April 29, 2003

94   Secretary Colin L. Powell, "The U.S.-Middle East Partnership Initiative: Building Hope for the Years Ahead," speech at the Heritage Foundation, December 12, 2002 (www.state.gov/secretary/rm//2002/15920.htm)

95   Robin Wright, "U.S. to Press a Four-Step Plan for Transforming the Mideast," *Los Angeles Times*, April 20, 2003

96   "Review & Outlook: Out of Arabia," *Wall Street Journal*, May 2, 2003

CHAPTER TEN
OIL, POWER AND EMPIRE

1   "Rumsfeld: It Would Be A Short War," *CBS News*, November 15, 2002

2   Office of the Press Secretary, "Press Briefing by Ari Fleischer," October 9, 2002 (www.whitehouse.gov/news/releases/2002); Sanger and Schmitt, *New York Times*, October 11, 2002

3   Woodward, Bush at War, 194; Frum, 282

4   For overall analysis of post-Soviet global economics, see Raymond Lotta, "Imperialist Globalization and the Fight for a Different Future," *Revolutionary Worker*, November 23-December 7, 1997 (www.rwor.org); Revolutionary Communist Party, USA, "Notes on Political Economy: Our Analysis of the 1980s, Issues of Methodology, and The Current World Situation" (Chicago: RCP Publications, 2000)

5   Khalilzad, From Containment to Global Leadership, 7-8

6   Jeffrey E. Garten, "A Worldwide Economic Stimulus Plan," *New York Times*, January 11, 2003

7   Al Hunt, "Our Way or the Highway," *Wall Street Journal*, February 27, 2003

8   David Leonhardt, "Jump in Oil Prices Puts New Strains on Shaky Economy," *New York Times*, March 2, 2003

9   Marilyn Rabler, "U.S. Energy Demand to Rebound in 2003 as Production Slides," *Oil & Gas Journal*, January 27, 2003, 67; Neela Banerjee, "Oil's Pressure Points," *New York Times*, April 13, 2003

10   Neela Banerjee, "Fears, Again, of Oil Supplies at Risk," *New York Times*, October 14, 2001; Daniel Fisher, "The Prize," *Forbes*, November 12, 2001

11   Alan Freeman, "The Economic Background and Consequences of the Gulf War," in The Gulf War and the New World Order, 161

12   Pollack, *Foreign Affairs*, July/August 2003, 2-4

13   Banerjee, *New York Times*, April 13, 2003

14   "Strategic Energy Policy Challenges For The 21st Century," Report of an Independent Task Force, Sponsored by the James A Baker Institute for Public Policy of Rice University and the Council on Foreign Relations (hereafter "Baker"), 19 (www.bakerinstitute.org/Pubs/studies/bipp_study_15/bippstudy15.html). The Baker Institute is headed by James A. Baker, III, Secretary of State under President George H.W. Bush.

15   Baker, 4

16   Frank Viviano, "Energy future rides on U.S. war: Conflict centered in world's oil patch," *San Francisco Chronicle*, September 26, 2001

17   Zbigniew Brzezinski, The Grand Chessboard: American Primacy and its Geostrategic Imperatives (New York: Basic Books, 1997), 52-53; Benjamin R. Barber, Jihad vs. McWorld (New York: Ballentine Books, 1995, 1996) 45, 47

18   Vernon Loeb, "New Bases Reflect Shift in Military: Smaller Facilities Sought for Quick

Strikes," *Washington Post*, June 9, 2003, A1

19 Baker, 16

20 Baker, 31

21 Neela Banerjee, "For Exxon Mobil, Size Is a Strength and a Weakness," *New York Times*, March 4, 2003

22 Neela Banerjee, "U.S. Oil Still Pours From a Mideast Barrel," *New York Times*, October 22, 2002, C1

23 "Reliable, Affordable, and Environmentally Sound Energy for America's Future: Report of the National Energy Policy Development Group" (National Energy Policy), May 2001 (www.whitehouse.gov/energy), ix

24 Danny Hakim, "Fuel Economy Hit 22-Year Low," *New York Times*, May 3, 2003

25 National Energy Policy, x; EIA, "Early Release of Annual Energy Outlook 2003" (www.eia.doe.gov/oiaf/aeo/), November 20, 2002

26 EIA, November 20, 2002; Simon Romero, "Short Supply of Natural Gas Is Raising Economic Worries," *New York Times*, June 17, 2003

27 National Energy Policy, xv

28 National Security Strategy, 19-20

29 Yergin, *Washington Post*, December 8, 2002

30 Timothy L. O'Brien, "Just What Does America Want to Do With Iraq's Oil?" *New York Times*, June 8, 2003

31 Pollack, *Foreign Affairs*, July/August 2003, 4

32 EIA, "Persian Gulf Oil and Gas Exports Fact Sheet," February 2001; Neela Banerjee, "U.S. Oil Still Pours From a Mideast Barrel," *New York Times*, October 22, 2002, C1

33 Baker, 75

34 Judicial Watch, "Cheney Energy Task Force Documents Feature Map of Iraqi Oilfields," July 17, 2003 (www.JudicialWatch.org)

35 "World Industry News: US sets meeting on exploiting Iraqi oil after Hussein," *Oil and Gas International*, October 30, 2002

36 Peter Beaumont and Faisal Islam, "Carve-Up of Oil Riches Begins," *The Observer* (UK), November 3, 2002

37 Thaddeus Herrick, "U.S. Oil Wants To Work in Iraq, Concerns Discuss How to Raise Output After a Possible War," *Wall Street Journal*, January 17, 2003

38 Felicity Barringer and Neela Banerjee, "Who'll Control Iraq's Oil? Tangled Questions Abound," *New York Times*, April 9, 2003

39 Barrionuevo, *Wall Street Journal*, July 9, 2003

40 Jeff Gerth, "U.S. Is Banking on Iraq Oil to Finance Reconstruction," *New York Times*, April 10, 2003. Bob Lawson, "NELPI's Langenkamp: What happens with Iraq's oil?" *Oil & Gas Journal*, October 28, 2002, 39

41 Baker, 17, 42

42 Neil King Jr., John J. Fialka and Bhushan Bahree, "In Oil Fallout From Iraq War, Iran Could Gain, Saudis Lose," *Wall Street Journal*, September 19, 2002

43 Baker, 23

44 EIA, "Country Analysis Briefs: Iraq," October 2002 (www.eia.doe.gov/-cabs/iraq.html); Tom Cholmondeley, "The Mother of All Legal Rows," *Guardian* (UK), November 22, 2002

45 O'Brien, *New York Times*, June 8, 2003

46 EIA, "Iraq," October 2002

47 Neela Banerjee, "Iraq Is a Strategic Issue for Oil Giants, Too," *New York Times*, February 22, 2003

48 EIA, "Iraq," October 2002; Lawson, *Oil & Gas Journal*, October 28, 2002, 38; Beaumont and Islam, *The Observer*, November 3, 2002

49 Daniel Yergin, "Gulf oil: How important is it, anyway?" *San Francisco Chronicle*, April 13, 2003

50 Banerjee, *New York Times*, February 22, 2003. See also, Chip Cummins, "Kuwait Feels Pressure to Give Companies Access to Oil Fields: Emirate Could Lose Out to Northern Neighbor If Iraq Is Opened Up to Foreign Investment," *Wall Street Journal*, February 27, 2003

51 Dreyfuss, *Mother Jones*, March/April 2003

52 Chip Cummins, Susan Warren and Bhushan Bahree, "Inside Iraq's Giant Oil Industry, A Maze of Management Tensions," *Wall Street Journal*, April 30, 2003, A1; Paul Krugman, "The Martial Plan," *New York Times*, February 21, 2003

53   Robert Collier, "Foreigners, exiles appointed to help run Iraqi oil ministry," *San Francisco Chronicle*, May 4, 2003; Peter Behr, "Iraqi Exiles Say Nation Must Double Oil Output: U.S.-Backed Study to Urge Openness to Foreign Firms," *Washington Post*, May 6, 2003, E1. The Pentagon named Thamir Ghadhban, a former Iraqi oil official, interim chief executive.

54   Behr, *Washington Post*, May 6, 2003; Keith Johnson, "Iraqi Officials Plan Program For Oil-Exploration Projects," *Wall Street Journal*, July 2, 2003

55   Warren Vieth, "U.S. to Let Iraq Manage Its Oil," *Los Angeles Times*, August 18, 2003

56   Rajiv Chandrasekaran, "Bremer Broaches Plans For Iraq's Oil Revenue Money Should Be 'Shared by All Iraqis,' He Says," *Washington Post*, June 23, 2003, A17

57   Lisa Girion, "Immunity for Iraqi Oil Dealings Raises Alarm," *Los Angeles Times*, August 7, 2003; Ruth Rosen, "As ordered, it's about oil," *San Francisco Chronicle*, August 8, 2003

58   Verne Kopytoff, "Which way to go? Iraq must choose a course for expanding its oil production: national or multinational," *San Francisco Chronicle*, May 25, 2003

59   Warren Vieth, "Postwar Iraq Would Need More Than Oil Funds, Experts Say," *Los Angeles Times*, April 3, 2003; Kopytoff, *San Francisco Chronicle*, May 25, 2003

60   Warren Vieth, "U.S. May Tap Oil for Iraqi Loans," *Los Angeles Times*, July 11, 2003; Janet Hook, "Republicans Want Iraq to Share Costs of Rebuilding," *Los Angeles Times*, September 19, 2003

61   Rosenberg, Horowitz and Alessandrini, *Middle East Report*, Summer 2003, 28

62   Robert Collier, "Saudis worry Iraq war could create oil rival," *San Francisco Chronicle*, February 16, 2003

63   David Ignatius, "Mending the Marriage With Saudi Arabia," *Washington Post*, July 29, 2003, A17; Stanley Reed, "Suddenly, the Saudis Want to Close Some Deals," *BusinessWeek* online, August 4, 2003

64   Leon Fuerth, "An Air of Empire," *Washington Post*, March 20, 2003, A29

65   James Surowiecki, "The Oil Weapon," *New Yorker*, February 10, 2003, 38; Bhushan Bahree and Thaddeus Herrick, "Saudis Plan to Ensure Oil Supply During War," *Wall Street Journal*, March 11, 2003; Peter S. Goodman, "U.S. Adviser Says Iraq May Break With OPEC: Carroll Hints Nation Could Void Contracts," *Washington Post*, May 17, 2003, E1; Oliver Morgan, "Iraq 'may have to quit OPEC,'" *The Observer*, April 27, 2003

66   National Security Strategy, 19

67   Cholmondeley, *Guardian* (UK) November 22, 2002

68   Rumsfeld, *Wall Street Journal*, May 27, 2003

69   Rosenberg, Horowitz and Alessandrini, *Middle East Report*, Summer 2003, 28

70   "Shadow Over the Oil Fields," *Los Angeles Times*, May 8, 2003; Elizabeth Becker, "Details Given on Contract Halliburton Was Awarded," *New York Times*, April 11, 2003; Karen DeYoung and Jackie Spinner, "Contract for Rebuilding of Iraq Awarded to Bechtel," *Washington Post*, April 18, 2003; David R. Baker, "Bechtel will employ 25,000 Iraqi workers," *San Francisco Chronicle*, July 23, 2003

71   Dan Morgan and David B. Ottaway, "In Iraqi War Scenario, Oil Is Key Issue," *Washington Post*, September 15, 2002, A1

72   EIA, "Iraq," October 2002; Cholmondeley, *Guardian* (UK) November 22, 2002; Gerth, *New York Times*, April 10, 2003

73   Warren Vieth and Elizabeth Douglass, "Gauging Promise of Iraqi Oil," *Los Angeles Times*, March 12, 2003

74   William Boston, "Europe shifts to post-war focus," *Christian Science Monitor*, March 20, 2003

75   Sabrina Tavernise, "Oil Prize Past and Present," *New York Times*, October 17, 2002; Jeanne Whalen, "Russia Tries to Salvage Iraqi Oil Pacts," *Wall Street Journal*, November 11, 2002; Vieth and Douglass, *Los Angeles Times*, March 12, 2003

76   Judicial Watch, July 17, 2003

77   Morgan and Ottaway, *Washington Post*, September 15, 2002; Sandy Tolan, "Beyond Regime Change," *Los Angeles Times*, December 1, 2002; John W. Schoen, "Iraqi Oil, American Bonanza?" MSNBC, November 11, 2002

78   Michael Dobbs and Susan B. Glasser, "Russian Oil Fears Play in Iraq Policy: Moscow Neutrality During War Sought," *Washington Post*, November 22, 2002, A1

79   Andrew Buncombe, "Russia Fears US Oil Companies Will Take Over World's Second-Biggest Reserves," *Independent* (UK), September 26, 2002

80   Keith Johnson, "Iraqi Officials Plan Program For Oil-Exploration Projects," *Wall Street Journal*,

July 2, 2003; Goodman, *Washington Post*, May 17, 2003

81   Tavernise, *New York Times*, October 17, 2002; "The Politics Of Iraqi Oil," *CBS Evening News*, February 20, 2003; Warren Vieth, "Oil Is Factor in Iraq War Equation," *Los Angeles Times*, October 16, 2002; Paul Richter, "U.S. Seeks to Calm Russian Fears on War, Oil Supplies," *Los Angeles Times*, January 10, 2003; Dobbs and Glasser, *Washington Post*, November 22, 2002

82   See, for example, "Russian Oil Power," *New York Times*, November 30, 2001

83   Alan Cullision and Jeanne Whalen, "War Shows Fragility Of U.S.-Russia Links," *Wall Street Journal*, April 1, 2003

84   Rosenberg, Horowitz and Alessandrini, *Middle East Report*, Summer 2003, 28; Jackie Spinner, "'Open' Contest Pledge For Iraq Subcontracts," *Washington Post*, April 18, 2003

85   Lee Gaillard, "Forget oil: Water is the crisis," *San Francisco Chronicle*, March 14, 2003

86   See also, Alwyn Rouyer, "Basic Needs vs. Swimming Pools: Water Inequality and the Palestinian-Israeli Conflict," *Middle East Report* 227, Summer 2003, 2-7

87   Stephen C. Pelletiere, "A War Crime or an Act of War?" *New York Times*, January 31, 2003

88   Brzezinski, The Grand Chessboard, 30-31

89   Thomas L. Friedman, "Our War With France," *New York Times*, September 18, 2003

90   National Security Strategy, 13; Tyler, *New York Times*, March 8, 1992

91   Khalilzad, From Containment to Global Leadership, 30, 7; CITE PROJECT; see, for example, "Open Letter to the President: A letter to George W. Bush about our nation's defense budget," *Weekly Standard*, January 23, 2003

92   Dreyfuss, *Mother Jones*, March/April 2003, 44, 46, Keith Bradsher, "Lacking Reserves, China Watches Flow of Oil," *New York Times*, March 22, 2003; Keith Bradsher, "China Buys Another Piece of Big Caspian Sea Oil Field," *New York Times*, March 12, 2003

93   Michael T. Klare, "New Global Hot Spot: Iraq War Will Redraw Strategic Map," *Pacific News Service*, March 14, 2003; see also, Stephen Blank, "Scramble for Central Asian Bases," *Asia Times Online*, April 9, 2003

94   See, "Afghanistan: The Oil Behind the War," *Revolutionary Worker*, November 4, 2001 (www.rwor.org)

95   Yergin, *San Francisco Chronicle*, April 13, 2003

96   Greg Jaffe, "In a Massive Shift, U.S. Plans To Reduce Troops in Germany," *Wall Street Journal*, June 10, 2003

97   Shanker and Schmitt, *New York Times*, April 20, 2003

98   Jaffe, "Pentagon Prepares to Scatter Soldiers in Remote Corners," *Wall Street Journal*, May 27, 2003; Vernon Loeb, "New Bases Reflect Shift in Military: Smaller Facilities Sought for Quick Strikes," *Washington Post*, June 9, 2003, A1; Shanker and Schmitt, *New York Times*, April 20, 2003; Donald H. Rumsfeld, "Why Defense Must Change," *Washington Post*, July 18, 2003, A19

99   Thom Shanker, "Officials Debate Whether to Seek a Bigger Military," *New York Times*, July 21, 2003

100   Greg Jaffe, "In a Massive Shift, U.S. Plans To Reduce Troops in Germany," *Wall Street Journal*, June 10, 2003; National Defense University and Institute for National Strategic Studies, Strategic Assessment 1999, 39

101   George Monbiot, "Why Blair is an appeaser," *Guardian* (UK), November 5, 2002

102   Paul Krugman, "You Say Tomato," *New York Times*, July 29, 2003

CHAPTER ELEVEN
THE BITTER FRUITS OF UNJUST WAR

1   Robert Fisk, "Anti-Colonial War," Znet (www.zmag.org), April 17, 2003

2   Bryan Bender, "CIA warned administration of postwar guerrilla peril," *Boston Globe*, August 10, 2003

3   Peter Slevin and Dana Priest, "Wolfowitz Concedes Iraq Errors," *Washington Post*, July 24, 2003, A1

4   David Stout, "Bush's Plans on Iraq Draw Criticism From Senators," *New York Times*, September 9, 2003

5   Tabassum Zakaria (Reuters), "Franks: 10-25 Attacks a Day on U.S. Troops in Iraq," *Washington Post*, July 10, 2003

6   Paul Richter and Esther Schrader, "U.S. May Seek U.N. Assistance in Volatile Iraq," *Los Angeles Times*, July 17, 2003; Thom Shanker, "Rumsfeld Doubles Estimate for Cost of Troops in

Iraq," *New York Times,* July 10, 2003

7   John Daniszewski and David Zucchino, "U.S. Toll in Iraq Higher Than in '91 Gulf War," *Los Angeles Times,* July 19, 2003; Associated Press, "U.S. Troops Killed in Postwar Iraq Exceeds Combat Deaths, *New York Times,* August 26, 2003; Vernon Leob, "Number of Wounded in Action on Rise," *Washington Post,* September 2, 2003, A1; Jason Burke and Paul Harris, "America's hidden battlefield toll," *The Observer* (UK), September 14, 2003

8   Greg Miller, "U.S. Has 'Closing Window' to Stabilize Iraq, Advisors' Report Says," *Los Angeles Times,* July 18, 2003

9   "Facing Reality in Iraq," *Washington Post,* July 8, 2003, A16

10   Tom Newton Dunn, "Ready to Explode: Hope for Future Fades in Iraq," *Mirror* (UK), July 3, 2003; David J. Andrus, "Aftermath of War: The next West Bank?" *San Francisco Chronicle,* July 17, 2003

11   "Text: Bush Defends Iraq Plan," *Washington Post,* August 26, 2003

12   Mark Forbes, "'Dumb' bombs used to topple Saddam," *The Age* (Australia), June 3 2003; Crawley, *San Diego Union-Tribune,* August 5, 2003; Jamie Wilson, "Mass graves to reveal Iraq war toll," *Guardian* (UK), August 19, 2003

13   N Laura King, "Baghdad's Death Toll Assessed," *Los Angeles Times,* May 18, 2003; Niko Price, "AP Tallies 3,240 Civilian Deaths in Iraq," *Associated Press,* June 11, 2003

14   Peter Ford, "Surveys pointing to high civilian death toll in Iraq," *Christian Science Monitor,* May 22, 2003

15   "Jodie Evans: Witnessing the U.S. Occupation of Iraq," *Revolutionary Worker,* August 17, 2003

16   Carol Rosenberg and Matt Schofield, "In bombed neighborhoods, everyone 'wants to kill Americans,'" *Miami Herald,* April 15, 2003

17   Thomas L. Friedman, "Starting From Scratch," *New York Times,* August 27, 2003

18   The looting may have been less spontaneous than it appeared, and no doubt further details about the war and U.S. actions and tactics in the course of it will emerge over time, as was the case after the 1991 Persian Gulf War.

19   Scott Wilson, "Bremer Adopts Firmer Tone For U.S. Occupation of Iraq," *Washington Post,* May 26, 2003, A13

20   Peter Slevin and Dana Priest, "Wolfowitz Concedes Iraq Errors," *Washington Post,* July 24, 2003, A1

21   Mark Fineman, Robin Wright and Doyle McManus, "Preparing for War, Stumbling to Peace U.S. is paying the price for missteps made on Iraq," *Los Angeles Times,* July 18, 2003

22   Edmund L. Andrews, "Once Hailed, Soldiers in Iraq Now Feel Blame at Each Step," *New York Times,* June 29, 2003

23   Mike Allen, "Bush Cites 'Progress' Being Made in Iraq," *Washington Post,* August 9, 2003, A9

24   Michelle Goldberg, "From heroes to targets," *Salon,* July 18, 2003

25   "Child sickness 'soars' in Iraq," *BBC News,* June 8, 2003

26   Rajiv Chandrasekaran, "Troubles Temper Triumphs in Iraq: Problems Persist in Reconstruction Despite Gains," *Washington Post,* August 18, 2003, A1

27   Amy Waldman, "For a Town Council in Iraq, Many Queries, Few Answers," *New York Times,* July 9, 2003

28   Robert Collier, "Iraqis growing impatient with U.S.: Lagging transition to independence stirs anger, frustration," *San Francisco Chronicle,* June 27, 2003

29   ABC Nightly News, July 18, 2003

30   Vivienne Walt, "Civilian deaths stoke Iraqis' resentment: Bitterness may widen resistance," *San Francisco Chronicle,* August 4, 2003

31   Helen Thomas, "Who's counting the dead in Iraq?" *Miami Herald,* September 5, 2003

32   Ahmed Hashim, "Iraqi Insurgency Is No Monolith," *Pacific News Service* (www.pacificnews.org), July 29, 2003

33   Robert Collier, "Shiite support for U.S. occupation of Iraq appears tenuous," *San Francisco Chronicle,* July 16, 2003

34   Pamela Constable, "Cleric Calls for 'Islamic Army': U.S. Authority Challenged by Shiite Leader," *Washington Post,* July 19, 2003, A12

35   Douglas Jehl and David E. Sanger, "Iraqis' Bitterness Is Called Bigger Threat Than Terror," *New York Times,* September 17, 2003

36   "Bush: 'We Will Do What Is Necessary,'" *Washington Post,* September 8, 2003, A16

37   Bush, *Washington Post,* September 8, 2003; "Rumsfeld Sees No Link Between Iraq, 9/11,"

Associated Press, September 16, 20003; Milbank, *Washington Post*, September 18, 2003

38 "Statement be David Kay on the Interim Progress Report on the Activities of the Iraq Survey Group (ISG) Before the House Permanent Select Committee on Intelligence, the House Committee on Appropriations, Subcommittee on Defense, and the Senate Select Committee on Intelligence" (Kay Report), October 2, 2003; James Risen and Judith Miller, "No Illicit Arms Found in Iraq, U.S. Inspector Tells Congress," *New York Times*, October 2, 2003; Dana Priest and Walter Pincus, "Search in Iraq Finds No Banned Weapons," *Washington Post*, October 3, 2003, A1; "The Elusive Iraqi Weapons," *New York Times*, October 4, 2003

39 Joseph Cirincione, "The Kay Contradiction," Carnegie Analysis: Carnegie Endowment for International Peace, October 3, 2003

40 "No Al-Qaeda link found to Iraq's WMD program: Kay," Yahoo! News, October 5, 2003

41 Tom Raum, "Weapons Report Adds to Bush Setbacks," *Associated Press*, October 3, 2003; David Stout with Terence Neilan, "Bush Cites Parts of Arms Report to Justify U.S. Action in Iraq," *New York Times*, October 3, 2003; Bob Drogin, "Botched Iraqi Arms Deal Is Detailed," *Los Angeles Time*, October 4, 2003

42 Julian Borger, "Revelation casts doubt on Iraq find," *Guardian* (UK), October 7, 2003

43 Borger, *Guardian* (UK), October 7, 2003; Risen and Miller, *New York Times*, October 3, 2003; Priest and Pincus, *Washington Post*, October 3, 2003

44 Drogin, *Los Angeles Times*, October 4, 2003

45 Maureen Dowd, "Is Condi Gaslighting Rummy?" *New York Times*, October 9, 2003

46 Slobodan Lekic, "Aide: Saddam purposely misled on arms," *Associated Press*, August 2, 2003; Gordon, *New York Times*, August 1, 2003, Interview with Scott Ritter, KPFA *Flashpoints*, October 2, 2003; Drogin, *Los Angeles Times*, October 4, 2003

47 Scott Ritter, "A Weapons Cache We'll Never See," *New York Times*, August 25, 2003

48 Raum, *Associated Press*, October 3, 2003; "President Bush's Speech on the Use of Force," *New York Times*, October 8, 2002

49 Tim Predmore, "Paths of Glory Lead to a Soldier's Doubt," *Los Angeles Times*, September 17, 2003

50 Ann Scott Tyson, "Troop morale in Iraq hits 'rock bottom,'" *Christian Science Monitor*, July 7, 2003

51 Jeffrey Gettleman, "Anger Rises for Families of Troops in Iraq," *New York Times*, July 4, 2003; Susannah Rosenblatt, "Families Join In Push for Troops' Return," *Los Angeles Times*, August 14, 2003

52 Thom Shanker, "Rumsfeld Doubles Estimate for Cost of Troops in Iraq," *New York Times*, July 10, 2003; Associated Press, "Postwar Iraq likely to cost more than war," *USA Today*, August 11, 2003

53 Richard W. Stevenson, "78% of Bush's Postwar Spending Plan Is for Military," *New York Times*, September 9, 2003

54 Rory McCarthy, "Foreign firms to bid in huge Iraqi sale," *Guardian* (UK), September 22, 2003

55 Edmund L. Andrews, "Budget Office Says 10 Years of Deficits Could Total $5 Trillion," *New York Times*, August 26, 2003

56 See Scott Wilson, "Bremer Adopts Firmer Tone For U.S. Occupation of Iraq," *Washington Post*, May 26, 2003, A13

57 Jason Leopold, "Dems scrap Plans To Look Into Claims White House Manipulated Intel On Iraqi Threat," Antiwar.com, September 13, 2003

58 Robert Baer, "We Pulled Out of Beirut. We Can't Abandon Iraq," *Washington Post*, August 24, 2003, B1

59 William Kristol and Robert Kagan, "Do What It Takes in Iraq," *Weekly Standard*, September 1, 2003

60 Avakian, *Revolutionary Worker*, March 17, 2002

61 Ahmed Rashid, "Ground Zeroes," *Outlook India*, September 7, 2002

62 Amy Waldman, "Violence Spreads Through Afghanistan, Killing Dozens," *New York Times*, August 13, 2003; Robyn Dixon, "Afghans on Edge of Chaos," *Los Angeles Times*, August 4, 2003

63 Alan Cowell, "Blair, Increasingly Alone, Clings to Stance, *New York Times*, February 17, 2003

64 "Bush: 'We Will Do What Is Necessary,'" *Washington Post*, September 8, 2003, A16

65 Jeff Johnson, "Ashcroft Promises 'Fair Trials' for Terrorists," CNSNews.com, December 6, 2001

66 "A Statement of Conscience: Not In Our Name" (www.nion.us)

APPENDIX
"A BODYGUARD OF LIES"

1   U.S. Department of Defense News Briefing, Presenter: Secretary of Defense Donald Rumsfeld, September 25, 2001

2   John Cochran, "Reason for War?: White House Officials Say Privately the Sept. 11 Attacks Changed Everything," ABC News, April 25, 2003

3   Romesh Ratnesar, "Iraq & al-Qaeda: Is There a Link?" CNN.com, August 26, 2002

4   Dana Milbank and Mike Allen, "U.S. Shifts Rhetoric on Its Goals in Iraq: New Emphasis: Middle East Stability," Washington Post, August 1, 2003

5   Robert Burns, "Deputy Defense Secretary Says Weapons Issue is Now Secondary in Iraq," Associated Press, July 21, 2003

6   Eric Schmitt, "Rumsfeld Says U.S. Has 'Bulletproof' Evidence of Iraq's Links to Al Qaeda," New York Times, September 27, 2002

7   Hugh Pope and Neil King, Jr., "U.S. Officials Discount Any Role by Iraq in Terrorist Attacks," Wall Street Journal, September 19, 2001

8   Bonner, New York Times, October 11, 2001

9   William Rivers Pitt with Scott Ritter, War on Iraq: What the Team Bush Doesn't Want You to Know (New York: Context Books, 2002), 49

10   Alan Simpson and Dr. Glen Rangwala, "Labour Against the War's Counter Dossier," September 17, 2002

11   James Risen and David Johnston, "Split at CIA & FBI on Iraqi Ties to Al Qaeda," New York Times, February 2, 2003

12   "Leaked Report Rejects Iraqi al Qaeda Link," BBC, February 5, 2003

13   Peter S. Canellos and Bryan Bender, "Questions Grow Over Iraq Links to Qaeda," Boston Globe, August 3, 2003

14   U.S. Department of Defense, "News Transcript: Deputy Secretary Wolfowitz Interview with The Laura Ingraham Show," August 1, 2003

15   Leopold, Antiwar.com, August 7, 2003. See also Matt Kelley, "Ex-Officials Dispute Iraq Tie to al-Qaida," Newsday, July 13, 2003

16   Sciolino and Tyler, New York Times, October 12, 2001

17   "Atta met twice with Iraqi intelligence," CNN, October 11, 2001

18   James Risen, "Prague Discounts an Iraqi Meeting," New York Times, October 21, 2002

19   "Full Text of Colin Powell's Speech," Guardian (UK), February 5, 2003

20   "U.S. troops search for chemical, biological weapons, Iraqi camp alleged to be source of ricin found in London," CNN.com, March 31, 2003

21   "Iraq War: Unanswered Questions," BBC News, April 17, 2003

22   Walter Pincus, "Alleged Al Qaeda Ties Questioned: Experts Scrutinize Details of Accusations Against Iraqi Government," Washington Post, February 7, 2003, A21

23   "Elusive Qaeda Connections," New York Times, February 14, 2003

24   Dana Milbank, "For Bush, Facts Are Malleable," Washington Post, October 22, 2002

25   Cam Simpson and Stevenson Swanson, "Story at odds with Powell's UN case," Chicago Tribune, February 11, 2003

26   Pincus, Washington Post, February 7, 2003

27   William O Beeman, "Colin Powell's Al Qaeda-Iraq Connection Tenuous At Best," Pacific News Service, February 6, 2003

28   Pincus, Washington Post, February 7, 2003

29   Pincus, Washington Post, February 7, 2003

30   "Ansar al-Islam leader threatens to document his links to US," Agence France-Presse, February 1, 2003

31   Johathan S. Landay, "Militant group allows tour of site labeled al-Qaida poison lab," Knight Ridder Newspapers, February 8, 2003

32   Jeffrey Fleishman, "An inside look at Ansar al-Islam," Los Angeles Times, April 27, 2003

33   Carla Anne Robbins, Marilyn Chase and Hugh Pope, "Spreading Fear: Sophistication of Anthrax Raises New Questions About Germs' Source"; R. James Woolsey, "The Iraq Connection"; "The Anthrax War" (editorial), all from Wall Street Journal, October 18, 2001

34   Michael Massin, "Seven Days in October," The Nation, November 12, 2001

35   For discussion of anthrax mailings, see: Sabin Russell, "Silica grains detected in anthrax letter are tiny clues," San Francisco Chronicle, October 30, 2001; Mark Schoofs, Gary Fields, and Jerry

Markhon, "Killer's Trail: Linguistic, Other Analyses Hint at Unabomber Type, Implying Long Search," *Wall Street Journal*, November 12, 2001; "Anthrax Attacks Likely Came from U.S. Government Laboratory Expert," *Dow Jones Newswires*, November 21, 2001; William J. Broad, "The Spores: Terror Anthrax Linked to Type Made by U.S.," *New York Times*, December 3, 2001; William J. Broad with David Johnston, "U.S. Inquiry, Tried, but Failed, to Link Iraq to Anthrax Attack," *New York Times*, December 22, 2001

36   Rick Weiss and Dan Eggen, "Lethal formula in anthrax mail points to labs of three countries," *International Herald Tribune*, October 26, 2001

37   White House, "President Bush, Prime Minister Blair Discuss Keeping the Peace," September 7, 2002 (www.whitehouse.gov/news/releases/2002/09/20020907-2.html)

38   Joseph Curl, "Agency disavows report on Iraq arms," *Washington Times*, September 27, 2002

39   IAEA Press Release, "IAEA Submits Six-Monthly Progress Report on its Verification Activities in Iraq," October 7, 1998

40   Priest and Pincus, *Washington Post*, October 3, 2003

41   Kay Report, October 2, 2003

42   "President Bush Outlines Iraqi Threat," speech delivered at Cincinnati, Ohio, October 7, 2002, (www.whitehouse.gov/news/releases/2002/10/20021007-8.html)

43   Sheelagh Doyle, "Fake document and exaggerations," *Independent* (UK), April 20, 2003

44   Mark Phillips, "Inspectors Call U.S. Tips 'Garbage,'" CBS News, February 20, 2003

45   "President Bush Outlines Iraqi Threat," October 7, 2002

46   Norman Dombey, "What Has He Got?" *London Review of Books*, October 17, 2002

47   Powell, *Guardian* (UK), February 5, 2003

48   Michael R. Gordon, "Agency Challenges Evidence Against Iraq Cited by Bush," *New York Times*, January 10, 2003

49   Dan Stober, "Nuclear inspectors reportedly angry," *San Jose Mercury News*, March 18, 2003

50   Phillips, CBS News, February 20, 2003

51   "Iraq's Weapons of Mass Destruction: The Assessment of the British Government," September 2002

52   "Bush's State of the Union speech," CNN.com, January 29, 2003

53   "Hans Blix: War Planned 'Long in Advance,'" News24.com, April 9, 2003. It is unclear who concocted the documents. New Zealand's *Herald* cites the *New Yorker's* Seymour Hersh, who speculates that British intelligence may have forged the documents to help Bush quell congressional opposition to the war: "In September, late September, before the Senate voted on a resolution authorizing the war, [the documents were displayed] at a series of top-secret briefings in a secure room over in the Congress." Roger Franklin, "Layers of deceit that built a case for war," *New Zealand Herald*, April 29, 2003

54   Bob Drogin and Greg Miller, "Top Inspectors Criticize CIA Data on Iraqi Sites," *Los Angeles Times*, March 8, 2003

55   Dana Milbank and Walter Pincus, "Bush Aides Disclose Warnings from the CIA," *Washington Post*, July 23, 2003

56   Robert Novak, "Mission to Niger," Townhall.com, July 14, 2003

57   Andrea Mitchell, "White House Striking Back?" NBC News, July 21, 2003

58   Mitchell, NBC News, July 21, 2003

59   David Harrison, "America Silences Niger Leaders in Iraq Nuclear Row," *Telegraph* (UK), August 3, 2003

60   Walter Pincus, "Bush Team Kept Airing Iraqi Allegation," *Washington Post*, August 8, 2003

61   Elisabeth Bumiller and James Dao, "Cheney Says Peril of a Nuclear Iraq Justifies an Attack," *New York Times*, August 27, 2002

62   "Statement to the United Nations Security Council by IAEA Director General Dr. Mohamed ElBaradei," March 7, 2003

63   "Bush's State of the Union speech," CNN.com, January 29, 2003

64   Alexander Higgins, "U.S. Accuses Rogue States of Developing Bio Weapons," *Associated Press*, November 19, 2001

65   Pitt and Ritter, 28-29, 33-37

66   Walter Pincus and Dana Priest, "Interim U.S. report on arms indefinite," *San Francisco Chronicle*, September 25, 2003

67   David E. Kaplan and Mark Mazetti. "Second Intelligence Report: 'No Reliable Information' Iraqis Stockpiling Chemical Weapons," *U.S. News and World Report*, June 13, 2003

68   Pauline Jelinek, "More than half of Iraq's top 'weapons sites' searched with no result," *Associated Press*, April 23, 2003

69   For example, see Bernard Weinraub, "Chemical Agents; American Soldiers Find Drums Possibly Storing Chemical Agents," *New York Times*, April 8, 2003

70   "Suspected Bioweapons Lab Found," MSNBC, May 11, 2003

71   Douglas Jehl, "Iraqi Trailers Said to Make Hydrogen, Not Biological Arms," *New York Times*, August 9, 2003

72   Louis Meixler, "U.S. troops said to have found evidence of sarin, blister agents north of Baghdad," *Associated Press*, April 27, 2003

73   Guy Taylor, "Final tests find no nerve agents in Iraqi chemical," *Washington Times*, May 2, 2003

74   Kay Report, October 2, 2003

75   CIA, "Iraq's Weapons of Mass Destruction Programs," October 2002, 13, 16 (www.cia.gov/cia/publications/iraqwmd/IraqOct_2002.htm)

76   Gordon, 48

77   CIA, October 2002, 16

78   John F. Burns, "Biological arms site reinspected: UN weapons checkers find little despite suspicions of renewed activity," *San Francisco Chronicle*, November 29, 2002

79   Powell, *Guardian* (UK), February 5, 2003

80   Judith Miller and Julia Preston, "Blix Says He Saw Nothing to Prompt a War," *New York Times*, January 31, 2003

81   "Hans Blix's briefing to the Security Council," *Guardian* (UK), February 14, 2003

82   Powell, *Guardian* (UK), February 5, 2003

83   Raymond Whitaker, "Revealed: How the road to war was paved with lies," *Independent* (UK), April 27, 2003

84   Miller and Preston, *New York Times*, January 31, 2003

85   Jo Warrick, "Despite Defectors' Accounts, Evidence Remains Anecdotal," *Washington Post*, February 6, 2003

86   Kay Report, October 2, 2003

87   Powell, *Guardian* (UK), February 5, 2003

88   Andrea Mitchell, "Where is the feared Iraqi arsenal," NBC News, May 1, 2003

89   "Iraq War: Unanswered questions," BBC News, April 17, 2003

90   Kay Report, October 2, 2003

91   Powell, *Guardian* (UK), February 5, 2003

92   Whitaker, *Independent*, April 27, 2003

93   Powell, *Guardian* (UK), February 5, 2003

94   Dafna Linzer, "Iraqis won't admit to banned weapons," *Associated Press*, May 3, 2003

95   Doyle McManus and Bob Drogan, "U.S. to step up its search for banned arms," *Los Angeles Times*, April 20, 2003

96   Powell, *Guardian* (UK), February 5, 2003

97   Gary Jones and Alexandra Williams, "Real Authors of Iraq Dossier Blast Blair," *Daily Mirror* (UK), February 8, 2003

98   "Timeline: The Gilligan Affair," *Guardian* (UK), July 18, 2003

99   Ian Urbina, "Broadcast Ruse," *Village Voice*, November 13-19, 2002

100   Powell, *Guardian* (UK), February 5, 2003

101   James Cusick and Felicity Arbuthnot, "America Tore Out 8000 Pages of Iraq Dossier," *Sunday Herald* (Scotland), December 22, 2002

102   Sgt. 1st Class Doug Sample, "Saddam Has 'Weeks, Not Months,' Says Security Adviser Rice," *American Forces Press Service*, February 16, 2003

103   Dr. Mohamed El Baradei, "Mission Possible: Nuclear Weapons Inspections in Iraq," *Wall Street Journal*, March 7, 2003

104   Blix, *Guardian* (UK), February 14, 2003

Index

A

Abdallah, Shadi, 307
Abraham Lincoln, 220
Abrams, Elliott, 212
activated charcoal, ban on, 183
Afghanistan
  at risk of anarchy, 296
  foreign military forces in, 272
  movement of Soviet troops in, 92
  Soviet invasion of, 87, 88
  strategic importance of, 271
  U.S. bases in, 274
Aflaq, Michel, and founding of Ba'ath Party, 68
Africa, oil potential of, 261
agriculture, changes to under U.S. occupation, 232
Ahtisaari, Martti, consequences of sanctions in Iraq, 171
air power
  as a policing method, 53
  See also Operation Desert Fox
al Beiruti, Dr. Ayman, 177–78
al Qaeda
  alleged links to Hussein regime, 7, 14–15, 287, 302–305
  goal of, 9
  links to Saudi Arabia, 15
  support of Iraq for, 194
Al Quds-Jerusalem, 177
al Saedi, Dr. Salem Mohammed, 153
Al-anfal campaign, 112, 113–14
al-Attar, Layla, 194
al-Bakr, Ahmad Hasan (General), 72
al-Hakim, Abdul Aziz, 287
al-Hakim, Ayatollah Mohammed Bakr, 280
al-Intifada in Iraq, 63
al-Islam, Ansar, Iraqi connection with, 307, 308–309
al-Majid, Ali Hassan, 112
al-Sabah clan, 45
al-Sadr, Moqtada, 287
Al-Shiraa, and arms-for-hostages expose, 110–11
al-wathbga, 63
Al-Zarqawi, Abu Musab, Iran connection with, 306–308
Albright, Madeleine Korbel
  and child mortality rate in Iraq, 185
  and lifting of Iraqi sanctions, 195–96
Algiers Agreement of 1975, 82
Ali, Rashid, 50
ALS (amyotropic lateral sclerosis).
  See uranium, depleted
aluminum tubes, 313
American Enterprise Institute, 5

American Gulf War Veterans Association, 156
American military presence, in post-war Iraq, 170
American occupation of Iraq, protests against, 221
American Type Culture Collection, 310
Amiriya shelter, bombing of, 148
Amiriyah Serum and Vaccine Institution, 319
Amnesty International, report of conditions of Iraqis in detention, 227
Amstutz, Daniel G., 232
Anderson, Jack, 92, 93
Anglo-Persian Oil, 39
  See also British Petroleum
anthrax
  and Tom Daschle, 310
  link to Iraq, 12
  shipments to Iraq, 102
anthrax letters, 310
anti-ballistic missile treaty, Bush administration rejection of, 24
anti-colonialism
  and effect on oil availability, 254
  support of United States for, 59
anti-Hussein uprisings
  American call for, 158–60
  lack of American support for, 160–63
anti-personnel cluster bombs. See cluster bombs
anti-personnel weapons
  use of by Britain, 53
  use of by United States, 54
Arab Independence Party, revolt against British, 41–42
Arab League, Iraq participation in, 208
Arab nationalism, 33, 41–42
Arab/Israeli peace talks, 164
arc of instability, 253
Arif, Abdul Salam, 72
Arkin, William M., 143, 213
Armitage, Richard, 212
Arms Control Research Center (ARC), environmental contamination from Gulf War of 1991, 156
arms inspections, as tool for maintaining sanctions, 187
arms intelligence, distortion of, 109
arms monitoring, creation of permanent system in Iraq, 189
arms sales
  from France to Iraq, 111
  from Soviet Union to Iraq, 111
  from U.S. to Iraq, 108, 115–16
  to Lebanon from Iraq, 123
  U.S. cessation of, 123
arms-for-hostages plan, 108

arms-for-influence plan, 108–109
Army Tactical Missile System (ATACM), 54
Article 54 of Geneva Convention, violation by
   United States, 146
Ashcroft, John D., definition of "terrorism," 298
Asia-Pacific region, oil potential of, 261
assassination of Saddam Hussein's sons, 286
assertive multi-lateralism, Clinton's support for,
   214
Associated Press, body count reporting, 281
Ataturk, 47
atrocities
   "Highway of Death" massacre, 152–53
   1st Infantry Division (Mechanized) assault,
      153–54
   firing on disarmed Iraqi prisoners, 154
   lack of reporting of in post war Iraq, 173
   use of human shields in Kuwait, 138
   See also biological weapons; chemical weapons
Atta, Mohammed, and Iraqi intelligence,
   305–306
attacks on Iraq, initial discussions about, 10–11
Austria, as source of chemical weapons, 102
Avakian, Bob, 19–20, 295
"axis of evil," 13, 217
   See also Iran; Iraq
Azerbaijan, U.S. bases in, 274
Aziz, Tariq, 105

B

Ba'ath government. See Ba'ath regime
Ba'ath officials, removal from power, 225
Ba'ath party
   as "apostate regime," 304
   historical background of, 68–69
   relations with Shi'a, 94–95
   suppression of party loyalists, 227
   taking over of assets of, 223
Ba'ath regime, 2, 81, 282–84
   anti-communism of, 70
   atrocities of, 70–71
   population support for, 278
   technical infrastructure, 189
babies in incubators hoax, 139
Babylon, 38
Baer, Robert, 294–95
Baghdad Centre (BOMVIC), 329
Baghdad Pact, 64
Baghdad, anti-American protests in, 221
Baker Institute for Public Policy, 252
Baker Report, 252–54, 260
Baker, James
   assessment of Clinton administration, 215
   call for cease-fire in Iraq, 150

meetings with Tariq Aziz, 137, 143
   threatened use of nuclear weapons, 143
Balfour Declaration, 42
Balfour, Lord, 41, 51
banned weapons, search for after Gulf War of
   2003, 222
Barber, Benjamin R., 253
Barzana, Mustafa, attempted assassination of, 81
Barzinji, Sheikh Mahmoud, 48
Basra, Iraq
   consequences of fall of, 100
   inclusion in Kuwait, 45
Bechtel National, Inc.
   contract to restore Iraqi infrastructure, 267
   subcontracting opportunities with, 271
Beinin, Joel, 242
bentonite, 310
Bessmertnykh, A., call for cease-fire in Iraq, 150
bin Laden, Osama
   and American's weakness, 220
   and creation of Iraqi Islamic state, 209
   links to Saudi Arabia, 244
   opinion of Saddam Hussein, 303
biological weapons, 102–104, 317–20, 322–23
biological weapons convention, 24
black boxes, as listening devices, 201
Blair, John, 51, 53
Blair, Tony, 315
Blix, Hans
   comments on Kay Report, 290
   inspections in Iraq, 322, 328–29
   uranium purchase from Niger, 314
   weapons of mass destruction, 19, 193
Blum, William, 65, 102
body counts
   in Gulf War of 1991, 154–55
   lack of in Gulf War of 2003, 299
Bolton, John, 212, 241
bombings of Iraq, 43, 280
   See also bunker buster bombs; cluster bombs
BOMVIC, 329
Bookman, Jay, 28
Boot, Max, 27
Bosnia, U.S. intervention in, 214
botulinum toxin, 317
botulism
   evidence of, 200
   shipments to Iraq, 102
Bradlee, Ben, description of Nixon White House,
   14
Bremer, L. Paul, 218, 222, 225, 226, 230, 233,
   293
   final authority over Governing Council (Iraq),
      223

implementation of laws for foreign investment in Iraq, 231
Brezhnev, Leonid Ilyich, 92
Bring Them Home Now campaign, 292
Britain
  anti-personnel weapons development, 53
  division of Persian oil with the United States, 59
  invasion of Jordan, 66
  role in Iranian nationalism, 60
  role in post rebellion Iraq, 44–45
  withdrawal from the Persian Gulf, 79
British Broadcasting Company, and Blair Dossier, 326
British intelligence services
  links between Iraq and al Qaeda, 304
  use of articles from "Jane's Intelligence Review," 325
British Petroleum, share of Iraqi oil, 52
Brzezinski, Zbigniew, 88-92, 252, 272
Bulgaria, U.S. bases in, 274
bunker buster bombs, 54
Burleigh, Peter, and Operation Desert Fox, 202
Bush administration
  arrogance of, 12
  classification of Kay Report, 289–90
  cover-up of war casualties, 146–47
  manipulation of war fervor, 135–37, 138–39
  rejection of Iraq peace offer, 150–51
  rejection of treaty commitments, 24
  reorganization of Iraqi oil industry, 258–59
  response to Saddam Hussein, 4
  subordination of status of foreign countries, 25
  use of language by, 288
Bush I. See Bush, George Herbert Walker
Bush II. See Bush, George Walker
Bush, George Herbert Walker
  as head of CIA, 84
  assassination attempt against, 194
  dismissal of Iraqi peace offers, 150–51
  encourages Iraqi uprising, 159
  need for ground war, 149–50
  new world order, 135, 163
  not another Vietnam, 142–43, 150
  on invasion of Kuwait by Iraq, 119
  post-Soviet global strategy, 134–35
  reaction to Iraqi withdrawal refusal, 137
  says no "green light" to Iraq, 123–24
  says U.S. does not seek conflict, 130, 144
  U.S. Iraq policy goals of, 133–34
Bush, George Walker
  allegations of Iraqi terrorism, 194
  allegations of Iraqi weapons of mass destruction, 15, 186, 291, 311, 312, 314, 317

cost of Iraq War, 293
  description of war on terror, 2, 8, 10, 248
  foreign policy of, 6
  Iraq as part of war on terror, 3, 27, 277, 293, 294
  on September 11, 2001, 1
  preparation for war on Iraq, 10–11, 13, 220–21, 242
  use of the word "terror," 288
  victory declaration by, 220
  See also Bush administration
Butler, Richard, site visits in Iraq, 201–202
Byrd, Robert, 106

C

Cairo Conference, 43
Campagnie Francaise des Petroles (CFP), 52
Canada, oil potential of, 261
capitalism in Iraq, 231–32
capitalism, and global energy sources, 249
capitalist globalization.
  See globalization
Cardoen, and cluster bombs, 102
Carroll, Philip, 263, 270
Carter Doctrine, 90–91
Carter, Jimmy, 87, 89, 90, 91, 97, 98
Casey, William, and anti-personnel cluster bombs, 102
Caspian Basin, as source of energy, 255
Caspian Sea energy fields, control of, 273–74
casualties, of Gulf ground war, 152–53
Center for Strategic and International Studies, 270
Central Intelligence Agency.
  See CIA
Chalabi, Ahmad, 226, 269
Chemical Ali. See al-Majid, Ali Hassan
chemical and biological weapons
  overview, 317–23
  U.S fear of in Iraq, 162
chemical weapons
  use in Iraq in 1920, 42
  use of Iran-Iraq war, 101–104
  See also biological weapons
Chemical Weapons Convention, and UN resolutions regarding Iraq, 188
Cheney, Dick, 8, 130
  "Defense Planning Guidance" document, 4, 214
  and attack on Iraq, 174–75
  and Office of Special Plans, 305
  assessment of Iraq threat, 133
  connection to Haliburton, 267
  defense of Kuwait, 126

Energy Task Force documents, 269
firing of Gen. Dugan, 130
Iraq as a festering problem, 213
media coverage of 1991 Gulf War, 153
on nuclear weapons threat, 291, 316
on U.S. position in the Middle East, 7
opposition to Clinton foreign policy, 214–15
support for Iraq war, 13, 278
trip to Saudi Arabia to secure troop deployment, 136
China
    as regional power, 273
    commercial interests in Iraq, 206
    dependence on foreign oil, 273
Chirac, Jacques President, 25
cholera, increase in post Gulf War of 1991, 173
Chomsky, Noam, 57
Christian Peacemaker observer delegation, 279
Christian Science Monitor, body count, 281
Chubin, Shahram, 95
Churchill, Winston, support for chemical weapons, 42
CIA
    and intelligence on Iraq's WMD, 314, 319, 320
    and Iraqi National Congress, 169–70, 197–98
    attempted assassination of Qasim, Abdul Karim, 68
    role in anti-colonial movements, 59
    role in establishment of Ba'ath government, 70–71
ciproflozacin, ban on, 183
Cirincione, Joseph, 288–89
civilian casualties, 281–82
civilian deaths, in Iraq-Iran war, 103–104
Clark, Ramsey, 126
Clayton, Gilbert, 40
Clean Break: A New Strategy for Securing the Realm, 216, 239
Cleland, Max (Senator), 15
Cleveland, William, 49, 73, 235–36
Clinton administration
    claims of Iraqi terrorism by, 194
    impeachment and global strategy, 216
    response to Saddam Hussein, 4
Clinton, President Bill, 31, 202–203
cluster bombs
    Cardoen, 102
    role in civilian deaths, 281
    use of during Gulf War of 1991, 158
Coalition for Democracy in Iran, 240
Coalition Provisional Authority, as mandate to administer Iraq, 221–23
Code Pink, 282
Cohen, Richard, 310

Collier, Robert, 232, 286–87
colonialism, in Iraq, 43, 221
Colombia, as source of energy, 255
compliance creep, as factor in sanctions against Iraq, 196
Control of Oil, 51
Core Principles for a Free Iraq, 226, 230
corporate globalization.
    See globalization
corporations, support for non-conventional weapons programs, 102–103
councils, local, prevention of formation of in Iraq, 223
covert counter-insurgency operations, 10
Cox, Sir Percy, 45
CPA.
    See Coalition Provisional Authority
cruise missile, as instrument of assassination, 200
Curzon, Lord, 40, 52
cyanide, use against Kurds, 112
cyclosarin, evidence of, 319

D

D'Arcy, William, 39
Daniel, Leon, 153–54
Daponte, Beth Osborne, estimation of body counts, 155
Daschle, Senator Tom, 30
    and anthrax letters, 310
debt forgiveness, in exchange for support of Gulf War, 141
Defense Advanced Research Projects Agency (DARPA), 115
Defense Intelligence Agency (DIA), 5, 317–18
Defense Planning Guidance, 4, 214, 272–73
Defense Policy Board, support for Iraq war, 12
Department of Homeland Security, 26
Desert Fox.
    See Operation Desert Fox
Desert Storm War.
    See Gulf War of 1991
Diamond, Jared, 37
diarrhea, increase in post Gulf War of 1991, 173
disarmament, 19
disease, in post war Iraq, 284
Djibouti, U.S. bases in, 274
Dobriansky, Paula, 212
doctrine of preemption, domestic version of, 26
double-speak, 23
Dowd, Maureen, 290
doxycycline, ban on, 183
Dreyfuss, Robert, 78, 262–63
dual containment policy, 167–68
Due, Torben, 181

E

E. coli bacillus, shipments to Iraq, 102
east Asia, as source of energy, 255
eavesdropping equipment, use during Iraq inspections missions, 199–200
Egypt
 and United Arab Republic, 63
 anti-colonial movements in, 59
 as source of chemical weapons, 102
 as U.S. ally, 28
 Islamist revolt in, 209
 nationalist movements in, 63
 resumption of ties to Iraq, 105
Egyptians, expulsions from Iraq, 163
Eisenhower Doctrine, 65
El Baradei, IAEA Director General Dr. Mohamed, 314, 316, 327–28
empire, as subtext for ongoing war, 2, 27–30
empires, rise and fall of, 31
energy gap, 255
energy security, as major U.S. goal, 255
energy sources, concentration in unstable areas, 252–53
energy supremacy, global struggle for, 256
Energy Task Force, 269
environment
 administration censorship of reports of, 156
 destruction of during Gulf War of 1991, 155
Eurasia, strategic importance of, 271
Europe, dependence on Persian Gulf oil, 256–57
Euros as petrodollars, 207
Evans, Jodie, 282
Executive Order 13303, 264–65
Exxon, 52
ExxonMobil, problems with "flat" production, 254

F

F-18 Super Hornet, 54
Fallujah II facility, 320
families, impact of UN sanctions on, 184–85
Farouk King, 1952 coup against, 59
Farouk-Sluglett, Marion, 44, 62
February revolution (Iran), 87
Feis, Herbert, 56
Feith, Douglas J., 5, 216, 239
Fertile Crescent, 37
Feurth, Leon, 266
Fisk, Robert, 278
Flour Daniel, 263
Foreign Suitors for Iraqi Oilfield Contracts document, 269
Forrestal, James, 57
Fourth Geneva Convention of 1949, violation by

Bush administration, 152
fourth world war.
 See war on terror
France
 and easing of sanctions, 206
 and UN Resolution 1441, 270
 commercial interests in Iraq, 206
 links to post Gulf War Iraq, 194
 oil contracts with Hussein's Iraq, 268–69
 relations with Iraq Ba'ath government, 77
Franks, Tommy, 279, 299
Free Officers group (Iraq), 64
free press, suppression of in post war Iraq, 227–28
Freeman, Alan, 251
Frelick, Bill, 164
Friedman, Thomas, 32, 272, 283
From Containment to Global Leadership, 5
Frum, David, 12, 248–49
fuel economy, 254
full-motion flight simulators ban, 183
Fuller, Graham, 106–107
Future of Iraq oil working group, 263
Future of Iraq project, 225
FutureMAP, creation of, 115

G

Galloway, George, 237, 246
Gang of Eight, 130
Garner, Retired General Jay, 223, 283
Garten, Jeffrey, 250
Gates, Robert H., 172
Gause, Professor F. Gregory, 190
genocide.
 See smart sanctions
gentamicin, ban on, 183
Georgia, 274
Germany
 as source of chemical weapons, 102
 manufacturing projects with Iraq, 77
Ghorbanifar, Manucher, Pentagon meetings with, 115
Gilligan, Andrew, 304
Glaspie, April, meeting with Saddam Hussein, 123–27
global capitalism and oil, 32–33, 58
 See also capitalism
global dominance, importance of Middle East to, 32, 235–39
global energy sources, and capitalism, 249
Global Hawk (unmanned spy plane), 54
global military build-ups, 295
global policy of the United States, after September 11, 2001, 7–8, 19–21
globalization

acceleration of, 2
corporate, 26
and effect on Iraqi people, 232
popular opposition to capitalist, 215
using military to advance, 25–26
Golan Heights, Syria and occupation of, 239
Gordon, Professor Joy, 172
Gore, Al, 213
Governing Council
creation and constitution of, 222–24, 229
makeup of, 228
protests against, 224
gravity bombs, inaccuracy of, 147
Greater Kurdistan.
See Kurds
Greenpeace
assessment of U.S. military strategy, 142
assessment of U.S. military strategy in 1991
Gulf War, 144
estimate of Iraqi military casualties in 1991
Gulf War, 152, 155
Guantánamo, treatment of prisoners in, 324
Gulboukian, C. S., 52
Gulf War of 1991, 28–29, 118
American body count, 155
coalition and tensions within, 141
costs and pledges from other countries, 140
destruction of non-military targets, 147–48
effects of, 177–78, 184–85
firing of oil wells, 156
ground war, 151
Iraqi body count, 154–55
Iraqi opposition to, 36
lack of peace treaty to end, 158
massacres, 153–54
new censorship during, 152–53
Persian Gulf anger over, 208–209
use of depleted uranium munitions in, 54
use of media in, 146–47
Gulf War of 2003, 118
cultural destruction during, 36–37
Iraqi opposition to, 36
See also specific topics about
Gulf War Syndrome, 157–58

H

Haass, Richard, 161
Hague Convention, violation by Bush adminis-
tration, 152
Haiti, U.S. intervention in, 214
Halabja, attack on, 112–13
Haliburton, no-bid contract in Iraq, 267
Halifax, Lord, 59
Halliday, Denis, 180, 183–85

Hamid, Ameed, Dr., 166
Hammurabi, 38
Hamza, Khidhir, 312
Harem, Ali, 285
Harriman, Averell, 68
Hashim, Ahmed, 286
Hassan, Ali al-Majid.
See al-Majid, Ali Hassan
Havel, Vaclav, 306
hawk central.
See Pentagon
Hellfire (missile), 54
Hersh, Seymour
exposure of post-1991 Gulf War massacres, 154
exposure of weapons inspections use for spying,
201
Nixon-Kissinger agreement with Shah, 80
repudiation of assassination plot, 194
Hezbollah, 239–40
Highway of Death, cover-up, 152–53
Hijazi, Farouk, 305
Hiro, Dilip, 88
Hoar, Army General Joseph P., 246
Homeland Security Act of November 2002, and
DARPA scandal, 115
hostage crisis.
See Seizure of U.S. Embassy (Iran)
humanitarian aid, minimization of approved
amount to Iraq, 182–83
Hungary, U.S. bases in, 274
Hussain, King (Jordan), 71
Hussein, Abdullah, monarchy of, 44
Hussein, Faisal Abdullah, monarchy of, 43–44
Hussein, Saddam
and Ba'ath party, 69–70
and fate of Iraq, 119
and Iraq's profile, 200
assassination attempt against, 2
connection to September 11, 2001, 288
coup attempts against, 197–203
and expansion of social welfare, 77, 128
impersonations of, 326
justification for invasion of Kuwait, 127
meeting with Ambassador April Glaspie,
123–27
plans to remove, 5, 6, 212
rise of, 72–73
U.S. support for, 100–101
Hussein, Sherif of Mecca, 40, 43, 44
Hussein-Glaspie meeting transcript, 123–26
hydraulic lifts, ban on, 183

I

IAEA, 311, 313, 316, 319

and Iraqi nuclear weapons development, 191, 311, 312, 316
ibn Saud, 44
Ignatieff, Michael, 30
imperialism.
    See United States, imperialism of
import duties in Iraq, revocation of, 223
independent Arab state, British promise of, 40
India, as source of chemical weapons, 102
Indyk, Martin, 168
infant mortality rate, under sanctions in Iraq, 184
infrastructure destruction, as deliberate strategy, 145–46, 174–75
inspectors, Iraqi refusal to allow, 203–204
Instant Thunder bombing assault, 143–45
intelligence information, use of by United States, 108–109, 136
International Atomic Energy Agency.
    See IAEA
International Criminal Court, Bush rejection of, 24
international law, revisions to, 2
International Red Cross, denunciation of sanctions against Iraq, 141
international sanctions, usefulness to United States, 140–41
invasion of Kuwait, use of human shields in, 138
Iran
    and possible Soviet invasion of, 92
    as a target for the 21st century, 28, 217
    effects of U.S. attack on, 271
    embassy rescue mission in, 91–92
    invasion of Iraq, 100
    link to Nicaraguan Contras, 111
    poverty in, 60
    seizure of U.S. embassy, 87, 88
    suppression of Iranian nationalism, 60
    suppression of Kurds by, 113
Iran-Contra affair, 111, 115
Iran-Iraq War
    as impetus for invasion of Kuwait, 119–21
    costs of, 99
Iraq
    administration case against, 14–15
    administration view of, 17
    anti-government demonstrations in, 63
    as a target for the 21st century, 217
    assassination of King and Crown Prince, 64
    border dispute with Kuwait, 46
    British support of monarchy in, 49–50
    commercial interest in, 206
    compliance with UN inspections, 195
    concentration of wealth in, 62
    consequences of failure in, 197

continued efforts for negotiated settlement with U.S., 137
creation of, 43
decline of veterinary diagnostic and control infrastructure, 17
demand for independence for, 41
demographics of, 49
destruction of cultural treasures, 36–37
destruction of offensive capability of, 149–50
development of "supergun," 122
diplomatic relations with U.S., 105–106
disappearance of middle class in, 175–76
disarmament program of, 169
distribution of power in under Ba'ath, 73
economic sanctions against, 169
formal independence, 50
goals of invasion of Kuwait, 131
government of in post Gulf War of 2003, 222–24
government suppression of self-determination, 61–62
"green lights" from U.S., 96-97, 123–27
historical overview, 39–45
illiteracy in, 62
increase in regional profile, 120
invasion of, 1
invasion of Iran, 96–100
links to al Qaeda, 7, 302–309
links to France and Russia, 194
misinformation circulated about, 12
nationalist movements in, 63–64
occupation of, 2
oil potential of, 261
oil production restrictions, 62
oil reserves, 29
oil-for-food program in, 169
pacification campaigns, 83
poverty in, 61
pre-war offers to withdraw from Kuwait, 136
reasons for U.S. war on, 29–30
relations with Israel, 121–23
relations with U.S., 95–97
resumption of ties to Egypt, 105
strategic importance of, 271
U.S. protection of Petroleum and Interior Ministries, 36
use of anti-personnel weapons in, 53
use of helicopter-launched missiles, 54
use of napalm in, 54
use of unmanned spy planes in, 54
used as test for new weapons, 54
See also al Qaeda; anthrax letters; chemical and biological weapons; Mesopotamia; nuclear weapons; refugees; scud missiles; weapons

inspections; weapons of mass destruction
Iraq (map), vi
Iraq Body Count web site, 281, 299
Iraq for the Iraqis, 44
Iraq hawks, 90
Iraq invasion, pre-September 11th plans for, 6
Iraq Liberation Act of 1998, passage of, 212
Iraq oil production, 179–80
Iraq oil sector
  prohibition on repair of, 179
  reshaping of, 258
Iraq Petroleum Company (IPC), 45
  as "spoils of war," 263, 267
  division of, 52
  nationalization of, 75–76
Iraq Survey Group, 192–93, 222, 311, 319
Iraq uranium purchase from Niger, 313–15
Iraq wars
  consequences of, 280–84
  early plans for, 11
  lack of formal decision making about, 13–14
  military planning for, 17–18
  protests against, 297–98
Iraq water resources, 271
Iraq's Nuclear, Biological, and Chemical Weapon
  and Missile Program: Progress, Prospects, and
  Potential Vulnerabilities, 318
Iraq-Kuwait war, U.S. support for, 123–24
Iraqi armed forces, downsizing of, 225
Iraqi children, psychological traumas and, 148–49
Iraqi Communist Party (ICP), 69
Iraqi deaths, tabulation of, 285
Iraqi economy, privatization of, 233–34
Iraqi education system, changes to, 234–35
Iraqi intelligence services, reconstitution of, 226
Iraqi National Accord (INA)
  and Governing Council (Iraq), 223
  CIA support for, 199
Iraqi National Congress (INC), 270
  and Governing Council (Iraq), 223
  and weapons of mass destruction information,
    324
  uprising against Ba'ath regime, 197–98
Iraqi National Monitoring Directorate, 290–91
Iraqi oil, as "spoils of war," 267
Iraqi post war militia, creation of, 228
Iraqi radio and television, suppression of in post
  war Iraq, 227–28
Iraqi reconstruction, American and British block
  of, 181–83
Iraqi resistance to occupation, 284–85, 286–87
Iraqi troops, casualties, 281
Iraqi water system, effects of destruction of,
  172–75

Iraqi, biological warfare program, 102
Islamic movements, rise of, 33
Islamic Mujahideen, support by U.S. of, 89–90
Islamic world, reformation of, 237–38
Israel
  creation of, 41, 60–61
  expansion of, 121–22
  response to Gulf War of 1991, 209–10
  settlements, 164, 209
  withdrawal from West Bank and Gaza, 136
Israeli colonialism, Palestinian resistance to, 33
Italy, as source of chemical weapons, 102

J

Japan
  dependence on Persian Gulf oil, 256–57
  manufacturing projects with Iraq, 77
Jane's Intelligence Review, 325
Jihad of 1920, 42
Johnson, Chalmers A., 158
Jordan
  and Iraqi oil, 208
  and Palestinian uprising, 28, 122
  invaded by Britain, 66
  Judicial Watch, access to Energy Task Force
    documents, 258
  June 1967 "Six-Day War," rise of Arab nation-
    alism due to, 74

K

Kagan, Robert, 5, 24–25, 216, 295
Kay Report, 288–89, 311, 319, 323
Kay, David, 222, 311
Kellogg Brown & Root.
  See Haliburton
Kelly, Dr. David, suicide of, 326
Kelly, John, on border disputes, 126
Kennan, George, 30–31, 57
Kenya, U.S. bases in, 274
Khalilzad, Zalmay, 4, 212, 215–16, 225, 250, 273
Khomeini, Ayatollah
  and February revolution, 87
  and overthrow of Ba'ath Party, 94
  death of, 106
  U.S. policy toward, 101, 106–10
  See also biological weapons; chemical weapons
Kingdom of Saudi Arabia, support of British colo-
  nization for, 44
Kirkuk, discovery of oil at, 45
Kissinger, Henry, 24, 29, 58, 74, 77–78,79–84
  See also Pike Commission
Klare, Michael, 132–33, 273
Klein, Naomi, 232, 234
Komal Islami group, 309

Kosovo, U.S. intervention in, 214
Krekar, Mullah.
  See al-Islam, Ansar
Kristol, William, 5, 216, 295
Krugman, Paul, 234, 263
Kurdish Democratic Party (KDP), 198
Kurdish insurgency, 68, 80–84, 112
Kurdish language, 47
Kurdish resistance, destruction of, 112–13
Kurdish state, British prevention of, 50
Kurdistan Democratic Party, and Governing
  Council (Iraq), 223
Kurds
  "safe haven" within Iraq, 164
  discrimination and oppression of, 80–81
  exodus of, 160–61
  forced resettlement of, 112
  gas massacres of, 111–14
  historical background of, 46–48
  Kurdish revolt of 1925, 48
  refugees, 83
  right to self-determination, 48–49
  status of in post war Iraq, 228–29
  suppression of, 113
  U.S. use of, against Iraq, 79–84
Kuwait
  and Iraqi debt, 120
  border dispute with Iraq, 46
  dependence on foreign protection, 121, 140
  economic decline of, 210
  historical background of, 45–46
  invasion of by Iraq, 118
  oil production of, 120
  recognition of independence by Iraq, 72
  relations with Iraq, 120–21
  restoration of Sabah family, 163
Kuwaiti tankers, reregistration of, 111
kwashiorkor, as an effect of diarrhea, 173
Kyoto agreement, Bush administration rejection
  of, 24
Kyrgyzstan, 274

L

Lake, Anthony, 198
land mines, use of during Gulf War of 1991, 158
Latif, Beshar, 284
Lausanne Treaty, 48
Law for Autonomy in the Area of Kurdistan, 81
Lawrence of Arabia (T.E. Lawrence), 40, 42
Layne, Christopher, 9
Lebanon, 28, 63, 65
Ledeen, Michael Arthur, 27
Lemann, Nicholas, 9, 237–38
Libby, Lewis, 4

liberation as neo-colonialism, 221
Lieberman, Joseph (Senator), 310
Lieven, Anatol, 242–43
Lilley, Sasha, 237
Lloyd, Selwyn, 66
looting, 283
  See also specific institutions
Lotta, Raymond, 58, 236
Lou Gehrig's disease, linked to depleted uranium,
  157–58
LukOil, 269

M

Majid, Hussein Kamel, defection of, 190
Mali, U.S. bases in, 274
malnutrition, in post war Iraq, 177–78
massacres.
  See atrocities; biological weapons; chemical
    weapons
Maude, Sir Stanley, 40
McCaffrey, Barry R., exoneration of, 154
McCain, Senator John, 310
McChrystal, General Stanley, 323
McMahon, Sir Henry, 40
Media
  coverage of sanctions, 173
  coverage of post-war destruction, 282–83
  protest of 1991 Gulf War military censorship,
    153
  role in popularizing Iraq war, 12, 13
Mesopotamia, 36–39
  See also Iraq
meteorological equipment, ban on, 183
Mexico, oil potential of, 261
Middle East
  as key to American imperium, 216
  as source of energy, 32, 255
  demonization of, 298
  nationalist movements in, 63–64
  reshaping, 5
  social reordering of, 219
  spheres of influence in, 51
  strategic objectives for, 238–39
  U.S. restructuring of, 28–29
Middle East (map), v
military bases, in post war Iraq, 228
military build-up in Persian Gulf, 130
military buildup by U.S., 21–22
military casualties, 279
Military Families Speak Out web site, 292
military supremacy, use of, 26–27
Ministry of Religious Endowment (Iraq), looting
  of, 36
Mobil, 52

mobile biological weapons laboratories, 318
Mohammed Baqir al-Sadr, assassination of, 94
monetary policy, in post war Iraq, 233
Morris, Roger, 66–67
Morse, Edward L., energy equivalent of nuclear
    weapons, 132
Mossadegh, Mohammad, coup against, 60
Mosul, anti-American protests in, 221
Mueller, John and Carl, 185
Mukhabarat
    usefulness of in post Gulf War Iraq, 226
    See also National Security Bureau
multi-lateralism, 24
Multi-Launch Rocket System (MLRS), 54
munitions
    use of depleted uranium in, 54
    See also Gulf War of 1991; Gulf War of 2003
Murdoch, Rupert, 5
mustard gas, use against Kurds, 112

N

Najaf, anti-American protests in, 221
Nagy, Professor Thomas, 174
Nasser, Abdel Gamel, 57, 59, 63
nation-building, 283
National Association of Black Journalists, 238
National Library and Archives (Iraq), looting of,
    36
National Military Strategic Plan for the War on
    Terrorism, 21
National Museum (Iraq), sacking of, 36
National Security Bureau, 73
National Security Directive 26, 114, 122
National Security Directive 45, 131
National Security Directive 54, 131
National Security Strategy (NSS)
    implementation, 26–27
    U.S. global strategy outlined by, 20–21, 23–24,
        250
national sovereignty, 23–24
National Strategy to Combat Weapons of Mass
    Destruction, 22–23
Navigating through Turbulence: America and the
    Middle East in a New Century, 239
neo-conservatives (neocons), 5
neo-Reaganites, 5
nerve gas
    shipments to Iraq, 102
    use against Kurds, 112
Netanyahu, Benjamin, 5
Netherlands, as source of chemical weapons, 102
New American Century, 29–30
new world order, 4, 135
New York Times, on sanctions, 171–72, 184

Nicaragua, link to Iran initiative, 111
Niger, as source of uranium, 313–15
Nimud (Iraq), plundering of, 36
Nixon, Richard, 80
no-fly zones, 170
non-conventional weapons programs (Iraq),
    102–103
North Korea, 217, 271
North, Oliver, 109
Not in Our Name Statement of Conscience, 300
NSD-26.
    See National Security Directive 26
Nuclear Non-Proliferation Treaty, 22
Nuclear Posture Review, 22
nuclear war, and seizure of U.S. embassy (Iran),
    92
nuclear weapon development, in Iraq, 102
nuclear weapons, 311–318
    as response to weapons of mass destruction,
        22–23
    Iraq's attempts to build, 143, 289, 291
    proposed use in 1957, 66
    proposed use of, 143
Nye, Joseph, assessment of Bush strategy, 250

O

occupation, 292–94
occupation-lite, 283
October Surprise, 97–99
Office of Special Plans, 16, 305
    See also Condoleezza Rice
Office of Total Information Awareness, 115
oil
    and global capitalism, 32–33, 58, 249–51
    as indicator of global economy, 250–51
    British monopolization of, 51
    control of, 4
    discovery of in Iraq, 39
    Iraq oil production costs, 268
    price increases effect on U.S. economy, 251
    privatization of Iraqi petroleum sector, 262
    production in mid-1970s, 76
    profitability of, 51, 57–58
    reallocation of Iranian oil, 60
    refusal to discuss as cause of Iraq war, 248
    retroactive pricing for, 183
    strategic importance in 1920s, 51
    strategic power of, 56–58, 132, 255–57
    See also Gulf oil; OPEC; Red Line Agreement
oil and natural gas, 29, 57
oil contracts
    use of for political ends, 207–208
    used to lift sanctions, 268–71
oil-for-food program, 178–79

oil income, recycling of, 76–77
oil leverage, under Saddam Hussein, 260
oil markets, volatility of, 251–52
oil potential of Iraq, 260–61
oil potential of United States, 261
oil revenues
  Iraq's dependence on, 259
  Iraqi share of, 179
oil wells, firing, 156
Oman, U.S. bases in, 274
OPEC (Organization of Petroleum Exporting
  Countries)
  formation of, 64
  price hikes, 84–85
  U.S. influence on, 266
Operation Desert Fox
  as cover for assassination of Saddam Hussein,
    202–203
  destruction of Iraqi munitions during, 289
  escalated air attacks on Iraq after, 212
  timing of, 203
Operation Desert Shield, 130
Operation Desert Storm, destruction of Iraqi
  munitions during, 289
Operation Iraqi Freedom, 1
Order Number 13, 70
Organization of Petroleum Exporting Countries.
  See OPEC
organophosphate pesticides, ban on, 183
Oslo Agreements (1994), 164
Ottoman Empire, 39
Owens-Fitzpatrick, Barbro, 315

P

Pace, Marine General Peter, 21
Pahlevi, Mohammad Reza Shah, 33, 34, 60, 79,
  87
Palestine, demand for independence for, 41
Palestinian Authority, 237
Palestinian Intifada (1987), 121
Palestinian Intifada (2002), 209–10
Palestinians
  and Arab self-determination, 241–42
  core issues of, 244
  Iraq's concerns about, 121
  reprisals against in Kuwait, 163
Palestinian-Israeli conflict, U.S. role in resolu-
  tion, 28
Patriot Act, 26
Patriotic Union of Kurdistan (PUK), 198
Patriotic Union of Kurdistan, and Governing
  Council (Iraq), 223
Pearl Harbor, need for another, 1, 217
Pelletiere, Stephen, 271

Pellett, Dr. Peter L., 177
Pelosi, Rep. Nancy, 30
Pentagon
  and longer term military relationship with Iraq,
    228
  Defense Intelligence Agency (DIA), 5, 317–18
  role in Iraq War, 11–12
People's Republic of China, Iraq's relation with,
  64
Performance-Based Road Map to a Permanent
  Two-State Solution to the Israeli-Palestinian
  Conflict.
  See U.S. roadmap to peace
Perle, Richard Norman, 5, 212, 216, 239, 242
Persian Gulf
  and world oil reserves, 32
  establishment of U.S. dominion over, 126
  strategic importance of, 90–91
  U.S. covert campaigns in, 89–90
Persian Gulf War of 1991
  See Gulf War of 1991
Persian Gulf War of 2003.
  See Gulf War of 2003
Persian gulf, regional distress in, 208–209
Persian oil, division of, 59
petro-dependence, and U.S. economy, 254
petro-dollars.
  See oil income
petro-dominance, role of Gulf States in, 131–32
petroleum output, 252
Philippines, U.S. bases in, 274
Picot, Francois Georges, 41
Pike Commission, 83–84
Pike, Otis, 81–82
Poindexter, John, role in Iran-Contra affair,
  108–109, 115
Pollack, Kenneth, 251, 256
  on global importance of Saudi oil, 132
  on Iraqi deterrence in 1991 Gulf War, 143
post-Cold War world, U.S. assessment of, 134–35
Powell, Secretary of State Colin, 246, 315, 317,
  321, 322, 324, 325, 327
  1991 Gulf War, 130, 131, 142, 143, 146, 151,
    152
  preparation for 2003 war on Iraq, 5, 8, 13, 18
pre-emptive self-defense.
  See double-speak
pre-emptive strikes, as foreign policy, 20–21
precision guided missiles, 54
Predator (unmanned spy plane), 54
Predmore, Tim, 292
Presidential Directive 17, 22
presidential palaces, UNSCOM inspections of,
  200

Prevention of Genocide Act of 1988, 114
Project for the New American Century,
    "Rebuilding America's Defenses, Strategy,
    Forces, and Resources For a New Century,"
    211-12, 216–17, 273
propaganda, as government policy, 86
psychological terror, use of, 149

Q

Qasim, Abdul Karim, 64, 67–68, 69
Qatar, U.S. bases in, 274
Qatari royal family, ties to Abu Musab Al-
    Zarqawi, 308

R

Rahman, Abdul, 72
Ramadan, inspections as espionage, 324
Rand Corporation, assessment of Middle East,
    237
Rapid Deployment Joint Task Force, 90
Rashid, Ahmed, 296
Reagan Corollary, 90
Reagan, Ronald, and collusion with Iran, 98–99
Rebuilding America's Defenses, Strategy, Forces,
    and Resources For a New Century, 217
Red Crescent, body count, 281
Red Line Agreement, 52
refugees, 112, 161
regime change in Iraq
    activities in 1990s, 4
    as motivation of war against Iraq, 195
    as stated policy in Clinton administration, 212
    See also Condoleezza Rice
Rendon Group, 326
Renner, Michael, extent of toxic contamination
    from Gulf War of 1991, 156
Republican Guards, retention of after Gulf War
    of 1991, 160
Republican party platform (2000), removal of
    Saddam Hussein, 5
Resolution 1441, violations to, 18–19
Resolution 660, U.S. lack of support for, 142
Resolution 687
    establishment of nuclear-weapons-free zone,
        187–88
    use of to advance U.S. post-war aims, 171
restructuring economy of Iraq, 230–31
Results in Iraq: 100 Days Towards Security and
    Freedom, 284
revolutionaries, suppression of, 227
Revolutionary Command Council (RCC), 73
Rice, Condoleezza, 238, 315
    and regime change in Iraq, 116–17
    "first words matter more…," 8

on post-September 11 geopolitical opportunity,
    9
Richard, James, energy equivalent of nuclear
    weapons, 132
Ritter, Scott, 113–14, 137, 190–91, 192, 204,
    290, 303, 317
Rodman, Peter, 212
Rokke, Doug, 157
Romania, U.S. bases in, 274
Roosevelt, Franklin D., 59
Rouleau, Eric, 144, 210
Roy, Arundhati, 26
Royal Air Force
    airstrikes again Shi'a rebels, 42
    bombing of Iraq (1920), 42
Royal Dutch Shell, share of Iraqi oil, 52
Rumsfeld, Donald, 6, 17, 23, 27, 240, 293, 301,
    303, 315, 325
    and "bodyguard of lies," 301
    "Core Principles for a Free Iraq," 226, 230
    as special Middle East envoy to Iraq, 104–106
    position on pre-emptive strikes, 21
    response to September 11, 2001 attacks, 7
    support for war on Iraq, 104
Russia
    access to Iraqi oil, 206
    commercial interests in Iraq, 206
    and easing of sanctions, 206
    and Iraqi National Congress, 270
    links to post Gulf War Iraq, 194
    "most favored nation status" with Iraq, 206
    as rising oil power, 257
    oil contracts with Hussein's Iraq, 268–69
    oil potential of, 261
    and UN Resolution 1441, 270
    U.S. concern for reemergence of, 272–73

S

Sa'dabad Pact of 1937, 82
sanctions in Iraq
    and development of Iraqi oil resources, 207
    dissatisfaction with policy of, 205
    effect on Iraqi economy, 175–76
    effect on Iraqi women, 176
    impact on families, 184–85
    imposition of economic sanctions, 170–72
sarin, 317
satellite dishes, ban on, 183
Saud, King, alliance with the United States, 59
Saudi Arabia, 28
    and American war effort in Iraq, 245
    and Iraqi debt, 120
    consequences of support of United States Iraq
        policy, 209

dependence on United States, 140
economic decline of, 210
expulsion of Yemeni workers, 163
links to September 11, 2001 attacks, 244–45
oil production capacity, 120, 132
retention of House of Saudi, 163
role in the world capitalist financial system, 133
sympathy for Palestinians, 210
viewed as enemy of United States, 245
vulnerability of, 88
See also King Saud
Schlesinger, James R., 163, 220
Schneider, William, 212
Schorr, Daniel, obtained Pike Commission report, 84
Scowcroft, Brent, 83, 123–24, 142, 165
criticism of NSC response to Kuwait invasion, 129
need for ground war, 149
post-Soviet global strategy, 134–35
public arguments for going to war, 138
strategy toward Iraqi uprising, 161–62
UN resolutions as political cover, 142
U.S. Iraq policy goals of, 133–34
scud missiles, 323
secular nationalists, suppression of, 227
Security Council Resolution 688, 170
Seizure of U.S. Embassy (Iran), 91, 92
September 11, 2001
alleged Iraqi connection to, 12, 14–15, 287
as another "Pearl Harbor," 7, 217
as impetus for war, 2, 3
Bush administration response to, 8
effect on U.S. Iraqi strategy, 213
Seven Sisters oil cartel, 75–76
sewage, percentage of in Iraqi water, 174
Shadow (unmanned spy plane), 54
Shah of Iran, 33, 34, 60, 79, 87
Sharon, Ariel, 240, 243
Shatt al-Arab waterway, importance of, 46
Shi'a, 42, 94
Shi'a Islamists, 227
Shi'ites, exodus of, 160–61
Shinseki, Eric, 279
Sick, Gary, 91
Sifry, Micah L., 66
silica, 310
Singapore
as source of chemical weapons, 102
U.S. bases in, 274
Sixth Fleet, 65–66
SLAM, 54
Sluglett, Peter, 44, 62, 70–71

smart bombs, inaccuracy of, 147
smart sanctions, 183–84, 185
smoking gun, lack of evidence of, 290
SOCONY, 51
Solberg, Carl, 57
Somalia, U.S. intervention in, 214
Soviet Union
and conflicts with United States in Middle East, 60
effect of collapse on Persian Gulf politics, 121, 128
effect of collapse on U.S. global strategy, 4, 134–35, 205, 213–17
invasion of Afghanistan, 87, 88
Iraq's relation with, 64
relations with Ba'ath government, 74–75, 77
See also Russia
Spain, as source of chemical weapons, 102
Special Security Organization (Iraq), 201
speedboats, ban on, 183
Standard Oil of New York (SOCONY), 51
Standoff Land-Attack Missile (SLAM), 54
State of the Union Address, 314, 315
Strategic Energy Policy Challenges For the 21st Century.
See Baker Report
strategic positioning, 271–74
strategies of war, 2
strategists, 5
streptomycin, ban on, 183
Sumerians, 38
Sunni peoples, 46
Sunni triangle, 286
Sykes, Mark, 41
Sykes-Picot Agreement, 41–42, 51
Syria, 28
and United Arab Republic, 63
conflicts with United States, 239
demand for independence for, 41
nationalistic movements in, 59

T

Tajikistan, 274
Talib, Sayyid, 44
Taliban government, 10
Teicher, Howard, 85, 89, 90, 105
telecommunications licensing power, 223
terrorism
as cause of Iraq War (2003), 1
definition of, 298–99
lack of definition of, 10
link of Iraq to, 194, 301–10
See also war on terror
Thielman, Greg, 304

Thomas, Helen, 285
Timmermann, Kenneth R., 96
TotalFinaElf SA, 206, 268–69
Toward a Neo-Reaganite Foreign Policy, 5, 216
Transjordan, 43
  See also Jordan
treaties, changes to, 2
Treaty of Sevres, 47
Truman Doctrine, and impact on Soviet Union, 60
Truman, Harry S, 60
Turkey, 274
  and establishment of Kurdish state, 208
  ban on Kurdish names, 48
  claims in northern Iraq, 48
  closure of borders after Gulf War of 1991, 164
  dependence on United States, 140
  suppression of Kurds in, 113, 163–64
Turkish nationalism, 47
Turkmenistan, 274
Twin Pillars, 79
Twining, Nathan (General), 66
typhoid, increase in post Gulf War of 1991, 173

U

U.S. advisory board, for Iraqi petroleum industry, 263
U.S. Agency for International Development (USAID), 267
U.S. arms sales to Iraq, 116
U.S. bombs, assessment of, 281
U.S. built helicopters, as delivery mechanism for chemical bombs, 113
U.S. control of Iraqi oil, effect of Saudi Arabia, 265–66
U.S. Council on Foreign Relations, 252
U.S. global hegemony, 4–5, 19–21, 26–27, 213–17
U.S. "green lights" to Iraq, 96–97, 123–27
U.S. intelligence services, politicization of, 304
U.S. policy of intervention, 89–90
U.S. Provisional Authority, 223
U.S. roadmap to peace, 243–44
U.S. Special Forces, elimination of Saddam Hussein by, 14
U.S. troops in Iraq, attacks on, 279
U.S. war crimes, "Highway of Death," 152
U.S., diplomatic relations with Iraq, 105–106
U.S.-Iraqi relations, 3
Ubaidullah, Sheikh, 47
UN Charter, legitimate reasons for war, 19
UN Children's Fund (UNICEF), incidence of disease in post war Iraq, 284
UN inspections of Iraq, 190–91

UN Monitoring, Verification, and Inspection Commission (UNMOVIC), 203
UN Resolution 1284, 203–204
UN Resolution 1441, 270, 326
UN Resolution 660, 140
UN Resolution 687, 167, 168–69, 188–89
UN resolution 715, 189
UN resolutions, loose definitions of goals in, 196
UN sanctions against Iraq, lifting of, 260
UN Security Council
  Bush administration and, 139–42
  divisions in after Operation Desert Fox, 203
UN Security Council Resolution 1483, 221–22
UN Security Council, Iran-Iraq War resolutions, 104
UN Special Commission (UNSCOM), 188–90
UN weapons inspections, and covert operations, 200
unemployment, increase in under U.S. occupation, 232
unexploded munitions, effect on Iraqi agriculture, 158
UNICEF/Iraq Ministry of Health, 1999 survey by, 184
Union of Soviet Socialist Republics.
  See entries beginning with Soviet and Soviet Union
United Nations.
  See entries beginning with UN
United States
  and Ba'ath regime atrocities, 71
  and conflicts with Soviet Union in Middle East, 60
  and conventional weapons sales to Iraq, 103
  and Iraqi nuclear weapon development, 102
  and support of King Saud, 59
  and weakening of global arms control treaties, 188
  as an empire, 28
  change in nuclear strategy, 22
  division of Persian oil with Britain, 59
  fear of European influence in Iraq, 207
  field testing of new weapons in Iraq, 54
  foreign economic interests, 31
  global strategy in post-Soviet world, 4–5, 134–35, 205, 213–17
  imperialism of, 30–32, 187–88
  Iraqi oil production manipulation, 62
  military buildup and deployment, 274–75
  oil potential of, 261
  oil production in, 56
  Persian Gulf alliances, 79
  policy in Afghanistan, 89–90
  policy of "no-contacts" with Kurds, 114
  policy of stalemate in Persian Gulf, 108–10

relations with Iran, Israel, and Syria, 240–44
reliance on petroleum products, 251
response to invasion of Kuwait, 129–30
response to nationalist movements, 65–67
response to OPEC price hikes, 84–85
share of Iraqi oil, 52
special relationship with Israel, 78
support for Ba'ath regime, 70–73
support for Iraq invasion of Iran, 96–100
support for Kurdish insurgency, 80–84
trade with Iraq, 114
use of military dominance, 187
use of oil as leverage, 57
use of precision guided missiles in Iraq, 54
weapons sales to Iraq, 102–103
weapons sales to Persian Gulf allies, 188
United States embassy in Iran, seizure of, 88–89
United States military
   involvement overseas, 9
   See also Afghanistan; Iraq; Saudi Arabia
UNMOVIC, 321
UNSCOM, 198–99, 203
uranium, depleted, 156–58
USA Today, 13
Uzbekistan, 274

V

Vance, Cyrus R., 96
Venezuela, 255, 261
Vietnam syndrome, 129
Vietnam, and approach to Gulf War, 142–43
Vincennes, attack on Iranian passenger jet, 111
von Clausewitz, Karl, 8
von Sponeck, Hans, 179, 180, 183, 196
   theft of Iraqi documents, 327
VX nerve agent, 317

W

Wald, Charles, 275
Wall Street Journal, advocacy of Iraq war by, 19, 237
war on Afghanistan, 10
war on Iraq, 279, 301
war on terror, 2, 8–10, 219–20
war reparations, effect of on Iraqi people, 180
war without the appearance of aggression, 135–36
war, legitimate reasons for, 19
Warden II, USAF Col. John A., on U.S. 1991 bombing strategy, 145–46
Warf, Professor James C., on depleted uranium, 157
Washington Institute for Near East Policy, 5
Washington Post, report on postwar Iraq, 279–80
water, policy of deliberate contamination, 172–75
weaponry, Iraqi surrender of, 227

weapons inspections, 327–29
   See also inspectors
weapons of mass destruction, 301–302, 311–29
   as a pretext for war on Iraq, 15, 287
   as excuse for intervention, 4
   depleted uranium, 157
   evidence of, 291
   fabrications about, 15–16, 288
   See also biological weapons; chemical weapons; cluster bombs
Webster, William, 121
Wilson, Joseph, 16, 127–28, 314, 315
Wilson, Woodrow, "Fourteen Points" of, 47
WMD.
   See weapons of mass destruction
Wolfowitz, Paul, 4, 211, 279, 304–305, 315
   on risks of inaction, 30
women, status of, 211
Woodward, Bob, 8, 126, 131, 248
Woolsey, R. James, 2, 11–12, 238, 310
World Trade Center bombing (1993), 7
World Trade Center bombing (2001).
   See September 11, 2001
World Trade Organization, Middle Eastern participation in, 246
World War I, role of oil in, 39–40
Worldwatch Institute, 156
Worldwide Attack Matrix. See covert counter-insurgency operations
Wurmser, David, 5, 216, 239, 242

Y

Ya'alon, Moshe, 243
Yemen, consequence of no vote on UN Resolution 678, 141
Yemeni workers, expulsion from Saudi Arabia, 163, 209
Yergin, Daniel, 56, 256

Z

Zaher, U., 70
Zakheim, Dov S., 212
Zarqawi, Abu Musab.
   See Al-Zarqawi, Abu Musab
Zilinskas, Raymond, 190, 323
Zionism, British support for, 41
Zoelick, Robert, 212

About the Author

Larry Everest has covered the Middle East and Central Asia for over 20 years as a contributing writer to the *Revolutionary Worker* newspaper. He has reported from Iraq, Iran, the Palestinian West Bank and Gaza, and India, and his articles and commentaries have appeared regularly in *Z Magazine* and Pacific News Service, as well as in publications across the country, including the *Boston Globe*, *Los Angeles Times*, and *San Francisco Chronicle*.

In 1986, he wrote *Behind the Poison Cloud: Union Carbide's Bhopal Massacre*, based on his on-the-scene investigation. In 1991, he traveled to Iraq following the Persian Gulf War and shot the video *Iraq: War Against the People*.

His writings can be found at www.larryeverest.com.